D0017948

11/22

COMMONWEAL
Confronts the Century

LIBERAL CONVICTIONS, CATHOLIC TRADITION

EDITED BY PATRICK JORDAN AND PAUL BAUMANN

A TOUCHSTONE BOOK
PUBLISHED BY SIMON & SCHUSTER

TOUCHSTONE
Rockefeller Center
1230 Avenue of the Americas
New York, NY 10020

Copyright © 1999 by Commonweal
All rights reserved, including the right of reproduction in whole or in part in any form.

TOUCHSTONE and colophon are registered trademarks of Simon & Schuster, Inc.

"The Primacy of Caring," by Daniel Calllahan, beginning on page 214, is Chapter 5 from the book *What Kind of Life: The Limits of Medical Progress,* by Daniel Callahan. It appears here with his permission and that of Georgetown University Press.

"On Becoming a Catholic," by Graham Greene, beginning on page 289, is from *A Sort of Life,* by Graham Greene, and is reprinted with the permission of Simon & Schuster, Inc.

Portions of this work have been previously published in *Commonweal.*

Manufactured in the United States of America
10 9 8 7 6 5 4 3 2 1

Library of Congress Cataloging-in-Publication Data

Commonweal confronts the century : liberal convictions, Catholic tradition / edited by
  Patrick Jordan and Paul Baumann.
      p.   cm.
    "A Touchstone book."
    1. Sociology, Christian (Catholic)   I. Jordan, Patrick.   II. Baumann, Paul.
  III. Commonweal (New York, N.Y.)
  BX1753.C525   1999
  261—dc21   99-35028
                                                                            CIP

ISBN 0-684-86276-X

A WORD OF THANKS

To all those who have helped see this project to fruition, in particular Margaret O'Brien Steinfels, Robert G. Hoyt, and the *Commonweal* staff; interns Christian Zwahlen, Grant Gallicho, Andrew Rosato, and Maurice Timothy Reidy; Susanne Washburn; and our editor at Simon & Schuster, Caroline Sutton.

A NOTE ON STYLE

We have maintained the use of pronouns as they appeared at the time of publication, and also the term "man." Otherwise, we have attempted to use current spelling, capitalization, and punctuation. A number, if not the majority, of selections have been shortened; our aim has been to enhance their readability while maintaining their substance and style. For the same purpose, paragraphs have sometimes been elided. Where breaks in the edited text might prove abrupt, we have provided ellipses.

In grateful thanks to Edward S. Skillin, *Commonweal* staff member, editor, and publisher (1933–98), and to James O'Gara, managing editor and editor (1952–84); to the Commonweal Associates, whose annual contributions make publication possible; and to our readers, whose loyalty has kept the magazine going for three quarters of a century.

CONTENTS

BELIEFS   **287**

ART   **369**

INTRODUCTION

PETER STEINFELS

The first issue of *The Commonweal* was dated November 12, 1924—a week after Calvin Coolidge was elected president of the United States, ten months after the death of Lenin, and barely six weeks before Adolf Hitler was released from the rather comfortable prison to which he had been sentenced for his failed putsch of the year before and where he had occupied himself in dictating the first volume of *Mein Kampf.*

Within the coming year, Eisenstein's *Potemkin* would appear, as would Charlie Chaplin's *Gold Rush,* Shostakovich's First Symphony, and Virginia Woolf's *Mrs. Dalloway* (receiving a rave review in *The Commonweal*). In 1925 Sinclair Lewis's novel of biomedical dedication, *Arrowsmith,* also positively received in *The Commonweal,* won a Pulitzer Prize—and F. Scott Fitzgerald's *The Great Gatsby* did not (in itself "a mediocre novel," wrote the *Commonweal* reviewer, but "an important stepping stone toward a literary excellence, which Scott Fitzgerald ought some day to achieve"). Alfred North Whitehead's *Science and the Modern World* was only one of that year's books on the meaning of science to get the magazine's attention. And why not? In the summer of 1925, Michael Williams, founding editor and presiding genius of the new magazine, trundled off to Dayton, Tennessee, where H. L. Mencken and a horde of other journalists were making a quasimythological event out of John T. Scopes's trial for violating a recent Tennessee ban on teaching human evolution.

This was the world that *The Commonweal* (the magazine's title was shortened simply to *Commonweal* in 1965) was created to engage. It was

PETER STEINFELS served in a variety of editorial positions at *Commonweal* (1964–72, 1978–88) and was the magazine's editor from 1984 to 1987. From 1988 to 1997 he was the senior religion correspondent for the *New York Times.* Since then, he has written the biweekly "Beliefs" column on religion and ethics for the *Times* and served as a visiting professor of American studies at the University of Notre Dame, and most recently as a visiting professor of history at Georgetown University.

a world that had superficially returned to the "normalcy" announced by Coolidge's predecessor and where, as silent Cal put it, "the business of the United States is business." It was also a world of promising but puzzling science and technology, of embryonic totalitarianism, of novel and disconcerting art, of new forms of mass entertainment. Finally, it was a world where much of the cultural elite and, in the United States, much of the populace viewed Roman Catholicism as an alien and sinister force. The magazine had scarcely begun publishing when it was caught up, somewhat reluctantly, in a controversy about whether the election of a Catholic as one of seven fellows at Harvard posed a danger to the republic. About the same time, the *Christian Century,* a voice of liberal Protestantism, recommended taxing religious institutions because that might prove particularly onerous to the Catholic Church and therefore contribute toward "removing that menace to democratic civilization." At a less polite level of society, the Ku Klux Klan was making anti-Catholicism a major plank in its agitation; the KKK's campaign to ban private (read, Catholic) schooling had succeeded in Oregon and was proceeding apace elsewhere, until the Supreme Court's landmark ruling *Pierce v. Society of Sisters* declared such measures unconstitutional.

Born in that climate, the new magazine felt compelled to defend the faith and its institutions, certainly with civility and a keen awareness that much united Americans across religious lines, but nonetheless with a great confidence in its beliefs. As it said at the end of its first six months of life, "nothing can do so much for the betterment, the happiness, and the peace of the American people as the influence of the enduring and tested principles of Catholic Christianity."

At the same time, some things immediately set *The Commonweal* apart from most other expressions of the largely immigrant Catholicism of that era. The magazine was unquestionably the creation of an educated elite, not scornful of the immigrant fervor that had built and filled Catholic parish churches but nonetheless convinced that something more was needed than the narrow understanding of "religious duties"— the fulfillment of ritual obligations and the avoidance of personal immorality—that often dominated popular Catholicism. What was that something more? It was to engage the faith with contemporary thought, literature, art, and public affairs, and to do so at a distinctly higher intellectual level than was then typical of American Catholicism. Indeed, the need for Catholic thinking equal to the culture's best would only increase, the editors believed, as the church prospered in the United States.

The Commonweal was not a "church organ," blessed or burdened by any official sponsorship. It was an independent journal edited by laypeople, and this, too, was distinctive. It reflected the further conviction that such a broad engagement in the political and cultural life of the society was preeminently the task of the laity and constituted a sphere of activity where Catholics could not carry out their religious calling without exercising a good deal of independent judgment.

Seventy-five years later, some aspects of that earlier world remain strikingly similar: The very first issue of *The Commonweal,* after all, carried an article by G. K. Chesterton titled "Religion and Sex"! Other aspects were fated to fester and turn gangrenous. The totalitarian regimes would wreak their cruelty on millions of bodies and souls; war would engulf the planet, and armaments swell to the point of potential global annihilation. Both developments put traditional codes of morality and their institutional representatives on trial but simultaneously stripped modernity of a confident glitter that not even the trench warfare of the Western front had quite dulled in 1920s America. And in a fashion virtually unprecedented for any religious body of such size and age, Catholicism itself would undertake a massive stocktaking at the Second Vatican Council (1962–65), deciding that among its "enduring and tested principles," not all had been, or deserved to be, so enduring, and some required new testing.

Throughout all of this, *Commonweal* strove to bring Catholic faith and modern life, especially the experience of American freedom and diversity, into fruitful contact. In doing so, it offered a unique perspective on its nation, its church, its century, a perspective that students of American politics, intellectual life, or religion cannot afford to ignore.

Over the years Catholic and non-Catholic readers have repeatedly testified to the excitement of their first encounters with the magazine and to the loyalty that resulted. Identification with the magazine and its special perspective was such that, within the church, the term "*Commonweal* Catholic" came into vogue. In a way, that enthusiasm might seem puzzling. After all, this was a journal distinguished precisely by moderation and nuance, not alarm and censure. The *New York Times* had greeted the first issue, as Rodger Van Allen notes in his invaluable two-volume history of the magazine—*The Commonweal and American Catholicism* (1974) and *Being Catholic: Commonweal from the Seventies to the Nineties* (1993)—as a journal that promised to pursue its purposes "with a moderation of language and a command of facts" that certainly contrasted with the church's critics. "Suavity not ferocity marks The Commonweal style," said the *Times,* and "the usual bitterness of theological controversy is missing."

For many readers of the magazine, this breadth of vision and tone of reflective reasoning was attraction enough. But more was involved. Although the initial issue included an admiring article on Louis Veuillot, the nineteenth-century archconservative French Catholic journalist, inevitably the magazine found itself thinking within the opposing tradition, often labeled "liberal Catholicism," that urged the church to build on democracy, freedom, and the spirit of change rather than doggedly battle them. Ultimately, *Commonweal* was known as a liberal journal; and even as the L-word, derided by sixties radicals and eighties conservatives alike, went into disfavor, the editors never backed away from it. From the Depression years on, the identification had been deepened by a commitment to government activism in regulating the economy and redistributing its benefits, a commitment quite in keeping with traditional Catholic social thought. *Commonweal's* liberalism was similarly reflected in its opposition to censorship and the anti-Communist hysteria of the McCarthy period, its consistent support for organized labor and for consumer and cooperative movements in their heyday, its condemnations of anti-Semitism (the magazine had launched a major campaign for an American boycott of the 1936 Olympics in Berlin) and of racial discrimination.

This liberalism frequently riled at least some vocal leaders of American Catholicism, particularly when a new generation of editors, taking over the magazine in 1938, pointedly repudiated the identification of Christian civilization with Franco's supposed crusade against communism in Spain. Within a year, the magazine lost more than 20 percent of its subscribers. The Jesuit weekly *America* was aghast at what it considered *Commonweal's* neutrality between "the champions of a Christian social order" and "the protagonists of a Sovietized state." *Commonweal* came under similarly fierce attack in the 1950s for its steady criticism of the anti-Communist antics of Joe McCarthy. In neither case was the magazine at all neutral between communism and Christianity or dictatorship and democracy. But looking to the positive American experiment in church-state separation and to the unhappy alliances of throne and altar in Europe, *Commonweal* believed that faith and freedom were endangered, not upheld, when temporal causes or social orders, particularly those enforced by state power or claiming priority over individual rights, were uncritically baptized as the work of God. Politics, the editors believed, was a worthy engagement on behalf of the common good, but it was also an all-too-human sphere of prudential judgment and compromise. One could not move directly from scriptural injunctions or church documents to specific political measures without carefully weighing the immediate circumstances and consequences. "Crusade" was not a good word in *Commonweal's* vocabulary.

This predisposition did not keep the magazine from taking definite positions. But to the disappointment of allies, it usually argued those positions in pragmatic terms, reserving the emotive power of endorsement or condemnation in explicitly religious language for only the most compelling cases. From the time of France's postwar attempt to crush Ho Chi Minh's movement for Vietnamese independence, for example, *Commonweal* had warned that Southeast Asia could prove a quagmire. Its early criticisms of American involvement focused on specific excesses—what the ethics of just and unjust wars consider the morality of means rather than the morality of ends. It was prepared to approve one of President Lyndon Johnson's bombing initiatives if that could facilitate a negotiated settlement. Only as the failures of both means and ends became overwhelming did the editors, in 1966, brand the war as flatly "unjust" and "immoral"—"a crime and a sin."

On another life-and-death question, abortion, *Commonweal* has consistently affirmed that the unborn human life deserves protection and strongly criticized those who strive assiduously to remove that reality from public debate. But recognizing that this debate could not be governed by norms derived from one group's revelation, the magazine has published arguments made in terms of general reasoning, and it has distinguished between the morality that any individual may observe and the morality that can be effectively written into law as an expression of a pluralistic society's moral consensus.

If *Commonweal's* liberalism did not always sit well with some Catholics, neither did it agree with some liberals. At issue, occasionally, was the journal's religious commitment. Of course, liberals disdained the entrenched Reformation claim that the pope was the Antichrist, but they were less resistant to the companion stereotype that the Catholic Church was deliberately breeding a mindless flock whose growing numbers, hopelessly in thrall to papal orders, imperiled American liberties. In the 1950s, Paul Blanchard's diatribes, arguing that Catholicism was no more compatible with freedom than was Soviet communism, appeared in the

Nation, and the historian John McGreevey has documented just how seriously they were taken among the country's intellectual elite, influencing
at least one member of the Supreme Court. *Commonweal* forcefully rejected
Blanchard's accusations at the same time as it warned Catholic advocates
of censorship or bloc voting that they were carrying grist to his mill.

Yet fissures between *Commonweal* and other liberal intellectuals were
more apt to open up over religion in general than Catholicism in particular. At least some forms of liberalism held that freedom was safeguarded
only by a rock-bottom skepticism about ultimate truth, or that separation of church and state implied separation of religion and politics or
even religion and society, so that religious convictions and institutions
might subsist, at most, as private sources of comfort and inspiration, but
with no legitimate role in public discourse about politics and social
norms. As liberalism shifted in recent decades from the egalitarian bread-
and-butter issues of the New Deal and the War on Poverty to the defense
of personal freedoms, especially concerning reproduction and sexuality,
it has relied more and more on the principle that the government should
scrupulously abstain from judgments about the good life (including decisions regarding its beginning and end), leaving them instead to the individual. This is a position that *Commonweal* has found faulty in
principle and illusory in practice. A gulf has accordingly opened between
it and much of American liberalism, without especially closing the gap
dividing it from conservatism.

■

Halfway through *Commonweal's* history, Roman Catholicism entered
a new era. In many ways, the Second Vatican Council was the fulfillment
of the magazine's hopes. It endorsed the vocation of the laity to be active
participants in the liturgy and bearers of the gospel in society. The council dismantled the barricades Catholicism had thrown up against the
modern world. The Eucharist and other sacraments were restored to the
center of the church's prayer life, where they had sometimes been over-
shadowed by popular devotions. Scripture was likewise restored to the
center of the church's consciousness, where it had sometimes been over-
shadowed by church decrees and various schools of theological and
philosophical reasoning. The council extended a hand to other branches
of Christianity, began purging Catholicism of the stain of anti-Jewish
ideology, and acknowledged the value of other world religions. It
solemnly affirmed the inviolability of conscience and the right to religious freedom.

To *Commonweal* this last affirmation was especially satisfying, a vindication of the editors' twofold defense of Catholicism's place in American intellectual life and of the significance of the American experiment, especially of religious freedom, for the church's life. The magazine was similarly vindicated by the council's elevation of dialogue over apologetics and polemics. Dialogue had been *Commonweal's* keynote from the start, and a chief reason some Catholics had periodically accused the magazine of lacking fervor. The first article of the first issue had been by a non-Catholic. That essay was sympathetic to the magazine's outlook, but the editors have always published pieces at odds with their own views, regularly resorting to the debate or symposium format. (For example, the defense of liberal Catholicism by William Clancy, included in this collection as representative of the magazine's viewpoint, was originally paired with an attack on liberal Catholicism by William F. Buckley Jr.) Individual editors have offered signed dissents to the unsigned editorials that express the editorial staff's collective judgment. The magazine often retained columnists who consistently challenged the prevailing editorial policy.

Vatican II was followed in detail by *Commonweal*—more than one editor traveled to Rome to observe the proceedings firsthand, and there were writers for the magazine, primarily Gregory Baum and Robert McAfee Brown, among both Catholic and Protestant experts and observers. But ironically this minute attention made it impossible to select any one or two articles among the many detailed dispatches for reprinting here. Even when an author like Hans Küng surveyed the forest rather than the trees at the end of the council in December 1965, he did so in almost telegraphic style, assuming perhaps that his readers had already studied the trees one by one. The council, in fact, appeared to be a culmination of *Commonweal's* hopes, so much so that Eugene McCarthy, a friend of the magazine since his days as a Minnesota congressman, once ruminated that it faced the problem of the March of Dimes after the polio vaccine: success had removed its raison d'être.

The reality proved otherwise. If the council is not represented here by any direct report or commentary, it is thoroughly reflected in the controversies it left in its wake. *Commonweal* published numerous articles on the impact of liturgical reform; the prolonged debate over contraception and widespread objections to Pope Paul VI's reiteration of its condemnation in his 1968 encyclical *Humanae vitae,* swelling into a full-scale crisis of authority; the role of women in the church, including their ordination (as well as that of married men) to the priesthood; new issues of church and state, morality, law, revolution, and resistance raised by liberation theology, by the war in Vietnam, by abortion and euthanasia. Meanwhile, the 1960s had erupted—in some ways quite to *Commonweal*'s liking, such as the religiously inspired civil rights movement and student activists' criticism of a liberalism that was strictly "procedural" and lacking in substantive commitments, but also in ways that grated against the journal's whole tradition, like the radicals' apocalypticism and the counterculture's exaltation of hedonism and immediacy over reason and reflection.

The council, the 1960s, and the tumultuous years that followed introduced two discontinuities into *Commonweal*'s history. In its first three decades, the editors had not focused much on the church's internal life except to defend it against its cultured despisers. They occasionally voiced disappointment in church authorities but rarely discussed doctrines, and only in the most deferential tones. By the middle fifties, the staff included editors trained in philosophy and theology and resolved to add a lay perspective where the ordained had long held a near monopoly. They were blunt about the church's historical failures. They probed basic questions of faith and morals. The difference can be measured by comparing the enthusiastic reception the journal gave Pius XI's condemnation of contraception in his 1930 encyclical *Casti connubii* with its frankly critical reception of *Humanae vitae*. Although "the new encyclical must be taken seriously and weighed soberly," the editors predicted that it would bitterly divide the church and "fail the test of history."

At the same time, *Commonweal*'s place on the map of American Catholicism began to shift. As long as demands for change in the church had to struggle even to get a hearing, *Commonweal* had provided a sympathetic forum. Only the anarchist, pacifist *Catholic Worker,* with which *Commonweal* shared many historical and personal ties, and the similarly allied but more academic quarterly *Cross Currents,* consistently stood to *Commonweal*'s left. The postconciliar period saw the flourishing of other independent lay platforms, especially the *National Catholic Reporter,* a weekly newspaper founded by Robert G. Hoyt, now a senior writer at *Commonweal.* More important, it saw the birth of enthusiasms, sometimes among friends who had looked to *Commonweal* for leadership, that now provoked the journal's skepticism. As never before, the magazine found itself caught between two fronts. Not only was there a Catholic right that had yet to come to terms with the council's reforms;

there was a Catholic left that seemed determined to push them over a precipice. *Commonweal* tried to keep its own counsel. It published misgivings about the reformed liturgy, criticized aspects of liberation theology, challenged the idealization of Sandinista Nicaragua, favored nuclear deterrence over unilateral disarmament, and cast a cool eye on optimistic proposals for new sexual moralities. At the same time, the magazine resisted the sweeping reversals of disillusioned neoconservatives who found happiness in Ronald Reagan's "morning in America" and backed Contra warfare in Central America and the Star Wars antimissile system in the stratosphere. *Commonweal* refused to organize its thinking around a dichotomous culture war that wrapped feminism, legalized abortion, gay rights, affirmative action, the ACLU, pop music, welfare, environmentalism, Hollywood movies, TV sitcoms, the network news, the National Endowment for the Arts, and liberal Democrats into a single, seamless enemy—or likewise recoiled from every exemplification of military intervention, the religious right, family values, right-to-lifers, means testing, work requirements, decency ratings, and sexual restraints in mass entertainment. Tellingly enough, when a group of scholars designed a major foundation-funded study mapping the "Catholic Right" and the "Catholic Left," they found it impossible to place *Commonweal* in either camp.

Independence, in short, has been a *Commonweal* hallmark, independence from church structure or subsidy, independence from liberal orthodoxy, independence from the post-sixties factions, whether Catholic or secular. For most of its history, this independence has made the magazine a financially precarious operation, disregarded by the wealth that backs many Catholic or liberal causes, sustained instead by the modest donations of loyal readers and by the thrift and sacrifices of its editors and writers.

■

For *Commonweal's* history is one of people as well as ideas, starting with the visionary and self-styled romantic Michael Williams. It was his genius and energy that launched the magazine, even if his mood swings and weakness for alcohol and Generalissimo Franco ultimately alienated him from his colleagues. George N. Shuster, educator and journalist, left the staff in 1937 after clashing with Williams over the Spanish Civil War but not before putting his own irreversible stamp on the magazine. His German-American roots prepared him to report on the conditions that bred Nazism and warn Catholics in no uncertain terms of the moral as well as political toxicity of German, Austrian, and Spanish fascism. He went on to serve as president of New York City's Hunter College, then the largest all-women's college in the world. After carrying out government assignments in wartime, he spent eighteen months in 1950–51 as state governor of Bavaria for the American occupation government. His final years were spent assisting the Reverend Theodore A. Hesburgh at Notre Dame, where Shuster had studied and taught before going to *Commonweal*.

Edward S. Skillin was one of "Shuster's boys," hired by the then managing editor in 1933 along with Philip Burnham. The two of them would take over the magazine as coeditors five years later, but Skillin would remain as editor and publisher, a quiet, unfailing caretaker of the *Commonweal* legacy, for no less than sixty years more, retiring in the summer of 1998 and ceasing his regular commute to the office only at year's end—at age ninety-four. From his home in New Jersey, he continues to proofread each issue.

Two more generations of editors deserve mention. A post–World War II generation was represented by John Cogley and James O'Gara, founders of a Catholic Worker house in Chicago who broke with Dorothy Day over pacifism and served in World War II. Unlike many of their predecessors on the staff, they were educated in parochial schools and, with the help of the G.I. Bill, Catholic universities. (Burnham and Skillin were Phi Beta Kappa graduates of Princeton and Williams respectively; and both had attended Eastern prep schools.) Cogley and O'Gara brought to the magazine something of the struggling, urban milieu of immigrant Catholicism, as did James Finn and William Clancy, two other 1950s editors, who combined liberal politics with strong literary interests. O'Gara remained at the magazine as managing editor and editor until 1984; he and Skillin, the two long-distance runners of *Commonweal*'s history, guided the magazine through the tumultuous years following the council. Cogley moved on to positions at the Fund for the Republic, the Center for the Study of Democratic Institutions, and the *New York Times*. Throughout the fifties, however, he continued his one-page columns in the magazine, and those assembling this collection had to struggle to include only three of these fine-cut gems of lucid, unassuming argument.

What could be called the Cold War–and–council generation was installed at *Commonweal* when I first worked there, in the summer of 1964. Daniel Callahan, prolific author and later a pioneering figure in the field of modern biomedical ethics, worked at one of the magazine's dilapidated desks, separated by a pea green metal and glass divider from John Leo, later a writer for the *New York Times* and *Time* and most recently a columnist for *U.S. News & World Report.* I arrived for work in the warren of "offices" created by those ugly dividers on the day that Richard Gilman, the magazine's drama critic, who was moving on to review plays for *Newsweek,* turned his book-strewn nook over to Wilfrid Sheed, three of whose novels were to be nominated for National Book Awards and who went from reviewing plays for *Commonweal* to reviewing movies at *Esquire. (Commonweal's* roster of drama critics has been particularly distinguished, starting with Richard Dana Skinner in 1924. By the 1960s, former occupants of that post—Walter Kerr, Gilman, Sheed, and John Simon—were reviewing plays or movies for the *New York Times, Newsweek, Esquire,* and *New York.*) A summer in such company did not make it easy to return to graduate school.

In 1964, too, William V. Shannon was contributing a regular "Washington Report" and taking a hawkish view of the nation's growing commitment in Vietnam. The opposing analysis (and more or less the magazine's) came from a former editor, William Pfaff, who would soon start submitting a regular "Foreign Affairs" column. Shannon, who changed his mind about Vietnam, was to join the editorial page of the *New York Times* and eventually serve as American ambassador to Ireland. Pfaff, a humanist operating in the world of think tanks, came to write essays on international politics for the *New Yorker* and produce a syndicated column; his book *Barbarian Sentiments* was nominated for a National Book Award.

My own connection with *Commonweal* went back, more or less, to the age of seven or eight—when I recall my mother being unaccountably more absorbed in a colorless, pretty much pictureless magazine than in my relentless explanations of why I needed a pair of cowboy boots (and a guitar and a pony . . .) in order to pursue my career as a future Gene Autry. Van Allen, in his history, states that I "was the first *Commonweal* editor whose parents had been readers of the magazine," but he thankfully refrained from any quasi-Freudian theory of why I was driven to serve on the magazine not once but twice—and to increase the use of color and illustrations. Since 1988 I have observed the life and struggles of the magazine from the novel perspective of the editor's spouse. I have seen it improve its financial situation to a somewhat more stable level of impoverishment. I have seen it pass through the astonishing changes of recent decades in typesetting and production, and lurch forward into cyberspace (www.commonwealmagazine.org). I have seen it address the new challenges of domestic and international politics in a world no longer polarized between East and West, and try to maintain dialogue within a church increasingly polarized between liberals and conservatives. People forget that I edited the magazine not long ago, so they don't understand the irony when they say, "Tell your wife how much *Commonweal* has improved in recent years."

This anthology is not, in the strict sense, a "Best of *Commonweal*" collection, although many of these articles could certainly qualify for such a volume. Nor have the editors simply chosen the pieces that were most notable from a strictly historical standpoint, although, again, many of these would qualify. Rather the anthology has been organized around certain themes, political, social, cultural, theological, that not only have preoccupied the magazine throughout its life but remain of pressing concern today. Remarkable reporting and superb writing and even arguments that were once of defining importance for the readership, but addressing topics long since settled or forgotten, had to be set aside. Even within those guidelines, many hard, highly subjective choices had to be made. The editors decided to cut articles, mainly to increase the number and range of topics in the anthology, but occasionally to save readers from being bogged down in time-bound references that would require footnoted explanations.

The four opening articles—"Setting the Scene"—capture moments and sound motifs: the shadow of totalitarianism cast over both faith and freedom; the social inequities of America and the wisdom-beyond-stereotypes of Americans in facing them; the liberal Catholic stance toward church and world. After that, the categories and questions are self-explanatory.

Reviews, a major element in every issue of *Commonweal* for seventy-five years, are a particularly difficult category to anthologize because they often depend on the reader's familiarity with the work or artist under consideration. Yet reviews—not just of books but of plays, films, and to a lesser extent dance, music, and painting—have always had an important place at *Commonweal,* a prominence reflecting a Catholic humanism rooted in the doctrines of creation and incarnation. The attention given the arts in *Commonweal* stood in opposition to a Christian hostility to matter and the senses that minimized beauty as a path to the divine and would harness the aesthetic impulse tightly to the plough of ethics.

Commonweal's challenge to an art-denying censoriousness regularly provoked criticism and ignited many of the most heated discussions in its
pages.

∎

The quest for thematic coherence and, of course, space limitations
have kept many important (and colorful) contributors to *Commonweal*
from this collection's table of contents. There is nothing by Hilaire Bel-
loc or G. K. Chesterton, the dynamic duo of Britain's Catholic intellectual revival. Jacques Maritain alone represents the parallel literary and
philosophical flowering on the continent; missing are *Commonweal* contributors like novelists Georges Bernanos and François Mauriac, poet
Paul Claudel, philosopher Etienne Gilson, Don Luigi Sturzo (the pio-
neer of Italian Christian Democracy, exiled under Mussolini), and the
uncategorizable French intellectual Emmanuel Mounier. John C. Cort,
the magazine's tireless chronicler of labor union struggles, is not here,
nor is Abigail McCarthy, another long-time columnist, nor Claire
Huchet Bishop, who regularly surveyed children's books with the eye of
an outstanding children's author.

Likewise missing are six priests essential to any history of American
Catholicism: Virgil Michel and H. A. Reinhold, two founding fathers of
liturgical renewal who aired their then-radical notions in *Commonweal;*
Monsignor John Tracy Ellis, dean of church historians; and three advi-
sors to the American bishops on social and political issues: the "Right
Reverend New Dealer" John A. Ryan, the noted labor priest Monsignor
George Higgins, and the Reverend J. Bryan Hehir, a longtime *Common-
weal* columnist as well as professor at Georgetown and Harvard. Miss-
ing, too, are many of the non-Catholic sages and scholars to whom the
magazine turned from its earliest days, like the distinguished architect
Ralph Adams Cram, Walter Lippmann, Lewis Mumford, Hannah
Arendt, Will Herberg, Harvey Cox, Robert Coles, and Robert Bellah.
The Reverend Andrew Greeley is not here, although his appearance in
the magazine's pages never failed to generate controversy.

Space limitations also dictated one of the editors' most reluctant decisions, to forgo reprinting any of the distinguished poetry the magazine
has published over the decades. Some of these poems, like "At the
Manger" (a section of W. H. Auden's "For the Time Being") and Robert
Lowell's "Christmas Eve Under Hooker's Statue," are easily found elsewhere. Still, the decision meant the absence of poems by Padraic Colum,
J. V. Cunningham, Josephine Jacobsen, Stanley J. Kunitz, Robert Lax,

Sister M. Madeleva, Phyllis McGinley, Ned O'Gorman, Mary Oliver, Anne Porter, Kenneth Rexroth, Theodore Roethke, Elizabeth Sewell, and John Updike, among many others. Three of the magazine's poetry editors, Rosemary Deen, Marie Ponsot, and John Fandel, who contributed their own poetry and criticism to *Commonweal*'s pages, are similarly missing.

Also unrepresented are several women who broke into a largely masculine editorial staff: Helen Walker, who left the *New Republic* to join the original staff; Mary Kolars, an assistant editor from 1927 to 1938; Anne Fremantle, a freewheeling member of the staff in the forties and fifties and a sterling example of the British traveler and essayist undaunted by topics from the Fabians to Mao's China; Oona Sullivan, who assisted the magazine in a year away from a long career at the Ford Foundation; and Karen Sue Smith, who went on to be editor of the quarterly *Church*. Many of the founding mothers of feminist theology—Mary Daly, Rosemary Ruether, Elisabeth Schüssler Fiorenza, for example—wrote in *Commonweal,* before moving on, in some cases, to territory where the editors chose not to follow; Elizabeth Johnson here represents those concerns.

■

I often puzzle about *Commonweal*'s future, as I suppose editors and ex-editors did throughout its history. I wonder how that future will be affected by the new generations whose Catholic formation and outlook differ dramatically from those of preconciliar Catholics. Their talents and their generosity are no less than those of past generations, but their institutional identification is reportedly much weaker. Can *Commonweal* generate the kind of loyalty—among readers, writers, and supporters—in the future that has sustained it in the past?

Even more, I wonder how that future will be affected by the extraordinary revolution in communications now under way, creating readers who dwell in cyberspace and converse by E-mail. What, indeed, will be the future of all similar "magazines of opinion" with relatively small circulations and slim financial backing?

But there is one thing I do not wonder about. As I write, a physically failing but spiritually forceful Pope John Paul II is in Mexico and about to visit the United States. Once again, the airwaves and news columns are full of talk about Catholicism and modernity. The U.S. Senate is on the brink of critical votes in the drawn-out drama, melodrama, of President Bill Clinton's impeachment. Once again commentators left and right, confounded by the citizenry's remarkable display of indifference, disgust, and support for the president, are trying to gauge the nation's moral reflexes. Iraqi and American military forces are exchanging fire daily; new massacres in Kosovo flout international justice; the gruesome reports from Africa, whether of marauding troops or devastating AIDS, have begun to blur one into another. Meanwhile, on a plane of activity that appears utterly distant from these fevered zones of violence and suffering, stock markets soar and fall, giant corporations merge and multiply, technological wizards perform dazzling feats with computers or genes. As I confront this phalanx of challenges to the mind, the imagination, and the soul, the one thing I do not wonder about is the continuing need, really the desperate need, for what *Commonweal* has provided for seventy-five years: the steady exertion of intelligence, compassion, candor, wit, appreciation, indignation, and all the resources of the magazine's religious faith on the mysteries of human conduct and the awesome events of the day. None of us can steer an intelligent course into the future without the guidance of the past. There are few better places to find it than in this anthology.

Encountering
the Twentieth Century

For the most part, Catholicism responded to the dominant forces of the twentieth century—total war, industrialization, scientific and material progress, communism, fascism, totalitarianism, liberal democracy, religious pluralism, and secularization—either with great ambivalence or with outright opposition. Many Catholic thinkers were convinced that the political instability, social and economic dislocation, and utilitarian morality of the modern age—with its widespread rejection of religion, tradition, and inherited authority—constituted a dire threat to the dignity of humankind. The unprecedented slaughter that convulsed Europe from 1914 to 1945 was seen as a confirmation of the church's warnings about the consequences of embracing the atheistic humanism and secularism of the French Revolution and the Enlightenment.

In 1864, after more than half a century of democratic and antireligious revolution in Europe, Pope Pius IX issued his notorious *Syllabus of Errors,* boasting that it was absurd to think that the "Roman pontiff can and should reconcile himself with progress, liberalism, and recent civilization." In the long battle against anticlerical European liberalism, followed in this century by the fierce struggle with Marxist materialism, Rome set its face against a modern world determined to put an end to the remnants of the church's temporal power and spiritual claims.

There was, however, a liberal strain within Catholicism, one that defended the church and hoped to reconcile Catholicism's traditional concern for the poor, social justice, and moral truth with the values of democracy and religious pluralism. In France this effort was led, paradoxically, by ultramontanes such as Henri Lacordaire and Charles de Montalembert. In England, Cardinal John Henry Newman and Lord Acton gave magisterial expression to a Catholicism confident enough to engage the intellectual challenges of the modern era. Still, Catholic liberals were few and suspect virtually by all. Within a church too often tied to aristocratic or reactionary interests, liberals' politics raised doubts about their orthodoxy. Outside the church, liberal Catholics found their theology raising equally grave suspicions about their politics.

As the essays and reportage that follow attest, those suspicions were often misplaced, but not entirely unfounded. Liberal Catholicism is rarely content with either the party or the church line. If men like Newman and Acton prized liberalism's devotion to freedom of conscience, they were also keenly aware of its exaggerated individualism, naive majoritarianism, and moral relativism. At the same time, Newman made enemies among his coreligionists with his reservations about Vatican I's declaration of papal infallibility. "I drink to the pope"—Newman famously explained—"but I drink to conscience first."

George Shuster, *Commonweal*'s managing editor from 1928 to 1937, possessed the same ability to make distinctions, to hold his loyalty to the church in tension with a skepticism about much that Catholics do in the church's name. He applauded, for example, the instinctive rejection of communism by German and Austrian Catholics, but their willingness to tolerate Hitler earned his uncompromising rebuke. At their best, *Commonweal* writers brought this kind of double-mindedness to the examination of the century's great conflicts. If some Catholics thought tradition or the Bible or prudence could justify racism, George H. Dunne, S.J., exposed their faulty logic and misunderstanding of elemental Catholic moral principles. If contemporary liberals assume that Catholics who support equal rights for women can look the other way when it comes to abortion, *Commonweal* editors have repeatedly tried to correct that false impression.

Whether the debate concerned a Catholic in the White House, a living wage for workers, a preferential option for the poor, the fate of affirmative action, or the role of government in our economic and social lives, the magazine has tried to present a realistic picture of how people actually live their lives in order to put flesh and bones on abstract moral principles. Policy studies of housing needs, working conditions, and welfare are of course necessary. But having Dorothy Day take us into the slums, Budd Schulberg map out labor strife on the Brooklyn waterfront, or Stuart Dybek show how the welfare system operates helps us to grapple with the abiding complexities of our time.

Setting the Scene

TERROR IN VIENNA

GEORGE N. SHUSTER

We have passed through a week of harrowing experiences, still so vivid in the memory that I can hardly bring myself to write about them. It is one thing to see blood spilled, and another to watch the soul of man writhe in torment and then die. On the fateful Wednesday evening when Dr. Schuschnigg announced that Austria was to pass judgment on its government and its future, I happened to be touring the provinces with an Austrian journalist. In so far as we were concerned the news dispelled any illusions we may have entertained concerning the fateful gravity of the situation. A blow was to be struck in favor of Austrian independence, but it could hardly succeed unless somewhere in Europe a promise of substantial aid had been given.

Information concerning that point was reserved to a handful of people. But we could see—and this the next day's travel was to make even clearer—that, in so far as the country itself was concerned, there was no room for doubt concerning the decision. The government had been everything but popular. It was based on an attempt to exercise a

GEORGE N. SHUSTER (1894–1977) was *Commonweal*'s managing editor (1928–37). He later served as president of Hunter College and U.S. representative to UNESCO. His books included *The Catholic Spirit in America* (1927) and *Religion Behind the Iron Curtain* (1954).

"Catholic dictatorship" in a notoriously anticlerical state, and such stability as it possessed was the result far less of its own innate strength than of the intense hatred which separated its enemies of the Right and Left. Nevertheless after Berchtesgaden a kind of miracle had happened. The Chancellor's plucky stand for independence and his promise to modify the rigid financial policies of his government had evoked a wave of popularity which was constantly growing more impressive.

There were Nazi demonstrations in almost all towns, but nowhere excepting possibly in Styria did they serve any other purpose than to show that the strength of Hitler's support had been greatly exaggerated. Workers, including many embittered former Social Democrats, were flocking to the Schuschnigg colors, and it seemed quite possible that in two weeks the gulf between the Catholic party and labor would be healed. Later on I was to regret having gone on this reconnoitering trip, but the fact that I went at least enables me to declare without any hesitancy whatsoever that the situation was fully under the government's control, that the plebiscite was being organized with the utmost fairness, and that every sign pointed to a severe Nazi defeat. All stories and rumors to the contrary are fabrications. It is true that some pressure was brought to bear on civil servants, and that the government was in control of most of the instruments of propaganda. But in every other respect the road to the polls was so unobstructed that one had difficulty in realizing that Austria was not a democratic state.

We drove on through mountainous and sparsely settled country, so that we arrived in Graz late at night on March 11, utterly unaware that the government had yielded to Hitler's ultimatum. There we ran headlong into a delirious Nazi demonstration. The car was surrounded by a crowd of schoolboys carrying any number of assorted weapons. "Jews! Jews!" resounded on all sides, and it was only by dint of displaying a measure of good feeling which I did not possess that we were able to extricate ourselves and leave for Vienna despite the hour and a blinding snowstorm. Almost every mile of what seemed the longest trip on record was interrupted with shouts. Boys armed with rifles and bayonets leaped from the roadside and insisted upon inspecting our passports and our political opinions. Once we lost our bearings and instead of keeping on the main highway drove up to a Franciscan monastery. When the error had been corrected, there gathered round us in that darkness a band of armed youngsters the oldest of whom was seventeen. They insisted upon searching the car for "treasures" which they thought we were escorting to safety.

At last we reached Vienna at five in the morning. The city, which had never boasted of more than a few thousand active Nazis, was asleep excepting for a small group of the faithful still congregated before the German tourist bureau in the Kaerntnerstrasse, inside which a huge portrait of Hitler was banked with flowers. But there was little time for slumber. An hour later German bombers began to "demonstrate" over the city. They swooped down so close to the housetops that every other sound was drowned out. Round about, groups of high school boys began to mount guard. Directly across the street from us, for example, two urchins in knee pants stood with rifles and bayonets looking for all the world like boy scouts run amok. The vanguard of the German army, seated in trucks and armed to the teeth, began to roar through the streets. Terrorization was in progress—the method adopted for enforcing submission by creating what can be defined as absolute insecurity.

In order to understand what this means one must remember that probably less than a third of Vienna's population can qualify as German according to Nazi principles. For all these people the borders had been hermetically sealed the night before. The coup had come so suddenly that Austria was a huge trap. By eight in the morning every resident American in the city had a swarm of visitors asking the impossible. They begged for aid in cajoling passports out of the embassy or in being smuggled out of the country. I have never seen so much despair and frenzy in all my life. Meanwhile more and more thousands of Germans were brought to Vienna. Police, black shirts and brown shirts, soldiers and officials—all these were impressive, but most striking of all were the masses of organized school children brought down by train and truck to demonstrate when Hitler arrived. Soon the otherwise quiet and dignified city became a veritable bedlam. All day and all night the roar continued, rendering sleep an incredible luxury.

The pogrom followed. Jewish shops were plundered and smashed. Houses were entered and ransacked. Individuals were pursued on the streets. Property was confiscated without a moment's warning. Whole streets looked as if a tornado had passed along. But far worse than all this was the horrible despair which unnerved hundreds of thousands—a despair so omnipresent that suicide was a normal recourse. People stabbed or shot themselves to death on the very streets. I shall say no more about it excepting this: An American monsignor and I walked along together wondering whether even Christianity can subdue the beast in man. Cruelty surrounded us, massed, exultant, and victorious. I know now what Calvary means. . . .

Nevertheless, when Hitler entered the city, the bells of St. Stephen's

Cathedral rang out in welcome. I do not wish to judge harshly, but I doubt whether in all history there is a more shameless incident. It was for many of my acquaintances who sensed the full moral ignominy of what was happening round about just as if Christ had really made a pact with Satan in the hour of temptation. . . .

I was so shaken by this experience that for hours I walked about aimlessly, hardly noticing the shouting and the roaring and the click of steel. All this was merely external. What mattered was not what had come, but what had gone—the values of Christendom no longer earned but merely inherited, now to be struggled for tenaciously again through long generations with quiet heroism, self-sacrifice, and martyrdom. These values must be rescued not only through the present difficult times but through the even more perilous days ahead. For there is nobody over here now who doubts that Europe is on the brink of irreparable disaster.

THE OTHER AMERICA

MICHAEL HARRINGTON

At twenty, most of us have painfully learned that stereotypes are a way of lying, of expressing the sprawl of reality, the contradictions of experience. By thirty, we discover the other side of the coin: that the stereotype is a way of saying a half-truth. To be sure, people and things are frozen, plucked out of time and history in the process, but there is always a wisdom at the center of the distortion.

When it comes to stereotypes of America, there is even more complexity, for all of them are partially true, even though many of them express polar opposites. Dickens's vision of revolutionists devoted to freedom and slavery is accurate; Blake's prophetic image of a liberating nation is too. More recently, the fashionable stereotype has been almost completely negative. "America" stands for gadgetry, rootlessness, in the tyranny of mass-produced *kitsch*. "Americanization" is the terrible fate which is befalling Europe as it produces an efficient industrial civilization. The symbol of Coca-Cola shall stand over all.

Another America is suggested by Robert Frank in his brilliant collection of photographs, *The Americans* (Grove). He has seen a nation of almost tragic spaciousness in which people are glimpsed at a moment of repose: looking out of windows, listening to music, sometimes thoughtful but always waiting, caught in a welter of experience (or, to make the metaphor photographic: riding an endless highway). His camera has defined an older stereotype, one which precedes the theories of mass culture and says the exact opposite of the grim thesis that posits "Americanization" as mechanized mindlessness.

In *The Americans,* one finds two main vantage points: the region and

---

MICHAEL HARRINGTON (1928–89) wrote *The Other America, The Accidental Century,* and other works. He served as national chairman of the Democratic Socialist Organizing Committee.

the working people. It is important to remember (or to be reminded) that families need not look as serenely vulgar as they do in a Norman Rockwell illustration, that there are still faces clearly marked by their experience, areas which defy any attempt to erect a huge stereotype. And people still work. The middle-class citizen, so distant from the plant and perhaps hypnotized by automation, can almost come to believe that the commodities of this society are produced invisibly and without human intervention. Frank's camera reminds one that this is not so. For there is an America which has perhaps been out of sight in the fifties. A feeling of helplessness, of frustration in a decade of conservativism and reaction, directed the eyes toward the neon sign and the infinite rows of Coke bottles. But another America remained. . . .

The most obvious, even defining, fact about the other America is its variety, the resourcefulness of its geography. One million signboards can be erected on the highways; hundreds of thousands of vistas can be blocked out of view; but a sweeping magnificence persists.

In Seattle, Washington, the people live in the presence of Mount Rainier. The Indians, it is said, once thought that this solemn peak was God. Their mistake is understandable. Driving in the city, one never knows when the turning of a corner will reveal the aspect of beauty. On a clear day, each hour, each period, is given a special definition by the mountain. And this geography enters into a culture. It is, of course, intermingled with the history of the region: logging, the I.W.W., the Seattle General Strike of 1919 (in this American city, they spoke of "Soviets" at that time), the weather-beaten and brawling tradition of a port.

Thus, the coffee cups in many restaurants in Washington are bigger than they are in the East. Their shape developed out of an outdoor, working world and they are part of the texture of life in the area. At the truckers' stop in the Cascade mountains where breakfast is ten strips of bacon, four eggs, and a pile of home-fries, these coffee cups are one of the forms defining a history and a way of living. They are related to the towering fact of the mountain.

Then there is a place like Stockton, California. This is the center of a lush, profitable farm land which for years has been dominated by huge growers. In the city, one suddenly confronts an unusual sight in contemporary America: a working class defined by its clothes. Someone remarked not too long ago that when the big factories in Detroit put up lockers for the workers, the existence of social classes became harder to see on the city streets. The men no longer went to the shop in their work clothes. Rather, they wore clean shirts and slacks and changed at the plant. This hasn't happened yet in Stockton. . . .

And there is an industrial geography, too. Outside of Pittsburgh, there are coal and steel towns with their slag heaps, their company houses, the perpetual shadow of the machine. Yet, when the plant gives out (as the mines in West Virginia have), the people cling to their tiny, dirty world. There are friendships, churches, traditions, a fierce way of life within the great world. Here, as in Seattle or Stockton, the region has made a culture. Even here.

One could go on and on, but the point is obvious. The other America is still a nation of regions, of scenic surprise (as the plane lifts over the mountains coming down from Denver, the city of Albuquerque and the desert on which it lies seem almost a Shangri-la). The other America is culturally heterogeneous: its coffee cups are different, so are its politics. Its vitality may well be a matter of cultural lag, of a historic impetus acquired in experiences which predate the era of mass culture. But the other America is real.

And yet there is a point of homogeneity. At its worst, it is a source of arrogant ignorance and bigotry; at its best, it is the persistence of something precious and fine. The other America is not simply a political democracy. It is a democratic culture as well.

Not too long ago, Dwight Macdonald wrote of America in *Dissent:* "*Here:* everybody is 'equal' in the sense that nobody respects anybody else unless he has to, by *force majeure;* the national motto should be not '*E Pluribus Unum,*' not 'In God We Trust,' but: 'I got mine and screw you, Jack!' or better, 'Brother'—('friend' and 'brother' being used to express extreme hostility and contempt)." Macdonald is quite right, quite fashionable, and quite wrong. Our democratic culture has led to anti-intellectualism, to an incredible egotism, and it lacks a European respect for tradition. All this is true, but this stereotype must have its counter-stereotype: the positive, driving force of the egalitarian ethos in the United States.

Take waiters. At the point of table service, a culture expresses its values profoundly. The English waiter "thanks" the patron at every moment in the process. There is a litany of servility. The German customer will call the lowliest bus boy "Mr. Headwaiter," but accompanies this by an imperiousness of the voice and, often enough, table pounding. The tone contradicts the form. And in America, waiters are often gallingly independent, slow, poised, and familiar; yet they are not overwhelmed by being waiters, they are as "good" as you are.

On another level, there are thousands of union locals in the other America where workers participate in a living democracy. This is the "other" labor movement (other than the one-sided, and often malicious, image of the union produced in the congressional hearings). In it, local presidents are regularly defeated for office, the rank and file produces its own leaders, and a sense of solidarity is real and alive. A famous European socialist once said to a friend of mine, "Your workers walk differently. They seem so confident."

In such an atmosphere, "Brother" is not a word of contempt but a token of a certain community. At times, it is even embarrassing to hear. Not long ago, a rank-and-file unionist in Lansing, Michigan, who had been on the losing side in an election, was shocked at the idea that this should lead him to distrust the union itself. His victorious opponent, he explained to me, was a union brother and despite their differences they were part of a common cause. The moment was, to be sure, sentimental (and, consequently, for the observer, not without its irony), but it happens in the other America.

All of this, of course, is not the product of some mysterious, genetic process whereby Americans were born different—or better. It comes out of our history. The frontier, the immigrant waves, the tradition of opportunity, the struggle of Populist farmers and C.I.O. workers—these are the creative moments of a democratic culture. They have not marked America with those ruins and layers of civilization which make the European tradition so visual. True enough, the other America is constantly tearing down buildings and putting up taller ones. But the continuity does exist in the manners, attitudes, and speech of the people, and this is another sense of the word America.

Perhaps what confuses so many people about the other America is that it is a maze of contradictions. The sense of solidarity can also become xenophobia; the egalitarianism can turn savagely on the representative of high culture. Or, by a peculiar paradox, the American sense of classlessness often becomes a support for the reality of social classes. It conceals antagonisms, it blunts the drive for social justice; the belief that we are "all" middle class is part of a mechanism of domination in which the people are submissive.

Yet these contradictions are but another expression of the expansiveness, the individuality of the other America. And taking the positive stereotype rather than the negative, this American egalitarianism is a more decent and human way of people meeting people than exists in societies which have impressive monuments to tradition. Indeed, this is probably *the* American monument.

It is important to understand the other America. For if the pessimistic theorists are right, we live in a nation which has been artificially homogenized, and where opinion is infinitely manipulable. That is the pejorative sense of America, and it expresses its own truth. . . . On the other hand, there is hope if one can see the other America. Take the Negroes in the Southern sit-ins for an example.

For some years, a great many Negroes in the South conformed to part of the racist stereotype. They were passive, they accepted their own degradation. This was accomplished through a political mechanism of terror, an economic system of harsh exploitation, a social reality of exclusion from the culture of the white man. But even then, the other Negro was developing. First of all, there was the enormous creativity which went into the Negro church. (To some, this seemed only quaint; in retrospect, it must be recognized that this was a momentous fact.) Then there came the slow contact with a broader world—with the radio, movies, television, the unions, and modern industry. Behind the stereotype, a new tradition was in the making. It burst out in the Montgomery bus boycott; it subsided; it has flared up, all the stronger, in sit-ins.

And what if this would happen, not only among the Negroes, but throughout the other America as well? The future, if it is to contain hope, is being prepared in the midst of the other America. Here, in that part of the nation which is not dominated by gadgets and mass media, is the source of our creativity. This sentiment, in its gutted form, is the commonplace piety of all the candidates and Fourth-of-July orators who have ever been. But it may be the expression of a reality, too; the reality of the other America.

THE CATHOLIC IN THE MODERN WORLD: A LIBERAL VIEW

WILLIAM CLANCY

William Buckley and I have met in debate three times this year. Each time, I have heard him describe my own "liberal" position, and have failed to recognize it. I still await some debate in which he will tell us what a "conservative" Catholic is. Because the "liberal" and "conservative" question is not one defined by the easy labeling and categorizing that are the stock in trade of many magazines—both on the left and on the right. It is a question that cannot be profitably discussed in Mr. Buckley's terms of easy blacks and whites, of "angels" and "devils."

This question of the Catholic in the modern world, of what the attitude of the Catholic should be toward problems of the modern world, is not a simple conservative question of rejecting the modern world or a simple liberal question of embracing the modern world—although, in the course of polemics, the question sometimes is reduced to this. It is not a question of being either "for" the modern world or "against" it. It is rather the complex, serious, and history-laden question of the general approach of Catholics to the modern world. It is a question of attitude. And here we must begin by making some basic distinctions.

In the first place, every Catholic—and this includes every "liberal" Catholic—is in a certain sense a conservative. And this is true by definition. It would be monstrous to maintain otherwise. The Catholic accepts a Revelation that was once and for all delivered to the Apostles; it is part of his patrimony to conserve this Revelation and to pass it on.

So the question here of the liberal and the conservative Catholic is not a doctrinal question. Doctrinally, every Catholic is a conservative, and is proud to be a conservative. The notion of a doctrinally liberal Catholi-

WILLIAM CLANCY (1922–81) was an editor of Commonweal (1952–55) and of Worldview. He was later ordained a priest. A collection of his essays, Time's Covenant (University of Pittsburgh Press), was published in 1987.

cism, if it ever existed, was disposed of once and for all in the condemnations of Pius IX and of Pius X.

The question here then is not doctrinal. It is: given these facts, given these distinctions, what should be the attitude of Catholics toward the modern world? And it is here, in the question of attitude rather than of doctrine, that the terms liberal and conservative assume meaning—at least as descriptions if not as definitions. It is from this standpoint that I wish to consider them.

Now, this question of the approach of the believer to the "modern world" is an ancient question; it is more ancient than the Christian church. This is the question that the psalmist asked in one of the greatest, most moving psalms of the Old Testament. The psalmist asked: "How shall I sing the Lord's song in a strange land?" And believers must repeat the psalmist's question in every age, because in every age there is a conflict between "the world" and the believer. The Prince of this World is at work through history, and any believer who thinks that he serves his faith by subjugating it to the moment, to the demands of the age or to the demands of the century, betrays his faith. The believer is always a stranger and a pilgrim; his question therefore will always be: "How shall I sing the Lord's song in a strange land?"

In seeking to answer this question, the believer faces two obvious temptations. The first temptation is simply to reject the city of man; and this is the temptation to utter transcendence. Certain Christians in every age have succumbed to this temptation. It is a temptation, I think, which historically is more at home with a certain type of Calvinism than it is with Catholicism; but Catholics succumb to it, too. They reject the world as evil; they turn their backs upon it and say: "Here we have our oasis of truth; outside there is the night. Let us build our walls. Let us hold fast to the truth we have. Let us not open the doors." This is the historic temptation of the conservative.

The second temptation comes most easily to certain forms of liberal Christianity, and finds its ultimate expression, I suppose, in such a form of liberal Christianity as Unitarianism; and that is the temptation simply to embrace the "modern" world, to tailor the demands of religion to fit the contingencies of the age. But this temptation also has been felt within the household of the faith. It was yielded to in the nineteenth century by the Abbé Lamennais, and it was the basis of the Modernist movement at the beginning of the twentieth century. This is the historic temptation of the liberal.

Both temptations are a betrayal of the church and of the world—that world which the church strives to save. As Christians, we betray our vocation if we succumb to either.

The extreme conservative merely rejects—his answer to the world is a simple "No"; the extreme liberal merely accepts—his answer to the world is a simple "Yes." If I may make a theological analogy, I would say that the extreme conservative, who merely rejects the world, analogically commits the sin of despair; and the extreme liberal, who says a simple "Yes" to the world, analogically commits the sin of presumption. Christian wisdom rejects both. Christian wisdom demands that in our response to the world we find a middle way. The ancient adage of Christian wisdom, *"Virtus stat in medio,"* "Strength stands in the middle," is true here as it is true in other aspects of our vocation as Christian citizens of an earthly city.

Although this question of the relationship of the believer to the age is a perennial problem, older than the Christian church, it is a particularly acute problem in our own age; and it promises to become even more acute in any age that we can foresee, because we live not only in a post-Christian age, but also in what is probably a postreligious age.

It is very easy, and very comforting, to talk about "religious revival" in America—about the strength of the church and the strength of the parishes in our land. We can take comfort in religious statistics, however, only if we fail to understand what is really happening in the world about us. Almost everywhere in the world, religion is in retreat. It is on the defensive. The world that is now being made is a world from which, tragically, religion is largely absent. And so, for the believer the question "How shall I sing the Lord's song in a strange land?" is more pressing today than it was two hundred years ago; and it will be even more pressing in the future.

The question that Mr. Buckley and I are debating, therefore, is not an academic one; it is very real. And it is not a new one; it is very ancient. It is a question that we can ignore only at great peril for religion itself. Because, since the French Revolution of 1789 (that watershed of history) the Christian, more than at any other time, perhaps, since the fall of the Roman Empire, has been forced, if he is to survive, to make a radical reassessment of his position toward the age and of his relationship to the power structures of the world.

This is the problem of conservative and liberal Catholicism. In making this reassessment, what should the Catholic's attitude be? What should his adjustment be, if any? Should he reject out of hand? Should he embrace? Should he attempt to find a middle way?

Now, I maintain that this problem is particularly acute, and the temptations particularly strong, for those Catholics in the modern world who call themselves "conservative." They have tended toward a complete rejection of the world that comes out of the French Revolution. They have tended to view the modern age simply as the dominion of the Prince of Darkness, and to say: "We have our oasis of truth. Here we will stay, and our only contact with the outside world will be to issue an occasional communiqué condemning it."

Such an attitude among Catholics presents terrible problems for the church, if only from the standpoint of the church's evangelizing mission. And it presents terrible problems for the Christian layman whose personal vocation, even as a layman, is to save the world. In the Epistle for the Mass of the twentieth Sunday after Pentecost, Saint Paul tells us, "See, brethren, that you walk carefully; not as fools but as wise men, redeeming the time, because the days are evil." We note that Saint Paul did not tell us to castigate the time. He told us to "redeem the time." And here, in the fifth chapter of Ephesians, Saint Paul briefly summed up what is the Christian's vocation in every age—to find himself in evil times and yet not to turn his back upon them but redeem them.

This certainly is relevant to one of the really horrifying things about our modern condition—the polarity that exists in modern culture between the world and religion—between man and God. In the words of a great contemporary Protestant theologian, Paul Tillich (Mr. Buckley, I trust, will forgive me for quoting a non-Catholic theologian): "The modern world sees Christianity as reaction pure and simple; and Christians see the modern world as rebellion pure and simple." In this tragic situation neither can effectively address a word to the other. And so, what has actually been happening under our very eyes and what is continuing to happen, at an ever faster pace, is that the world goes on building its city, from which we, as Christians, are absent; and we Christians, smug in our own wisdom and in our own virtue, are content to let that city, quite literally, go to hell.

Father John Courtney Murray, one of the most distinguished contemporary Catholic theologians, addressed himself to this problem a few years ago when he asked whether, in the face of modern secular civilization, the Catholic's attitude should be to stand fast, holding out his hand in an attempt to stop this civilization's progress, all the while looking over his shoulder at the ever-diminishing figure of Isabella II of Spain. "What a peculiar stance for the universal church," Father Murray observed.

My criticism of those Catholics who call themselves conservatives is that they do precisely this. In their major attitudes toward modern civilization, in the last one hundred and fifty years, they have been vehemently negative. And in this, I think, they have helped to create that image of the church as a mere nay-sayer which pervades the modern world. This image is essentially a caricature of the church, but it prevents modern men, almost en masse, from seeing the church as that community of creative love and salvation which the church really is. Historically, too many Catholic conservatives have fallen into a habit of mere nostalgia, of mere defensiveness; they have thus seemed, at least, unconcerned for any of the great battles for which the modern world has fought. With Father Murray I would say: What a peculiar stance for the universal church!

It seems to me that the error of conservative Catholicism has been its failure to distinguish—and whatever may be the intellectual failures of Catholics, the last should be a failure to distinguish! And, because of their failure to distinguish, conservative Catholics have condemned everything for which the modern world has struggled because the *reasons* for which the modern world has struggled have been wrong. Who in the modern world, for example, has fought the great battles for equality and for freedom? (These are easy words, I know.) Concretely, who has fought the battles for racial justice? Was it the Catholics of Europe who stood most strongly against anti-Semitism? In this country, has it been Catholics who have led the battle for Negro rights? No, in both cases it has been the despised liberals. Who has fought the battles for freedom of the press and for freedom of conscience? Has the Catholic community either in this country or in Europe been famous for these things? I fear the answer is obvious. And again it is No.

The picture of modern history is largely the opposite. The Catholic community, on the whole, has either held back from the battles through indifference or has been content to condemn those who fought for these causes because their philosophy was a secularist, a non-Christian, or even an anti-Christian philosophy. But if the modern world has fought these battles for the wrong reasons, it seems to me that in these matters the Christian's proper role should be to supply the right reasons, rather than to turn his back upon the battles themselves.

Certainly, in modern history the battleground for the major arguments between liberal and conservative Catholics has been France. It was French conservative Catholics who, through the entire nineteenth century, insisted on involving the fortunes of the church with the fortunes of the French monarchy. And it was a great "liberal" Pope, Leo XIII, who finally ordered these conservative Catholics to cease tying the hopes of the church to anachronistic political institutions and admonished them to come to terms with the republican institutions of their age, if they were to have any hope of speaking to their age at all.

Again, in our own century, it was another Pope, Pius XI, who condemned the conservative French political movement, *L'Action Française.* In this movement conservative Catholics once more sought to tie the church to a rightist nationalism. At the cost of great bitterness among many Catholics, Pius XI demanded that they cease their efforts to involve the church with authoritarian politics.

And we may recall the recent, poignant letter that close to two hundred Spanish priests circulated among their bishops, warning of a dark future for the church in Spain unless, more than they had in the past, Spanish Catholics entered into and showed some concern for the causes of social justice and civil liberties—causes for which, once again, the Spanish liberals seem to be struggling alone.

In considering these things, in our tendency to damn causes for which we should have fought (and which should now be our causes) because they are the causes of men with whose philosophy we cannot agree, we might recall the wisdom of John Henry Newman, who once observed: "If they say to me, this cannot be Christian because it is found in paganism, I reply, this cannot be pagan because it is found in Christianity."

In these matters the Catholic liberal distinguishes. He recalls the words of the contemporary French theologian, Henri de Lubac, who has reminded us that in every age the Christian has a dual vocation. He faces two tasks: to conserve and to adapt. If he merely conserves and fails to adapt, then he has betrayed his duty as a Christian to the world. I believe it is the tragedy of conservative Catholicism that it has so completely polarized itself, and built such thick walls around itself, that it has forsaken the Christian's second vocation, which is to adapt the truths he has conserved to the unique needs of the present.

The Catholic liberal, however, believes that God's providence did not stop at some point in history—in the sixteenth century at the Reformation or in 1789 at the revolution. He believes that God works *through* history. Because our God is a God of history, and he does bring good even out of evil.

It was a nineteenth-century French theologian, Dupanloup, the bishop of Orleans, who said something that I think we should remember today. He asked what Catholics should say to the men of our age— the liberals, the secularists—who accuse us of reaction and of failure to accept the facts of modern liberty. Dupanloup replied, "We must say this: we accept, we welcome the liberties for which you have fought. You made the revolution without us. Indeed, you made it against us; but you also made it for us. In spite of you, God willed it so."

Modern liberalism has fought and won battles for which we Catholics should have fought but which, in our blindness, we too often opposed. Thus does God's providence work in man's affairs. Those Catholics who are described as "liberal"—who are "open" toward modern civilization— are at their best, I think, when they are in search for the evidences of God's providence in history, even in movements where they may least expect to find God's hand.

THE POLITICAL CRISIS

E. J. DIONNE, JR.

There are two large arguments going on right now in politics. One is over what happened last November. The other is over what ails us as a country. . . .

The most popular view among Republicans is that November's vote was the big bang, the real revolution, the final fulfillment of the promises of Ronald Reagan's election. In this view, the country has decided that government is the problem and wants the federal government cut down, chopped up, shipped off to the states. The most interesting iteration of this argument sees the 1994 election as the logical outcome to the end of the cold war. For a sixty-year period, beginning with the New Deal response to the Great Depression, continuing through World War II and then through the cold war, all of the pressures were to increase the power of government and in particular the power of Washington. Some conservatives will even concede that this whole process of aggrandizing government was necessary. But now, they will argue, there is no Depression, no Hitler, no Soviet Union—and thus no need for a big government in Washington. We are, in this view, returning to "normalcy," which is a normalcy of limited government and decentralized power. . . .

This is a serious argument . . . but it is not, I think, the whole story. An alternative view of 1994 sees the election in terms much less grand. In this view, voters were not dissatisfied with big government so much as with bad government, or, more precisely, disappointing government. This view attributes the election not to the strength of Republicanism or to the power of the conservative idea, but the failure of Democrats and liberals. In 1992, Bill Clinton did indeed offer a promising synthesis aimed at updating the old Progressive and New Deal vision and accept-

---

E. J. DIONNE JR. (1952–   ), a syndicated columnist for the Washington Post Writers Group, is the author of *Why Americans Hate Politics* (Touchstone).

ing some corrections. The older vision was embodied in an effort to complete the New Deal and Fair Deal by passing health-care reform and to respond to economic change with various initiatives in job training and job placement. The corrections were designed to deal with the public's legitimate anxieties over the functioning of government—thus the reinventing government project—and the importance of being clear that social policy needed to embody certain values—thus a welfare-reform plan that embodied greater generosity on the side of education, training, and work opportunities, but also a sense of responsibility embodied in a work requirement and an emphasis on the need to reduce the number of out-of-wedlock births and fatherless families.

Yet in the first two years of the Clinton administration, the administration and a Democratic Congress failed to deliver the basic components of the program: Health-care reform failed, welfare reform never got off the ground, political reforms in lobbying and campaign-finance law died, and the administration's quite popular job-training initiatives never got financed at anything like the levels implied during the campaign.

Moreover, the benefits of the economic recovery in its first two years were unevenly distributed. The well-educated posted substantial income gains. Those without college degrees and especially those with only high school diplomas or less held their own at best, and in many cases continued to suffer income losses.

The notion that disappointment rather than ideological realignment was the real story in 1994 is underscored by several facts. First, the Republican victory was, indeed, historic, but it was also narrow. There is no denying that taking over the House of Representatives was a very, very big deal. . . . Yet the fact is that Republican House candidates took only 51 percent of the vote. . . . What is most revealing . . . is that the Democrats' 1994 losses were concentrated in the groups that had suffered a long-term decline in their economic fortunes. Between 1992 and 1994, the Democratic share of the House vote dropped a staggering twenty points—from 57 percent to 37 percent—among white male high school graduates who never went on to college. The Democrats also fell fifteen points among white males who attended college but never got a degree. Both groups are suffering in this economy. . . . Labor Secretary Robert Reich and Ruy Texeira, a political analyst at the Economic Policy Institute, pointed to these figures as demonstrating that the Democrats' 1994 defeat was largely the result of disaffection among Americans who are suffering in the new economy.

This analysis of the election, with its emphasis on the performance of government and the economy rather than on conservative ideology, feeds into the second large argument going on in the country. That argument is over what it is that most troubles us. Conservatives have a clear answer: The country is bothered by too much government and, above all, by a moral crisis. William Bennett put it very forcefully. "Our problem is not economic," he said in a speech to the Christian Coalition. "Our problems are moral, spiritual, philosophical, behavioral . . . crime, murder, divorce, drug use, births to unwed mothers, child abuse, casual cruelty and casual sex, and just plain trashy behavior."

The other view, put forth among liberals and the Left, is that the fundamental crisis is economic. It relates to the falling living standards of many in the middle and the economic catastrophe in the inner cities. What riles the country most, in this view, is that those who work hard and play by the rules have discovered that many of the rules have been repealed and that no one let on what the new rules are. Many are working harder for less, as the president likes to say, and are understandably resentful. Technological change and the globalization of the economy have kicked out many of the supports for a middle-class standard of living. For very large numbers of people, there is no longer such a thing as what the Catholic church has called "the family wage."

What struck me and many of my colleagues in talking to voters was their anxiety over the impact of economics on their family lives. With both parents having to work, sometimes more than two jobs between them, they felt they were cheating their children. A great many felt they were being forced to choose between providing for their family financially and having the time they needed to spend with their children. Increasingly, they were finding they could do one or the other but not both.

This second argument is central to the future because buying into one side or the other leads to quite different policies and approaches. Catholic social thought could help prevent this argument from becoming a dialogue of the deaf. There is no way forward but to acknowledge both crises. The plain fact is that we will get nowhere if we deny that there is a very real, very troubling moral crisis in the country, a crisis that is destructive to families and especially to children. Anyone who cares about social justice must be concerned with the future of the family because one of the overwhelming forces increasing inequality and immiseration is the rise of fatherlessness. If we don't figure out ways of putting parents and kids back together, most of the problems that everyone on all sides worries about will get much worse. It is also important to find new structures outside of government to help solve these problems. In the area of teen motherhood, the churches have played an enormously constructive role in trying to create shelters and what Progressive Policy Institute analyst Kathleen Sylvester has called "second chance homes" where teen mothers can live with their children in safe, supportive environments. More broadly, the churches can speak with a clarity and forcefulness about moral obligations and personal responsibility in a way that governments never can.

But the churches can do something else, and the Catholic bishops have done this with great courage: remind us that degrading economic circumstances can lead to a degradation of the moral climate. They can remind us in particular that there is no way to help the impoverished solve their own problems in the absence of money. It has been argued that by stepping into so many areas, the government has sapped the energies of private institutions to help the poor. Some government actions, indeed, may have undermined the sector of civil society, the churches, and voluntary institutions. Those policies must be reversed. But . . . those who run the voluntary institutions organized by the churches fear that they would simply collapse under the pressure of huge new burdens if government withdrew large amounts of support for the poor. The costs of providing food and shelter and those second-chance homes are enormous. By all means be open to new ways of helping the poor and acknowledge the social catastrophes in our midst. But let us not pretend that simply having government walk away from these problems will lead to a miraculous solution. . . .

Father Philip Murnion, director of the National Pastoral Life Center, offers a powerful insight from his own experience. After his dad died, Murnion's family was on welfare for several years. But it was, he noted, a very different time. Back then, there was a kind of triad that provided a foundation on which poor people could build themselves up. There was government to provide resources—cash. There was the family to provide love and nurture. And there was the church, with its authority to provide moral guidance. Now all three legs of the stool are in danger. There is family breakdown. The churches enjoy less authority than before. The money is still there, but it is now under threat. Murnion argues, and I think he's right, that we will not solve the problems that trouble us without paying attention to the need to strengthen all three supports.

I would add that we will also not solve these problems unless we take seriously the hugely disruptive effects of the economic changes we are passing through. The issue is not to stop technological change and the huge globalization process in its tracks. This is neither possible nor, in the long run, desirable. But periods such as this one of enormous economic change produce huge disruptions in the lives of families and communities, substantial new opportunities but also substantial problems. Those who are doing well because of these transformations have a particular obligation to think about how they, how the community, and how the government can ease the burdens on those from whom this transition period is extracting the largest costs.

My conclusion about what awaits us in politics and public policy in the future is that a policy of laissez-faire, of pure hands off or anemic government, will not finally satisfy the country because it will not deal with the underlying economic and moral crises so roiling us. But those who believe in something other than laissez-faire will not make their case successfully unless they acknowledge the personal and moral dimension of this problem to which William Bennett among others speaks so forcefully.

Robert McAfee Brown offered what I think is a brilliant insight on how the gospel speaks to us. The gospel "speaks different words to different times," he said, "and even different words to different participants in the same times." The church must preach responsibility to fathers who abandon their families and to teenagers contemplating the obligations of parenthood. It must teach the virtues of self-discipline, work, and perseverance. But it must also preach to those blessed with the world's riches about their responsibilities to their neighbors and their communities and their country, to the poorest among us. We have individual responsibilities. We have social responsibilities we cannot abandon either.

Religion and Politics

MARCH 15, 1928

IS MR. SMITH DANGEROUS?

THE EDITORS

The *New York Herald Tribune* has interested a great many people in an editorial which appeared in the *New World,* official organ of the Archdiocese of Chicago, on January 27. In many respects the document is worthy of even more attention than it has received. After saying that there are "intelligent, courageous" Catholics who are anxious not to stir up bigotry at the present time, the editor in question averred that "the impending nomination of a Catholic for the presidency" would supply enemies of the church with an incentive to rant. . . .

It is difficult to see, however, how all this sordid reality can be anything more than a reason for hoping that Governor Smith becomes the nominee of his party and draws nationwide scrutiny toward his record. The church, of course, would not be greatly served by the fact that one of its members attained to the presidency. A succession of Catholics in the White House could convince nobody of the validity of the Petrine claims. The most one could expect is that if all were radiant with virtue and urbanity, the good example given would win respect and sympathy. . . .

For the real significance of Governor Smith's prominence lies not at all in any imaginary service he may render the church. It lies rather in the circumstance that he is preparing the way for more complete and enthusiastic work by Catholics for the nation. Our Constitution laid down principles of religious freedom, and of every citizen's right to aspire to the presidency. Yet here we are, more than one hundred and fifty years after the signing of the Declaration (to which one Catholic affixed his signature) running amuck over the chance that a man whom New York respects as the greatest governor it ever knew, whom citizens of every class and type admire for integrity and intelligence, and to whom the regeneration of Tammany Hall is in great measure due, may become a "Catholic" president! Who has a right to expect Americanization of an immigrant people if we persist in setting before them so flagrant a case of anticonstitutionalism and antitolerance?

It is because we desire so strongly a freer and more devoted participation by Catholics generally in the national life that we have welcomed so heartily the coming forward of "Al" Smith. Let his fearlessness ignite a general Catholic fearlessness. But beyond that let us examine his credentials frankly, and honestly make up our minds as to whether the party to which he belongs is pledged to the preferable form of government. All this is the genuine American style of action. The rest is weakness, catering to ignorance and stubborn prejudice, cowardice before the only devils who have it in their power to destroy the republic.

THE TOTALITARIAN TEMPTATION

JOHN A. LUKACS

Every century has its theme, and the theme of the twentieth is totalitarianism. To deny this amounts to complacency; and the main concern of this article is with complacency. I wish to establish the proposition that the relationship between Catholics and totalitarianism is by no means as unequivocal as is generally thought. (That I am speaking of Catholics and not of Catholicism is a distinction the appropriateness of which should become clearer later in this article.)

Our understanding of the roots of totalitarianism has hitherto been rather inadequate, yet there is no doubt that the totalitarian appeal of the twentieth century rose out of the deficiencies of an Age of Reason. From an unduly optimistic view of the nature of man and, consequently, from many unwarranted illusions about the nature of politics and of societies, failure has come in many places. From this failure the totalitarians have prospered. An uneasy perception of the same broken illusions has also drawn the attention of many to the Catholic church, a church that always has maintained a wise skepticism about the meaning of material progress and man's ability to transform the world into a Garden of Eden. For both—the church with immense sadness, the totalitarians with blatant joy—register the failure of the Age of Reason.

From this parallel attraction—to totalitarianism and to the church—a conclusion immediately suggests itself. Its logic, at first sight, seems very compelling. It forms the basis of the popular liberal-broad-minded view of the problem. It reasons that the appeals of totalitarianism and of Catholicism are not only parallel but that, in many instances, they actually merge. It claims that the appeal of Catholicism, like the appeal of totalitarianism, is emotional rather than spiritual. There are men and

JOHN A. LUKACS (1924–   ) is author of numerous works, including *The Great Powers and Eastern Europe* and *The Hitler of History*.

women, it is said, who, for various reasons, yearn for guidance, for authority; who, in our troubled world, are not brave enough or willing to rely on their own intellectual judgment and spiritual resources. These are people with an authoritarian frame of mind. They need the inner comfort of an absolute religion. And this is illustrated by those former Communists who, in joining the church, merely sought refuge, in the words of many critics, in another authoritarian faith. It is a seemingly convincing argument.

This argument—at its best, aligning, at its worst, equating, the authority of the church with the authority of Bolshevism—extends from psychology into politics. It is pointed out that the Catholic record against totalitarianism is, essentially, a negative record. Nowhere, it is said, does communism flourish more than in Catholic countries, where the innate lassitude and corruptibility of the Latin character is coupled with many social inequalities, countenanced by a church that clings to the remnants of the aristocracy: obviously it is in Italy and France and not in Germany or Sweden where Western European communism is strongest. And, it is said, even though the church—for evident and selfish reasons—has been consistent in opposing communism, it has been notably deficient in opposing fascism. Spain, and always Spain, is advanced as the prominent example. Some Latin American nations and the Italy of Mussolini follow. It is again, at first sight, an impressive listing.

The standard Catholic defense is, however, no less impressive and convincing. To the unique opposition of the church to communism, Catholics may point with pride and justification. It shows a constancy, compared to which the record of other religious or secular organizations is singularly pale. When it comes to social justice, the Catholic defense stands, again, on solid ground. There are the papal encyclicals, prescient and wise, notably contrasting with the social ethics of their day; there are the numerous Catholic warnings against the material and spiritual evils of industrialism and capitalism. And while for a variety of reasons, the opposition of the church to Fascist regimes has not always been visible on the surface, this opposition has nevertheless been unique and effective: the church earned the thorough hatred of Mussolini and especially of Hitler.

From a historical perspective this is very impressive. For the strongest political defense of Catholicism is always a historical one: there are very few thinking men today, including those critical of Catholic politics and states, who would still claim that the liquidation of the Catholic Hapsburg monarchy in 1918, a liquidation then proposed and supported by many sincere Protestants, impeded rather than hastened the cause of totalitarianism in Europe.

. . . [And] there is another aspect of all this. It is not visible on the surface. It lies and moves with those darker undercurrents of the human heart which, more than ever, make history in this era of emotional mass movements. The illumination of these currents, however momentary, however difficult, reflects a picture that is painful in its truth. It destroys the complacency with which the usual Catholic rebuttal to the charges that link Catholics with totalitarianism is often made. It is, in brief, the fact that Catholics have been, and indeed, sometimes still are, the pacemakers of totalitarianism.

Catholics, I say again, and not Catholicism. Catholics, mostly, who have fallen away from the church, but also some who regard themselves as very good Catholics and staunch members of the church militant. What is more, these Catholics often assist the totalitarians not in a negative but in a positive way. For they are not in a reactionary mood. They are, so they think, on the side of progress. . . . [M]any of these people were born Catholics and later abandoned their faith. There were, however, a great many Catholics (and not only in Germany), who, though they continued receiving the sacraments, complacently overlooked and, at times, even approved, the actions of the SS. And this is a fact with which we should be concerned, for it has a terrible relevance to the present and the future of the West. Relevance, that is, if we accept the political assumption of this essay: the assumption that communism is not the only totalitarian movement that is a present danger to the Western world and to its Christian traditions, and that, in the long run, other totalitarian movements may prove more attractive and even more successful. . . .

If we consider, then, the interrelationship of communism, fascism, National Socialism, we should, after some thought, reach a conclusion that further strengthens my central assumption. This is the conclusion that, in the 1950s, it is not communism and not fascism but National Socialism that provides the only common denominator to all totalitarian states and movements. To equate Communists with Fascists is a false and tawdry generalization, practiced by many liberals; yet one adjective, the National Socialist one, fits all totalitarian tendencies in our day. Tito, Hitler, Stalin; Perón, Mao, Mossadegh: all have a common trait; they all are national socialists. For they all exploit and prosper from the emotional tendencies of the masses. In different degrees they all are against old-time capitalism. And they all are extreme nationalists.

That the opposition of many Catholics to totalitarianism has not been as clear as we might wish is one thing. Curiously, however, our own recognition of this unpleasant fact does not make the case of our critics stronger. Rather, the contrary is true.

The reason for this is the concentration of the whole dialogue upon arguments which are neither relevant nor correct. "Catholicism and democracy are essentially opposed," say the critics. "They certainly are not," say the defenders. But the questions are not these. Their proper phrasing should be: "Catholicism cannot accept the principle of majority rule." And the answer should be: "For a principle of justice, it cannot indeed." "Good," the critics reply, "thus you admit that the Roman church is essentially authoritarian." To which the true answer should be: "Authoritarian, yes. Totalitarian, never."

Here we arrive at a most essential distinction.

For this is the paradox: In our century, hasty and impatient, Catholicism stands accused of being too rigid, too authoritarian, too disciplinary, clinging to traditions of an outmoded past. But this is the same perception which, foolishly enough, views the totalitarians, and especially those of the "right" (in itself an outmoded categorization), as "super-reactionaries." The very opposite is true. And thus the full paradox emerges that the Roman Catholic church will ultimately stand in the way of all totalitarians, including National Socialists, precisely because of its ancient principles, traditions, and "reactionary" skepticism. On the other hand, Catholics will march along with, if not ahead of, the totalitarians at times and in places where the climate of the mass-man has triumphed, where provincial ideals have come to rule, where the function of the majority principle as a means to promote individual dignity and liberty ceases to be recognized; where the ends and means have already been reversed; where the material and social status of the majority has alone come to define progress and democracy.

This is a very interesting, though immensely sad, phenomenon. Catholicism, with its great emphasis on free will and on individual conscience, has never been inclined to accept the majority principle as a yardstick with which to measure the progress of societies. The majoritarian concept of the primacy of the community over the individual was, essentially, a Puritan idea. When Paul Blanshard accuses Catholicism of totalitarian tendencies, what he really means is authoritarianism and not

totalitarianism; he wishes to defend not liberty but the majority principle. And all this would be well if only the majority principle and liberty
always went hand in hand. The terrible lesson of the twentieth century is
that, unfortunately and often enough, they are mortal enemies.

In other words, it could be said that when and where Catholicism de-
fends ancient liberties it is not because then and there the Catholic
church has finally swallowed the lessons of democracy; it is because it has
maintained its reservations about democracy.

That our intellectuals are beginning, uneasily, to sense this cruel
dilemma, is true. But to sense does not mean to perceive, let alone to realize. Hence their fearful confusion. To them the acknowledgment that
the principles of liberty and of majority rule might diverge, would be a
painful admission. Not to thinking Catholics, however; and this is why
among those very few who, already in the pleasant Victorian age, had
sensed and forecast the climate of the totalitarian century, thinkers with
a Catholic temper predominated: Newman, Acton, Donoso, Péguy were
some of these very few. What to others would have amounted to painful
admission, to them was but sad truth. They recognized it.

Yet many Catholics—and, it may be said, most American Catholics—
have not. Their failure of recognition does not, however, come from confusion. It is that failure which comes from complacency. And one of the
facets of this complacency is the ideology of anticommunism. . . .

I do not wish to be misunderstood. It is necessary to oppose communism, any time, anywhere. But, for an American Catholic to oppose it is
not a special virtue. (It was not a special virtue for a German Jew to oppose Hitler.) It is rather a simple duty, a duty which, for most Catholics,
calls for very little sacrifice. In a prosperous America, amidst the political
and social circumstances of our day, it calls for no sacrifice at all. And because it does not call for sacrifice, in these circumstances, this opposition
to communism should not become a central ideology. Yet it does.

It is here that the hidden dangers lie. For this central and wrathful
preoccupation with communism obscures the existence and potential
power of other totalitarian appeals. . . . And this is a delusion over whose
ethical emptiness tower its dark and tangible portents; for, as I said earlier, Hitler may be dead but National Socialism certainly is not.

The importance of these portents, then, becomes immediately evident when we consider that, to Hitler, anticommunism proved not an
end but a political means. That the war, in which he first annihilated
Catholic Poland, which war then destroyed Europe, and which ulti-

mately resulted in the great advance of Soviet Russia, was launched by Hitler in secret and greedy connivance with Stalin is one fact; the other is that the true antitotalitarians have been the men who fought *both* Hitler and Stalin, such men as DeGaulle, Mihailovic, Anders, De Gasperi, Adenauer, Mindszenty. . . .

Catholics are human. And because they are human, they are apt to reflect the temper of their times. In the eighteenth century, when the world was obsessed with the illusions of rationalism and enlightenment, Catholics were prone to be hesitating, apologetic. During the last century, which was obsessed with the illusions of national self-determination and scientific progress, Catholics either went along with a weakening faith or fell back to an introverted attitude that was reactionary in the true sense of the word. This century is the century of totalitarianism. It cannot but affect many Catholics.

The recognition of this state of affairs is a matter of supreme importance, for the church cannot truly prosper in an era of complacency and hypocritical "tolerance." It is the uniqueness of the church that imposes a special burden on Catholics in this age when there is not only a constant clamor for justice but also a constant neglect of injustice; when rights are stressed but duties are not.

Here we arrive at the ultimate conclusions.

I wished to demonstrate that there is no reason for complacency about the relationship of Catholics to the totalitarian trends of the day. But what is so curious is that, while emphasizing what to them seemed the fruitless and negative attitude of the church to totalitarianism, even the critics of the church have largely failed to understand how Catholic populations and individuals have sometimes aided the totalitarians.

One reason for the critics' failure to emphasize the positive contributions of Catholics to totalitarianism may be that, after all, the Catholic over-all record has been singularly good; the noble resistance of many Catholics and the spiritual survival of Catholicism have been evident amidst circumstances where other religious and social doctrines have been far more compromised. For, while there were many provincial Catholic compromisers, there were many Catholic martyrs with an aristocratic frame of mind, men who simply recognized not the promised privileges but the essential burdens which their Catholic principles required from them in a tottering world.

Many Catholics, and many American Catholics, do not understand totalitarianism. Because of this misunderstanding, the weapons of many

will misfire. Because of other misconceptions, and moved by the un-
charitable temper of self-righteousness, many will make way for other,
and infinitely more popular, totalitarians. Because of that complacent
self-righteousness, many will abandon the last shreds of the Catholic
habit of self-questioning and will support the new totalitarianism of
some anticommunist ideology. Some will even wind up among the leaders of this ideology. But, if the totalitarians are going to be true to their
own bent, there will come a point—or, rather, two, five, ten, twenty minor, and sometimes invisible, points—where they, perhaps unwittingly,
will have to conflict with the church. Then those Catholics who wish to
remain with them will have to be, necessarily, ex-Catholics.

For, while it is certain that there are many Catholics who truthfully
reflect the totalitarian tendencies of our awful age, it is even more certain
that the last opposition to the totalitarians will have to come from men
and women who, always and everywhere, uphold Catholic principles.

They may be few; and they may perish. Even then, in a new age of
the catacombs, the church will prosper; and, ultimately, it will be again
the examples of these few Catholic Christians that will, silently and
from the dead, save the world by exhorting future generations to sacrifice.

THE CHRISTIAN IN POLITICS

EUGENE J. McCARTHY

I
s there a Christian politics? . . . Neither history nor political theory establish any basis for the application of the label "Christian"
in any absolute sense to politics. Recognition of Christianity by
the state does not make the state itself "Christian," nor does official approval of certain Christian forms and practices. Neither does the
fact that all citizens of a state are Christians make that state a Christian
state. A government might be distinguished as more or less Christian to
the degree that it has either succeeded or failed in establishing a greater
measure of justice; or, a form of government called Christian to the extent that it depends upon the inspiration of the Gospels for its fulfillment, as does democracy. Such qualified application sets the limits of the
use of the word "Christian."

Although the existence of a purely Christian politics cannot be established, there remains an obvious need for Christians in politics, that is,
for Christian politicians. Every human society is political and every adult
member of such a society must of necessity assume political obligations.
A Christian must assume these obligations as a citizen, and more particularly as a Christian citizen. He must, as Pope Pius XII pointed out in his
message correcting the misinterpretations of the directive "Return to the
Spiritual," be actively present in political life—"wherever vital interests
are at stake; where laws concerning the worship of God, marriage, the
family, the schools, the social order, are being deliberated; wherever
through education the spirit of a nation is being forged. . . ."

The calling of a Christian is not to judge the world, but rather to save
it. In the conflict between good and evil, in which great advantage is
given to evil by neglect, the Christian cannot be indifferent to so important an area of conflict as that of politics. Not everyone has an obligation

---

EUGENE J. MCCARTHY (1916–), politician, educator, and poet, served in the United
States Congress as representative and senator from Minnesota.

to run for public office, or even to become active in party organization. The measure of participation required of an individual depends on many conditions of personality and circumstances. There is no excuse, however, for complete neutralism and detachment. It is not even possible, under all circumstances, to justify the position of the "independent voter," or of the nonpartisan citizen. These forms of political activity can be enjoyed only because others are actively engaged in party politics. It is important to keep in mind the testimony of history to the need for party politics in domestic government. In the United States party factions preceded the adoption of the Constitution itself, and government, since that time, has depended upon political party activities. Good government depends on good political parties.

In approaching politics, the Christian must be realistic—politics is a part of the real world. In politics the simple choice between black and white is seldom given. The ideal is seldom realized, and often cannot be advocated. For example, a Christian politician in a society in which many marriages are broken may have to advocate and support divorce laws for the sake of public order. Trade, diplomatic relations, and cooperation with nations whose conduct he condemns may be made necessary by circumstances. Political leaders may, in what Maritain describes as "regressive or barbarous" societies, have their freedom of choice reduced to the point where they must take a position which is questionable, rather than the alternative which is simply and completely bad. Prudence may require the toleration of evil in order to prevent something worse, and may dictate a decision to let the cockle grow with the wheat for a time. In making decisions of this kind, the Christian in politics, whether he is the official who makes the decision, or the citizen who supports the official and his decision, runs the risk of being called un-Christian or anti-Christian. This is a risk which he must be willing to take.

Despite these difficulties and complications it should nonetheless be possible to distinguish the Christian in politics. If such distinction could not be made there would be no point in urging the participation of Christians in political life.

What are the marks of a Christian politician? He is not necessarily the one who is seen most often participating in public religious activities, or conferring with religious leaders. He is not necessarily the one who first and most vociferously proclaims that his position is the Christian one and who attempts to cover himself and his cause with whatever part of the divided garment that is within his reach. He is not necessarily the one who makes of every cause a "crusade" presenting himself as Carlyle described the crusader as "the minister of God's justice, doing God's judgment of the enemies of God."

The Christian in politics should be judged by the standard of whether through his decisions and actions he has advanced the cause of justice, and helped, at least, to achieve the highest degree of perfection possible in the temporal order. He has available to him a great body of teachings on secular matters. He should know and understand those teachings and should seek to apply them.

When a political problem can be reduced to a simple question of feeding the hungry or of not feeding them; of ransoming the captive or of refusing to ransom him; of harboring the harborless, or of leaving him homeless—there should be no uncertainty as to the Christian position. Problems of overpopulation, of displaced and expelled peoples, of political refugees, and the like are in reality not always reducible to simple choices. As a general rule the inclination of the Christian should be to liberality. His mistakes and failures on problems of this kind should be as a consequence of leniency rather than of a fearful self-interest; of excess of trust, rather than of excess of doubt and anxiety.

The Christian politician must, of course, hold fast to the moral law remembering that the precepts of morality do not themselves change, even though the way in which they are applied to concrete acts may be modified as society regresses or is perverted.

On the basis of moral principles, he must strive to separate good from bad even though the line may be blurred or shifting. He must remember and honor in action the rule that the end does not justify the means. He should carefully avoid confusion such as that which is manifest in Cromwell's reply to Wharton's protest of Pride's purge and the execution of the King. "It is easy to object to the glorious actings of God, if we look too much upon the instruments. Be not offended at the manner. Perhaps there was no other way left."

The Christian in politics should be distinguished by his alertness to protect and defend the rights of individuals, or religious institutions and other institutions from violation by the state or by other institutions, or by persons. He should be the first to detect and oppose a truly totalitarian threat or movement and the last to label every proposal for social reform socialistic.

He should protect the name of Christ from abuse and profanation, and should himself avoid unwarranted appeals to religion. He has a very special obligation to keep the things of God separate from those of Caesar.

The Christian in politics should shun the devices of the demagogue at all times, but especially in a time when anxiety is great, when tension is high, when uncertainty prevails, and emotion tends to be in the ascendancy.

The Christian in politics should speak the truth. He should make his case in all honesty—aware that any other action is as C. S. Lewis states, to offer to the Author of all truth the unclean sacrifice of a lie. He should not return calumny and slander in the same token, but combat them with truth and honesty, risking defeat for the sake of truth. He should not resort to the common practice of labeling, which by its falseness violates justice, and by its indignity offends charity. Powerful personalities may be able to stand against these forces. The weak are likely to be destroyed. It is these who must be the concern of Christians.

In addition to distinction on the basis of actions the Christian in politics should be distinguished by his manner of approach. He should normally be optimistic rather than pessimistic. The optimism would not be blind or foolish, without awareness or recognition of reality, but rather manifesting hopeful confidence, despite the difficulties of a situation and the potentiality of men and human society for failure.

The Christian should show respect for the opinion, judgment, and motives of others. This he can do without any abject denial of the certainty of his own position and without agreeing to disagree, or conceding that those who disagree with him may be right.

The Christian should be humble, reflecting in his actions his awareness of the great mystery of redemption, and the shared mystery and dignity of all men.

Altogether these seem to be difficult standards and demands. Their fulfillment requires sanctity. There is, however, no other measure which is valid for Christians in politics or in any other way of life. As the great politician and saint, Thomas More, observed, "It is not possible for all things to be well, unless all men are good—which I think will not be this good many years."

KENNEDY THE CATHOLIC

JOHN COGLEY

N ow, after his tragic death and less than a full term in the White House, it is possible to see that John Fitzgerald Kennedy served his church as brilliantly as he served his country. He did so, not by being the first Catholic president but by being the first American president who was a Catholic. The distinction was clear in the president's mind from the first days of his campaign and he observed it loyally throughout his years in the White House.

Five years ago, in a controversial article for *Look,* he stated that whatever his personal religious views might be, nothing transcended an officeholder's obligation to uphold the constitutional oath. There was an outcry in the religious press at the time, not only the Catholic but certain sections of the Protestant press as well, reminding Mr. Kennedy that God is to be served before man and that the Christian conscience is to be obeyed before the Constitution. The reminders were unnecessary. Mr. Kennedy, though he certainly was no theologian, had a steady grasp of basic Christian morality. The statement appearing in *Look* was carefully worded, especially the term "officeholder."

Mr. Kennedy's problem was that he overestimated the political, and perhaps even the theological, sophistication of his co-religionists. What he wanted to say of course was that ours is a government of laws not of men and that the president cannot, even in the name of his personal conscience, set aside the Constitution. Later, in his confrontation with the Houston ministers, Kennedy spelled out his position more clearly, stating unequivocally that if as president he ever felt conscientiously obliged

---

JOHN COGLEY (1916–76) was a *Commonweal* editor from 1949 to 1955, and a columnist until 1964. Later he served as an editor at the *New York Times,* as a presidential campaign adviser for John F. Kennedy and Eugene McCarthy, and as founding editor of the *Center Magazine.*

to act contrary to the Constitution, he would resign rather than betray the oath of office. He added with considerable vigor that he anticipated no such difficulty nor was he ready to concede that there would be any conflict between his Catholic conscience and the oath of office.

John F. Kennedy was never at ease with what-would-you-do abstractionism of this kind, and he frequently showed his impatience with it. To be sure, he had to take account of it in order to get elected, but his natural inclination was to put a much higher premium on the pragmatic and the historical and what his theological critics would call prudence but which he thought of simply as politics. These personal predilections were at once a handicap and a strength to the first American Catholic elected president.

They were a handicap, especially during the campaign when he was required to talk rather than act. He had to state his position incessantly, but the terms of the argument shaped by the theological-minded were simply not within his frame of reference. "It is hard for a Harvard man to answer questions in theology," he wrote to me once. "I imagine my answers will cause heartburn at Fordham and B.C. [Boston College]."

As a result of this shyness in an unfamiliar intellectual world, his Catholicism was at first widely suspect. Catholics, ignorant of or hostile to the intellectual climate of a Harvard, were as uncomfortable with Kennedy's pragmatism as he was with the scholastic-flavored thought of the Catholic universities. Protestants, starting from their own stereotypes of how a "good" Catholic should operate intellectually, were put off, as were a good many Jewish and humanist intellectuals. When Kennedy first began to be taken seriously as a contender for the White House, not a few Catholics were disappointed that one who was so untypical had reached such prominence as a spokesman for their community. Certain Protestants talked the same way. More than one was heard to say that he wished that if there were to be a Catholic president, it would have been a "good Catholic" rather than Kennedy. The name of another, more theologically sophisticated politico was frequently cited as the kind they had in mind.

But after the president got to the White House, emphasis on his faith was muted. If the school question had not flared up as it did, the religious issue might have been quietly buried. But this of course did not happen automatically. The president himself always had to take into consideration that his religion was a factor that might cause a blowup at any time. He went to some pains not to show any signs of favoritism or to give any indication that he was dominated by the hierarchy of the church. Inevitably, this circumspection was churlishly noted from time to time in the Catholic press. As some had predicted before his election, Protestants, as well as Catholics, began to say that Catholic influence was weaker under Mr. Kennedy than it would have been under a man of a different faith.

Catholics, then, had to pay a price for the fact that one of their body sat in the White House. Theodore Sorensen admitted as much in a lecture at Columbia, when he acknowledged that President Kennedy was handicapped by the circumstances of his being the first Catholic in the White House when it came to dealing with federal aid to parochial schools. From the very first days of the campaign, the president gave it as his opinion that such aid would be deemed unconstitutional by the Supreme Court. But until the end, the suspicion lingered in Catholic minds that because the issue was politically explosive for Kennedy, they would have fared better in getting it tested under a non-Catholic president.

Despite his lack of interest in abstract theological matters, though, John F. Kennedy probably had more influence on the future of the American church than any Catholic, lay or clerical, in the history of the nation.

There are, first and foremost, the sheer facts of his life. He was the quintessential modern man, a product of the twentieth century, gifted with a good mind, a graduate of the most respected schools, a sophisticate, and a universally admired statesman. He had a horror of the pietistic and avoided moralism as if it were poison. (The only "un-American" traits in his character.) Yet, his Catholicity was as much a part of him as his modernity. He wore both of them as unselfconsciously and elegantly as he wore his London clothes. John F. Kennedy was a living refutation of the argument of those who used to hold that Catholicism was an anachronism in the modern age. He did not claim to be a saint, nor was he ever mistaken for one, but he was a man of faith and of steady, unspectacular loyalty to his church. Finally, he died an authentic hero in the minds of millions of young Americans. That will go a long way toward shaping the image of Catholicism in the years ahead.

Secondly, whatever theoretical issues remain to be solved, President Kennedy showed by his career that American Catholicism as a matter of fact has long since come to terms with religious pluralism. Not even his bitterest critics ever accused him of personal prejudice, and the only serious criticism of his handling of religious issues during his years in the White House came from fellow Catholics. Certainly now the symbolic exclusion of Catholics from the highest office in the land has come to an end. Nor, after John F. Kennedy, can one imagine the nation embroiled in the kind of controversy that swirled around his candidacy only four years ago.

Finally—and this is a more controvertible personal view of mine—President Kennedy more than any other leader rescued the day-by-day politics that makes democracy possible from the disdain in which it had been held in America. Only a few years ago, there was a disturbing poll taken which showed that a very high percentage of Americans regarded politics as a dirty business unfit for their children. I doubt that a similar finding would be turned up today. For Kennedy took public pride and satisfaction in his vocation, and he did not identify his calling merely with the proposal of noble goals but also with the hard work and earthy craft necessary to turn those goals into reality. This latter meant compromise, frustration, wheels and deals, and, above all, the responsible use of power. And the president employed all these means shamelessly and candidly. Frequently in doing so he brought down upon his head the charge of being cynical, timid, power-hungry, and shallow. Ideologues on both left and right found him anathema. Purists and utopians, who forever confuse rhetoric with leadership and propositions with proposals, frequently expressed their "disappointment" with him, though their expectations from the beginning were minimal. But lead he did, and as became clear at the time of his death, he also educated millions of people to the realities of the nuclear age.

It was here, I believe, that he made his most distinctive "Catholic" contribution to American life. Not that he was self-consciously Catholic in his attitude toward the uses of power. If his approach to this difficult problem was essentially Thomistic, as I believe, it was a Thomism learned not in a classroom but absorbed from his Irish forebears who were untutored in philosophical schools but were blessedly free of the burdens posed by a "Moral Man, Immoral Society" view of the political order. The criticism might justly be made of that generation of politicians that they were too little aware of the corruptive tendencies attached to the possession of power. But, to their credit, it can also be said that they never flinched from political responsibility nor did they think of themselves as less worthy Christians because they had to face up to the consequences of Original Sin in public life.

The traditional American religious attitude, on the contrary, had never quite come to terms with the responsibilities of power. It had accepted Lord Acton's famous phrase as a dictum rather than a warning. Acton said that power *tends* to corrupt; he did not say that power is itself an evil thing, though that is how he is usually interpreted. His insight resulted from a Catholic not a Calvinistic view of life.

So deeply rooted in the American mind was the idea of power itself as corruption that even Catholics were persuaded of its truth and, in formal statements, frequently sounded more Puritan than Thomistic. But at the theoretical level at least, Catholicism was spared the agonizing reappraisal of power that American Protestantism, under the guidance of Reinhold Niebuhr, undertook a generation ago when the nation was drawn, against its will, into the world community. Though it never accepted the notion of society as inescapably "immoral," Catholic theory provided for the kind of social responsibility that Dr. Niebuhr encouraged.

Just as it was John F. Kennedy rather than John Courtney Murray who dealt the death blow to the notorious Catholic church-state "thesis" as a factor in American politics, so was it Kennedy more than Reinhold Niebuhr who finally instructed the nation in the responsible use of power. For example, he saw no need for the pietism that John Foster Dulles used to sugarcoat the harsher aspects of foreign policy during the Eisenhower administration. He was not coy about the employment of American power, ever. As a result, he shocked some people, but many more were relieved of an intolerable burden of false guilt under his easygoing tutelage. (Among the most shocked, incidentally, were many who had long endorsed the Niebuhrian insights.)

In spite of, and maybe because of, his "Catholic" attitude toward power, President Kennedy, at the time of his death, was mourned primarily as a leader who had made world peace a more feasible ideal and who could be trusted to negotiate honorably with the Soviets in the effort to achieve it. Though there were some doubts about his possible rigidity at the time he was elected, based on another stereotype about Catholics, rigidity was foreign to his temperament and he was leery of anti-Communist crusades. The key to his administration was probably summed up in his famous warning that we should neither negotiate from fear nor ever fear to negotiate. That statement, to my mind, was a dual recognition of the two foundations of Catholic political thought: an appreciation of power, on the one hand, and recognition of the preeminence of reason, on the other.

John F. Kennedy's historic role in the history of the church, then, was like everything else about him: low-key, more subtle than apparent, more pragmatic than propositional, more indirect than intrusive. Such was his understanding of the American political system *and* of Catholicism that he did not regard himself as any less a Catholic because he was impartially the president of all Americans, whatever their faith or lack of faith. Just as he suffered from anti-Catholic bigotry, so did he benefit from Catholic tribalism in the 1960 election. It is a measure of his accomplishment that three years later there is much less of both. He knew that in the second-term campaign he looked forward to, he could not depend on either as a stable fact of American political life. That did not sadden him. He had no doubt that he would win the election, not on the basis of his religion, any more than he would lose it on that basis, but on his record as a public servant.

RICHARD J. DALEY—
A PERSONAL MEMOIR

MICHAEL McAULIFFE

He never understood me and Christ knows I never understood him. Neither did anyone else with the possible exception of his wife. Meanwhile, dozens of alleged pundits have had a go at him and several wrote the definitive words many hours before they got him into his grave at Holy Sepulchre.

Richard J. Daley laid several bribes on me about forty-five or forty-six years ago. I took them, and I never paid off, so this is a last attempt. His and my code demand at least the effort.

My father's sister, Nora Guilfoyle, a widow with ten children, lived down the road from us on Throop Street, in a neighborhood called Bridgeport, in Chicago, Illinois. It is two-and-a-half miles southwest of the Loop and its back door was the stockyards. No literary luminary, from Upton Sinclair to James T. Farrell to Saul Bellow, has ever succeeded in recapturing or even evoking the recollection of the stench that pervaded our little world from the blood, entrails, and hides of the slaughtered animals on a hot summer's day.

It was a ramshackle place, we were all poor. One of the few ways up or out if you weren't brilliant was politics. Most of us, including Dick Daley, were not brilliant. We were Polish, Irish, Czech, a few Germans. Each group had its own church, usually Catholic. Blacks and Jews there weren't. We were urban provincials often crude, sometimes tough, rarely well-educated, probably scared, and we had needs—many of them.

Although I was an altar boy, I still spent a lot of time in the temporal world of those humble houses, that awful stench, the capacious emptiness of my schoolboy pockets. I developed a racket. I needed one.

My father was a city employee. During the Depression they paid in scrip and the boys downtown were cashing it for the boobs at a nice 15 to

MICHAEL McAULIFFE, a communications consultant in New York, wrote for the *Chicago Sun-Times* and *Billboard* magazine.

20 percent discount because the city stood behind it. In those days, people seemed to believe in cities . . . *"urbi et orbi"* as each new pope says when he lays on the first *barucha*.

With the cashed-in scrip we managed a cash flow. It wasn't a flood but one of the few working trickles in the block. From about '30 to '34 our dinner table kept expanding in direct proportion to the number of unemployed bricklayers, steamfitters, carpenters who were our cousins, brothers-in-law, uncles, aunts, nieces, and old friends. I lived in this world and also in a ten-year-old's world of needs—for ice cream cones, candy bars, caps for my toy pistol, with the ultimate a bleacher seat at Comiskey Park, home of the last-place White Sox.

Aunt Nora's daughter, Sis, was being courted by a short, heavy-set guy already in politics. He was going to night school and was also secretary to "Pighead Joe" McDonough, our neighbor and county treasurer, so named I guess because he was fat, bald, and had distended nostrils. I didn't say we were nice; we had these needs for jobs, food, spending money, and to call each other names.

Pretty soon I knew this young pol's schedule better than his intended, my cousin, Sis. So, I would saunter down to my aunt's living room and get very talkative with the young couple as my aunt hovered a discreet room or two away. The young pol never failed to lay a nickel, dime, and, as the romance waxed, sometimes a quarter on me together with a suggestion about where one might get the best ice cream cones in the neighborhood—not the closest place, mind you, but the farthest store where they had the best.

It was an on-going contract. Sometimes I was suffered for five, ten, fifteen minutes, actually conversed with about school, baseball, family news. But, in the end I always got my tribute and they got their privacy. I may well be the only guy on earth who ever grafted Dick Daley for something approaching hard cash with anything resembling consistency.

Please forgive me for the subjective, egotistical bunch that I knew Richard Daley longer, better, and in a more human context than most biographers, commentators, obituary writers, critics, and even lackeys.

To me, the essential thing about him was that he took care of his own. This can be seen as a narrow, xenophobic, and far from purely philanthropic trait. But it is not necessarily a negative one. How many humans, told as the shadow approached that this was to be the inscription on their tombstone, would rail against it?

He was short, overweight, a disastrous orator. He was more Catholic than the pope—detested divorce, couldn't tolerate a dirty joke, practiced the deceptive art of nursing a single highball for hours on end with the aid of quarts of soda, pounds of ice. His public relations were abominable. He had the sure, unerring knack of taking on the role of the heavy. He didn't give a good goddamn what anybody thought, and one of his few but frequent vulgarities was to tell, or indicate to those in his disfavor (often journalists), that they "can kiss my ass."

It is difficult for me to enumerate a single relative in a typically numerous Irish family who is not now, or did not spend most of his or her working life on the city, county, state, or federal payroll thanks to his intercession, or "clout" as the numerous observers so often and so aptly described it.

And yet, and yet, there was that day in the fifties that I passed through Chicago, dropped by to see him, and spent about ninety minutes closeted with him and a man named Harry S. Truman. I got up to go a half dozen times but was sat back down—Dick Daley somehow knew that such a "favor" meant more to me than any job he could ever give me and he fulfilled the contract right over any objection I might raise.

There was the man who worked with my father who once joined an insurgent political movement back in the forties and soon found himself a pariah and out of a job. My father went to see the then patronage-dispenser four or five times. "Dick, he's a hot head and a fool. But he's a good worker and he needs the job." Four times Daley told my father to tell the guy to "Go to hell." But after the sixth visit my father came home in triumph. The man was reinstated. I asked him how he did it.

"I told Dick he was punishing the fellow for his manhood and, goddamnit, I'm his uncle, ain't I?"

Once Richard Daley took the time to tell me his version of John Kennedy's narrow, imperative, eight-thousand-vote victory over Richard Nixon in Illinois in 1960. The story is as arcane as a shyster's spiel but as honest and legal as a page torn from Blackstone.

Few people could look as bad to some, as good to others, as he did because few people have so central a base and the whole nation as a canvas to move around in. He was largely responsible for giving us Adlai Stevenson; at the same time he never seemed to appreciate the towering moral stature of Martin Luther King Jr., despite many firsthand opportunities to do so. He would likely have done anything save strike a priest for John Kennedy, yet he continually put forward narrow, limited party hacks for local office—men so inept at campaigning and lacking in appeal that they couldn't win with the machine delivering a solid base of votes for them.

My God, he was human—loaded with limitations, foibles, blind-spots, prejudices, ego, and a power drive combined with a sense of om-niscience that rivaled de Gaulle's. But underneath all that flesh, those warts, the jumbled sentences, the cold fury visited on the ward commit-teemen who didn't deliver on election day, the cute Irish "poll" and the rectitudinous Catholic prude, there existed a man whose patron saint was really Santa Claus.

I think one of the reasons he got into the power game was to help all the slobs he knew and was related to who didn't have a notion about how to get their noses near the trough. I believe his will and estate, if made public, will reflect no more wealth than his official earnings and I know that Sis still bakes a lot of her own bread.

So, the fat little autocratic power broker who often looked like Bud-dha on the tube is gone and are any of us the better for it? I'm not, al-though I haven't lived in his city for nearly thirty years and hadn't talked to him in a year or so.

Boys and girls, there once was a Santa Claus. He lived in a city he loved and he ruled it for a long, long time. He took care of a lot of slobs who were white, black, Protestant, Catholic, Jewish, most of them a lot like him—finite, hypocritical, often mean, sometimes splendid. Every 1,460th day or so, he asked that they repay the favors. The last time out, about 75 percent of them turned out to say, "Yeah, for duh Mair. . . ."

Cunning, loving, sentimental, brutal, devious, honest, loyal to the point of being a neurotic, unforgiving and generous, all these words could be applied to Richard J. Daley. In short, he was a man and, as such, had something in common with da Vinci, as well as Al Capone.

What a pity he died so close to Christmas. He had the reindeer ready to go, he knew every chimney in town, and his bag—well, let me tell you, it was a big one. I know, I got my first present from it nearly fifty years ago. Nor am I ashamed to say that in an atypical, detached, and distant way, I have always been "one of his own."

The Bottom Line

CATHOLIC INDUSTRIAL PRINCIPLES

EDWIN V. O'HARA

A full generation has passed since Pope Leo XIII issued his epoch-making encyclical on the condition of labor. . . . His encyclical . . . concludes by explicitly placing on the clergy, in union with their bishops, the task of persistent and energetic action in behalf of the laboring class. He writes: "Every minister of holy religion must throw into the conflict [in behalf of social justice and charity] all the energy of his mind and all the strength of his endurance." Similar injunctions have been addressed to the clergy by Pius X, Benedict XV and Pius XI. In fulfilling these injunctions, the pastor will find that his activities in behalf of his working men will fall into three general channels, the currents of which flow largely in the same direction and frequently converge. These channels are education, organization, and legislation.

It will be the duty of the pastor in industrial centers to explain to his people clearly and frequently the Christian laws of justice and of charity as they affect employer and employee. He will point out with Leo XIII that a great error in the discussion of industrial problems is to possess oneself of the idea that class is naturally hostile to class; that rich and

EDWIN V. O'HARA (1881–1956), an associate chairman of the Social Action Department of the National Catholic Welfare Conference, served as the bishop of Kansas City, Missouri.

poor are intended by nature to live at war with one another. On the contrary, each requires the other; capital cannot thrive without labor, nor labor without capital. He will go on to teach that religion requires the laboring man to carry out honestly and well all equitable agreements fairly made; never to injure capital, nor to outrage the person of an employer; never to employ violence in representing his own cause, nor to engage in riot and disorder. Religion, he will continue, teaches the employer that his working people are not his slaves; that he must respect in every man his dignity as a Christian; that labor is nothing to be ashamed of, but that it is shameful and inhuman to treat men like chattels in order to make money, or to look upon them as merely so much muscle or physical power; that the employer must see that his workmen have time for their duties of piety and the obligations of their family life; that they must not be taxed beyond their strength or employed in work unsuited to their sex or age; that the workmen are entitled to a living wage, and that to exercise pressure for the sake of gain upon the indigent and destitute, and to make one's profit out of the need of another, is condemned by all laws, human and divine.

It will devolve on the pastor to undertake to assist his working men by organization and legislation. Most of the progress made by the working classes in recent times has been due to organization, and it will be the duty of the clergy to encourage every form of work association which legitimately promotes the workmen's interests. Much has been written concerning freedom of contract and the importance of allowing each man to bargain for himself. After a long and painful struggle, the working man has realized that there is no equality of bargaining power when the individual workman is pitted against the large employer. For freedom of contract, it is necessary that the working men combine and bargain collectively with their employers, so that there may be some semblance of equality between the two contracting parties. The so called American plan whereby the employer refuses to deal with labor collectively is, under a specious pretense of liberality, merely a hollow sham. The power of the employer to withhold bread is a vastly greater advantage than the power of the individual employee to refuse to labor. To speak of freedom of contract between the individual employee, whose family may be on the verge of starvation, and the modern accumulation of capital that seeks to employ labor, is simply grotesque humor.

The importance of workmen's associations is set forth by Leo XIII and the encouragement of labor unions will properly claim the interest of the minister of religion. It will, however, not be sufficient to encourage the organization of labor associations and to promote an increase of their membership, but it will be necessary for the pastor to impress upon the members of the unions who belong to his own congregation the importance of electing good men to leadership, and of recognizing that the union is not merely an economic institution, but has moral aspects as well. No small injury has been done to the cause of labor in our time through unprincipled leaders and a disregard of the moral principles which must provide the basis of permanent association.

In the field of cooperation, laboring men have successfully maintained stores which have proved a boon to their members. One form of cooperation deserves special attention; namely, the establishment of a co-operative credit association in a parish which will free the laboring man from the clutches of the loan shark, and will enable him to secure necessary advances of money on reasonable terms and without placing him in the power of the lender. Finally, the establishment of parish study groups among laboring men will be found of great service as a means of inculcating Christian principles in regard to these economic issues.

The utility of organization cannot be questioned. Nevertheless, there are limits to its successful activity. There are great groups of working people whom it is difficult to organize, and up to the present only a comparatively small percentage of workers are actually organized. It is the duty of the state to prevent any class of the population from becoming submerged, and consequently the pastor will, in his solicitude for his people, urge the necessary legislation to protect them. The problem of the inadequacy of women's wages is present in most American cities, and the program for minimum-wage legislation should secure the hearty cooperation of the clergy.

A similar interest will be manifested by the pastor in the limitation of hours of labor, both of women and men, especially in the prohibiting, as far as possible, of Sunday work and of late-night work. I recall that when the Industrial Welfare Commission of Oregon first entered a ruling prohibiting work for women in the department stores after six o'clock in the evening, many young women had for the first time in months a reasonable opportunity to go to church and hear Mass on Sunday morning.

Workmen's compensation legislation has now come in most of our states, and with it the abolition of the common law pleas of contributory negligence and assumption of risk, which enabled the liability insurance companies to prevent the injured workman from receiving compensation; but the principle of compensation needs to be maintained and extended, the importance of safety devices on machinery insisted upon, and many occupational diseases should be brought under the operation of compensation.

The pastor will be concerned, also, with the living conditions of his working people, and will feel it his duty to promote an adequate housing code, which will require the home of his people to be furnished with sufficient sunlight and fresh air, and open spaces for children's recreation. It will be necessary to resist the wild and unscrupulous advertising of city commercial clubs, which lead multitudes of unskilled laborers to congregate in congested centers, flooding the labor market and overcrowding the tenements. I have attended dying men in workingmen's hotels in rooms where no light but that cast by the flickering flame of the gas jet ever penetrated. Such conditions will be found wherever there is a lack of adequate housing legislation, or a neglect of its enforcement.

The pastor, too, will be interested in the promotion of legislation regulating employment bureaus and preventing the exploitation of men who pay for their jobs. The old story of the three groups of men on a job, the one going, the one coming, and the one working, is a grim commentary on unregulated employment offices.

Thus under the guidance of the principles enunciated by Leo XIII in his immortal encyclical, *Rerum novarum,* the Catholic church is seeking to establish the reign of social justice throughout the world of contemporary industry.

FOR THE TRULY POOR

DOROTHY DAY

Maria has come in from the country where she has been living for the past years, and we are going out to look for an apartment for her. It is for herself, her two children and husband. Without money they could no longer get along in the country. The city offers Alan a job at $15 a week and now the problem is, finding a home. The family of four cannot live on $15 a week, you say? Nonsense! With courage and determination, one can do anything. Well, of course, if they are used to it. . . . But they are not. They are used to owning their own home, to having a car, to sending their children to a private school.

But Maria meets problems with a fine spirit and refuses to be defeated.

It is one of those keen, clear January days with a faint warmth in the air—a good day for a brisk walk. Starting south on Avenue A, we face a sharp wind and a dazzling winter sun which hangs low over the houses. It is early, only two o'clock in the afternoon, and it is amazing how much light and sparkle there is in that sun which hangs so low in the sky.

We have no set plan, Maria and I, that is to say, we do not really know where we are going to look. We are just setting out to walk up one street and down another until a likely place presents itself. Nevertheless, I more or less know what I am doing, for I have placed the whole matter in the hands of Saint Joseph. He is a fine one to find a home for you, I tell Maria.

Maria is a Communist, but she is very fond of me, and if I think Saint Joseph is going to guide us, well and good.

He should be especially helpful, I add, since he had so much trouble himself in finding a place for Mary and the Child, and in consideration

---

DOROTHY DAY (1897–1980), cofounder of the Catholic Worker movement with Peter Maurin, was a writer and activist.

of the fact that we are modest in our demands, not expecting much more than a stable for the rent we can pay, he will surely guide us.

On 15th Street, just across from the Immaculate Conception Church, there is an empty flat. But though the outside of the building is clean, the inside is not, and the rent is exorbitant. Twenty dollars for four rooms, no heat, no hot water, no bath! Impossible. We are not being finicky, we just know we can do better.

As I say, we had no plan on setting out, but we did intend to confine our researches to one area—that large sprawling part of the East Side, bounded by the Williamsburg Bridge on the south, 14th Street on the north, the East River and Avenue A. This is a section apart from subways and elevated trains and accessible only by meandering buses or crosstown cars, which means that to get anywhere you have to pay two fares. But Maria likes to walk and so does Alan, and he can get up a half-an-hour earlier to make the long crosstown hike and save carfare, and the walking will be enlivening and he won't miss the country so much.

We are finding the walk enlivening ourselves, and as we go, we peer through doorways, looking for back-yard houses.

Did you know that all over the East Side there are hidden streets, accessible only through front buildings or obscure alleys, and on these hidden streets there are sometimes stables or little houses or rows of apartment buildings hidden from the world? These are quiet places, away from the noise of the street, away from trucks and taxis and street cars, and often, if the houses in front are high and those in back low, away from sunlight and air too. But sometimes the position is reversed, the houses in back are high and those in front low, and there is apt to be a bargain there.

One such place we found, back of Avenue A. It was a tall, slim back-yard house, four stories high, an apartment to a story, and each apartment renting for $14 a month.

But the janitor's husband reeled at us dangerously, and the smell of alcohol sent us fleeing to the street.

We cut over through Tompkins Square, to get to Avenue B, and it was good to feel the spongy earth under foot, though the feel of it brought a nostalgia for the fields.

Down on 8th Street past Avenue C there was an old house (not a back-yard house) facing north and south, with a trampled back yard. But the rooms were large and light and high-ceilinged, the house was a well-built one, and despite the neighborhood, which was teeming with children, one felt the luxury of space and nobly proportioned rooms. There were well appointed bathrooms, good electric fixtures, a well outfitted kitchen. But the rent for this place was too high, $25, and the gas bill would bring it up to $35, what with the heating of both house and water; and a man getting $15 a week cannot afford that, said Maria firmly.

Cutting across Avenue C which is a wide sunny street, we passed the pushcarts piled with artichokes, tomatoes, mushrooms and all kinds of fruits. "A penny a piece for artichokes," I cried, buying some, "and mushrooms only fifteen a pound. One can always eat anyway."

"We got a letter from our cousin in Russia," Maria said, "and he writes that nowadays when the people talk about America they don't want to hear about our industries or high buildings, but about the food for sale on the pushcarts where all can buy. They say, 'Can you really buy all the bread and butter you can eat? Can you really have fresh fruits and meats? And it is cheap?' It is very sad."

We cut back along 7th Street toward the part where the school children are beginning to gather for play. This street is not as crowded as 11th, 12th, or 13th. Those are supposed to be rough streets. Seventh Street has synagogues and women sitting out in the sun with baby carriages. On one side there is a public school. Around the corner on the square is Saint Bridget's Church, with a parochial school in back.

We were nearing the corner when we passed a wide passageway leading back to a long, irregular-shaped yard where there are a half-dozen five-story buildings. In front, facing the street, the houses are only three stories high.

The son of the Russian janitor, a clean, spectacled student, opens the door to one of the houses and shows us the apartments. There are three rooms, of fair size, all of them light and sunny on the top two floors. The living-room has a fire place and two many-paned windows facing south. The bedroom and kitchen face north and there is a window in each. There is a little toilet off the kitchen. Instead of a wash-tub, the boy says, the landlord will put in a bathtub. There is no heat, no hot water, no electricity, but the rent is only $10 a month.

The houses are sordid, grim, and look as though they belong in a Dickens novel. But Maria, who believes in scrubbing with strong yellow soap, is thinking of blue-and-white check curtains at the windows and her blue rag rugs on the floor.

"Blue, the psychologists say, is a happy color," she says cheerfully, not at all taken aback by the seven years accumulation of dirt in the apartments, for it is long since they were occupied, the janitor's boy says.

"Blue is the color of the sky and the Blessed Virgin's robes."

"If we take the top floor, we can use the roof. There'll be plenty of blue then. Alan can build a fence to make it safe for the children."

Her mind is pretty well made up—Saint Joseph has helped us in our search, for really, the rooms envisaged with fresh paint, curtains, scrubbed floors, rag rugs, and children's toys, are not so bad. A clear eye and a courageous spirit has transformed them into a home.

But it is too fine a day not to continue our walk, so we venture further into the depths of the East Side, down to Stanton Street to visit the model tenements of the Lavanburg Foundation. There had been stories in the paper a few weeks ago of the celebration of the fifth year of these model homes, built by the philanthropy, or shall we say, the loving kindness of a Jew, with the cooperation of his Catholic partner, two of whose sons are still on the board of trustees. Here there are roof gardens and basement club rooms, a kindergarten, and community activities. But the rents are $30 for three rooms, $34 for four rooms, and $42 for five rooms, low rents it is true, but too much for working people these days, when fathers of families are working half or full time for $10 and $15 a week and glad even of that to hold body and soul together.

"What should be done," said Maria, "is this. Landlords with the cooperativeness or sense of duty or whatever you want to call it, of Mr. Lavanburg, should take their old houses where the poor are still forced to live because they can't pay more than $10, $15, or $18 a month, and utilize the basements and roofs. There could be mothers' and fathers' clubs, and children's play clubs to meet in basement rooms for their activities. Community spirit and cooperation would be fostered. And the roofs could be made into playgrounds where they could gather together in summer instead of on crowded front stoops and garbage-filled streets, where the children are in continual danger. It wouldn't take much to make these reforms: only a landlord who has a social conscience and a few tenants who would cooperate and get things started. You don't have to have a million to do it. You don't have to have steam-heat and hot water. The poor are used to hardship. Small beginnings," she ruminated, as we walked back through dusky lamp-lit streets, for it was now five o'clock and twilight was upon us. "The roof playground first. We'll see what we can do. . . ."

WATERFRONT PRIEST

BUDD SCHULBERG

Last winter, when waterfront racketeering was front-page news, a tall, intense, youthfully balding New York Irishman wearing the cassock of a Jesuit priest aroused the curiosity of millions of TV and radio fans of Dave Garroway, Tex and Jinx, and other prominent programs.

"The mob is tryin' to scare the men off from giving the Crime Commission the facts on waterfront extortion, kick-backs, shakedowns, pilferage and all the rest of the mess that's been infecting our great port of New York," Father John Corridan told his audience. "They're boastin' already that when the Crime investigation is gone and forgotten, there'll be bodies floatin' in the river. Well, that's a good sign, in a way. It means the fast-money crowd who muscled in on our honest hardworking longshoremen are feelin' shaken and desperate. It may not come today or tomorrow or next week, but little by little the harbor workers, and the union leaders and the politicians are waking up. It's a long, uphill pull, but one of these days we're going to see law and order, job security, regulated hiring and union democracy raise our longshoremen to the level of dignity reached in other key industries."

"Is he real," a friend of mine actually asked me after having seen Father Corridan on the Garroway show, "or is he a young Pat O'Brien made up as a priest for a movie part?"

I laughed, but sympathetically, for I had had a similar reaction three years earlier. At that time, in the course of some research for a forthcoming movie, I asked some newspapermen how I could get the feel of the waterfront as it really is. Much to my surprise their answer was: "Go down and see Father John Corridan, the waterfront priest. He's been on top of it for years."

BUDD SCHULBERG (1914–) is the author of, among other works, *The Disenchanted, What Makes Sammy Run,* and the screenplay for *On the Waterfront.*

Next day I was having lunch at Billy the Oysterman's with this chain-smoking, ruddy-complexioned man in his early forties who looked fit enough to swing a hook with the best of them. He was too full of his subject to do much eating. It seemed to me the most unusual talk I had ever heard, combining the gritty language of the dock workers with mob lingo, the facts and figures of a trained economist and the teachings of Christ.

Listening to Father Corridan with growing amazement, I felt myself entering a world I would not have believed possible in America, just as I might have cried "fake!" if I had seen a movie about a Catholic priest who becomes a leader among rough-and-tumble dock-wallopers, as tough in his own way as the Mickey Bowers, Anastasias, Clementes and other criminal elements who have been allowed to gouge longshoremen and grab off an illegal $350 million annually from the port.

For the past six years, as assistant director of the Xavier Labor School, Father Corridan has put in as much as eighteen and twenty hours a day studying the waterfront problem. He has studied the figures pier by pier. He has talked to hundreds of longshoremen in his small office, which is littered with waterfront clippings and reports. He has gone into the homes of the dock workers to talk over the meat-and-potatoes problem with their wives. He has talked to cops, district attorneys, port officials, union officers, rank-and-file leaders, state employment people, congressional investigators, government labor authorities.

Call off a pier on either side of the river and Father Corridan can tell you who controls it; he's got the name and number of the hiring boss, the boss loader and the treasurer of the local who never bothered to keep books. He has traced their political connections. For years, while there was a general hush-hush policy regarding the fabulous "Mr. Big," William J. McCormack, who parlayed a horse-and-wagon into a hundred-million-dollar waterfront empire, Father Corridan has been studying the connections between him and such unsavory characters as strong-arm specialist Albert Ackalitis and the notorious gunman Linky Mitchell.

Full of the nervous intensity of the waterfront he serves, Father Corridan understands, and hopes by this understanding eventually to correct, the brutal and desperate measures used by hunters and hunted alike in the industrial jungle of New York harbor. "What I try to do—what all the waterfront priests try to do—is to help 'em learn how to defend themselves, how to bargain for themselves, in a lawful, intelligent way.

What they need down here, if we're ever to see this mess cleaned up, is their own, strong, honest organization. That way they won't get pushed around by the union racketeers, the shipping companies or the Commies."

That's the key to the unique labor class Father Corridan conducts at the Xavier Labor School in the Chelsea area that has been spearheading the revolt against the Anastasias, the Bowers mob, and the other labor racketeers who have been terrorizing the waterfront. Men come in off the docks in their work clothes, their faces still grimy from the hold or sweating from the heavy work. Because the Jesuit is known for his fearless stand against mob rule on the docks, attending his class is not considered healthy by the bully-boys who have muscled in on so many locals. "Sometimes our men have to slip in the back way after dark," says Father Corridan.

During one of his talks a heckler kept interrupting. As a Corridan man described it, "Father John had his number right away. He spotted him as one of the boys. So right in the middle of his talk he stops and goes up to this sharp-looking character. Cool as a cucumber, he says, 'I know who sent you, so go back to your bosses and deliver this message for me: tell 'em that if anything happens to the men I'm trying to help here, I'll know who's responsible, and I'll personally see to it that they are broken throughout this port. They'll pay and I'll see that they pay.'"

Father Corridan doesn't talk religion to the longshoremen who slip into Xavier to plan their resistance to open crime and union corruption. "It's straight bread 'n butter, dollars 'n cents," he says. "I try to pick the men who are natural leaders and who have the guts to talk up for honest trade unionism on the docks. I try to put them wise to the stuff they ought to know."

It was Corridan, for instance, who enlightened the men as to their rightful claim to some ten million in unpaid overtime under Article 7B 1 of the Wage-Hour Law. He wrote a letter to every senator and to all the key representatives explaining in detail the legal and moral justification for the longshoremen's case, at the same time urging a thorough investigation of the chronic infection that has paralyzed the greatest harbor in the world.

The only way that the priest touches on religion directly in his labor class is to ask his students what they consider the basis of economics. Invariably, they name "money," "bread," "profit," or "labor supply." And invariably Corridan's answer is, "Man." "Only man is capable of knowing and loving," he says. "In other words I teach 'em the dignity of man." The Christian strictures against man's inhumanity to man are brought up to date in the pope's encyclicals on social justice and Father Corridan always has this in the back of his mind, but, as he says, "We don't want to bog 'em down with a lot of theories, religious or otherwise. These are men with a problem—the problem of how to live like human beings— and they're looking for help in how to solve it. They want practical stuff, not a lot of heavy water."

The antiquated system of hiring known as the "shape-up," (outlawed in England over a century ago, Corridan points out) is not only un-American, a menace to our efficiency and security, but un-Christian, Father Corridan believes.

Christianity, for him, is not merely abstract dogma but a living force. The most cynical agnostic could not help but feel the presence and the power of Christ when Father Corridan describes the inhuman conditions he has seen on the waterfront. "I figured out, on a basis of yearly income and man-hours, that there is about enough work to support seventeen thousand longshoremen and their families," he says. "There are more than twice that many shaping-up. The uncertainty, the humiliation of having to stand there and beg with your eyes for work twice a day while ex-cons look you over like you were so much meat in the butcher shop—no wonder the men who get passed over at the morning shape wait for the bars to open and see how many belts they can get into 'em before they shape up again at noon." In a memorable sermon on the docks one of the few times when he revealed the spiritual passion behind his interest in human welfare on the waterfront, he said:

> I suppose some people would smirk at the thought of Christ in the shape-up. It is about as absurd as the fact that he carried carpenter's tools in his hands and earned his bread by the sweat of his brow. As absurd as the fact that Christ redeemed all men irrespective of their race, color, or station in life. It can be absurd only to those of whom Christ has said, "Having eyes, they see not; and having ears, they hear not." Because they don't want to see or hear, Christ also said, "If you do it to the least of mine, you do it to me." So Christ is in the shape-up. . . .
>
> He stands in the shape-up knowing that all won't get work and maybe he won't. What does Christ think of the efficiency argument of the shape-up? . . . Some people think that the Crucifixion took place only on Calvary. Christ works on a pier and His back aches because there are a fair number of the "boys" on the pier. They don't work, but

have their rackets at which so many wink. What does Christ think of the man who picks up a longshoreman's brass check and takes 20 percent interest at the end of the week?

Christ goes to a union meeting. Sees how a meeting is run. Sees how few go. Sees how many don't speak. Sees a certain restraint. At some meetings he sees a few with hundred-fifty dollar suits and diamond rings on their fingers drawing a couple of expense accounts. . . . Christ walks into a tenement and talks with the wife of a longshoreman. Her heart is heavy. . . .

As an audience, there's nothing tougher than longshoremen. They're edgy and suspicious, quick to smell a phoney. They gag easily on verbal syrup. They've *had* the silver-tongued orators, from the president of their International *up* and down, trying to sweet-talk them out of their rights. Their name for former Mayor O'Dwyer was "Weeping Willie." "Maybe we don' have too much education," a docker told me in a Chelsea saloon, "but you don' hafta go t' collich t' know who's with ya and who ain't. Father John is with us. He ain't tryin' t' sell us out like these itchy-finger boys posin' as organizers. And he ain't signin' us up for some phoney peace pledge like the Commies either. He's one of us. We believe in God up there and a fair shake down here."

Corridan didn't learn about gnawing poverty and the cause of humanity out of any book. His father, an immigrant from County Kerry, died when John was nine, leaving his mother Hannah to raise five boys. "The old man didn't leave any money—he was an honest cop," the priest explains. "He was always pounding beats in out of the way places like Rockaway because an honest cop cramped their style."

Mrs. Corridan worked as a cleaning woman, helped out by a small pension and Child Welfare. The boys learned how to handle themselves in the scrappy, competitive world of the hungry West Side. They had to hustle for every nickel in the incessant free-for-all of tenement life. . . .

One Christmas there wasn't enough money in the house to buy any real presents for the Corridan boys. John didn't care so much for himself—he was now eleven and prematurely wise in the ways of the tenement. But he worried about his little three-year-old brother. He knew the tot had asked Santa Claus for a fire engine—he had been talking of nothing else for weeks. As Christmas approached, the little boy's eagerness, and confidence that Santa would answer his prayers reached such proportions that John felt himself overwhelmed with temptation.

He went to a toy store—a chain store, he recalls, for he had figured with a Robin Hood's logic that they could best afford to absorb the loss—and priced a beautiful red fire engine. Two dollars. He hid out until the store was closed, then sneaked up to the cash register and jimmied it in a way he had learned from the hoodlum element of the neighborhood. The drawer shot open. "I looked at all that money," Father Corridan remembers. "I could have taken it all. But I just wanted that two dollars."

Later John had the problem of telling the priest in confession. "That was a turning point for my relations with the church," Father Corridan says now. "Seeing how much that fire engine meant to my little brother and knowing what an empty Christmas it would have seemed if Santa had let him down, I made up my mind that if the priest really gave me hell I was through with the church. So I went to confession that day with my knees trembling." The priest was understanding. "I did penance," Father Corridan recalls, "but I didn't have to give the fire engine back."

When he grew up to become a priest himself, he never forgot this incident. He does not condone dishonesty and disrespect for law. But he feels his own brief adventure in using bad means to a good end helps him to understand the desperate measures his parishioners can sometimes be driven to when poverty pins them to the wall, especially when their families are made to suffer for reasons of greed and indifference.

"I'm an apple-eater," he says, referring to the early days of the Depression when he and his brothers saw the humiliation his proud, hardworking mother suffered at the hands of officious social workers. Yes, Father Corridan doesn't have to draw on any books or second-hand knowledge when he describes the life of a longshoreman's wife in her cold-water railroad flat, pinching pennies to feed her kids. That's why he made up his mind that he would serve God among the poorest of his children, and that he would devote his life to social justice.

Five years ago a group of rank-and-filers came to Xavier and said, "Father John, a strike is brewing on the waterfront, whether the official leadership knows it or not. The men want a welfare fund and a vacation clause. If we don't try to get it for 'em, the Commies will grab the issue and try to make themselves the heroes."

Characteristically, Father Corridan's response wasn't to fly off the handle in an emotional way. First he sat down with an experienced insurance man and worked out a practical welfare plan on the Blue Cross model that could be operated for less than four cents an hour. Then he went down to Washington and managed to see Cyrus Ching, then head of the National Mediation Board. Corridan did not rely on a spiritual, humanitarian appeal. He had carefully marshalled the facts and figures to prove his case. The needs of the dock workers had never had such specific presentation. When the strike did break out, just as the priest knew it would though official leaders had refused to take it seriously, he wrote an article for the Jesuit magazine *America* detailing the case for the longshoremen. Then he had twelve thousand reprints of it distributed on the waterfront.

The program Father Corridan laid out responded exactly to the long-frustrated desires of the majority. His name became a by-word on the waterfront. When the Conciliation Service met to settle the strike, a copy of his article was placed before every negotiator. When the board approved both the welfare fund and vacations with pay, Father Corridan was widely credited with having won something for the men that they had been after for twenty-five years.

He just grins when you mention this. "All I did was tip the conciliation boys off to the pitch."

Holding services for striking longshoremen three years ago, Father Corridan offered this prayer:

"For those longshoremen who are straight and are good family men, God be praised; for those who slip every once in a while and lose hope, God have mercy; to *those responsible,* God grant the grace to see things as Christ sees them on the waterfront, for the time is growing short when God will have no mercy. . . ."

OUR RESPONSIBILITY TO THE POOR

JOSEPH L. BERNARDIN

The church does not claim any special expertise in the political, economic, or social order; as the Second Vatican Council reminded us, its mission is religious. But its social teaching does provide an indispensable framework within which to make a moral analysis of today's problems. It also can give the direction and motivation needed to work out viable solutions. . . . [I]t clearly spells out what the basic rights of people are, as well as the responsibility of the various elements of society, both private and public, to protect those rights. In recent months an increasing amount of emphasis has been placed on the responsibility of the private sector and, in particular, the churches, to provide for the needs of the poor. . . .

I am the first to admit that the churches, as well as all segments of the private sector, need to do more, and I will return to that point further on. But I wish to affirm as forcefully as I can that government also has a responsibility from which it cannot escape. Important as voluntarism is, it cannot alone resolve the problem of poverty. In his 1979 address to the United Nations, Pope John Paul II spoke about the need for creative collaboration among nations to overcome the global causes of poverty. That evening, in his homily at the Mass in Yankee Stadium, he challenged American Catholics in a very direct way. He first talked about the charitable work of the church, which he commended and encouraged. Then he added:

> But this is not enough. Within the framework of your national institutions and in cooperation with all your compatriots, you will also want to seek out the structural reasons which foster or cause the different forms of poverty in the world and your own country, so that you can apply the proper remedies. You will not allow yourselves to be intimidated

JOSEPH L. BERNARDIN (1928–96) was the cardinal archbishop of Chicago.

or discouraged by over-simplified explanations, which are more ideological than scientific, explanations which try to account for a complex evil by some single cause. But neither will you recoil before the reforms—even profound ones—of attitudes and structures that may prove necessary in order to recreate over and over again the conditions needed by the disadvantaged if they are to have a fresh chance in the hard struggle of life.

These powerful words call not merely for more charity but also justice. They are rooted in the thinking of Pope John XXIII who, in *Mater et magistra,* addressed the issue of the role of government in developing public policy in two crucial sentences: "To safeguard the inviolable rights of the human person and to facilitate the fulfillment of his duties, should be the essential office of every public authority. . . . One of the fundamental duties of civil authorities is to coordinate social relations in such fashion that the exercise of a person's rights does not threaten others in the exercise of their own rights nor hinder in fulfillment of their duties."

It is clear, then, that there are two sides of the coin. The common good, which civil society is obligated to defend and promote, requires that the individual's rights be respected. But it also requires the public authority to take action as needed and appropriate to defend those rights.

It is important, I believe, that we assume a position of advocacy for the poor, by insisting on a just economic and social order and by providing for their immediate needs. This is a work of justice and charity. The Latin American bishops at Puebla spoke about a "preferential option" for the poor. "We affirm," they said, "the need for conversion on the part of the whole church to a preferential option for the poor, an option aimed at their integral liberation." Such a preferential option would seem to call for the following:

1. In all matters of public policy, but especially those affecting the poor, we must insist on the truth. The problems are so complex that it is difficult enough to arrive at a clear analysis of their causes and possible solutions. We must, therefore, demand that the facts not be slanted or manipulated for political, ideological, or personal motives, as so often happens in the political process today. The urgency of the situation demands that everyone rise above the prejudices, divisions, and myths which delay solutions or make them impossible. Insisting on the truth—both in analyzing the facts and presenting the consequences of the pro-

posed solutions—will bring about a clarity that will be immensely helpful.

2. As a church, as I indicated before, we do not have any special expertise in the political, social, and economic orders. While all may share
a common goal, there may be a number of legitimate ways to achieve it.
Moreover, we must acknowledge that there are real problems and limitations which must be taken into account. In 1975, the American bishops
outlined seven principles which should guide our citizens and policy
makers as we plan and provide for the human rights and dignity of all
our people. Each flows from the church's social teaching as it has evolved
over the past ninety years. All are so essential to the issue of poverty that
they deserve repetition:

- Economic activity should be governed by justice and be carried out
  within the limits of morality. It must serve people's needs.

- The right to have a share of earthly goods sufficient for oneself and
  one's family belongs to everyone.

- Economic prosperity is to be assessed not so much from the sum
  total of goods and wealth possessed as from the distribution of
  goods according to norms of justice.

- Opportunities to work must be provided for those who are able
  and willing to work. Every person has the right to useful employment, to just wages, and to adequate assistance in case of real need.

- Economic development must not be left to the sole judgment of a
  few persons or groups possessing excessive economic power, or to
  the political community alone. On the contrary, at every level the
  largest possible number of people should have an active share in di-
  recting that development.

- A just and equitable system of taxation requires assessment according to ability to pay.

- Government must play a role in the economic activity of its citizens. Indeed, it should promote in a suitable manner the production of a sufficient supply of material goods. Moreover, it should

safeguard the rights of all citizens and help them find opportunities for employment.

The church as an institution must find new ways of increasing its own charitable outreach to the poor. . . . The Holy Father put it very bluntly in his Yankee Stadium homily. "We cannot stand idly by," he said, "enjoying our own riches and freedom, if, in any place, the Lazarus of the twentieth century stands at our doors. In the light of the parable of Christ, riches and freedom mean a special responsibility. Riches and freedom create a special obligation. And so, in the name of the solidarity that binds us all together in a common humanity, I again proclaim the dignity of every human person: the rich man and Lazarus are both human beings, both of them actually created in the image and likeness of God, both of them equally redeemed by Christ at a great price, the price of 'the precious blood of Christ' [1 Pt. 1: 19]."

. . . How should the church carry out its duty to make a preferential option for the poor, in light of the fact that its efforts tend to become counterproductive to the extent they are perceived as merely "political" in nature? How, in other words, can we speak to real issues—employment, housing, education, federal budget, and the rest—without being ignored or resisted by precisely those whom we need to reach and persuade?

These are complex, difficult questions, but I believe the church should lead the way in raising them and encouraging the search for answers. Our preferential option for the poor must be as informed as it is wholehearted, as realistic as it is sincere, as oriented to the eradication of poverty as to its relief, and rooted at all times in a vision of the integral dignity of the human person. For this purpose let us make our own the conviction of Pope John Paul II, that . . ."this difficult road of the indispensable transformation of the structures of economic life is one on which it will not be easy to go forward without the intervention of a true conversion of mind, will, and heart."

CHARITY

STUART DYBEK

The Agency assigned me to a slum on the south side of Chicago. There among mind-staggering problems I encountered a small problem everyone faces in one way or another. People kept hitting me for handouts. Walking around the shabby streets in my white skin and blue suit made me appear wealthy. I *was* relatively rich.

Sometimes a group of black guys my own age standing outside the Record Shack gesturing and laughing would see me coming and spread out across the sidewalk. By the time I got there they were staring in stony silence—some jiving blankly to the music, some amused, a few with open hostility.

"Hey social worker, you got some loose change?"

"I wanna buy me some cigarettes, man."

"Gimme a quarter."

After a while I realized they didn't want the money so much as they wanted to see how I'd react: scared that if I didn't give they'd kick my ass, or would I try to be cool and joke it off ("Money! man, I'm paid in food stamps,") or would I be professional and digging out my wallet distribute cards instructing them where to go for adult education classes (maybe then they *would* kick my ass, waiting creaky on the fourth-floor landing of some mine-shaft dark tenement). Or maybe I wouldn't say anything, just walk on by like the caseworker chicks did sometimes— downcast eyes, smiling the martyr's half-smile—and they'd watch her hips swing into the distance discussing whether or not she was out here looking for it.

Sometimes some drunk would latch onto me, follow me down the street clutching at my elbow, stumbling, slobbering, explaining he was

STUART DYBEK (1942–), the author of *Brass Knuckles* and *Childhood and Other Neighborhoods*, was formerly a caseworker with the Cook County Department of Public Aid.

colored and I was white and what the hell did I know about it, and he was old and I was young and man when you're old everything hurts every minute. Telling me anything he could think of, all the memories and stories flooding into his head through the sluice of alcohol, but always amounting to the same tragedies and hard luck, the same line manufactured out of past realities: he needed winter clothes for his little baby, or money for carfare so he could get a job, or for his TB—here he'd cough up a hoker and lay it on the sidewalk, green among pecking crowds of pigeons.

Or a few had a better approach: look man, I ain't gonna bullshit ya, I need it for a drink. Maybe they'd walk away if you shook your head no. But many were persistent believing if they just bugged you long enough you'd pay to get rid of them. And if that didn't work they'd beg because if there's one thing a man can't stand it's another man begging him—particularly in public with everybody watching.

For lunch I'd usually go to McDonald's Hamburgers. It was a drive-in, all glass, tile, and stainless steel gleaming under neon. I didn't have a car but there were benches where you could sit outside and eat your hamburger and fries. Across the street the city was moving mountains of tenements. "Pardon this inconvenience, Another Improvement being made for a Greater Chicago, Richard J. Daley, Mayor," the signs said. Workmen drove muddy, yellow bulldozers over fields of rubble. Drills clacked their prophecies of new foundations while kids chased up and down the huge mounds of dirt around the excavation pits. Blocks behind the site, modern high-rise housing projects rose up like walls. Usually a bunch of kids would come up and mooch dimes off me for Cokes. After they bought them they'd stand around discussing the White Sox with me, munching the ice after the drink was gone.

When I was new to the job—my first few months—constantly getting hit for money used to bother me. First I tried the open-handed approach and gave something to whoever asked. Usually all they wanted was a quarter. But I guess the word got out because everybody on the street began asking me for money. Each day I was out there the same people would show up. The handouts began adding up. But what was worse, I worried about being thought of as something no self-respecting caseworker wants to be thought of as—a sucker.

So then I made myself judge. Decided I'd only give money to people who really looked like they needed it. To whoever needed it! This, of course, was symptomatic of getting so close to the madness of the slum that your actions become absurd. But my absurdity was accepted by the neighborhood as something to be expected. When I'd refuse to shell out they argued: "Look man, I know you gave something to Clyde Jones. How come you give to him and not me? Is he a better friend, man? His problems bigger than mine? Or howbout yesterday! Lucy Winters says you layed a half a buck on her. What she doin' that I ain't?"

I could have said, "Look man, it's my money to do what I want with." But somehow this seemed to lead down The Lord Giveth The Lord Taketh away path of Miss Trainer's lectures.

Miss Trainer had a repertoire of lectures painstakingly collected over many years of service. Each new worker got to hear the one about "and I'm sick and tired of hearing young people knocking The System in front of recipients when it's The System that puts clothes on their backs and YOURS too!"

I'd dismissed her as just another of the frustrated old bitches The System was full of, who'd been rewarded for years of mediocrity and compliance with supervisory positions. It wasn't until the day I heard her lecture in Intake that I realized the extent of her power. The lecture began with a command for silence—her throat cleared into a pinched Kleenex—while all around her unwed mothers shushed illegitimate children.

"I hope none of you down here can work because if you can you won't get a cent out of US. I have to work for my money; you don't think the taxpayers pay me for staying home and having babies, do you? Of course not. If you are found eligible for Public Aid you will be expected to co-operate with our many programs to rehabilitate you. After all, friends, Public Aid, though a privilege of our great country, is not charity. We don't want you to feel like you're receiving a dole—no one with any pride wants that—feel rather that we are making an investment in your future and through that in the future of democracy."

I needed another approach but there never seemed time enough to figure one out. It was a minor problem—one that didn't pertain to the majority of cases on my load. Most of the requests came from their friends and neighbors—cripples, old people, kids, addicts, con men—all those who had failed to qualify or had successfully avoided the welfare rolls. When my clients asked me for money it was usually as a loan which they insisted on paying back. They weren't interested in testing me. They needed the money, maybe for a pair of shoes for the kid who was starting Head Start or just for a pack of cigarettes at the end of the month when the money from their unbelievably small aid checks ran out. There never seemed to be time to figure out an approach to anything. The office was a madhouse. My desk tottered beneath stacks of ragged case records I was always going to read.

Name: Julie McCall
Case #: ADC 1795502
Address: 3915 Cottage Grove
Birth Place: Greenwood, Mississippi

After clearing a space to write on I'd sit and try to concentrate on a letter to the mental health service worded strongly enough so that Julie McCall might be moved up a few ranks in the infinite line of people waiting for free therapy. I had to be careful not to word it too strongly so that when it passed under the bifocaled inspection of the archenemy, my supervisor, she didn't initiate proceedings to remove the children from the home. Such proceedings would never conclude. Their only effect was to divert energy away from dealing with the problem; their only purpose was to cover the supervisor in case something should happen. The telephones rang constantly like burglar alarms as if we were in a continual process of being robbed. Occasionally the hysterical voice of a caseworker could be heard above the din shouting into the phone that he had been ordered to hold the client's check because she had not shown up for housekeeping training.

Dear Mental Health Service,

I am writing in reply to your letter regarding ADC 1795502. A waiting period of six months before therapy is inconceivable given the current situation. Mrs. McCall undergoes weekly "epileptic fits" which have been diagnosed as possibly hysteric in nature. In recent interviews she has become increasingly despondent and has indicated powerful anxiety associated with past experiences. She was fucked frequently by her father between the ages of twelve and sixteen. Her two oldest children are reportedly his. Her husband, a man thirty years older than Mrs. McCall, is threatening desertion because he can no longer support her and the children plus his family of ten by a previous marriage. Unknown to Mrs. McCall, her oldest son, Charles, a boy of twelve who is still in fourth grade, offered to blow the caseworker for a quarter during the last home visit. Due to rapid deterioration of the home

It was always at such a point that my phone would ring. Perhaps it would be Mrs. McCall herself, calling as she did at least once a week to tell me she was going to kill herself and the kids.

"Don't, Mrs. McCall."

"Why not? What we got to live for?"

"Things will get better."

"You crazy! I'm gonna turn the gas on and kill us all!"

"Please don't do it, Mrs. McCall."

"I'm gonna do it this time for sure."

"But your children want to live."

"How do you know?"

"Anybody can see that . . . they're great kids. You've done your best raising them so far. They love you."

"They ain't happy—they just ain't sure how bad it is yet. I can't get 'em nothin. They lucky if they got enough to eat."

"But you give them love."

"Love?! What good's that without something to eat, some new clothes once in a while like other kids get?"

"You can't just give up."

"I sure can. My head hurts all the time, all I do is cry and worry about my kids—that they'll grow up like me. My head keeps hurtin. You my worker. You suppose to do somethin."

I tried to do something. I talked a friend of mine, a psychiatrist with a private practice, into giving her a half an hour of his time a week free. I paid the fifty-cents carfare and two-fifty childcare that it cost for her to get there. This arrangement lasted about a month and then she stopped going to see him.

"What the hell happened, Bill, you were suppose to do something," I complained.

"I tried to," he said, "but going back to that environment screwed everything up. Analysis is for the middle class, man. What she needs to solve her problems is fifty bucks more a week."

"Why'd you stop going?" I asked Julie McCall.

"It was wastin the money," she said, "nothin but talk. Besides that man is crazy, he tole me not to feel so bad about what my daddy done to me."

Walking downstairs from her apartment I almost trip over Charles McCall sitting crouched on a stair beside the bannister. He's holding himself like he's got a stomach ache.

"What are you doing here, Charlie?"

"Listening. Look what I got." He holds up a new looking transistor radio. The earplug dangles from his ear.

"Nice . . . one of those Japanese ones?"

"You wanna know how I got it, right?"

We step out of the piss-damp hallway. The sun bounces into our eyes off windshields and windows.

"I didn't steal it, heh-heh, it's a present."

He stares up at me with his translucent twelve-year-old face, eyelids wizened by sunlight. He winks. "You dig? What kinda music you like?" He turns the little radio on full blast and won't talk anymore, strolling past other kids down the street, dangling earplug plugged back in.

Once after hours I went to a bar to hear Muddy Waters with a friend of mine who'd started out with the Agency but ended up working full-time for "the Movement." We'd both been drinking a lot all afternoon. It was hotter than hell at the end of August and we were drinking cold beers and at the point where after every beer you have to get up and piss. Muddy was great singing one blues after another, sweat beaded on his face, his sportshirt hanging out. All the instruments were electric and they kept blowing fuses so they had to turn the air conditioner off. The drummer worked before a microphone; the guy who played harp cupped it against a microphone and when he fanned it the cord lashed around so it looked like an instrument with a long black tail. They had the doors open at both ends of the bar to catch the draft. It wasn't very dark yet. The windows still held some orange. The bar was loud and packed with a few couples trying to dance pressed against the wall and dripping beer bottles being passed over the heads at the bar. Kids squirmed through the tunnel the bar stools made on the pretense of shining shoes. After getting back from a trip to the john I find this guy in my seat talking in Al's ear. Al's just sitting there smiling with his money spread out before him on the bar.

"Give me a buck, man. C'mon, brother, this is one of your own askin ya . . . don't be a cheap mother. We got to help each other. I'm thirsty too, man. Fifty cents? . . . okay, just buy me a beer."

Al says, "Don't bother me, man, I don't have time for that shit."

The guy shrugs and moves down the line.

I tried it in the district a few times and it worked pretty well on drunks. There was something cavalier about the "I don't have time for that shit" part that got them. But it obviously wasn't an all-around technique. The "Reversal" was even more limited—just as the guy has his timing down and is about to ask you for something you turn and face him eye to eye with your palm extended and say, "Hey, friend, can you spare two bits?"

What I finally did arrive at was a common-sense approach. Somebody would hit me for money and I'd say, "Look, man, I'd like to help you but do you have any idea how many times a day I get asked out here? If I started giving to everybody who asked me I'd have to be a millionaire."

That usually worked. It was much better than asking, "Why should I?" because then they'd say, "'cause you got something extra and I ain't got enough." It had the effect of depersonalizing the request, of lumping them in with a group which made it seem like the odds were against me.

But the best thing about it was that I believed it the most. There was the part about "I'd like to help you." That was true. I would. And yet it was realistic. I was making about $500 a month before taxes and the caseworkers were getting ready to go on strike. Who knew how long that might last. I had nothing saved. My rent was $85 a month. I ate my meals out. I was paying $100 a month tuition, going to grad school full time at night in order to stay out of the draft. Whatever was left disappeared, mostly on drinking. If I got hit for a quarter five times per day and was in the field three times a week and about forty-nine weeks a year—I was entertaining the thought of the Agency giving us so much per month to give to moochers just the way they reimbursed us for transportation expenses. I mentioned the idea to Joe Faigabank who was union treasurer.

"We can't ask them to do that," he said.

"Why not—don't you have to loan out money when you're out in order to do your job sometimes?"

"Yeah, but look, trace the idea out to its logical conclusion. If you can do that why can't you just go out there and start giving the money away? You give the caseworker a wad and he just walks around poor neighborhoods handing it out. Even the Commies wouldn't support that."

"At least I'd know what the hell I'm suppose to be doing out there."

"You're suppose to be rehabilitating the disadvantaged by filling out forms in triplicate," Joe said.

"And looking for their boyfriend's shoes under the bed. Well, bring it up at the next meeting anyway, will you?"

Joe just stood there for a while punching staples in a random case record. When he figured enough time had elapsed to convince me he'd thought it over he said, "Okay, figure it out and write up some statistics."

"When do you think we're going out on strike?"

"They're going to discuss it at the next meeting," Joe said. "They gotta give us more bread, man, I'm barely making it."

"Can you believe it's possible for an ADC mother with five kids to make it on $250, man?"

"Has to be something on the side. Boyfriends. That's the only way. The people who make up those budgets have Ph.D.'s in Home Economics."

"We ought to get the recipients out on strike with us."

"What? A hunger strike?"

The hell with it, I thought, if we don't strike I'm quitting. It had been a year-and-a-half now that I'd been representing the bureaucracy, promising people aid they never got, jobs where there weren't any, medical care from butchers, sending them to psychologists who tried to help them accept their poverty, poking my nose in, spying—that's what the job basically was—the spying. But hell, I thought, at least I'm trying to do something. Then Bertha Williams called me up.

Actually she had called me up about a month before and asked me to drop over. She wanted some advice. She was a lovely, gentle woman whose husband deserted her five years ago, leaving her with four kids to support. She had worked in a factory stuffing jock straps in boxes until she was knocked down by a lift truck and her spine injured. Somehow the company screwed her out of getting any compensation. We were friends, or as Miss Trainer preferred saying, we had rapport. I had been very lucky in helping Mrs. Williams out of a jam she should never have been in during my first winter as a caseworker.

It had been a very bad winter with many spells of zero weather. Mrs. Williams made the mistake of moving from a condemned building. Her case record was lost and her aid checks undelivered. When she first contacted me her new landlord had given her a five-day eviction notice. She'd been surviving for two months on what she had been able to borrow from relatives and friends, most of whom were little better off than she was. Her apartment had no furniture—some boxes and a mattress on the floor, a hot plate, but no refrigerator. She had been keeping her perishable foods on the windowsill, pulling them in at intervals so they wouldn't freeze, until someone got wise and stole them. I managed to talk the landlord into turning her heat back on and lifting the eviction notice. When I went to the office her case had been supposedly transferred from, I found her case record and checks among the myriad memoes that had accumulated on the desk of her previous worker. He had quit over a month before and still hadn't been replaced. I had a violent argument with my supervisor who took the position that since Mrs. Williams had managed to exist for two months without aid then apparently she didn't need it. She was overruled, however, and the Agency approved $15 for a refrigerator. Her landlord, astounded at receiving his back rent, got us a good deal on a "hot" Frigidaire.

Mrs. Williams trusted me. She wanted some advice on her ten-year-old son, Irwin. He had a hernia, she explained, and she wondered whether she should have corrective surgery performed now or wait until he was older. I told her that was strictly a medical decision which I couldn't make, but that I did know that scar tissue heals faster at a young age. We talked about the possible effects growing up with a hernia might have on the boy like affecting his interest in sports or his entrance into puberty. I advised her to discuss it with a doctor. When I returned to the office I wrote out a referral to County Hospital for Irwin and mailed it to Mrs. Williams.

At first I didn't recognize her voice.

"Who am I speaking to, please?"

"This is Mrs. Williams." Her voice was flat and hollow at the same time.

"How are you, Mrs. Williams? How did Irwin make out? Did he have his operation?"

"Yes."

"How's he doing?"

"He's dead."

I had an impulse to hang up. The phones were ringing. "He's dead? How could he be dead from a hernia operation? It's not that serious." For some reason I didn't believe her.

"He's dead," she said, "that's all I know. He died on the operating table."

"But how!—didn't they tell you how?"

"I guess they did. They said they had to cut a hole in his throat but that it didn't work. I don't know; I didn't understand them."

"I'm sorry," I said.

"I'm calling to find out about the funeral," she said. "Are you all gonna pay for it?"

"Yes . . . tell the undertaker to call me and I'll make out the forms. . . . I'm sorry, Mrs. Williams."

"Thanks," she said and hung up.

I listened to the phone buzz for a while and then dialed County Hospital. I asked for information about Irwin. They gave me the runaround until I started hollering about an investigation. I didn't tell them I was a caseworker. I said I was with the Mayor's Office. A doctor explained that the boy had a heart defect which had gone undetected and his heart failed during the operation. They did all they could—performed a tracheotomy and massaged his heart but he died. There was nothing anybody could do, he said. It was one of those things.

I hung up and my phone rang almost immediately.

"This is Mrs. Williams again. I hate to bother you but on our budget for next month . . . do you have to take Irwin off right away. I could use his twenty-five dollars to buy us some clothes for the funeral."

"I'll leave him on," I said.

"Thanks," she said. "I appreciate it."

I was coming back from the funeral. It was early in spring and tiny blades of grass were pushing up from mud, through broken glass from beer bottles, among cracks in the sidewalk. Papers that had been buried in snow dried yellow and blew around. It was my last day in the district. Joe Faigabank asked me to organize my ideas on a handout fund before I quit. He figured it would be a little something extra the union could concede over the bargaining table. Rumors of a public employees' strike against the Agency continued to circulate. Newspapers carried articles predicting riots in the Negro community during the coming "long, hot summer."

I thought on my last day I would remember my first day and see everything vividly again, but I didn't. I was walking down the street adding up one quarter times five per day times three days per week times forty-nine weeks per year times how many years per life when I saw this panhandler coming a block away. I see him getting ready to mooch and automatically prepare my excuses: I'd like to help you, man, but do you realize how much I'd be spending if I gave to everyone who asked for it, not just you, man, but all the charities for orphans and war victims and mental illness and cancer and the heart fund and kidney disease and the Panthers and the Peace Movement and I'm hardly making it myself, brother.

No socks. At half a block I see his red-rimmed eyes behind cracked foggy glasses, a crushed hat, baggy pants with dragging frayed cuffs, a too-thin even for this spring day topcoat, limping like a scarecrow assembled at a Good Will store. He blinks at me and says, "Can you give me one cent?"

Race and Justice

APRIL 12, 1940

NATIVE DAUGHTER

ELLEN TARRY

As a Negro, I have been greatly pleased to note the haste with which the literary world has acclaimed Richard Wright, author of the book *Native Son,* as the greatest writer of his race. I rejoice not only because, like Richard Wright, I am a Negro, but because I am also familiar with the obstacles that confront young Negro writers. Even in the literary world, there are those who find it hard to visualize a black Bernard Shaw or a Louisa Alcott with kinky hair. For us, therefore, Richard Wright's triumph is signal.

However it is not Richard Wright's laurels that concern me so greatly. It is rather that in Catholic circles many have lamented the fact that the Negro writer who has arisen as the spokesman for his race should be a Communist.

When Mr. Wright addressed a group of book lovers at the 135th Street branch of the New York Public Library on Thursday, March 7, I have been told that the young writer said he was a God-fearing Communist. Be that as it may, if the young man said it, it only stresses his conversion to communism. I confess, by the way, that this is my first inkling that the Communists included God in their ideology. I had also believed that these people *feared* Stalin only.

ELLEN TARRY (1906–) lives in New York City, where she has taught, written, and worked for social justice.

Yet as an American Mr. Wright is entitled to his own political and religious beliefs. And we must accept, even if regretfully, the fact that Richard Wright, acclaimed America's most powerful Negro writer, is a Communist.

But Richard Wright was not born a Communist. Existing social, economic, and political conditions have made him so. I also doubt, very much, that Mr. Wright was taught to fear God by his Communist mentors. We learned about *Him* long before the Communists *discovered* us. And it is this inherent belief in God—only—that has kept all of us from turning to the *isms* that accept us as men and women, despite our black skins.

There may be Catholics who will not read *Native Son* because its author is a Communist. But, did you ever stop to think that Catholics may be among those who are responsible for some of the conditions that have led Richard Wright and scores of others into the ranks of the Reds?

The time has come for Christian America to shed its coat of hypocrisy and admit its sin. Even today, years later, I sicken as I remember the manner in which the Negro's lack of human rights was etched upon my memory. It was soon after I had returned to Alabama from a school conducted by the Sisters of the Blessed Sacrament. While well aware of the fact that I was a Negro, being colored did not seem strange, for so were my friends. True, I knew white people, but they were the nice white people whom my parents served. From them we received nickels, toys, and many useful gifts. The atmosphere in our home was such that it gave no hint of the bitterness that corrodes so many black breasts.

There was the time, I'll admit, when I heard talk of a race riot. But being a dramatic child who welcomed any new excitement, I was intrigued by the hushed whispers and drawn shades. Being too young to understand the consequences, I was really disappointed when the scheduled riot failed to take place.

A Ku Klux Klan parade had been another one of the highlights of my childhood. How well I remember my mother taking me from bed in the middle of the night and carrying me into the parlor. Father, in an old-fashioned nightshirt, with his fists clenched, was standing at a front window. On a couch sat the old woman who nursed my little sister, praying as she clutched the tiny baby to her breast. Outside there was the clatter of horses' hoofs. As the light from a fiery cross, held high by white-robed men on horseback, flashed its warning of destruction to all Catholics, Jews and Negroes, I saw my father open the drawer of a nearby table.

The reflection of the light glistened on the steel of a pearl-handled revolver. My mother tightened her hold upon my arm. But, childlike, I
broke away and pressed my nose against the window pane—the better to
see the men in white robes who rode fine horses and carried fiery crosses.
As the last clop-clop died in the distance, there was a dreadful silence.
My mother shook the old nurse. "Davie," she said, "you can stop praying now. They've passed us by."

Time passed and there followed years under the watchful eyes of
white Sisters. I returned to my parents a young lady. Ready to take my
place in the world, the Sisters had said. And on that memorable night,
when the plight of my race was so clearly explained, one of the neighborhood boys had borrowed a car and called to take me to my first party.

Now the business section of our town had spread until it fringed our
neighborhood. This had caused most of our friends to move to other sections of the city. The people who had moved into the houses they left va-
cant were unknown to us and, on the whole a pretty motley lot. Even
Aunt Lizzie, who had lived in the next house as long as I could remember, had moved to "the hill." And not only did we have a new next-door
neighbor, but my mother said she feared they were "a wild bunch."

So on this particular night as I prepared to sally forth to my first party
I was not wholly surprised to see a car, occupied by two white officers of
the law, drive alongside an automobile that was parked in front of the
next house. But I was anxious to be on my way and called to my escort
to come along.

"Wait!" my mother fairly hissed. And having the sort of mother who
meant what she said, I waited.

"Get out of that car!" I heard one of the police call to the two young
Negroes who were sitting in the parked auto. "And get out with your
hands in the air!" the other officer instructed, as he leaped from his car
with drawn gun. "You boys got corn [whiskey] in this car and we're
gonna find it tonight," said Officer No. 1.

"Well," asked the second officer, "what you standing there like two
dummies for? You *have* got whiskey, *haven't you?*"

"No, Sir!" the Negroes cried in unison, their arms stretched heaven-
ward.

"Well, we'll see!" and the policemen began searching the car.

As we watched from the porch, it seemed to me that they were making that car into a swell job for some junk dealer. Cushions were thrown
in the street. Tools were scattered about and boards ripped from the

floor. But this was all in vain, for the zealous officers found nothing that bore evidence of any violation of the law.

"Well," one of them admitted, as he pulled out a handkerchief and wiped the sweat from his brow, "we didn't get you tonight, but we'll catch you yet!"

The sight of the white men working so hard—and in vain—must have amused the smaller of the two Negroes (they called him "Shorty"), for he giggled.

"So it tickles you, eh?" said one of the officers. "Well, laugh this off!"

There was a succession of thuds, as the butt of the officer's service revolver cracked against the little Negro's skull again and again. Finally, his form lay crumpled on the asphalt street, as his friend stood helplessly by—his black hands high above his head.

"I reckon this'll teach you not to be so smart next time," laughed the other fiend who wore a policeman's badge, as he walked over to the Negro's prostrate form and began kicking him. His laughter only increased as the Negro feebly groaned.

To me, it had all seemed like a page from some terrible story book. But that Negro's groan struck a note of reality.

"Why you dirty dog!" I screamed, "you're kicking a man who's flat on his back!"

Quickly a hand was clasped over my mouth. "You little simpleton!" my mother muttered, "don't you know that they can do the same thing to you and I can't do a thing about it?"

In that moment, I fell heir to my heritage. I understood the whispers about the race riot. Again I saw white-robed figures and heard the clatter of horses' hoofs, as an old Negro woman prayed and clutched a tiny baby to her breast. I understood why my father could not look me in the eye after the Ku Klux Klan had passed by.

And if that Negro who was kicked, at the point of a gun, as he lay flat on his back, is today a member of any organization pledged to overthrow the brand of order that allows such atrocities—*who is to blame?*

It is readily admitted that Shorty was no civic leader. I doubt if he was affiliated with any movement dedicated to human betterment. Yet he was a young man and might have been any number of things. Out of this same town came the Negro who, I am told, is the vice-president of the Communist party in America. That is another example of the effect that unwarranted brutality has had upon many Negroes.

Most of us are familiar with the National Association for the Advancement of Colored People and the wonderful and constructive work it has done. We black folk enjoy many privileges that might not be ours if there had not been such an organization as the NAACP. Right now, however, I am thinking of one of the cases in which the NAACP was helpless; there is no organization under the sun that has the power to breathe life into the dead. And that is the only solution that would have satisfied those of us who loved Edna D———.

Edna came to our home from a nearby school. The City Federation of Colored Women's Clubs had been contributing to the support and educational expenses of Edna and her sister, Nobie. Neither of these girls were particularly interested in an education. As they were orphans, Edna felt she had been dependent upon others too long and left the institution. Nobie, who had lost both arms during early childhood, realized her handicap and remained at the school.

In those days there was a weekly deadline against which I had to write, and before long, Edna became the "head-lady" around our house. Two years went by with this happy arrangement. Then one day we were discussing the idea of my going to New York.

"If I go away, what will you do?" I asked Edna.

"Oh," she replied, "you go ahead. If you go to New York and study, maybe you'll get to be a real good writer. But be sure and send for me just as soon as you get a place for us to stay." Though the girl was usually slow of comprehension, she had found out that we needed each other. Little did she realize, though, that she was slated for martyrdom.

Like most literary moths, I came on to New York. But life in the big city was not as easy as it had been pictured in the books I had read. Months passed and once in a great while there was a letter from Edna. Each one contained the same question: "Don't you think you'd better hurry and send for me?"

But the winds of winter were cold and there were times when my daily crust of bread was not enough for me, let alone another. So I didn't send for Edna.

Then one day a newspaper clipping fell out of a letter that my mother had sent on by airmail. The clipping was an account of the fatal shooting of Edna D———, a Negro woman (she was barely 18) by Detective ——— for resisting an officer of the law. Once more I had been forced to swallow the bitter brew of America's farcical justice!

Edna, as the story goes, had attended a party. In the course of the evening one of the young women present had drunk a little more than wisely. Then someone lost a pocketbook and, after several heated discussions, the majority of the merrymakers decided that the lady who had tilted her cup so often had also taken the pocketbook. It seems that Edna had, for some reason, decided that someone else took the pocketbook. When the crowd began beating the silly woman, Edna became furious. And a furious Edna was something to reckon with.

Lacking about three inches of being six feet tall, with a frame well covered with flesh, Edna looked much like some African princess who had never been contaminated by the various bloods that race through the veins of most of us. Though slow to comprehend, right and wrong dictated the course of Edna's actions. When she saw the crowd beating a woman she believed to be innocent, she went to the aid of the unfortunate woman and, single-handed, subdued the rest of the crowd. Innately kind, with more than her share of maternal instinct, Edna then went home taking the woman with her.

Of course the people at the party were very angry with Edna. And they decided to play a trick on her that they knew would give the girl a good scare. They called police headquarters and told the officers to go to "913 North Street. There's a bad Negro woman there."

In a few moments the police walked into Edna's room. She had put the intoxicated woman to bed and was changing her shoes. You see Edna persisted in wearing shoes that were smaller than her generously proportioned feet. Her first act upon entering the house was naturally to seek comfort for her feet.

And so when the officers said, "Put up your hands!" Edna, intent upon changing her shoes and always slow to comprehend, simply looked up to see what was happening. That was the resistance that caused an officer of the law to shoot Edna.

There was an investigation, all the findings of which I do not know. I do know, however, that Edna's slayer kept his job and received no legal punishment.

Meanwhile, I prayed and waited. If this man escaped all punishment, I reasoned, surely I was following the wrong path.

Still I prayed and waited. Time passed. Then last year another clipping came in a letter I received. It was an account of the death of the man who had slain Edna D——. He met his death at the hand of another culprit who had resisted arrest. "Vengeance is mine!" saith the Lord. *He* had charted my course.

These unfortunate and inappropriate experiences have been recorded here not to spread hatred, stir up sectional strife, or arouse ill feeling. Neither have they been easy to share with you. But the cause for which I have written about these experiences is the salvation of millions of souls, and any suffering these memories might have recalled is only a small part of the contribution hundreds of us are ready to pay so that our more handicapped and less articulate brothers may enjoy the inherited rights of every man created to the image and likeness of God.

I would not have you believe that I have sought to paint a picture of a barbarous South. Indeed not I, for I love my home and some of my most highly esteemed friends are white. But my nice white friends, who are thoroughly familiar with these conditions, allow public officers to brutalize and murder helpless and inarticulate Negroes. It is this silence of kindly intentioned America that is causing Negroes everywhere to demand that those who call themselves our friends take their stand and let the world know about it.

Without a doubt Mr. Wright is recording the harvest of hate that white America has, perhaps unwittingly, sown. Can you honestly blame him?

THE SIN OF SEGREGATION

GEORGE H. DUNNE

The racist mind has contrived an almost limitless number of evasive analogies to justify the unjustifiable. They are evasive because they all ignore the crucial point which makes racial segregation essentially different from other kinds of segregation. It is said that if racial segregation were a violation of justice it would follow that I must admit into the circle of my intimate friends anyone who demands admittance and that I must keep perpetual open house to the whole world. The ancient sophists were more subtle than this.

We choose our friends for a variety of reasons, some good, some bad, and according to a variety of tests, some consciously apprehended, some known only to the subconscious. We may offend against charity by excluding certain individuals, but no one pretends that every individual has a fundamental right in justice to be accepted as an intimate friend of everyone else. You may not like my looks, you may not like my personality, you may not like my ideas. I may resent this, but I shall not charge you with injustice. I shall probably say: "Everyone to his tastes; and in any case, the feeling is mutual." But if you like everything about me except the fact that my ancestors were Irish and for this reason alone shut the door in my face, I shall charge you with injustice. In such an event, however, I shall not desire your friendship, because your attitude reveals a shallowness of mind that is distasteful to me. Only the snob is anxious for the friendship of snobs.

When we look honestly at this question we see that it is the advocate, not the antagonist, of racial segregation who impugns our right to choose our friends. The pattern of racial segregation and the prejudices which are a part of it say to me who am white: "We deny your right to

---

GEORGE H. DUNNE, S.J. (1906–98), served as a missionary to China and worked with the World Council of Churches in Geneva. He was a strong supporter of labor and civil rights causes.

include among your friends or to open your home to anyone who is of Negro ancestry. If you violate this taboo we shall cast you out of society." The social ostracism imposed upon me by a racist society is clearly an effort to interfere with my freedom to choose my own friends.

It is said that the elimination of racial segregation will mean miscegenation on a grand scale. This is the grand-daddy of all red herrings. Apart from the fact that its roots lie in a pride of race and blood that belongs properly to the Nazi, not to the Christian, philosophy of life, this sophism assumes that with the elimination of segregation there will be an end to freedom of choice in the matter of marriage. It conjures up in the minds of frightened mothers the fantastic image of thousands of screaming girls being carried off triumphantly to undesired marriage beds. Or if this be denied, then it must be admitted that it conjures up the image of thousands of delighted girls rushing happily into marriage with Negro boys. If the former image is fantastic, the latter image is hardly flattering to white boys; or, for that matter, to Negro girls. The fact is, of course, that it takes two to make a marriage and that we have the right to marry whom we choose. Again, it is not the opponent of segregation, but its advocate, who questions this right. The racial pattern says to me: "I deny your right to marry anyone of Negro ancestry. If you violate this taboo, society will mobilize the full force of social ostracism to punish you for your transgression."

Those who are fond of raising the spectre of miscegenation will say that I have unfairly represented their position. They will say that all they mean to affirm is that if the racial bars which now separate them are let down, whites and Negroes, as a result of familiar association, will lose their color consciousness and cases of intermarriage will multiply.

Nothing could better expose the artificial foundation of their entire position. It is they, not their opponents, who affirm that with the elimination of segregation inter-marriage will become common. What is this but an explicit confession that race prejudice can only be kept alive by setting up artificial barriers which prevent white people from really knowing colored people? It is an admission that once the former are permitted really to know the latter they will immediately perceive the fallacy of racism. It is a frank avowal that the grand illusion of our racial superiority can only be maintained by manufactured social contrivances. It is to admit that prejudice inevitably dies once knowledge supplants ignorance. It is to recognize that segregation is not the necessary consequence of any real inferiority, but the artificial device whose function is to create the illusion of inferiority.

It is said that people have the right to protect the value and desirability of their homes by preventing undesirable characters from invading the neighborhood. The tattered shreds of this well-worn argument ill conceal the naked sophistry underneath. Like all the other analogies, it ignores the essential difference between racial segregation and other kinds of segregation. Granting, for the sake of argument, the right to keep moral delinquents or slovenly housekeepers out of the neighborhood, the question is: Upon what ground do you refuse admittance to one who is neither a moral delinquent nor a slovenly housekeeper and whose only "offense" is that he has Negro ancestors? And the answer is: It is because you falsely and unjustly assume that the fact of Negro ancestry is itself a form of uncleanness. Establish your residential restrictions upon whatever other basis you choose—moral conduct, social grace, physical cleanliness, domestic propriety. (Whether or not the civil law will support them has nothing to do with the question at issue.) None of these restrictions implies the existence of a people whose nature is itself unclean.

The sophistry and hypocrisy of those who defend residential segregation by appealing to their right to maintain a proper standard of morals, of cleanliness, of beauty surrounding their homes is made manifest by the undoubted fact that these same people, for the most part, would prefer a white neighbor who violated all of their standards to a Negro neighbor who more than measured up to their most stringent demands. A white debauchee will be admitted when a Negro saint would never be tolerated.

It is said that a school commits no injustice in refusing to admit those who cannot meet its intellectual or financial requirements. It is said that a school commits no injustice which says that it will not admit students who live west of Thirty-second Street. *A pari,* so the argument runs, a school commits no injustice which says that it will admit only students not of Negro ancestry.

As in all the other analogies, the evasiveness is cheap, the sophistry transparent. Establish your intellectual, financial, or geographical tests. It is the Negro who can pass every one of these tests except the racial test whose case exposes the essential difference and the essential injustice of racial segregation.

Do you or do you not believe that this is a race tainted and inferior in nature, so much so that any individual belonging to this race, whatever his personal qualifications, is by the fact of race alone rendered unfit to associate with those of other races? If you do not, then upon what ground do you exclude this Negro who can pass all your course examinations, who can pay his tuition, and who lives east of Thirty-second Street? If you do, then you profess a doctrine which is branded as false by science, forbidden by the inspired word of God, condemned by the Vicar of Christ, and which, by denying that the Negro as a human person is fully equal to every other human person, violates a fundamental principle of justice.

There is another aspect of this which reveals unmistakably that segregation is not based, as the racist pretends, upon concern for purity of morals or physical cleanliness but upon the refusal to admit the equality of Negroes as human persons. The same person who will fight tooth and nail to prevent a Negro from living in his neighborhood will not hesitate to employ a Negro maid or a Negro cook. If he believes that Negroes are lacking in moral integrity, why does he permit a Negro maid to take care of his children? If he believes that Negroes are physically unclean, why does he permit the Negro cook to handle his food? The answer is obvious; he does not really believe either of these things; but he does believe that no one of Negro ancestry is his equal as a human person. To allow a Negro maid to bathe the baby or a Negro cook to handle the food implies no recognition of the equality of the Negro as a human person. But to allow a Negro to establish his home in the same neighborhood does imply a recognition of that equality and is therefore not to be tolerated.

It is difficult for the mind to emancipate itself from widely accepted social patterns. The history of the polemics about slavery provides a striking example of this. Today the Christian conscience instinctively repudiates slavery and without the necessity of recourse to involved casuistry recognizes it as incompatible with the dignity of man. Yet less than one hundred years ago the pattern of slavery was so woven into the social fabric that its protagonists found no trouble enlisting in its defense the support of many reputable moralists. The treatises they wrote make interesting reading today. One does not know whether to admire their ingenuity or pity their ingenuousness.

It is probable—at least we must think so if we are not to despair—that one hundred years from now the Christian conscience will repudiate with equal decisiveness the whole pattern of racial segregation. In that happy event the lucubrations of mid-twentieth-century apologists for Jim Crow will make interesting, if sad, reading.

Then there is the moralist who, in discussing racial segregation, includes in his enumeration of the specific rights in justice which belong to all men whether "white . . . black, yellow or red" the "right to the pursuit of happiness, that is to say, to such equal opportunities as are required for the pursuit of happiness." And a few pages further on he blandly denies, without giving any supporting argument, that the exclusion of a Catholic Negro boy from a Catholic school is a violation of justice, provided that there is another Catholic school which will admit him.

How is this trick performed? It is easy: one forgets the principle of justice one has already admitted, looks the other way when the spectre of racial segregation (the really pertinent point) looms up, and pretends that the only question at issue is the right to an education.

Yet none but the obtuse and insensitive can pretend for a moment that a people subject to a pattern of racial segregation enjoy equal opportunities with others for the pursuit of happiness. This pattern is a dark cloud over the happiness of every Negro who has not already been brutalized by subjection to the pattern. And the more sensitive the Negro, that is to say, the more he has succeeded in perfecting his personality (another fundamental right recognized by the moralists), the darker becomes that cloud. It is impossible to know Negroes without knowing this. It is impossible to look into the South without knowing this. It is impossible to put oneself imaginatively in the Negro's place without knowing this. And if nothing else will do, it should be enough to read Richard Wright's autobiography to realize this.

One of the most naive sophisms which the unavowed Catholic racist invokes to defend Jim Crow is the assertion that Catholic schools, since they are institutions, have the right to admit or exclude whomsoever they choose. It is a proof of the allure of sophistry that sincere men, themselves no friends of racism, have sometimes been beguiled by this far from subtle play on words. Casuistry, properly understood and practiced, is a respectable and useful form of dialectics. It is the most widely accepted method of teaching the law. Its object is to develop facility in applying legal or moral principles to concrete cases. But it is precisely the kind of equivocation here manifested and whose purpose is to rationalize violations of principle that has brought casuistry into disrepute and given it its bad name.

In what sense is a Catholic institution a "private institution"? In the sense that it is not a state supported or controlled institution. Therefore, should the state attempt to enforce a practice which violated Christian principles—as, for example, the practice of racial segregation—the Catholic institution is not obliged to submit; is obliged, on the contrary, to resist. In no sense is the Catholic institution a "private institution" as against the church regardless of what order or congregation or ecclesiastic authority directs it. Because it is a private institution, may it teach sexual promiscuity or birth control or hatred for one's neighbors? It is a Catholic institution and therefore under strict obligation to conform to Catholic principles. Among those principles is the uncompromising repudiation of racism in all its forms: "The *only* road to salvation is definitely to repudiate *all* pride of race and blood." (The words are those of Pope Pius XII; the italics are added.) If Jim Crow is not the natural offspring of pride of race and blood, whose offspring is it?

The mind which is bent upon defending racial segregation is inevitably forced to take refuge in equivocation, subterfuge, evasion, and rationalization. The passages through which this leads are tortuous and labyrinthine and warp the logical processes of the mind. No conclusion which it reaches, however absurd, should be surprising.

There are other distressing features to be found in the discussions of this question which one hears among some Catholics. One would suppose that they were pagan Greek philosophers instead of Christian moralists. The argument nearly always proceeds in terms of natural ethics.

There are certain questions which these people need to be asked. Is the morality of human actions in no way affected by the fact of the Incarnation? Is every action which would have been permissible to a Greek permissible to a Christian? Does the supernatural have no bearing upon our moral actions? Does the Christian, by reason of the supernatural order and specifically because of the reality of the Mystical Body of Christ, have no obligations binding under pain of sin which he would not have in a natural order or in an order presumed to be natural? Is it proper for a Christian moralist to formulate his discussions in terms proper to Greek philosophy only?

It is curious that it does not seem to occur to such people that Christ's identification of himself with every victim of injustice and uncharitableness has anything to do with the matter. "Whatsoever you do unto one of these my least brethren you do unto me." For the Christian who is not wholly dead to the real meaning and nature of Christianity these words give the complete and final answer to the race question. There is no need for statistics, no need for distinction and subdistinction. It is Christ who is turned out of your school, out of your church, out of your hospital. It is Christ who is ordered out of your restaurant, out of your neighborhood, out of your Pullman car. It is Christ who is insulted, humiliated. Yet often it has been my experience in discussing the question with certain Christians that reference to these words of Christ is met with blank looks all around. There is an embarrassed pause such as would ensue were I to dunk my cake at a musical tea. I have evidently committed a dialectical *faux pas.* In the silence of the pause one can almost hear the minds behind the blank faces working. And they are all busy with the same thought: "Now whatever possessed him to introduce that irrelevant note into the discussion?" Then someone will clear his throat and quickly act to bring the discussion back to the solid ground of good sense: "Now whether you look at it from the point of view of commutative justice or distributive justice. . . ." At that point for some curious reason I always think of Dostoevski's Grand Inquisitor.

"Whatsoever you do unto one of these my least brethren, you do unto me." Has this fact no impact upon the morality of Christian actions? Perhaps it could not affect the moral discussions of the Greeks, but surely the moral discussions of Christians cannot prescind from it.

The penalty exacted of those who do these things to Christ's "least brethren" was hell. It must seem rather pointless to them whether or not the Greeks could prove their actions no violations of strict justice in terms of natural ethics. Perhaps most curious of all, however, is the common assumption that only justice imposes strict obligations upon the Christian conscience. So long as it is thought possible to prove that strict justice is not violated, it is assumed that any action is permitted to a Christian. Charity can recommend, but apparently it cannot oblige. It can recommend that the authorities of the Catholic school admit the Negro applicant. It cannot oblige.

This is a remarkable evacuation of the essential content of Christian morality. Sins against charity are sins and therefore immoral no less than are sins against justice. Christian morality does not recommend that we not offend against charity. It obliges us under pain of sin not to offend against charity. Many seem to suppose that charity is a work of supererogation, something that is nice to observe if we find it not inconvenient, but which we can ignore or directly wound with impunity if we choose to do so.

This fallacy is but one of the many consequences of the influence of the dehydrated moral notions of a capitalistic society which has substituted mere caricatures for the fullness of the Christian virtues. Instead of charity we have philanthropy: the rich man who with a lordly wave of the hand and an inner warmth of self-satisfaction bestows a generous alms upon the beggar. A nice gesture if he is capable of it, no sin if he is incapable of it.

It has been sufficiently proved that racial segregation violates strict justice. But the point here being made is that, even if justice were not violated, no one would pretend that charity is not grievously wounded. Racial segregation is certainly a sin against charity and, in the Christian dispensation, is certainly immoral and not to be tolerated. We can go to hell for sins against charity as easily as for sins against justice, perhaps more easily.

THE CASE OF MR. Y.

PETER STEINFELS

I came to know Mr. Y. several years ago. Some tenants in our building had responded to a precipitous rise in the mugging rate by organizing a "watch" by the front door. Mr. Y. helped mount the operation not for himself, he assured us, but for the others. Despite his years, he was a large, strapping man, and anyone who tried to mug him was promised, with suitable references to many years of soccer, "a good kick in the teeth." Mr. Y. had been born in Vienna, the son of a cantor. He had studied dentistry, then left Austria for the United States in the mid-thirties; what he did here I never quite found out, though I always imagined it had something to do with the music which was the love of his life.

When another tenant and I would take our turn at the "watch," Mr. Y. would often join us. He would lean against one wall of the front hallway, puffing, scraping, knocking his ever present pipe, and address us, his audience, seated in folding chairs against the other wall. Mr. Y. had been struck not long before by a great personal tragedy in his family, and about this he would talk obsessively, his severe psychological distress in painful contrast with his physical vigor and the absolute certitude with which he pronounced on all subjects. At times like this, not daring to contradict him in his sorrow nor wishing to encourage it, I steered the conversation elsewhere. We talked about that period of history when fascism was on the rise in Central Europe and when all the artillery, ideological as well as military, was being drawn up for the war and the Holocaust; about the Austrian Socialists and the trade unions; about the assaults of the anti-Semitic youth squads on the Jewish students at the university.

Eventually the "watch" disintegrated and I saw Mr. Y. less frequently.

PETER STEINFELS (1941–), formerly the editor of *Commonweal*, writes the "Beliefs" column for the *New York Times* and teaches history at Georgetown University.

We greeted him or his wife in the hallway, or more often simply noted, by the strong aroma of his tobacco, that he had just used the elevator. There were rumors that Mr. and Mrs. Y. were going to move. Friends in the two apartments across from his, also Jews of Eastern origin, had left for safer districts; and the apartments were occupied by large families of Haitian blacks. Though one of the Haitian families had already lived in our building on another floor, Mr. Y. told me his wife was afraid to go out into the hall or the elevator because she could not recognize the strange faces.

Actually safety in our building seemed to increase, but that did not render the city safe. Late one evening, for instance, I found Mr. Y. pacing in front of the building in an agitated state. He had missed his wife when he went to pick her up after an opera. Eventually she arrived, via taxi, in danger of nothing graver than her husband's sputtering combination of relief and irritation. But we knew that such was not always the happy ending.

It was some time after that when I sensed a decline in Mr. Y. For one thing, he actually appeared without his pipe clenched in his teeth. Again we heard that he and his wife were buying an apartment elsewhere. Finally the day came when they moved out; I met him in the lobby on my way to work, and with honest regret I said good-bye.

We met again, however. Last week. It was in a neighborhood bank, and Mr. Y. looked ill. But he spoke enthusiastically of his new apartment in a semi-suburban section of New York—eighteenth floor, balcony overlooking the city, absolutely modern kitchen.

"But the best thing," he added vehemently, "is that I never have to see any more black faces." (There were several within earshot, but Mr. Y. had no concern for lowering his voice.) "No black faces—that's been the best thing for my wife, too."

I felt ambushed by his outburst, angry too, yet I knew how futile any reply might be. I turned away momentarily. Mr. Y., however, continued: "Ten years ago, I was a liberal too. But we made the mistake of opening the gates to *them*. All my life liberalism has been losing." And then, perhaps picking up a thread from our past encounters, he began to talk about the Social Democrats and the outbreak of World War I and Benito Mussolini. He was interrupted by a bank attendant (black) who said she could help him now.

A decade ago the liberal reflex might have been to say that Mr. Y. is a racist, and to leave it at that. But the foundering of many liberal hopes pointed to the importance of understanding people like Mr. Y. in their full complexity. Indeed, of complexity a man like Mr. Y. has almost no end. I believe, for example, that even in his salad days of liberalism, Mr. Y. probably believed black people generally inferior; but then it is difficult to sort this out from the impression that Mr. Y. thought most of mankind inferior. No doubt, the surfacing of Mr. Y.'s racism is linked to the suffering which private events wreaked upon him in recent years, to the dissolution of the small community he had enjoyed in our building and our neighborhood, and even to the apparent sapping of that physical vigor which was so much a part of him. But the anti-Semites of Mr. Y.'s youth in Austria were also people who had personal sufferings, who underwent social disruption, and who faced physical ills—what excuses do we make for them?

The very real problem of city crime—and the special terror it holds for the elderly—is also an element in Mr. Y.'s racism, although racism was just as clearly an element in magnifying these fears. Crime and terror, however, is no less a reality for Mr. Y.'s and my black neighbors; they too are mugged in the elevator and sometimes wait anxiously for wives to return at night; unlike Mr. Y., they do not have the option of finally fleeing to safer areas.

Mr. Y.'s racism is as much a racism as that Austrian anti-Semitism which provided the seedbed for Adolf Hitler's warped views and the ultimate consequences of which Mr. Y. escaped by only a few years. What conclusions flow from this fact, I am not sure. I doubt that politicians have much to gain by denouncing Mr. Y., or liberal programs by trying to convert him. I am not particularly interested in blaming him—though Mr. Y. is a moral adult and therefore not beyond blame. I write of the fact of his racism only because, in a season when new confusions are being hurriedly constructed, mirror-like, on old ones, it happens to be true.

AFFIRMATIVE ON AFFIRMATIVE ACTION

DON WYCLIFF

Nothing in the current debate over affirmative action has rankled me more as a black person than the question: "Isn't thirty years enough?" It has been asked by many people, but perhaps most prominently by Jesse Helms on the floor of the Senate in March. "Isn't thirty years enough?" Helms intoned, as he announced that he was introducing legislation to end all federal affirmative-action programs.

Isn't thirty years of affirmative action enough?

To put that into perspective, recall that the first black settlers arrived here as slaves in 1619. In the 376 years since, African-Americans have enjoyed two periods of relative normalcy, two periods of about thirty years each in which they were subject to neither involuntary servitude nor officially sanctioned second-class citizenship. And those two periods were separated by about seventy years.

Sixty good years out of 376—and people have the nerve to ask whether thirty years of affirmative action isn't enough. Incredible!

Nevertheless, the political facts of life suggest to me that thirty years will have to be enough. Because affirmative action, at least insofar as it means efforts to overcome the historically imposed disadvantages of black folks (and definition is part of the problem in this debate), looks like a goner.

My personal crystal ball says that 1996 will bring a watershed event of some sort in American race relations—a Supreme Court decision? passage of the California Civil Rights Initiative? the election of Phil Gramm?—that will be the symbolic equivalent of *Plessy v. Ferguson* in 1896. That, of course, was the Supreme Court decision that made "separate but equal" the law of the land, marking a kind of official end to Reconstruction and laying the juridical foundation for Jim Crow. The new

---

DON WYCLIFF (1946–) is editorial page editor of the *Chicago Tribune*.

event, whatever it turns out to be, will ring down the curtain on the most recent period of black advancement. God willing, we'll not regress as far as Jim Crow.

I fear that the foregoing suggests I am much more an unqualified supporter of affirmative action than I am. The fact is that it has troubled me for a long time and for a number of reasons, although none of them is killing.

It really can foster doubt about the legitimacy of the achievements of those it's meant to benefit—not just in the minds of white males, but also in the minds of the blacks, women, or other beneficiaries. I don't think this is a crippling defect. (It certainly doesn't seem to have crippled the white men who benefited from affirmative action in decades past by not having to compete with excluded portions of the population.) As Stephen Carter observed in his book *Reflections of an Affirmative Action Baby* (Basic Books, 1991), what's critical is not how one comes to the opportunity, but what one does with it.

Affirmative action imposes obligations on its beneficiaries, and no one has demonstrated that, on balance, those beneficiaries don't measure up as well as those from the traditional talent pools. (Of course, there's no reason they shouldn't measure up. Affirmative action has never been about hiring, promoting, admitting, or selecting unqualified persons. Rather, it is about looking for qualified persons in unaccustomed places.)

Another troubling aspect of affirmative action, at least at one time, had to do with the message that I perceived was being sent to young black people. During the bad old days before the civil rights movement, young black folks used to be told, "You've got to be twice as good as the white boy to get half as far." After the advent of affirmative action, the message sometimes seemed to be, "Don't worry, you've got an ace up your sleeve—you're a minority."

As a matter of historical equity, that may have been satisfying. After all, for centuries having white skin has amounted to having a whole deck of aces up one's sleeve. Turnabout is fair play. But in terms of its effect on the motivations of individual young black people, this could not be a healthy message to send.

I cannot know how widely or deeply this message may have been absorbed. But that it was a legitimate concern and not just a figment of my imagination became clear to me at a Congressional Black Caucus seminar in Washington in the late 1980s. A young black man, a college student, rose and naively asked a question in which he raised the possibility that affirmative action might be detrimental to the efforts of blacks to help themselves. The distinctively unappreciative response from the panelists, all defenders of affirmative action in higher education, suggested that he had touched a sore spot.

But however large or small this problem once may have been, I doubt, given the temper of recent times, that it has been one at all lately.

A far more substantial affirmative-action concern is the expansion of the number of groups and categories who are counted as "excluded" or "disadvantaged" and therefore qualify as beneficiaries. It's not that I would withhold from others an advantage that I enjoy. Rather, such an expansion was bound to undermine support for the concept of affirmative action itself, by diluting the sense that this was an obligation to justice. Remember, affirmative action (at least as originally conceived) was about compensation—reparation?—for disadvantages stemming from massive, unique, and undisputed historical wrongs. In this society, those criteria qualify two groups: African-Americans and Native Americans. Any others are a stretch.

The addition of women as a disadvantaged group and the broadening of the pool of disadvantaged minorities—however defensible these things may have been on an intellectual basis—undermined the emotional support necessary to sustain affirmative action as a matter of compensatory justice. When everybody is a victim, nobody is.

But the problem for affirmative action now is not just that it has lost support, but that it inspires opposition, and even anger. Far from being a device to achieve compensatory justice, its opponents say, affirmative action has itself become a source of injustice. "Reverse discrimination" has become the battle cry of the opponents.

By any objective, empirical standard, such complaints have to be counted as vastly overblown. A world in which the median wage of white men exceeds that of any other ethnic or gender category by at least a third has hardly been turned upside down by affirmative action. A world in which white men still possess 90-plus percent of all the top-level management jobs is hardly one in which white male hegemony is threatened by affirmative action.

(Of course, these same figures cut the other way as well. If, after thirty years of affirmative action, this is all the beneficiaries have to show for it, then why is it so important and valuable?)

But to argue over objective, empirical evidence—statistics—is to miss the point of the opposition to affirmative action. The point is philosophical: Affirmative action, involving government-sanctioned preference on the basis of accidental characteristics, represents a departure from principles of individual merit and achievement and equal protection of the laws that are the essence of America. (At least they are the essence in recent years, after the historically favored groups have gotten theirs and largely arranged things so they can keep it.)

Americans find it hard to rest easy with such exceptions to principle—whether they be malignant ones like slavery and Jim Crow, or a benignly intended one like affirmative action. In the case of affirmative action, toleration could be sustained only as long as the sense of it as compensatory justice—not political entitlement—could be kept alive. When that sense evaporated, so did the support.

So what is to be done?

Not much, I suspect. President Bill Clinton may, with his present review of affirmative-action programs, find a way to split the difference and cool the passions surrounding this issue. But I doubt it.

The fact is that an era is ending, the latest thirty-year window of opportunity for black folks in America. Affirmative action, I suspect, will end with it. I say that not happily, but resignedly.

For black people, the loss will be more symbolic than substantive. To be sure, affirmative action has wrought some genuine successes—I count my own education and career among them. But overall, in terms of bringing black people to parity with whites, it has not overwhelmed.

In the most important sense, affirmative action has always been more a spirit and a disposition than a program or a policy. It is that spirit that needs to survive. For the sake of America's soul, that spirit must survive.

Church and State

AUGUST 5, 1960

RELIGION IN THE CAMPAIGN

THE EDITORS

As this editorial is being written, Senator Kennedy stands before the country as the presidential nominee of the Democratic party. By the time it is read, Vice-President Nixon will—barring the totally unexpected—be the Republican candidate. This interim period before the campaign gets under way, then, provides a good opportunity to reiterate certain basic points about "the religious issue" in the election.

The possibility that the campaign will bring with it a sharp increase in religious tensions is so obvious it needs no belaboring. This is the reason a certain number of Catholics have always been uneasy about Senator Kennedy's candidacy, fearing that it is "too soon" for a Catholic to seek the presidency. Aside entirely from any question of Senator Kennedy's qualifications, these Catholics are afraid that the campaign will bring with it a rise in religious bigotry across the country; in addition, they fear that Catholics will be "blamed" for any national setback or mistake in judgment Senator Kennedy might make if elected. There is, of course, nothing they can do about it, but if the doubters had had their choice they would have preferred that the inevitable facing of the religious issue be postponed until some indefinite later date.

Another group of Catholics—one which we believe is much larger and in which we would count ourselves—understands but does not share these fears. Again leaving aside the merits of Senator Kennedy or any particular candidate, those who hold these views would like to see the religious issue in presidential elections laid to rest once and for all and they think this is as good a time as any. They take the constitutional ban against a religious test for public office seriously, and they think it a betrayal of the American idea to give this ideal only lip service. To put it simply, they want to see the end of the time-honored political dictum that any American boy can grow up to be president—as long as he is a white, Anglo-Saxon Protestant.

This goal is, we think, an estimable one on all scores. For it to be achieved, it is not necessary that Senator Kennedy be elected president of the United States. It is necessary only that the campaign be a fair one, argued on the real issues, and that if Senator Kennedy is defeated his religion should not be a major factor in that defeat.

In the campaign that lies ahead, it will help if all concerned are clear on a few fundamental facts. It is undoubtedly true that Catholics will take a special interest in Senator Kennedy's campaign, whether they are Republicans or Democrats. How could it be otherwise, when Catholics have never seen one of their co-religionists president and when religion played a part in the defeat of the only previous Catholic nominee? Nonetheless, as Senator Kennedy has noted on several occasions, he is not "the Catholic candidate" but a candidate who is a Catholic. The difference is a significant one.

In American elections, there really is no such thing as "the Catholic candidate," nor should there be. It is, surely, one of the blessings of the American tradition that our political parties are not divided along religious lines. Many American Catholics, for example, may disagree with current interpretations of the First Amendment on certain issues like school bus transportation for parochial school children, federally financed lunch programs, and the like. However, they certainly do not feel that they are confronted with a hostile and antireligious government, in the face of which the formation of political parties along religious lines is necessary—a step both Catholics and Protestants have sometimes found necessary elsewhere.

Indeed, quite the contrary situation prevails here. American Catholics do not feel beleaguered or in need of Catholic candidates or Catholic political parties. They have always supported the Constitution of the United States, including the First Amendment, and they do so today, beyond any question. However fascinating theoretical discussions about church-state relationships may be, this seems to us the central political fact of the matter.

For our part, we have always felt that questions on the church-state issue were legitimate enough in connection with Senator Kennedy's candidacy. In recent months, however, Senator Kennedy has made his views on this subject quite clear—so clear, in fact, that we think those who now profess to be in doubt simply choose not to understand. It is therefore time, we think, to leave the subject of church-state, on which Senator Kennedy has done all he possibly can to make his position clear, and to take up those vital issues of foreign and domestic policy which are really at stake in the election.

As to how much influence religion will have in the election, only time will tell. But Senator Kennedy is not Al Smith, and 1960 is not 1928. In his acceptance speech to the Democratic convention, Senator Kennedy said: "I hope that no American, considering the really critical issues facing this country, will waste his franchise and throw away his vote by voting either for me or against me solely on account of my religious affiliation." Here, it seems to us, Senator Kennedy spoke in the best American tradition, and the hope he expressed is one we share as the nation prepares to pick the next president of the United States.

DO CATHOLICS HAVE CONSTITUTIONAL RIGHTS?

THE EDITORS

The First Amendment, prohibiting the establishment of religion and guaranteeing freedom of religion, speech, press, and political activity, is not to be tampered with. Yet that is exactly what is occurring in a little-publicized civil suit now moving toward a decision in the United States District Court in Brooklyn. The argument in that suit is aimed specifically at the First Amendment rights of American Catholics, but ultimately it endangers the rights of all religious believers and in fact of all who hold deeply and dearly to values they would like to see reflected in our political life. Curiously, this argument is being advanced by groups whose own tenets ought to place them squarely on the other side of the issue.

The suit in question is *McRae v. Califano,* a class action challenging the Hyde Amendment, the Congressional rider on HEW's budget that restricted Medicaid reimbursements for abortion to a very narrow range of cases. Among the plaintiffs challenging the Hyde Amendment is the Women's Division of the Board of Global Ministries of the United Methodist Church, and among the plaintiffs' representatives are attorneys from Planned Parenthood and the American Civil Liberties Union.

The Hyde Amendment and the right-to-life politics surrounding it raise a host of complicated questions. . . . Some of them we have taken up at other times, and will probably address again. They are not our concern at the moment.

Likewise we are not concerned with the whole range of grounds on which the plaintiffs in Brooklyn have challenged the Hyde Amendment. . . . The fact, however, that the Supreme Court has already rejected most of these arguments as grounds for overruling the decisions of legislators to restrict abortion funds has led to the emergence of a novel, and extremely mischievous, line of reasoning.

The plaintiffs in *McRae* maintain that the Hyde Amendment is equivalent to the establishment of a religion, Roman Catholicism in particular but also of other religious viewpoints opposing abortion (Orthodox Judaism, Mormonism, various currents of belief among Lutherans, Methodists, Baptists, etc.). At the same time, by not funding abortions the Amendment restricts the free exercise of religion on the part of poor women whose religious affiliations might lead them, or even require them, to a conscientious choice of abortion. In short, it is argued that the concern for unborn human life reflected in the congressional action has no other basis than a sectarian theological one. The restriction on abortion funding has no properly secular purpose, advances one religious viewpoint at the expense of another, and finally involves excessive government entanglement with religion.

To support these allegations the plaintiffs' attorneys have produced a mass of evidence illustrating conflicting religious views on abortion, the leading role of Catholics in the anti-abortion forces, the militancy of the right-to-life movement, the divisive effects of its fervor and its single-issue approach to politics, and the role of Catholic Congressmen and lobbyists in formulating the Hyde Amendment.

It is, of course, fascinating to learn just how many times the Catholic lobbyist passed notes to a congressional aide during the House-Senate conferences on the Hyde Amendment. . . . But virtually all of this material is irrelevant to the crucial issue.

. . . As Lawrence Tribe writes in *American Constitutional Law,* "If a purpose were to be classified as nonsecular simply because it coincided with the beliefs of one religion or took its origin from another, virtually nothing the government does would be acceptable; laws against murder, for example, would be forbidden because they overlapped the Fifth Commandment of the Mosaic Decalogue."

In fact, we do not know precisely on what grounds voters who oppose government funding for abortion actually base this position. We do not know on what basis the representatives and senators supporting the Hyde Amendment reached that conclusion. It is quite possible, indeed quite likely, that many who are not opposed to abortion itself are nonetheless opposed to *government funding* of abortion—the real issue at hand—because of a political attitude about government's role in morally controverted issues or a pragmatic belief about compromise in a pluralistic society. Whatever the mixture of beliefs behind it, Congress's decision to protect fetal life is as secular on the face of it as its decisions to protect tracts of wilderness from spoilation, unknowing consumers from toxic drugs, or laboratory animals from cruel experimentation.

. . . [I]f the leading proponents of cutting off funds for the war in Vietnam had organized and agitated on religious grounds, would that have made a congressional refusal of further funds for that war a religious and not a secular policy decision? As the philosopher Baruch Brody reminds us, "Opposition to torture in Brazil does not become a religious moral position just because that opposition is now being led by the Catholic bishops."

In their zeal to outflank Congress's decision, what the Hyde Amendment's opponents have done in *McRae* is to inflate the notion of religion, and therefore of establishment and of religious infringement, beyond anything relevant to the First Amendment. Indeed, at times their brief reaches to sociological and theological definitions of religion as whatever draws upon religious imagery and references or whatever is of ultimate concern or, quoting Paul Tillich, "what you take seriously without reservation" or, more operationally, whatever is deeply divisive and produces emotional accusations and uncompromising behavior.

The first consequence of this inflation is to render their own argument contradictory. If both positions in this controversy are equally religious ones, if the withholding of government monies amounts to the establishment of the anti-abortionists' religious viewpoint and an infringement on the religious practice of those for whom abortion, in certain circumstances, might be religiously mandated, then would not the payment of government monies likewise amount to establishing the religious views of the latter group and infringing on the practice of the former? Indeed, if one is to talk of "entanglement," both the courts and common sense concur that providing taxpayers' funds for some purpose is far more entangling than simply withdrawing from the area altogether.

The second consequence of their reasoning is the disenfranchisement of American Catholics of their rights to political activity. "We do not contend," say the plaintiffs, "that any of the picketing, lobbying, or any other pastoral or political activities by churches is unconstitutional and we do not seek to prohibit these activities." What they do seek, however, is that the results of those activities be declared unconstitutional, and that *largely on the basis that it was Catholic picketing, lobbying, etc., which produced the results*. This is Catch-22 with a vengeance.

The third consequence of their reasoning is to disenfranchise all religious viewpoints from an active engagement in the political process. Their argument, it seems, would apply as well toward Jewish mobilization on behalf of Israel, the broad mobilization of the religious community for civil rights legislation, the nineteenth-century agitation by religious leaders against slavery. The only legitimate viewpoint in politics would be what the late Frederick S. Jaffe of the Alan Guttmacher Institute called a "secular ethics." And maybe not—given the plaintiffs' worry about "deeply held beliefs" and political divisiveness—even that.

It so happens that the plaintiffs in *McRae* cite *Commonweal* at several points, quoting editorials and articles that complained of the narrow vision or untoward tactics of the right-to-life effort. We assume they will take to heart our equal distress at their own vision and tactics. . . .

CORRESPONDENCE: ABORTION AND THE CONSTITUTION

Undermining the Court

As one of the attorneys from Planned Parenthood addressed in your editorial "Do Catholics Have Constitutional Rights?" my answer is that the lawyers for plaintiffs in the *McRae* litigation have never questioned and indeed would strongly defend the constitutional rights of Catholics as we would those of any other group. The issue in *McRae v. Califano* is not freedom of speech, but whether it is appropriate within our constitutional system for a basically religious point of view to be imposed on the entire population.

The Supreme Court decided in *Roe v. Wade* that a woman, in consultation with her physician, has a right to an abortion unqualified in the first trimester, and subject, until the fetus becomes viable, only to restrictions imposed for the protection of her health. The Court held that, since physicians, philosophers, and theologians cannot agree on the question of when life begins, the state cannot impose on all women the belief that an unborn fetus is a person.

Two days after the *Roe v. Wade* decision, the National Conference of Catholic Bishops Committee for Prolife Affairs declared, "As religious leaders, we cannot accept the Court's judgment and we urge people not to follow its reasoning or conclusions."

Since then, not only Catholics but other spokesmen for absolutist religious views have engaged in a concerted campaign to undermine the Supreme Court's decision.

That campaign led to enactment of the Hyde Amendment, which denies medically safe abortions to poor women even when a physician believes such abortions to be medically necessary. The legislative history shows that the amendment was not passed for any reason except the religious belief that life begins at the moment of conception. It does not save the government money, and indeed ends up being extremely costly in those instances where it in fact prevents the termination of pregnancy. It imposes severe hardship upon women whose religious beliefs do not prohibit abortion, including women whose religious beliefs mandate abortion under some circumstances.

Congressional proponents of the Hyde Amendment all justified their position by religious references. Introducing the Amendment, Mr. Hyde said, "The essential question [is] the humanity of the unborn. Abortion . . . is the calculated killing of an innocent, inconvenient human being."

The fact that some Congressmen who supported the Hyde Amendment did so, not from personal religious conviction, but, as your editorial points out, "because of a political attitude about government's role in morally controverted issues or a pragmatic belief about compromise in a pluralistic society" does not change the essentially religious bias of the legislation, any more than Protestant votes for federal funding of parochial education in Catholic or Jewish schools would change the religious bias of such legislation. On the contrary, it simply shows that some legislators are prepared, for political reasons, to vote for legislation favored by one religious group in exchange for that group's support. That is hardly the "secular purpose" for legislation which our Constitution requires.

Eve W. Paul
Director of Legal Services, Planned Parenthood Federation

Widening the Gap

Your editorial "Do Catholics Have Constitutional Rights?" has succeeded in widening the gap of understanding of the abortion rights crisis among religious groups. You have misrepresented the position of this organization.

As a plaintiff in the suit *McRae v. Califano,* The Women's Division, Board of Global Ministries of The United Methodist Church, has attempted to present to the court these basic points:

1. That a conscientious decision whether to terminate or continue a pregnancy in accordance with the principles of responsible parenthood is a religious obligation for us.

2. That the efforts of some religious groups to enact the absolutist position on abortion in *effect* would enforce one religious belief on those who believe otherwise; and, thereby interfere with our free exercise of religion.

3. That the tragic effect of the Hyde Amendment on poor women to coerce unwanted and health threatening childbirth, extra legal abortion, and sterilization is inconsistent with our moral and ethical practice of religion.

In your attempt to describe our position, you have caricatured our faith stance with insensitivity. You do not seem to comprehend the depth of our faith commitment in a matter such as this, which has compelled us to plead before the court for *our* right *to free exercise* of religious conscience and that of other women who hold similar beliefs. . . .

We would fight just as hard against a reverse Hyde Amendment that only paid for abortions and sterilization to preserve the religious and conscientious decision of pregnant women for whom childbirth is the moral course.

In no way is our organization attempting to "disenfranchise all religious viewpoints from an active engagement in the political process," as you claim. Our history as an organization which views social concern as resting at the heart of Christian mission would preclude such a stance.

The issue here is not a question of valid religious participation in societal concerns, but rather one of control. When there are so many varying religious viewpoints on abortion, our concern is that the force and power of government in the Hyde Amendment supports one religious viewpoint to the exclusion of all others.

Theressa Hoover
Associate General Secretary, Board of Global Ministries, The United Methodist Church

Baring Their Clause

The thoughtful editorial on *McRae v. Califano* lifts up most of the crucial questions in a case that has received all too little attention. In this suit I was one of the witnesses for the defense who attempted to document the many and necessary ways in which moral judgment informed by religious belief interacts with public policy in a democratic society. I was struck by the uncanny climate of a hearing in which socially activist Christians—in this case Methodists—were pleading that the government should prohibit precisely the kinds of activities in which they are themselves so deeply engaged. The assumption, not very well hidden, is that of course their engagement is different; they act out of enlightened and universal principles rather than sectarian motives, and they act as free citizens not under intellectual duress. In short, they are not Roman Catholics.

Then, too, it seems to some of our separated sisters of the Methodist Women's Division that anxiety about the unborn or about the definition of human life is so patently nonrational that it could only be prompted by dogma reinforced by ecclesiastical coercion. They do not challenge the bishops' more reasonable efforts to influence legislation on housing, unemployment, and a host of other issues on which "People of good will" are of like mind. The influence of religion should not only be countenanced but should be celebrated when it advances what I want advanced.

Since *Commonweal* is edited by and (mainly) for Catholics, it is understandable that your editorial is titled "Do Catholics Have Constitutional Rights?" As your editorial suggests, however, the challenge—while tainted by anti-Catholic impulse—is directed against all believers and even nonbelievers who understand that democratic polity requires a living relationship between public policy and the most deeply held convictions of the people. Without such a relationship, the moral legitimacy of the polity is thrown into question. . . .

The importance of *McRae v. Califano* goes far beyond the abortion debate, as important as that debate continues to be. It dramatically poses the questions whether, or in what sense, is ours a secular society, and whether, or in what ways, is the state to exclude the beliefs of the citizenry from its deliberations?

Richard Neuhaus
Senior Editor, *Worldview*

Religious Liberty for All

Your editorial "Do Catholics Have Constitutional Rights?" distorts not only the First Amendment challenge to the Medicaid abortion restrictions we are presenting in *McRae v. Califano,* but also the principles of the First Amendment itself.

It is clear from the legislative history of the Hyde Amendment that the purpose of the legislation was to protect what its proponents believe to be actual human lives. According to this view any fetus—one minute old, one day old, one month old—is fully human, and indistinguishable from an infant, and therefore abortion is murder.

But when human life begins is essentially a religious question. There is no scientific consensus on this question, and no religious consensus either. Most religions teach that a fetus is not a human being. Other religions, such as the Catholic religion, believe, as a matter of faith, that the fetus possesses or may possess a soul from the moment of conception. The current controversy over abortion is therefore a controversy over religious doctrine.

No one of us questions or challenges the right of Catholics voluntarily to observe the Catholic teaching on abortion. Nor does the lawsuit challenge the rights of Catholics to petition, demonstrate, lobby, or sermonize against the right to abortion. But antichoice Catholics, like Mormons, Orthodox Jews, or fundamentalist Protestants who support the present campaign to restrict abortion for the most vulnerable—poor pregnant women—have no more right to enact their religious beliefs into law than Jehovah's Witnesses who view blood transfusions as a sacrilege or fundamentalist Protestants who were responsible in the 1920s for the "monkey" laws prohibiting the teaching of evolution in the schools. Just as today's opposition to anti-abortion laws draws accusations of anti-Catholicism, so in the 1920s opponents of the "monkey" laws were labeled "anti-Christian."

Unfortunately, the cry of religious bigotry is a smoke screen for religious intolerance. Absent from your editorial and from the anti-abortion mobilization is respect for the dictates of religious faith and conscience which teach that abortion may be a moral, loving, and religiously required choice.

Let us start from the premise, which I trust we share, that the goal of the Medicaid program to provide comprehensive health-care coverage for the indigent is necessary, just, and humane. A cardinal principle of the program is that no one may be coerced or pressured to abandon conscientious beliefs affecting necessary medical care. Thus, a Jehovah's Witness is entitled to refuse a blood transfusion, and a woman of Catholic faith or otherwise is guaranteed this same freedom, to refuse or to choose, with respect to family planning services.

In the entire Medicaid program, only the woman whose faith and convictions dictate abortion is denied this right to conscience. The indigent Protestant woman who believes that responsible parenthood necessitates a decision whether or not to continue a pregnancy is pressured to forego her religious duty; so is the Jewish woman whose faith teaches that she place her health and well-being and that of her existing family above the existence of the embryo.

The state does not remain neutral by withdrawing funding for abortion. Nor does it, as you suggest, "subsidize" the free exercise of those who believe in the necessity and right of choice. The abortion restriction discriminates based on religious or conscientious choice just as would paying for health-care needs of children attending Orthodox Jewish schools but not those attending Roman Catholic or public schools. Neutrality is preserved only by allowing freedom of choice in accordance with individual conscience. . . .

Rhonda Copelon
Counsel Center for Constitutional Rights
Ira Glasser
Executive Director, American Civil Liberties Union
Janet Benshoof
Counsel to the Reproductive Freedom,
American Civil Liberties Project

ABORTION, RELIGION, AND POLITICAL LIFE

THE EDITORS

Two months ago, when *Commonweal* warned that the First Amendment rights of Catholics and other believers were threatened by the arguments advanced in a class action against the Hyde Amendment, a headline on the magazine's cover asked, "Are the ACLU and Planned Parenthood Listening?" The correspondence in this issue, as well as a thoughtful reply by Aryeh Neier, former director of the American Civil Liberties Union, in the December 30, 1978, *Nation,* indicate that they are. This is gratifying. The difference of viewpoint subsists nonetheless; and we are tempted to complain that though our correspondents are listening, they are not listening *well.* In fact, a reading of these letters persuades us that the difficulty goes deeper than that. What is, to begin with, a dispute over the wisdom of a legal tactic in a Brooklyn District Court, finally leads us to some much larger questions about abortion, religion, and the future of American politics.

But first the immediate issue. Despite the claims to the contrary by our correspondents, we do not think our editorial "distorts" or "misrepresented" their position. . . . We do not question, let alone "caricature," the depth of the Methodist Board of Global Ministries' "faith stance" and "faith commitment." Our problem is not with the sincerity and depth of the plaintiffs' *intentions* but with the actual argument they advance and with its possible *consequences.* . . . It is not a question of distortion, then, but of disagreement. And these letters, like Mr. Neier's response, do make clear exactly where the disagreement lies. For these correspondents, the Hyde Amendment's suspension of Medicaid funding for abortion expresses "a basically religious point of view," "the religious belief that life begins at the moment of conception"; it involves "essentially a religious question," "a controversy over religious doctrine." Or as Mr. Neier sees it, it is a view "exclusively rooted in theology and supportable only by an act of faith" and which therefore "lacks a valid secular purpose." . . . He finds that no valid secular purpose can be discovered behind the Hyde Amendment unless one accepts "those theologies that teach that actual human life exists from the moment of conception."

A rather fanciful exchange between Mr. Neier and a *Nation* reader further defines the issue at hand. This reader, a professor of law, a supporter of abortion, and an opponent of the Hyde Amendment, found Mr. Neier's conclusion "not just wrong, but absurd." He argued that one by no means had to consider fetal life equivalent to human life to find that its protection was a valid secular enterprise. "Assume with me for a moment that a fetus is nothing more than a fish. Does that mean that Congress could not constitutionally legislate to protect it? Of course not. On the contrary, Congress has enacted valid legislation to protect not only whales but snail darters." To which Mr. Neier replied, as law professors will, "Assume the existence of a religious society, Porgyism, which venerates fish and which secures the passage of an anti-abortion law in order to preserve the fetus in its fish stage. . . . *If that view is not generally shared and it is discovered to be grounded exclusively in the doctrines of Porgyism,* the law should be susceptible to attack as a violation of the First Amendment. . . ." (Our emphasis.)

This is to travel far from the tragic dilemmas that are at the root of the controversy over abortion and especially over the Hyde Amendment. But at least it clarifies something about the kind of "religious" belief that the First Amendment prohibits from translation into civil law. Is the desire to protect fetal life, even by withdrawing government funds for abortion, not generally shared? Is it grounded exclusively in the theological doctrines of one or several religious denominations?

The first problem that the plaintiffs' argument must confront is that not one but three major religious groups—Catholics, Orthodox Jews, and Mormons—are stringently opposed to abortion, and that they are joined in this outlook by a sizable number of Protestants. While all these faiths reach similar conclusions about abortion, moreover, they do so by a variety of theological routes. All of this suggests that the concern for protecting fetal life, like the concern for racial equality or for aiding the poor, ought to be treated as a general question of human justice, quite apart from the particular theological rationales that have been presented to support it. Such an impression is reinforced when one looks at public belief in the United States about fetal life and government funding of abortions. In 1975 . . . 43 percent of men and 58 percent of women believed that human life began at conception—far more than chose any other moment. But let us go directly to the question at hand. In 1975 Gallup also asked its cross section whether they were for or against providing abortions at government expense. Fifty-seven percent were against, 35 in favor. This figure compares with the findings of a poll of 9,000 voters leaving voting places last November. Only 44 percent of Democrats and 37 percent of Republicans favored government funding for abortion. In addition, both belief in the "humanness" of early fetal life and opposition to government funding of abortion appears to be increasing, not declining.

Why cite these statistics? Neither morality, nor law, nor constitutionality can be determined by public opinion polls. . . . The wording of polls can always be faulted. A majority, or a plurality, does not settle a profound moral question. The Hyde Amendment may be an unwise or unjust measure even though a clear majority supports it. But the sentiments it represents are obviously widely held throughout American society. There is no evidence that they are held "exclusively" on the basis of the theological doctrines of one or several "Porgyisms." There is no evidence for the theme that runs throughout the plaintiffs' case: that a narrow or particular theology is being "imposed" on the mass of citizens.

This brings us to another critical point. While abortion can be debated in strictly theological terms that demand what Mr. Neier calls "an act of faith," it can be, and is widely, debated in terms accessible to any rational person. In this, it nowise differs from debates about basic human equality, warfare, torture, capital punishment, and a host of other public issues. The plaintiffs in *McRae* considerably confuse this matter by pointing out that there is no "scientific consensus" on the value of fetal life and suggesting that the only alternative to a "scientific consensus" is a "religious consensus." Since there is no "religious consensus" either, for society to take any position at all on the question is to prefer one religious view over another. (Presumably, however, if there were a "religious consensus," that would be equally illegitimate in their reading of the First Amendment.) But science simply does not provide any answers at all to many of the deepest human questions. Throughout history, there has been no "scientific consensus" that individuals, or races, are fundamentally equal. If anything, the "scientific consensus" has been the other way. (And in many times and places—colonial America, Nazi Germany, South Africa today—there has been no "religious consensus" either.) To conclude that society must therefore abstain from judgment on these questions is nothing less than disastrous.

There are volumes upon volumes written on abortion, pro and con, which do not draw upon theologies "supportable only by an act of faith" but on science, philosophy, and legal and ethical traditions. The plaintiffs are fond of an analogy with the Jehovah's Witnesses' belief about blood transfusions, but they cannot point to any comparable literature about the morality of blood transfusions. The Witnesses' belief, based on their special understanding of divine revelation in Scripture, is like the Catholics' belief in the Real Presence—a distinctly theological issue. The morality of abortion, like the morality of capital punishment or of the Vietnam War, is not in the same category. There is a kind of moral reasoning, informed by science, informed by philosophy and political thought, informed by religious traditions, that can legitimately be the basis for majority decisions in a pluralistic society. To somehow place this kind of reasoning—and the politics that, in rough and ready form, accompany it—under the ban of the First Amendment's no-establishment clause would be to abandon much of our political and moral heritage and to reduce political life to technocratic engineering.

We are now squarely up against the larger issues signaled in the *McRae* case. We do not pretend that anything about the abortion debate sits comfortably with us. There is no shrugging off the tragic choices to which our correspondents refer, tragic choices that in the instances affected by the Hyde Amendment are intertwined with a poverty that is unwarrantable in the first place. We understand the reasoning of the right-to-life movement that it must take a stand against abortion wherever it can. But it is more than slightly troubling that the most notable case of its effectively taking a stand should bear, not on the well-off, but on precisely those whom life has already burdened and who have, again and again, been the objects of society's disdain and neglect. It is even more troubling when the right-to-life movement aligns itself so thoroughly with those forces which have been most recalcitrant about social welfare. . . .

Of course, the Left . . . makes little effort to understand the position of abortion opponents, writing them off as "absolutist," a curious adjective that one never finds applied to those who will brook no anti-Semitism, no sexual inequality, or no corporate bribery. The Left becomes utterly careless in its language about the issue of abortion, using terms like "coercion" or "compulsion" (as in "compulsory pregnancy") whether referring to the flat prohibition of abortions or (a distinguishable matter) the refusing of public funds for them. The Left repeatedly insists that those opposed to abortions are free to have them or not, which is to miss the whole point of the conflict, namely their belief that the life of another party is at stake. . . .

The Left has every reason to be solicitous about the roots of the moral impulse in politics. Without that impulse the Left itself is bankrupt. . . . One of the roots of the moral impulse, if not the tap root, is religion. The Left has not attended much to this fact, partly due to the historical conflict between the Enlightenment and the churches, partly due to the Left's concentration on problems of physical deprivation, often and unfortunately to the neglect of questions of meaning, identity, and integrity.

In our original editorial, we asked why the First Amendment argument against *McRae* would not equally apply to various other struggles, honored or supported by the Left, in which religion and organized religious groups have taken leading roles. Our correspondents have not answered this question. . . .

Our complaint against the plaintiffs in *McRae,* then, is essentially our complaint against the bishops and so many right-to-lifers. In their single-mindedness about one concern, they are running roughshod over numerous other values to which they owe responsibility. It is noteworthy that the First Amendment argument which these letters treat as so obvious did not figure in their original legal action. It was added to their case only after the Supreme Court appeared to reject their other grounds for the Hyde Amendment's unconstitutionality. We don't think they have pursued this unfortunate course because of any conscious wish to infringe the rights of believers and put up obstacles to the exercise of Americans' deepest values in the political arena, but because their zeal for the immediate cause has blinded their larger vision.

War and Peace

t often seems that the history of the past century can be captured in the litany of its wars. From the First World War to the collapse of the Soviet Union and the uncertainties of the post–Cold War world, the twentieth century saw human carnage on an unprecedented scale, as well as a steady and now almost unimaginable increase in the destructiveness of weapons. The stark fact of the existence of evil remained unchanged, as did the moral obligation to oppose those who use violence to destroy human life and freedom.

Throughout its history, *Commonweal* has defended the traditional Catholic just-war doctrine, willing to assume the moral responsibility of waging war yet determined that those with a just cause employ proportionate means in pursuit of a realistic end. Just cause and proportionate means are always, of course, the subject of intense dispute. The magazine supported war against Germany and Japan, for example, but was forthright in condemning the indiscriminate Allied bombing of German cities and the use of atomic weapons against the civilian populations of Hiroshima and Nagasaki. Just-war teaching forbids the intentional killing of noncombatants regardless of any alleged strategic need or utilitarian calculus.

Employing a similar logic, *Commonweal* supported the political and military containment of the Soviet Union and the need for the United States to maintain a plausible nuclear deterrent. Rejecting the campaign for unilateral disarmament popular in many religious and progressive circles, the editors argued that unilateral action by the United States would make war more, not less, likely. "We say this with fear and trembling," the editors confessed; but "maintaining the potential of waging [war] precisely to prevent it from ever occurring" was judged the morally prudent course. That did not prevent the magazine from giving space to those who reasoned that weapons of mass destruction make just-war thinking obsolete or absurd.

Ready to defend the use of force and the positive role played by the

United States in world affairs, the magazine never hesitated to oppose wasteful military spending or to judge particular wars and military involvements unjust. Declaring itself against the war in Vietnam in 1966, the magazine became something of a forum for the often widely differing views—from pragmatic to pacifist to apocalyptic—of those in the antiwar movement. Still, if there has been a consistent *Commonweal* perspective, it has been an unwillingness to resort to politically or morally reductionistic thinking. Distancing itself from the widespread American Catholic support for Franco in the Spanish Civil War, the magazine early on insisted on historical complexity, not ideological fideism. "To be strongly partisan . . . is indeed to aggravate a current intellectual disease: the conviction that we are going to be forced to choose between fascism and communism." That same temperament is evident in the magazine's engagement with all the great issues of war and peace over the last seventy-five years. It is perhaps best captured in John Cogley's measured tribute to Dorothy Day's public protests against nuclear weapons: "I could not conscientiously advise the U.S. government to strip itself of nuclear defenses," he confessed. "And as long as I want America to maintain these fearful weapons I must share the moral burden; I cannot join the pacifists though I can be glad they are around to say no."

CIVIL WAR IN SPAIN AND THE UNITED STATES

THE EDITORS

Most discussion of the Spanish question to date in the United States, by supporters of both sides, has been distinguished more for its heat than for any light cast upon the significance of events. But the war continues, and the manner of waging it, both in Spain and here in our own country, seems to change very little with the passage of time. As long as "total" war continues on the Spanish peninsula, it will continue to torment all of us, both in America and in Europe.

A Spaniard, unless he is one of the few who are determined—and able—to make the "double refusal," seemingly must choose between two governments whose characters are mixed and are impossible to know from here with any comprehensiveness. One government, or part of it, has instigated, or at least permitted, the murder of priests, nuns, and lay people; has utilized ruthless methods of accomplishing social and political and economic ends; and has chosen, as far as it is possible to see, many objectives in all these fields that should be condemned. Its alliance with Russia implies some, if an unknown, degree of identification with the evils of the Soviet regime.

The second government, which gives the church open support, yet, in its conduct of warfare, repeatedly and despite protests from the Holy Father, destroys defenseless civilians, particularly by its air raids upon cities. Air raids made by one side cannot cancel out those made by the other. Many of its leaders give utterance to totalitarian views very similar to those which have been condemned by the church in other countries. The system of government it utilizes and favors, so far as can be seen, contains elements that should be sharply rejected. Its alliance with the Fascist and Nazi nations implicates it to some, if an uncertain, extent in the evils of those regimes. . . .

In this country there has been violent partisanship either for the Spanish Nationalists or for the Madrid-Barcelona government. We feel that violent American partisanship on either side with regard to the Spanish question is bad, not only because the facts are obscure, but chiefly because both sides include elements that no American wants imported into this country.

To be strongly partisan concerning the Spanish Civil War is indeed to aggravate a current intellectual disease: the conviction that we are going to be forced to choose between fascism and communism. This is a dangerous disease; sufferers from it are blinded by it to the truth that both systems are anti-Christian and secularist.

It is for these reasons that we believe that the wisest, as also the most charitable and perhaps the most difficult, policy for Americans is to maintain that "positive impartiality," a sanity of judgment toward both sides in Spain. Above all, we must avoid fostering the growth of totalitarianism and hatred of Christianity by avoiding all activities that even faintly encourage that spirit of hysterical opposition and human distrust which is the very life blood of both of those systems.

JUST WAR

JACQUES MARITAIN

With what power events, when they involve suffering and bloodshed, challenge the spirit. More than ever reason has a duty to see clearly. But in the fire of such events ideas are quickly put to the test.

Many people thought that under modern world conditions there could no longer be a just war. . . . Of course it is true that the criteria for a just war established by the theologians of the classic age need revision, for war itself has radically changed: the war of armies has become the war of peoples, and is something which more closely resembles a cosmic cataclysm than the "last recourse" (*ultima ratio*) of those theologians. Yet in this cosmic cataclysm human beings are engaged, and hence the rules governing what is just and what is unjust remain. Confronted with the joint action by which the two peoples of France and of England—in order to challenge the frightful passion of violence and pride which thrust out against Poland and in order to prevent the world's being enslaved to the lust for brutal domination by which Hitler's totalitarianism is obsessed—decided to go to war against Germany, what man of right judgment would not say in conscience: this war against Germany is a just war?

Here is no question of an ideological war. It is not to serve an idea or a divinized abstract principle that France and Great Britain are giving the blood of their children and jeopardizing their heritage of civilization. It is rather for the elementary realities in the absence of which human life ceases to be human.

Nor is there here any question of a holy war. The people of this country have enough common sense, they know well enough what every war brings with it and after it, in misery and in poison and in the intensification of the most vile as well the exaltation of the most noble in our

JACQUES MARITAIN (1882–1973) was professor at the Institute Catholique of Paris and the author of *Man and State, Art and Scholasticism, The Things That Are Not Caesar's, The Degrees of Knowledge, The Peasant of the Garonne,* and other works.

earthly life, to guard themselves against enlisting the sanctity of the ineffable Name in the temporal war which they are fighting.

It is a question of a just war. Fighting for justice—suffering and dying so that a bestial barbarism may not rule over the earth—they know (at least those who have the light of faith know) that they may count upon the help of God. They do not say: our cause is divine, our cause is the cause of God, we are the soldiers of God. They say: our cause is human, it is the cause of that human community desired by God in the natural order and which is called our fatherland, and which, hating war, has been forced to resort to war against an iniquitous aggressor; and because our cause is just, God will have pity on us.

And yet if ever a war could seem bathed in the reflections of supernatural struggles, as though already assigned its place on this side of the "threshold of the Apocalypse," as Léon Bloy used to say, it is certainly this war which has just begun. The enemy with whom we are dealing holds high the banners of blasphemy and of pagan empire; the alliance of atheism with idolatrous racism has uncovered its true countenance. But if it acts in its true character of iniquity by swallowing and by absorbing the things of God into the things of Caesar, we act in our true character of justice by maintaining the distinction between them, even though the temporal cause which we defend is in closest relation to the sacred welfare of souls.

What I would now like to point out is that the question of the justice of a war—which relates to a specific act and a dispute between men—and the question of its distant origins—which relate to the endless concatenations and crisscrossings of many acts and a dispute between the human conscience and the Master of history—are two quite different questions. For one thing, we know that sin is the cause of all the evil that happens on earth and that all men are sinners; for another thing, we know that a man may defend a just cause against an unjust adversary. And these two things are both true at the same time.

That which makes a war either just or unjust is, in essence, the immediate purpose and motive which determined it. The war against German National Socialism has for its immediately determining purpose and motive to resist the aggression of which Poland has been the victim, and to resist unbridled imperialist greed: it is a just war.

The remote origins of every war—which, moreover, involve the interior life of each people just as much as the relations between peoples—consist in accumulated moral evil. They consist in egoism, forgetfulness of the commonweal, an inordinate love for material goods, hardness of heart, a refusal to recognize the very existence of others; they consist in stupidity or folly, the weakness or ambitious fury of those in power, and that scorn for justice and for love, that scorn for God which is the boast of a politics holding itself aloof from natural ethics and the law of the gospels. They consist in the seven deadly sins which, having flourished for a certain length of time, at last bear their fruit, in accordance with the very laws of that nature which they try to spoil.

Certainly in all this there are unequal responsibilities; the infinite Spirit recognizes these and weighs them; they may be immensely different, one from the other. In the last analysis, one way or another, to one degree or another, and without permitting the man of blood who has unleashed war in any way to clear himself of his crime, nobody, when it comes to the remote origins of a war, is altogether innocent before God.

Germany wages an unjust—a manifestly, monstrously unjust—war; and to the extent that she has yielded to Hitler and given herself over to him, her part in the underlying causes and the remote origins of the war is enormous. Yet she is not alone in carrying the burden of the sins from which the war sprung. That her war should be unjust and criminal does not free the other peoples from the duty of making themselves humble before God. That the other peoples should have some share before God in the remote origins of the war in no way makes Germany innocent of the crime of the unjust war she is waging nor of the barbarous fashion in which she is waging it.

The hard lessons of the last war and of what came after must not be lost. The German people became auto-intoxicated by the idea that not only must it recognize—what was strict truth—that it had in 1914 undertaken an unjust war, but admit that it alone—like a damned soul—carried the whole burden of the sins from which that war arose. The mistake which made possible this fatal auto-intoxication will not be made again. Nor will we once more identify the German people—however great its moral complicity—with Hitler and his totalitarianism. The Fuehrer's fundamental fraud, his glory as Antichrist, is to believe and to wish to be the incarnate Word of his people. Down with this false glory, this lie! He is not the incarnate Word of his people; he is their vampire.

Sane politics requires the distinctions of which I speak; they have a major political importance. It is terribly manifest how a sane and truly realistic politics needs, if it is to preserve its clear insight, that feeling, which Christianity gives, for common human misery and at the same time for moral realities and the requirements of justice.

CITIZEN SOLDIER

JAMES FINN

In the course of his fine article "A Soldier's Legacy" (*Commonweal,* December 5, 1997) Robert Ostermann, a veteran of World War II, asserts: "Who says war is not criminal . . . speaks an inexcusable lie." That assertion is not as clear as it initially appears to be. For if war is criminal, who are the criminals, which of the participants? I ask the reader to keep the question in mind during the following description of my own personal reaction to reading *Citizen Soldiers* by Stephen E. Ambrose (Simon & Schuster).

Citizen Soldiers is the history—chronological, statistical, descriptive, anecdotal—of the American soldiers who fought in Europe from June 7, 1944 (D-Day), to May 7, 1945, when Germany surrendered. Ambrose is a trustworthy historian, a fine writer, with a remarkable empathy for the men and women about whom he writes, particularly those in the front lines of the battle. He has produced an exciting but harrowing story. I could read it only in short installments.

In turning to this book, I was breaking an unformulated rule of not reading or recalling any particulars of World War II. But after more than fifty years I thought I could finally afford to do so, to learn the path I had taken as a member of Regiment 328, 26th (Yankee) Division, Third Army. For as a lowly infantry private during that conflict, I was as ignorant of the "big picture" and as unsure of where I was most of the time as any of the bewildered soldiers described by Tolstoy or Stendhal.

Almost every soldier who fought agreed that only those who actively engaged in combat could truly understand what it is like, but Ambrose, I believe, comes as close as any writer-historian can to communicating that experience. Drawing upon historical sources, interviews, and oral testimony he weaves together strategic plans, tactics, and actual incidents, the successes and the failures—including massive intelligence fail-

---

JAMES FINN (1924–), formerly a *Commonweal* editor, is chairman of the Puebla Institute.

ures—the cowardly, the heroic, and the accidental, into a coherent narrative.

The reader is led through the fighting among the hedgerows of Normandy, the rapid advance across more open ground, the crossing of the Rhine, the deadly, useless, ill-advised push through the Hurtgen forest, the Battle of the Bulge, the surge into Germany, and the stunned entry into concentration camps. Along the way he encounters the various ground troops; the pilots of bombers, fighters, and Piper Cub spotters; officers and enlisted men, nurses and medics—all of the citizen soldiers of a democracy who had to be welded into the fighting unit whose courage and ability were the object of Hitler's early contempt.

Ambrose inquires into why these citizens of a democracy persevered and overcame. What were the principal motives that guided them? Was it patriotism? Simple necessity? Learned hostile response? Mutual trust and reciprocity among the soldiers? He makes insightful comparisons with the soldiers of the Civil War who invoked ideals of patriotism, honor, the cause, the flag, and with those of World War I, during which such ideals were shot down.

Sideways, crabways, I approach those same questions. What did the army want with the skinny, nineteen-year-old kid I was when I was inducted? Could they plunk him into infantry training, teach him to take twenty-mile hikes loaded down with combat equipment, to take apart and reassemble an M1 rifle blindfolded, to cross a swift-flowing river, turn him into a sharpshooter, then into a scout who would take the lead as his platoon advanced into unfamiliar ground, who would go on night patrol behind enemy lines? They not only could but they did, each step seeming as unreal as it was unlikely to that soldier in the making. Ambrose offers snapshot glimpses of soldiers in combat. I offer some of that skinny kid, memories which return to me with the force and clarity that some vivid dreams have, sharp in detail but slightly surreal.

- On guard duty somewhere in France on a bright moonlit night, the shadows black and sharp-edged. I distract myself by kicking a stray GI boot down the slight slope in front of me. That is, I try to, for the boot scarcely moves and I gradually realize that it still encases a foot that is, in turn, firmly attached to the body that lies in its shallow grave.

- Lying flat on the ground in a thinly wooded grove, my ears filled with the noise of bullets and shrapnel passing overhead, my eyes fixed on the bloated dead body in front of me, I begrudge the thin layer of leaves that prevents me from hugging the ground even closer. I realize that I am not afraid of dying but that I am deathly afraid of being painfully wounded.

- In a small house in a deserted village perched on a hillside, we find a very large, flat-bottomed, clear green bottle practically filled with wine. As we drink it we look out over the valley and see planes firing at targets below them. The tracer bullets make beautiful abstract patterns against the dark sky. We have no idea if the planes are ours or theirs.

- After a long march, we pause in a relatively open field and are told to dig foxholes. Since we believe that we are likely to push on in only a few hours, most of us make only half-hearted efforts to dig deep. But an officer standing in a jeep, pistols visible in his holsters, drives around examining the area. Soon an order comes down. General Patton says we had better dig those #@%*$+ holes deep, and right now. A short time later we are glad we did. A couple of German planes that seem to have strayed into the area spray down bullets that thud heavily into the ground around us.

- On one of the few sun-brightened days I am by myself—although I don't know how that could have been—as I enter a small, empty church. The roof has been partly destroyed. Shafts of sunlight pass through the jagged opening and pick out the gilt edges of the altar and meager ornaments. A great silence has fallen on the air and a great feeling of peace comes over me. It persists for some days.

- In the dark, our company has entered a rather dense forest heavy with rain mixed with snow. My then-buddy shares the surname Savage with a pulp-magazine hero and is automatically called "Doc," that character's nickname. Doc and I do our best to find a patch of ground where we can dig a foxhole big enough for both of us. In the bottom of the foxhole we make a small trench to hold the rising pool of water that gathers and, although our feet are already soaking wet, we try to keep them on the ledge each side of the trench. In spite of the fact that we can hear German voices not far from us, our weariness is greater than our fear, and we trust to our guards and the pitch-black night to provide security for us. I wake to hear gasping moans at the edge of our foxhole. Doc had waked with the morning light and had gotten out of the foxhole to look around. A sniper had shot him in the stomach. He dies soon afterward.

- In the same forest, the snow and cold continue. We have advanced almost not at all, expected supplies do not arrive, we cannot get dry, and we cannot take off our boots because putting still-wet socks and feet back into frozen boots is impossible. Getting out of my foxhole one morning, I stumble and fall in the snow. Getting on my feet, I repeat the performance. And yet again. I notice others performing similar antics. We are unable to walk. Some of us are driven to a barn where we are told to remove shoes and socks and dry our feet. Even if it's only to be a few hours we all feel a blessed relief. But our waxy-white feet begin to swell and turn colors. In what was to turn into a nine-months' passage through a string of hospitals, six months of which I can neither stand nor walk, my own turn into purple, then black, scaly balloon-like appendages that cannot suffer even the weight of a bed sheet. I learn that I have trench foot, a World War I term I had never heard before.

- In a hospital in Bournemouth, near the south coast of England, we hear the drone of V-bombs, the silence, and then the explosions. The brief periods of silence are the most frightening. In late December, casualties from what was to be called the Battle of the Bulge begin to stream through our ward and I learn that my outfit has been thrown into that battle. Alternating and intermingling waves of guilt for not being with them and gratitude that I'm not sweep over me. But as if to underline the difference between those on the front line and those in the rear, when the chickenshit officer in charge of our ward comes through for inspection, those of us who cannot stand are ordered to lie at attention in our beds. (Ambrose quotes Paul Fussell: "Chickenshit refers to behavior that makes military life worse than it need be, petty harassment of the weak by the strong . . . small-minded and ignoble.")

- Home again. As our hospital ship pulls into New York Harbor, we can hear and see through a porthole the band that greets us. As we wait to be taken off the ship, kindly Gray Ladies—so named because of the gray outfits they wear—pass through with their welcome-back gifts. I am thrown into a frustrated, impotent, and incoherent rage as our smiling Gray Lady extends to me, and I silently accept, her gift of chocolate and comic books. Comic books! My feelings are only compounded when my three cabin mates pounce on them eagerly.

• Months later, at the hospital center at Camp Carson, Colorado, I receive my honorable discharge, one line of which reads: "EAME Ribbon, I Bronze Service Star Good Conduct Ribbon Combat Inf Badge." Like most other soldiers, I go back to pick up the loose threads of my former life.

My experience in the war was not as prolonged or as intense as many of those of whom Ambrose writes, nor the damage I suffered as severe. It qualifies me, however, to respond personally to the question of why we fought, of what forged us into fighting units, and to the question of the criminality of the war. Ambrose himself makes severe judgments of particular decisions and individual soldiers, not excluding the highest-ranking officers, even of Dwight Eisenhower whom he much admires. He notes, for example, that once battle lines became relatively stable, officers above the rank of captain rarely visited the front lines. From the rear echelons they ordered soldiers to fight in conditions they knew nothing about. As a consequence, thousands of young American and German soldiers died needlessly. The push through the Hurtgen forest was based on a plan that "was grossly, even criminally stupid."

The replacement system, Ambrose writes, was criminally wasteful and could have been easily corrected. "Its criteria was the flow of bodies. Whose fault was this? Eisenhower's first. He was the boss. And Bradley's. And Patton's." Ambrose adds that it could only be that "they had no conception of life on the front lines." The importance of this issue is indicated by the high turnover in different units. My division had a 119-percent turnover, far from the highest.

Ambrose confirms what I previously knew only as rumor. I got trench foot because General Omar Bradley had decided, in September 1944, that the campaign would be over before December. Instead of needed winter clothing, other supplies were pumped into the pipelines. As a result, the infantryman's clothing was "criminally inadequate" for Northern Europe's worst winter in forty years. Those who were ill-supplied and not rotated so they could get dry and warm, got trench foot. "Trench foot put more men out of action than German 88's, mortars, or machine-gun fire . . . some 45,000 men had to be pulled out of the front lines because of trenchfoot—the equivalent of three full infantry divisions." Many lost toes, feet, and, if gangrene set in, the entire lower leg.

Here some distinctions are in order. Rape, murder, theft, desertion— the seemingly inevitable accompaniments of war—are surely criminal. But the criminally stupid? The massively wrong decisions? The complacent ignorance of the rear-echelon commanders? The war itself? Here, rather than immediate labels, some legal and moral analyses are called for. And a return to the question of why we fought is helpful.

I believe the most common judgment to be correct. In combat we depended upon each other. Without thought or reflection, soldiers risked their lives for each other. Those ties were among the strongest they ever had or would have. We fought for each other. This is what joined us and transformed us into fighting units. But we also had implicit trust, I believe, in the decisions our country was making. Along the way, some soldiers learned additional reasons, like the major who said, when he first saw the inhuman concentration camps, "Now I know why I am here." And some of us learned later. Again, I believe a common judgment to be correct: What Hitler unleashed on the world was monstrously evil and it would have been criminal not to have opposed it. And I like to think that if that nineteen-year-old kid could have known more than he did and fully grasped this fact, he would have fought not only because he was called upon to do so, but because it was the right thing to do.

HORROR AND SHAME

THE EDITORS

Two months ago (June 22) we were writing about poison gas. We said: "To the Orient we are bringing the latest inventions of our civilization. There is only one we have not brought. It is gas. If we use that we will have brought them all. Gas is no worse than flame. It is only that it is one more weapon. The last one we have to use. Until we invent a new one." And then we said: "The time has come when nothing more can be added to the horror if we wish to keep our coming victory something we can use—or that humanity can use."

Well, it seems that we were ridiculous writing that sort of thing. We will not have to write that sort of thing any more. Certainly, like everyone else, we will have to write a great deal about the future of humanity and the atomic bomb. But we will not have to worry any more about keeping our victory clean. It is defiled.

There were names of places in Europe which from the early days of the war were associated with a German idea that by disregarding the rights of civilians you could shorten a war. These names of places—Rotterdam, Coventry—were associated, and seemed likely to be associated in men's minds for a great number of years, with a judgment of German guilt and German shame. There was a port in the Pacific which sheltered American naval power. It was attacked by air without warning and the name Pearl Harbor was associated, and seemed likely to be associated for many years, with a Japanese idea that you could win a war by attacking the enemy before declaring war on the enemy. The name Pearl Harbor was a name for Japanese guilt and shame.

The name Hiroshima, the name Nagasaki are names for American guilt and shame.

The war against Japan was nearly won. Our fleet and Britain's fleet stood off Japan's coast and shelled Japan's cities. There was no opposition. Our planes, the greatest bombers in the world, flew from hard won, gallantly won bases and bombed Japanese shipping, Japanese industry, and, already, Japanese women and children. Each day they announced to the Japanese where the blows would fall, and the Japanese were unable to prevent anything they chose to do.

Then, without warning, an American plane dropped the atomic bomb on Hiroshima.

Russia entered the war. There was no doubt before or after Russia entered the war that the war against Japan was won. An American plane dropped the second atomic bomb on Nagasaki.

We had to invent the bomb because the Germans were going to invent the bomb. It was a matter of avoiding our own possible destruction. We had to test the bomb and we tested it in a desert. If we were to threaten the use of it against the Japanese, we could have told them to pick a desert and then go look at the hole. Without warning we dropped it into the middle of a city and then without warning we dropped it into the middle of another city.

And then we said that this bomb could mean the end of civilization if we ever got into a war and everyone started to use it. So that we must keep it a secret. We must keep it as sole property of people who know how to use it. We must keep it the property of peace-loving nations. That is what we said about the atomic bomb—together with odds and ends about motors the size of pin points which would drive a ship three times round the world—that is what we said about it, after we had used it ourselves. To secure peace, of course. To save lives, of course. After we had brought indescribable death to a few hundred thousand men, women, and children, we said that this bomb must remain always in the hands of peace-loving peoples.

For our war, for our purposes, to save American lives we have reached the point where we say that anything goes. That is what the Germans said at the beginning of the war. Once we have won our war we say that there must be international law. Undoubtedly.

When it is created, Germans, Japanese, and Americans will remember with horror the days of their shame.

LONELY PROTEST

JOHN COGLEY

A few weeks ago a reader said that I had a blind spot on Christian pacifism. He may well be right. I admit I have never been persuaded by the pacifists' arguments, and I have heard them all. However, it is only fair to add that since Hiroshima I have been equally unimpressed by antipacifist arguments, and I have heard them all, too. For if the pacifists are guilty of arrant utopianism, they are not alone; the vaunted "realism" of their opponents has little to do with the realities of the nuclear age.

The moralists who talk of modern war as if it were subject to rational controls must know that their theories are the stuff of textbooks, no more. Sure as shooting, another general war will mean the use of nuclear weapons.

Even America dropped the atom bomb, and at a time when victory was within sight. What power, especially what totalitarian power, will hold off from using the hydrogen bomb with defeat in the offing?

I take for granted, then, that another general war will mean nuclear warfare and wreak unimaginable horror and destruction. What will follow from this destruction civilized men cannot envisage. Certainly it will not be world order or "peace" as the word has been understood. And a war that does not reestablish order and peace is not a just war.

If you believe this, my pacifist friends ask, why aren't you with us? I have to answer with a "logic" that is not logical: I am not with you because I am involved in the general evil. I know that America's "militarism" has kept us from destruction. Under the stresses of the past decade, would the world still be intact if only the West knew the secret

---

JOHN COGLEY (1916–76) was a *Commonweal* editor from 1949 to 1955, and a columnist until 1964. Later he served as an editor at the *New York Times,* as a presidential campaign adviser for John F. Kennedy and Eugene McCarthy, and as founding editor of the *Center Magazine.*

of nuclear war? I don't know. I am sure, though, that we would be wiped out if Russia alone had the secret. Therefore what peace we have had is the bitter fruit of mutual fear. I could not conscientiously advise the U.S. government to strip itself of nuclear defenses. And as long as I want America to maintain these fearful weapons I must share the moral burden; I cannot join the pacifists though I can be glad they are around to say no.

Such reasoning will not pass the test of textbook investigation. In an ethics class debate I would lose my shirt. But it seems that the only way to win that debate would be to talk as if the traditional criteria for a just war were actually relevant; I know they are not. Or one could take the position that they are not relevant and urge the government to dismiss the Marines; in the interests of peace, I am not willing to do that, either. So I will have to keep on losing arguments and count each day that Armaggedon is held off as another victory. That is a hell of a way to live. But, under the circumstances, no one can doubt that this is a hell of a world we live in.

None of these personal views is important except as a context in which to discuss the imprisonment of Dorothy Day and ten of her followers. The Catholic Worker people were jailed because they refused to take shelter during an air-raid drill. They refused in order to protest against the very moral dilemma that leaves me—and my pacifist friends too, for that matter—without a debater's point to our names.

I don't know what to do about the dilemma. If the pacifists actually had responsibility, I don't believe they would, either. But Dorothy Day and her friends want to do something. They are not like me; they are not willing to live without a murmur in a morally ambiguous situation. I think they have more faith in God than I do; I know they have more faith in men. By the simple act of resisting the nation's periodic preparations for doomsday they hope to point up the importance of life over death.

Whether the government may declare a synthetic "emergency" and suspend civil rights for the duration of a period arbitrarily set by decree should surely interest the upper courts. But it would do less than justice to Dorothy to treat the affair as a civil-liberties case. Miss Day acts in the spirit of the prophets; she is indifferent to legalities. Only a plea of guilty made sense to her, for she and her friends saw their protest not as an exercise of a civil "right" but as a religious duty; imprisonment was something to be accepted not as a legal injustice but as "penance" for the sins of the world.

Imagine surviving a hydrogen bomb and, sitting among the ruins, remembering the case of Dorothy Day and her friends. With millions dead and other millions grotesquely injured, what would we think then about their small, pitiful effort to cry out their protest in the days when we rehearsed for annihilation? Who among the survivors would have an unkind word to say about their lack of "prudence"? How would the echo of the judge's words—"a heartless bunch"— sound to those in the wasteland?

They were sent to jail because out of the 10 million they alone said no; they took their harmless soap-box way to say that something has to be done. And, to our shame, there was scarcely a protest from the Catholics of America when one we call a saint was put behind bars. She protested against the destruction of mankind. Those who protest against risqué movies are given Catholic Action medals.

ON NUCLEAR DISBELIEF

THOMAS POWERS

I have never seen a nuclear weapon. But last spring I visited the Atomic Museum at Kirtland Air Force Base on the edge of Albuquerque, New Mexico, and saw a great many bomb casings. When you look at them your eye says bomb! but your mind says they are just hollow shells. The bomb guts are missing. Still, you get the idea. Some match your idea of what a bomb ought to look like—Fat Boy, for example, the 9,000-pound bulbous monster which destroyed Hiroshima. The one in the Kirtland Atomic Museum is painted olive drab. The one at the Bradbury museum at Los Alamos is painted white. Both are grossly fat and thoroughly lethal in aspect.

But scariest of all is the Mark 17 bomb casing. According to the sign this was the first hydrogen or fusion or thermonuclear bomb which could actually be dropped from an aircraft, but it's hard to credit. It's hard to imagine anything could get it off the ground, short of a derrick. It is twenty-one feet long and five in diameter and it weighs twenty-four tons. But the numbers don't suggest the impression. The designer of the Atomic Museum had talent and a flair for the dramatic. The displays are in a great cavernlike hall, dramatically lit from below, and the Mark 17 looms up in the gloom like a . . . well, quite a lot like the great blue whale which hangs from the ceiling in the American Museum of Natural History. The thing is so huge, the casing is so massive you simply can't believe it could get off the ground. But like all the others it's hollow. It's not really a bomb at all, just a suggestion of the bomb, nothing more than a teaching aid.

At Vandenberg Air Force Base a year ago I saw a Mark 12-A re-entry vehicle, a black cone-shaped object, perhaps three feet high, with a car-

---

THOMAS POWERS (1940–), a Pulitzer Prize winner and *Commonweal* columnist from 1975 to 1983, is the author of *The War at Home, The Man Who Kept the Secrets,* and other works.

bon-carbon skin and a polished nose cone of specially heat-resistant al-
loys which erode away in the terrible heat and wind of re-entry at ten
thousand miles an hour. It was sitting in a classroom where Air Force officers take an introductory course in ballistic missiles. One of the in-
structors began to rattle off statistics and then stopped abruptly. "Sir," he
said, "what is your clearance?" I said I was a journalist and didn't have
any sort of clearance. That was the end of the lecture. But I marveled at
the RV all the same. It was so small, light, and sleek. Is there any limit to
human genius? Somehow the guts of the Mark 17 leviathan had been refined and reduced and squeezed into this neat package a couple of men
might cart off in a wheelbarrow.

So I've never really seen a bomb—just drawings, photographs, and
the outer skins of bombs. Most people haven't seen the skins. For us the
bomb is a purely mental thing, an abstract concept, a kind of pocket of
anxiety in the mind. I *know* the New York City subway system is going
through hard times because I ride it every day. I *know* the price of gaso-
line is up. The sting in my eyes tells me Los Angeles has an air pollution
problem. No one has to tell me that blacks and Puerto Ricans live in a
different world because I brush their alien shoulders on the city's streets.
Things physically present announce themselves unmistakably, but the
bomb is like the knowledge of death. It comes and goes, a kind of mood.
A story in the paper, or a siren late at night, can bring it heaving up out
of the unconscious part of the mind. But then it sinks back, like other
things we know but can't bear to think about.

In the last two years I've talked to a lot of military people about nuclear weapons, strategic policy, what the Russians are up to, and the like.
For the most part, they have been an impressive group of men—sober,
intelligent, knowledgeable, and orderly in their habits of mind. They did
not seem at all warlike. Nothing they said suggests that the defense of the
United States is in careless or reckless hands. The motto of the Strategic
Air Command, which has authority over bombers and land-based inter-
continental ballistic missiles, is "Peace Is Our Profession." As I remember it's carved on the lintel over the main entrance to SAC headquarters
at Offut Air Force Base near Omaha. This is the sort of thing to invite a
bitter smile, everything considered, but so far as I could tell, SAC people
take it seriously. I asked a colonel at Offut if he thought the ICBMs
would ever be launched, and he said no—they *all* say no—and added,
"If that happened we would have failed in our job." It's tempting to poke
ironic fun at such earnest remarks, but it wouldn't be fair. The officer

wasn't being smarmy. He really meant it. His job was preventing wars, not winning them.

The military men involved in nuclear weapons policy—and their civilian colleagues, too, for that matter—don't believe it's ever going to happen. For them, I suspect, no belief is deeper and stronger. Their assurances on this point have none of the tinny quality of budget officials, say, telling you the federal deficit will disappear in 1984, when they know full well this barely qualifies as even an honest hope.

When you think about it, the equanimity of military people makes perfect sense. They know the United States and the Soviet Union have got 15,000 strategic nuclear weapons between them. They've been trying to figure out a way to fight a genuinely limited nuclear war for thirty years, and haven't come up with anything convincing yet. They know the Pentagon periodically tries to plan for the postattack world but always throws up its hands in despair because there is simply no way of projecting how bad it would be. The destruction would be too general. The normal means of recovery and reconstruction would be threatened in too many ways to calculate.

Take transportation. Airfields, ports, railway marshaling yards, and major highway intersections would be destroyed. Aircraft, ships, rolling stock, and large numbers of buses, trucks, and cars would be destroyed. Many of the factories which might build more would be destroyed. If factories remained, the workers might be dead or too sick to work. The breakdown in transportation would make it hard to feed or care for them. Power lines would be out. Most petroleum refineries would have been destroyed, fuel would be in short supply, and the little remaining would be hard to distribute. And so on and so forth. How can you predict how long it would take to get things moving again when so many factors are involved, which overlap in so many ways? The answer is you can't. The government goes on churning out civil defense and reconstruction plans, but the Pentagon has never made a serious official guess how well they would work—or even if they would work at all—because the computers can't factor in all the variables.

This is the sort of thing military men know, generally in great detail, and none of it is encouraging where the subject of nuclear war is concerned. On top of that, they know we shall never get rid of nuclear weapons. Arms agreements *may*—even that is in doubt—limit their number and type, but disarmament is not on the horizon. It is not *over* the horizon. When you put these two things together—knowledge of what nuclear weapons can do, and a conviction we shall always have them—you can see why military men tell themselves, and everybody else, the bombs will never be used. They are flesh and blood, after all. Their wives and children all live in target areas. They can't *bear* to think anything else.

It's difficult to remember how I thought about things a couple of years ago, when I first started to read seriously about nuclear weapons. A lot of things came as a shock then which seem familiar now. I made lots of errors in writing about the subject. Once, for example, I wrote that the bomb dropped on Nagasaki was the last one in the American inventory. In late August 1945, I thought, there were no bombs in the world at all. But later the man who assembled the core for the fourth bomb told me I was wrong.

After two or three months of reading I went through a period of intense sadness. At first I didn't know what it was. I thought the source might be worry about my father, who is eighty-nine, or a friend whose marriage was breaking up, or chronic financial anxiety, or something else of the kind. Then I told myself I was an idiot. Of course I was sad. I had finally schooled myself in the numbers and knew for the first time that we *really had* built weapons enough to break the back of our civilization. I'd gotten the details straight about radiation sickness, theories of war-fighting which all imply any nuclear war will go the limit, the steady march of technical improvement in weapons design which makes military people so jumpy, and so on and so forth. I had read or been told *nothing* which suggested we were going to learn to get along without these weapons. It was quite clear, in fact, that we were going to go on pointing them at enemies until we used them or the world came to an end. Since the news on the geological front is all good, and the planet can expect to survive another couple of billion years, that meant, as a practical matter, we would go on as we were until we used them. In short, it seemed to me as clear as night follows day that it is going to happen.

But everybody I talked to took the contrary view. Everybody, that is, professionally involved in defense matters. Ordinary citizens often entertain foreboding of the darkest sort. In a quite matter-of-fact way they will say, "What else were they built for?" Defense community people *never* say that. What they say is, "It doesn't make sense. There is nothing to be gained. No rational man would ever use nuclear weapons. They can serve no useful purpose in war."

That, of course, is true enough. But does that mean they won't be used? You might have said all those things about the great armies of Europe in 1914. Indeed people did say them. Reasons for not using nuclear weapons are also reasons for not having them. Citing the litany of their horrors is an argument against their possession or use, not an argument we won't use them—given we have them. Such arguments are really an expression of hope, and we depend on hope because there is nothing else. I have heard dozens of defense people explain why nuclear weapons will never be used. I have never heard a note of fear or despair. Their confidence is sunny and unshakable. If we just stick to our guns and make sure we've got a weapon for every weapon they've got, then there's nothing to worry about. There is a soothing quality to these reassurances, as if we were being told that airplanes really do work, and it's safe to fly.

But now comes the curious thing. After a year or two of seeing things in this light, for the first time I feel the tug the other way. I find myself wondering if perhaps the military men aren't right after all. They say it would be crazy, and are absolutely right. We worry about so many things that fail to come to pass. Two hundred years ago Malthus was worrying that the world's population had already stretched the planet's resources to the groaning limit. Maybe fear of nuclear weapons is enough to keep everyone sober and cautious. Maybe the only danger is falling behind, just as the Pentagon says. Maybe all those people in Washington are right, and I'm wrong. I devoutly hope they are right. Maybe it just won't happen.

This is a mood I'm describing, not really an argument. I don't believe it for a minute.

The problem is disbelief. An argument is the ephemeral stuff of the mind. It has no solidity. It surrenders to the world, over time, and the world tells us tomorrow will be much like today. It is a considerable undertaking to go out and see the Air Force bases and atomic laboratories and missile-launching centers. But even there the note of the lethal is missing. The bomb casings are all hollow. The missiles are all mock-ups used as teaching aids. The military men work eight to four and go home to their families. Nobody shows any sign of fear. Everything suggests tomorrow will be much like today.

We know we are mortal but we don't feel mortal and we live, generally, as if there were plenty of time for everything. The moments of recognition are few and they fade. We know that nothing lasts, nations die, the continents move, atmosphere whirls off into space, suns burn out—but not here, now, to us. These things we can't believe. It is the same with the missiles in their silos. We know what they will do. Most people don't even have to be told. They know. But knowing and believing are very different things. The world has its disconcerting way of going on from day to day, just as if nothing were ever to change. Belief is frail and fades away.

The people in the defense community have all had their ghastly moments, from the president on down to the missile launch control officers reading paperback novels in their steel cubicles suspended on springs forty feet beneath the Great Plains. Every last one of them, I am convinced, has looked it in the eye at one time or another. Even Nikita Khrushchev had his dark moment. He once told the Egyptian journalist Mohammed Heikal, "When I was appointed First Secretary of the Central Committee and learned all the facts about nuclear power I couldn't sleep for several days. Then I became convinced that we could never possibly use these weapons, and when I realized that I was able to sleep again." Thus we all go on, sustained by disbelief.

IS DETERRENCE MORAL?

THE EDITORS

The question is more pressing than ever. In the months since Reykjavik, Mr. Gorbachev has been pelting the West with proposals for getting rid of nuclear arms. So far, the West has been capable of responding with little more than, "Yes, but . . . Yes, but . . ." even to the zero-option proposal of its own devising. Eventually, one hopes, embarrassment will concentrate the collective mind of Washington and NATO. Does the West really want a Europe free of intermediate-range missiles, as it said seven years ago? Does the West really want to get rid of the threat of Warsaw Pact short-range missiles, as it said only a few weeks ago? Does the West really want Europe denuclearized altogether, as various peace movements have been vigorously urging and most European leaders vigorously denying? Does the West really want to do away with all ballistic missiles—or even all nuclear weapons—as Gorbachev and Reagan grandiosely proposed at Reykjavik?

These should not be rhetorical questions, meant only to taunt Western leaders for their apparent timidity. There are good reasons why some veteran arms-control advocates who were once aghast at the Reagan administration's unreceptive stance toward East-West arms negotiations are now rubbing their eyes and shaking their heads at the same administration's sudden lurches toward sweeping reductions in nuclear weapons. Would a totally denuclearized Europe make the outbreak of conventional war there more or less likely? If the answer is more likely, then ultimately won't nuclear war between the superpowers be rendered more likely as well? In Mr. Gorbachev's world of the year 2000 where nuclear weapons have been reduced to zero, the nation that cheated would pose a tremendous threat. That is why Robert McNamara, even while he affirms the desirability of a nuclear-free world, points out that it would require a virtually perfect method of detecting any building of nuclear weapons "by any nation or terrorist group." Otherwise, "an agreement for total nuclear disarmament will almost certainly degenerate into an unstable rearmament race."

To raise problems like these is not to defend the *status quo* of fifty thousand nuclear weapons as anything resembling a rational system of "peacekeeping." Quite the contrary. No one should dismiss the present opportunities on the grounds, say, that Mr. Gorbachev is only pursuing Soviet interests. Of course he is. An agreement serving Soviet interests will be a lot more solid than one based on some unlikely outburst of Kremlin benevolence. The question is whether Soviet interests can be made to coincide in this area with the interests of the West and the interests of peace and human survival. And thinking this through obviously requires clarity in the U.S. and Europe about basic objectives. Political leaders are being forced back to an old truth: Getting rid of nuclear weapons is not exactly the same thing as getting rid of nuclear war. It's no good reducing the superpowers' capacity to destroy civilization from five times over to two times over if, in the process, the likelihood of such a catastrophe is actually increased.

Faced with a moment like the present, we are forced back to basics in moral as well as strategic terms. Four years ago, for example, the Catholic bishops declared a "strictly conditioned moral acceptance of nuclear deterrence." Yet it is not unfair to say that in many of the circles where the bishops' nuclear pastoral has been most warmly welcomed and actively promoted there is more tolerance than enthusiasm for both the letter's reaffirmation of just-war doctrine and for the bishops' acceptance of deterrence. Indeed, when *Commonweal* recently published an article characterizing the bishops' (and the pope's) acceptance of deterrence as a blank check, a soft pitch to the military-industrial complex, and "a bleak day for the gospel," reader response was almost unanimously favorable.

Why is this issue posed more emphatically today? Precisely because the flurry of arms talks between East and West, following upon the ambiguities in the Reagan Star Wars initiative, has raised the question of whether we should be pursuing arms control on the basis of strengthening deterrence or simply dismantling it. Not only that. The visions of a nuclear-free world entertained by the two protagonists at Reykjavik actually served to remind many people of how problematic such notions really are. Between the very plausible goal of deep cuts in nuclear arms and the grander goal of abolishing such arms entirely, whether by treaty or strategic defenses, the leap is enormous. Given an ideologically divided and distrustful world, and the fact that the knowledge needed to recreate nuclear weaponry will not disappear, reliance on deterrence of some sort or another looks less like a temporary resort on the way to total nuclear disarmament than a semi-permanent fact of life. Even a world government with peacekeeping powers might have to maintain some kind of deterrent. But should we then be striving, in our arms reduction efforts, to shape a moral nuclear deterrent? Or should we agree with those who believe such a thing is a contradiction in terms at best, a blasphemy at worst?

It is not hard to make a strong case against the morality of nuclear deterrence. For some, that case is only an extension of the incompatibility they see between the gospel and *any* use of violent force. But many others who don't consider themselves pacifists equally reject any use of nuclear weapons on the grounds that they immediately perpetrate death and destruction on an indiscriminate and disproportionate scale—or they threaten almost inevitably such death and destruction through escalation. Deterrence, they would allow, is not use; indeed, it is justified as a means of forestalling use. But deterrence, should it fail, involves a future risk of unjustifiable deeds; and indeed, if it is not to fail, it requires an immediate readiness to commit the horrendous acts that effectively deter.

That is the moral argument, but opposition to deterrence is both more and less than an argument. It is a deep-seated recoiling from all the calculations of threat and anticipated destruction on a vast scale that deterrence theory ultimately entails. It is an almost visceral conviction that this sort of thinking can only be corrupting and ungodly, can only undermine peace, even "peace of a sort," rather than assure it.

The logical conclusion of an antideterrent posture is unilateral nuclear disarmament. And the logical conclusion of that is probably a rejection of any armed resistance (except possibly guerrilla warfare) against a determined nuclear power. If deterrence is immoral, then nuclear arms will become the monopoly of immoral nations. These are not very palatable conclusions for the average citizen, and only the boldest American opponents of deterrence are apt to follow this logic to its end. Most find ample scope for their overall rejection of deterrence in active opposition to particular excesses of U.S. military policy, of which there are plenty.

What, then, is the bishops' alternative? No one, of course, and certainly not the bishops themselves, would claim that their argument concerning deterrence is without considerable ambiguities. It leans heavily on a papal pronouncement and does a better job of yoking together certain reasonable conclusions than of supplying a coherent moral rationale to justify them. One result has been the widespread belief that the bishops advocate a species of "bluff deterrent": that they condemn all possible *uses* of nuclear weapons as immoral but nonetheless allow the state to maintain a nuclear threat, which our leaders are under moral obligation never actually to carry out. It is reasonably objected that such a deterrent not only implicates the military and the citizenry (who are presumably unaware or uncertain of their leaders' ultimate determination never to use these weapons) in the intention to carry out vastly immoral actions, but it also stands doubly condemned for being so transparent a bluff as in fact to increase the danger of nuclear war. A close reading of the pastoral and the debates that shaped it would show that this interpretation is inaccurate. Nonetheless grounds for it can be easily found in the text, as well as in other episcopal statements. And, most significantly, the bishops themselves have done little to clarify the matter.

If the bishops have avoided resolving this ambiguity, that may reflect a reluctance to exacerbate differences within their own ranks or alienate the constituency that has, in many respects, been the most devoted to the pastoral's message. It also reflects sensitivity to the danger of reinforcing popular complacency about the nuclear *status quo* or lending support to the marketing of ominous or wasteful new weapons systems in the name of deterrence. It is a healthy thing when bishops shy away from appearing to bless weapons, especially weapons of mass destruction.

Nonetheless, the moral case for nuclear deterrence needs to be voiced. The bishops were right to express "profound skepticism" about the moral acceptability of any use of nuclear weapons; that put the burden of proof where it belongs. But they were also right in refusing—as the record of their debate shows—to rule out all use definitively, in particular retaliatory strikes against military and economic, not primarily civilian, targets that would not involve disproportionate noncombatant deaths. Do such targets actually exist? Does the word "proportionate" retain any meaning in the case of nuclear strikes? Is escalation so inevitable that all restraint would be lost? These are "empirical" questions—concerning facts that, if deterrence serves its purpose, can never be ascertained with certainty. But the first question is whether, always within the severe limits of our knowledge, we will explore these questions at all. Should we be comparing targets; sizing up the historical and psychological evidence concerning escalation in war; asking ourselves what level of "incidental" casualties have been accepted as legitimate in wars that, with hindsight, we might consider just? Dare Christians even enter this kind of moral discussion?

Most opponents of deterrence instinctively say "no." We say "yes." And we say that the evidence concerning targets, casualties, and escalation is at least mixed enough that the search for a moral deterrent is not doomed to self-contradiction but is, on the contrary, morally preferable to the immediate and complete rejection of nuclear deterrence.

We say all this with fear and trembling. Any truck with nuclear war—even maintaining the potential of waging it precisely to prevent it from ever occurring—risks asserting an arrogant degree of control over our destiny that some would say belongs only to God. What are the limits of human responsibility for the world, what is the point beyond which we must leave everything to God's sovereignty rather than be complicit in profound evil?

But we believe that *any* position on nuclear deterrence must be held with fear and trembling. The stakes are enormous. They include not only the preservation of freedoms and institutions of enormous significance, but also the prevention of continental holocaust itself. Unilateralism is often said to risk the former. More to the point, should it ever begin to be widely accepted, unilateralism would create instabilities making nuclear war more, not less, likely. That, too, is a tremendous challenge to any conscience.

The search for a moral nuclear deterrent is not equivalent to the acceptance of *any* deterrent. The demand to reduce the wasteful, dangerous mountain of weapons; the opposition to new, destabilizing systems; the insistence on a political component that would complement the military dimension of East-West relations—all this is implied in the idea of an acceptable deterrent. Those who refuse to reject deterrence in principle face no small task. Starting, for example, with Star Wars.

NUCLEAR WAR AND CHRISTIAN RESPONSIBILITY

THOMAS MERTON

We are no longer living in a Christian world. The ages which we are pleased to call the "ages of faith" were certainly not ages of earthly paradise. But at least our forefathers officially recognized and favored the Christian ethic of love. They fought some very bloody and un-Christian wars, and in doing so they also committed great crimes which remain in history as a permanent scandal. However, certain definite limits were recognized. Today a non-Christian world still retains a few vestiges of Christian morality, a few formulas and clichés, which serve on appropriate occasions to adorn indignant editorials and speeches. But otherwise we witness deliberate campaigns to eliminate all education in Christian truth and morality. The Christian ethic of love tends to be discredited as phony and sentimental.

It is therefore a serious error to imagine that because the West was once largely Christian, the cause of the Western nations is now to be identified, without further qualification, with the cause of God. The incentive to wipe out Bolshevism may well be one of the apocalyptic temptations of twentieth-century Christendom. It may indeed be the most effective way of destroying Christendom, even though man may survive. For who imagines that the Asians and Africans will respect Christianity and embrace it after it has apparently triggered mass murder and destruction of cosmic proportions? It is pure madness to think that Christianity can defend itself with nuclear weapons. The mere fact that we now seem to accept nuclear war as reasonable is a universal scandal.

True, Christianity is not only opposed to communism, but is in a very real sense at war with it. This warfare, however, is spiritual and ideological. . . .

THOMAS MERTON (1915–68), Trappist monk, author, and poet, was a longtime contributor to *Commonweal*.

We must remember that the church does not belong to any political power bloc. Christianity exists on both sides of the Iron Curtain and we should feel ourselves united by very special bonds with those Christians who, living under communism, often suffer heroically for their principles.

Is it a valid defense of Christianity for us to wipe out these heroic Christians along with their oppressors, for the sake of "religious freedom"? It is pure sophistry to claim that physical annihilation in nuclear war is a *"lesser evil"* than the difficult conditions under which these Christians continue to live, perhaps with true heroism and sanctity preserving their faith and witnessing very effectively to Christ in the midst of atheism. . . .

GETTING OUT

THE EDITORS

The United States should get out of Vietnam: it should seek whatever safety it can for our allies; it should arrange whatever international face-saving is possible; and, even at the cost of a Communist victory, the United States should withdraw. The war in Vietnam is an unjust one. We mean that in its most profound sense: What is being done there, despite the almost certain good intentions of those doing it, is a crime and a sin. At a moment when claims of military victory are drowning out quiet admissions that the war cannot be settled for years, this conclusion must be affirmed and reaffirmed.

We have not reached this conclusion because we are pacifists. The moral problem of warfare is bound up with the moral problem of the existence of evil. And the almost incredible apparitions of evil mankind has witnessed within the last half-century, in this nation as well as others, convince us there are moments when force must be met with force.

Nor do we believe there is nothing at stake in Southeast Asia. Vietnamese—on both sides—are fighting for their lives and for their right to live unmolested in their homeland. The threat presented by China, swiftly adding nuclear weapons to its chauvinist ideology and cult of the will, is a real one, not the product of anti-Communist imaginations. To measure these stakes against one another, and against the horror of the war, is a miserable and difficult task, but it is not "blasphemy, while the killing goes on," as a few have maintained. It involves surveying a host of often contradictory political and military reports; it involves numerous subjective judgments; but it remains the only way we know for men to make moral decisions in an ambiguous world.

Measured not by declared intentions but by past performance, a Communist victory in South Vietnam would most likely mean a rigorous dictatorship, bloody liquidation of dissenters, and a certain amount of social and economic reform. By the same standards, a Saigon victory will probably mean a looser form of authoritarian government, suppression of radical dissent rather than its liquidation, and little alteration in the *status quo*. On the level of world politics, a U.S. withdrawal could lead China tragically to miscalculate American determination in some "eyeball to eyeball" nuclear confrontation of the future. But to be honest, one must admit that any nearly total success of American policy in Vietnam is as likely to lead to a tragic miscalculation on our side. Already some dismiss all too cavalierly China's willingness to fight beyond its borders. However important the fate of the Vietnamese people and the balance of power in Asia, it seems they are but ambiguously served by American policy.

In brief, the outcome in Southeast Asia will make a difference. But not the decisive difference needed to justify a war which may last longer than any America has ever fought, employ more U.S. troops than in Korea, cost more than all the aid we have ever given to developing nations, drop more bombs than were used against the Japanese in World War II, and kill and maim far more Vietnamese than a Communist regime would have liquidated—and still not promise a definite outcome. The disproportion between ends and means has grown so extreme, the consequent deformation of American foreign and domestic policy so radical, that the Christian cannot consider the Vietnam War merely a mistaken government measure to be amended eventually but tolerated meanwhile. The evil outweighs the good. This is an unjust war. The United States should get out.

But is there not a "third way," a negotiated compromise which means less than total success and less than total failure for both sides? Indeed over the years numerous "third ways" have been proposed. An independent South Vietnam joined to the North (and to the U.S.) in a great Mekong River development project was one such conception. Today many contemplate a neutralized Vietnam with a coalition government in Saigon including the National Liberation Front—another "third way." But none of these proposals has become a reality. And none appears likely to do so. More and more doubts surround the expressed willingness of Washington to negotiate a settlement; but there is even less evidence that Hanoi has wanted to talk, at least since 1965 when near-victory slipped out of Vietcong fingertips. To demand a negotiated settlement, supporting the war only in the meantime and only to this end, makes sense if a negotiated settlement is truly in sight. Otherwise, the "meantime" stretches out into five, eight, ten years. One's moral and political judgment is rendered hostage to the fanaticism of Washington and Hanoi.

This does not mean that opponents of the war should cease to point out and encourage every move toward settlement. They should simply make clear that the basic injustice of this war consists in things other than whether it is the fault of Hanoi or Washington that an attempt at negotiation may break down. There are things that Washington could do, even within the narrow range of its present policy, to bring the Vietnamese War closer to an end.

The holiday cease-fire should be prolonged as long as possible. The bombing of North Vietnam should be halted, and the Russians assured there will be no threat of renewing it if they apply all their influence to bringing Hanoi to the negotiating table.

The Saigon military regime tail must cease to wag the U.S.—or for that matter, Vietnamese—dog. There is currently much talk about a "new" war in Vietnam, one in which U.S. troops are winning the day militarily. If only, adds a weak, small voice, social and political reforms can now get under way! That weak, small voice has been repeating the same message for years. And despite the current burst of enthusiasm for retraining and redeploying the South Vietnamese army for "pacification" purposes, there is little hard evidence that this latest effort will be different from past ones. Saigon must dedicate itself to a genuine land reform benefiting the peasants, pledge the maintenance of land distribution carried out by the Vietcong, and develop an honest administration.

At the least, measures such as these will benefit the Vietnamese people; at the most, they might strengthen the Saigon government to the point where the Vietcong would decide it had better negotiate quickly before all is lost, and where Saigon itself would consider a coalition government a possibility.

Saigon need never take such steps, of course, as long as it knows the United States will stay no matter what. Washington should privately warn the Ky administration that it had better produce results soon lest the U.S. reconsider its commitment. Rumors of such a warning might indeed delay negotiations while the Vietcong and Hanoi waited to see whether Saigon could do the job, but at present it looks as if the Vietcong and Hanoi are doing exactly this anyway. Furthermore, such rumors could prepare U.S. public opinion for greeting any eventual withdrawal as justified, not because "our boys" couldn't win but because the Saigon government didn't do its share.

Finally, the United States must de-escalate its settlement demands. So must Hanoi. But de-escalation on the American side would mean a frank and open willingness to negotiate with the National Liberation Front. It would mean acceptance of the fact that there must be a recognized role for organized left-wing and Communist forces in the political life of any postsettlement South Vietnam.

These suggestions are not new nor are they at all sure-fire. Should they fail, they do not justify going on with this immoral war. They are simply the very least that can be done.

NOTES FROM THE UNDERGROUND

DANIEL BERRIGAN

May 7 marks exactly a month since I packed the small red bag I had bought in Hanoi, and set out from Cornell, looking for America. So far, it has been a tougher and longer voyage than the one which set me down in North Vietnam some two years before.

In the course of that month, I have changed domicile some six times; this in strict accord with a rule of the Jesuit Order, making us, at least in principle, vagabonds on mission: "It is our vocation to travel to any place in the world where the greater glory of God and the need of the neighbor shall impel us." Amen, brothers.

It may be time for a modest stock-taking. What can I hope to accomplish, on the run as I am, having to improvise and skimp and risk being ridiculous, or plain two-cents wrong? How can I reject honored presumptions of conduct, like "the good man is responsible for his actions"; he "pays up on demand"? Or the older Socratic dictum: "One owes the state restitution for broken law, violated order"?

The method of Martin Luther King, violation of local or state law and submitting to jail, had a great deal going for it; circumstances supported the principle. Being in jail was invariably an appeal to a higher jurisdiction. It brought the attention of national authorities to the fact of local or state violations; it brought pressures from above.

Alas and alas, how could such a tactic apply to me and my friends? What superior jurisdiction would rush to action, on the occasion of our jailing? To whom could we appeal? To the International War Crimes Tribunal? To the United Nations? To the World Court? . . . As far as national due process is concerned, the highest appeal courts duly swept aside the issues we tried to raise. That, of course, did not remove the issues; they grow hotter and more lethal every day. The war is mounting in

---

DANIEL BERRIGAN, S.J. (1921–), is a Jesuit priest, author, and peace activist. He wrote this while a fugitive from the FBI.

fury. The Congress, the universities, the churches, bankers, workers, decent citizens of all stripes, separately or in concert, are talking to stone-deaf power. For at least the past six months, when jail was becoming a nearer and larger threat, the students with whom I worked for three years, and for whom my decision seemed to be of some import, said to me time and again, with imploring: When they come for you, don't go in!

The festival at Cornell offered a delicious opportunity, too good to let pass. Some 10,000 students had come together for a post-Woodstock festival of arts, politics, communal living, all in honor of non-violence and Catonsville.

Irresistible. At 7:40 P.M. on Friday, April 17, I ended ten rustic days in hiding on the land, and entered the great Barton Hall. The Freedom Seder was in progress. The moment arrived when Elias the prophet is summoned, figure of providence for all those in legal jeopardy. Supposing that I qualified, I walked on stage.

The next hour and a half were stormy indeed. I recall a sense of weightlessness, almost of dislocation; the throng of young faces, singing, dancing, eating, the calls of support and resistance. Much love, many embraces, the usual press of journalists. Then, in a quiet moment, a friend whispered: Do you want to split?

It was all I needed. Why not indeed split? Why concede, by hanging around, that wrong-headed power owned me? Why play mouse, even sacred mouse, to their cat game? Why turn this scene into yet another sanctuary, so often done before, only delaying the inevitable, the hunters always walking off with their prize?

When the lights lowered for a rock group, I slipped off backstage. Students helped lower around me an enormous puppet of one of the twelve apostles, in use shortly before by a mime group. Inside the burlap, I had only to hold a stick that kept the papier-mâché head aloft, and follow the others, making for a panel truck in which we were to pack the costumes. The puppets were pitched aboard; I climbed in, blind as a bat, sure of my radar, spoiling for fun. It was guerrilla theater, a delight, just short of slapstick. An FBI agent ran for the phone, our license plate was recorded, the chase was on. But our trusty van, hot with destiny, galloped for the woods, and we made it.

The first month has been an interesting experiment: the breaking of idols. That myth of omnicompetence surrounds almost any large federal authority, a myth inflated despite all sorts of contrary available evidence (the successive CIA fiascos in Southeast Asia and elsewhere, the wrong

Marines on the wrong beaches, the utter inability to touch the sources of unrest at home). Was there something here to be dramatized? The FBI is quite possibly composed of earnest, stern, honorable Romans. (I am always made to feel secure when meeting them, there are so many Catholics; even when they stoop to conquer, poking under beds for priests, they never forget their folklore; it is always; "Are you there, Father Dan?")

Still I suggest my case offers interesting evidence of a striking failure of power, beginning with the FBI and extending even to Vietnam. It is a failure of overkill technology, of pacification, of search-and-destroy missions, of Vietnamization, of indiscriminate trampling of national boundaries.

. . . I could go on, but perhaps a point is made. A dizzying thought occurs to me, shaking my hand as I write. Could it be that your humble servant, without script or staff, might be an instrument for demythologizing Big Bro Justice? I like the idea, even as a voice reminds me it is fraught with presumption.

Mr. [John] Mitchell, it is reported, was recently presented with a shiny night stick by a local police department. It was inscribed: "To the top cop." He carried it home under his arm, grim with satisfaction. Now the head of the Justice Department has at his disposal, directly or through others, some hundreds of thousands of night sticks and assorted other hardware, goods, and services, plus the hands itching to wield them on command. I contemplate all this vast panoply of power; and I am not shaken, any more than Buddha under his plane tree. For I have other armaments, resources and visions, of which Mr. Mitchell can know little. My friends, in the main. I number among them, for a start, professors, resisters, priests and nuns, some black Panthers, a deceased corpulent pope (pregnant with a new world), many men and women at present serving time, Kurt Vonnegut, David Smith and his sculpture, Corita, my mother of eighty-five years (a woman of rare fiber and beauty), John of the Cross and his road map for a dark night, Paul Goodman (crotchety and visionary), the Vietnamese. I could go on, Mr. Mitchell, but you get the idea. From the swamps of Asia, from the American underground and jails and campuses a word goes forth: "When the chips are down," the little people ask, "Who are your friends?" And further: "Who owns this land anyway?"

The question burns like a night flare. The night sticks come running. But the night sticks can do nothing; they do not signify. In the deepest sense (forever lost to top cops) they are ersatz; wooden limbs in place of living ones. They substitute woodenly and hardly at all, for lost friendship, lost communion, contemplatives and activists, for friends and countrymen and dreamers, open minds, closed mouths, the network of men and women who at need can be counted on to "harbor, aid and abet," and, as the saying goes, generally mother up the works and agents of power.

My being at large is thus related, in some quirky way I leave to others, to an infinitely more striking historical occurrence. Simply, Vietnam cannot be defeated. I take the fact to heart, an article of human faith, constantly buttressed by news out of Asia and Washington. In public places and private, I cherish it, and smile and smile to myself, the delight of a man to whom sanity is surprise, gift, delight. . . .

It's because we own the land. The night sticks of the chief cop are no apt substitute, given the real world, for organs, limbs, compassion, brain, historical sense, patience, courage, the nonviolent resources of good friends. The top cop, even as he invents more and more electronic junk, censors, intercoms, copters, taps, bugs, computers, *et al.,* becomes less and less able to be a man; spontaneous, free-spirited, humorous, spunky—liturgical. I think we can match him, by being some of these things, at least some of the time. I think as a result, we can liberate even top cops, causing them to commit what one ex-agent assured me was the most heinous of internal crimes: embarrassing the Bureau.

Finally, if they do run me down, I will claim a win anyway. I will go off to jail in better spirits than my captors.

The first month is over, the future is charged with surprise. Come, Holy Spirit.

SHOULD WE GO TO WAR WITH NICARAGUA?

THE EDITORS

Never mind that for several years we have been at war with Nicaragua. This fact has been conveniently obscured, if by no means hidden, by the denials oozed from the White House while a plan to train a 500-man guerrilla force for interdicting weapons going from Nicaragua to El Salvador swiftly blossomed into the care and feeding of a full-fledged *contra* army 15,000-strong. Once Congress stopped playing along—prodded by embarrassments like the mining of Nicaraguan harbors and the revelation of a CIA-sponsored lesson book in assassination and terrorism—the administration increasingly shed its own obfuscations and uncertainties. Talk of interdicting arms faded; talk of "freedom fighters" and making the Sandinistas cry "Uncle!" increased. When Congress first balked at a new round of *contra* funding, Secretary of State Shultz promptly hinted that the administration might have to commit U.S. troops to combat in the region. . . . In short, the administration is now putting the proposition bluntly to Congress and to the American people: preferably by proxy but if need be by U.S. troops, we *should* go to war with Sandinista-led Nicaragua. What the administration is not saying—at least not clearly—is why.

And Congress? In an extraordinary display of muddle-headedness, it seems to be replying, "Why not?" War is evidently a matter of some casualness, to be determined by episodes of the weightiness of President Ortega's "embarrassing" visit to Moscow. One would think that if there were reasons to justify the bloodshed and destruction of war these would be apparent whether or not the head of Nicaragua's government, like the head of Italy's government or the head of India's government, openly consulted with the Kremlin. Nor does the charade about "humanitarian" aid to the *contras* provide any excuse for not looking at those reasons. The rationale for backing our proxies today will be the rationale for sending U.S. forces tomorrow.

That rationale has two main components, emphasized differently by various administration officials and supporters, and sometimes juggled quickly enough to impress the public and hamper scrutiny. The first component is *security.* The Sandinistas are undeniably pro-Soviet; however much U.S. policy has cemented this orientation, it was evidently their own choice from the start. But swollen as their military capacity is—both as a consequence of their own revolutionary vision and as a realistic response to U.S. measures—it poses no genuine threat to American security. The argument then becomes that this nation of less than three million people is a *latent* danger—a potential Soviet base threatening Gulf of Mexico supply lines to Europe—as well as a base of subversion and a destabilizing factor in Central America. Does such a latent danger justify U.S. intervention? The principle of nonintervention in international affairs may not be absolute, but to amend it to justify military measures against all sorts of *latent* dangers is to grant powerful states the privilege of exercising vetoes over the makeup of any government within their reach.

The conclusion to be drawn from the potential threat of a pro-Soviet Nicaragua is that Washington should negotiate a *modus vivendi.* The outlines of such an agreement have been clear for some time. They involve bans on certain kinds of weaponry as well as Soviet ports. They require guarantees for Nicaragua's neighbors. They may limit support to fellow revolutionaries. Absent the complicating factor of a U.S.-sponsored insurgency, drawing these lines—and enforcing them—is not an insurmountable problem. Enforcement would best be accomplished by regional or international authority. But at the outside it could revert to the U.S., whose forces—at an unknown cost to Honduran political development—are already thoroughly implanted in the region.

The second component of the rationale for war is *democracy.* Certainly evocations of "freedom fighters" play better with the public than calculations of security, especially since the latter appear far-fetched to many Americans. But no doubt the appeal to democracy has a real moral force within the administration and to liberals and centrists as well. And it should. It is a large step, however, from backing democracy to funding the *contras* or planning a U.S. invasion.

This is not the place for a full-scale appraisal of the Sandinista regime. Nicaragua, *pace* the president, is *not* "a totalitarian dungeon." Nor is it, *pace* some of its supporters, the last, best hope of the poor and oppressed. Its leaders, insofar as they have a guiding philosophy, appear captives of an outlook that scorns "bourgeois" liberties and has a worldwide track record of economic failure. Yet five years into Sandinista rule, independent centers of power, undisguised manifestations of political opposition, checks on human rights abuses, and even rudiments of parliamentary election and debate remain more real in Nicaragua than in numerous other third-world regimes, including some with close U.S. ties. Part of the tangled debate centers on how much of this moderation has survived because of American pressure and how much despite it.

But objections to a war for democracy in Nicaragua do not end with inevitably ambiguous conclusions about the ultimate drift of the Sandinistas. The men who control the guns in the anti-Sandinista insurgency are men whose past careers as Somoza henchmen abundantly disqualify them as standard bearers of democracy. That thousands of disaffected *campesinos* and a number of honorable democratic politicians have felt compelled to join with such dubious leadership reveals the extent of Sandinista failure. But there are no reasonable grounds for belief that a *contra* military victory would initiate anything but another round of dictatorship, bloodbath, and prolonged insurgency.

The debate about U.S. policy toward Nicaragua is scandalously unserious, as though war were only political campaigning carried on by other means. War in Central America is not the necessary, not even the plausible, means to assuring security and democracy in the hemisphere. For a tradition in which war can only be a last resort, justified by stringent criteria, current developments demand an unmistakable protest.

A WAR ABOUT AMERICA

GEORGE WEIGEL

Forgive what may seem an impertinence: but this proponent of the just-war tradition, who supports the use of armed force against Iraq, also believes that America needs a genuine peace movement—which is precisely not what has been in the streets (and in many ecclesiastical venues) these past months. Why do we need it? Because the alternative is an anti-American power movement that will, like its Vietnam-era antecedent, debase the coinage of political discourse for years to come.

What would a peace movement worthy of the name have been teaching since the war began on August 2, 1990?

It would have unambiguously condemned Iraqi aggression, telling Saddam Hussein that he could not play the Vietnam card in American domestic politics.

It would have focused its disarmament concerns on the Iraqi dictator's relentless build-up of weapons of mass destruction, and demanded their dismantling under international inspection.

It would have avoided Saddam Hussein's strategic trap: the establishment of a fictional moral equivalence between the Iraqi invasion, occupation, and plunder of Kuwait and Israeli policy in the Occupied Territories.

It would not have posed the moral argument on U.S. Gulf policy as one between the morally concerned and the morally obtuse, but rather as a complex democratic deliberation in which the central virtue is prudence.

It would have refused to indulge in ritualized corporation bashing, and it would have disciplined itself to reject slogans like, "We won't fight

GEORGE WEIGEL (1951–), past president of the Ethics and Public Policy Center in Washington, D.C., is the author of *Tranquillitas Ordinis: The Present Failure and Future Promise of American Catholic Thought on War and Peace* (Oxford).

for Texaco." It would have linked legitimate concerns about America's dependence on foreign oil to an acknowledgment that the countries that would be hit hardest by Saddam's control over this basic commodity would be the poor countries of the third world and the emerging democracies of Central and Eastern Europe.

It would have avoided excuse-making for the embrace of Saddam Hussein by the PLO.

Finally, it would straighten itself out on the subject of America. Has there ever been so reluctant a superpower as the United States? Has there ever been a great power, at the pinnacle of world politics and economics, that put itself through such rigors of self-examination before committing its citizens to battle? U.S. foreign policy is, of course, neither omniscient, omnicompetent, nor fully satisfactory from a moral perspective. The failures of U.S. policy toward Iraq are well known; a genuine peace movement would urge that, in thinking through the postwar politics of the Middle East, we learn from some profound errors of analysis and judgment.

But to argue, as one demonstrator in Washington did in January, that the United States is "a much greater danger to the Middle East" than Saddam Hussein is a position so desperately wrongheaded that it can only derive, not from a thoughtful calculus of policy failures (and successes), but from the deep-set alienation that has been both the distinguishing hallmark of the "new movement," and its temporal and ideological linkage with "Vietnam." The war is also about America.

Life, Death, and the Dignity of Persons

The modern scientific and democratic age has brought great, even undreamed of, benefits to humankind. Americans enjoy remarkable levels of education and material prosperity, as well as increased life spans and better health—including ostensible control over human reproduction. In addition to secure political liberties, a profound respect for individual autonomy and personal choice pervades nearly all aspects of American society.

Commonweal has championed these improvements in our common condition while warning of the simultaneous and sometimes subtle erosion of the values and institutions—such as the family and community—on which such achievements are built and sustained. Can a mature acceptance of religious and political pluralism avoid moral relativism? How can all share fairly in the enormous wealth created by a capitalist economy? Can a conception of the common good guide modern medicine, or are we doomed to the pursuit of expensive high-tech medical interventions that only the wealthy can afford? Is abortion on demand the necessary foundation of equality for women? Is marriage essentially a private contract between two consenting adults, or as Jo Mc-Gowan writes, "a community-building act from the very beginning"?

Perhaps no contemporary issue has so vexed relations between Catholics and the larger culture as has abortion, which has brought the Catholic conviction that moral truth cannot be determined by vote into sharp conflict with the American instinct for privacy and pragmatic compromise. The magazine protested the 1973 Supreme Court decision legalizing abortion, noting that the ruling "diminished the whole concept of what it means to be a person." At the same time, the editors judged the church's anti-abortion efforts counterproductive and unpersuasive. In typical *Commonweal* fashion, Peter Steinfels (editor, 1984–87) argued against the absolutism of both sides of the abortion issue. Given American political realities, the decades-long practice of abortion, and the ambiguities inherent in the biology of early embryonic development, abolishing abortion is not a realistic possibility. A respect for the reasoned views of Americans who do not share the church's belief that life begins at conception requires compromise. He proposed a ban on abortion after the eighth week of pregnancy, while encouraging Catholics to continue working to convince their fellow citizens of the dignity of all unborn human life.

Sensitive to the value of pluralism, the magazine has nevertheless opposed the further privatization of decisions about life and death, such as physician-assisted suicide and euthanasia. In American culture, wrote Rand Richards Cooper about the right-to-die movement, "the appeal of rights is so compelling that it leaves scant room for realities and interests not easily expressed as rights. And with assisted suicide that means leaving out way too much." Reflecting on his grandmother's prolonged illness and death, Cooper worried that legalizing euthanasia would subject the dying to enormous pressures to end their lives, while leaving the rest of us with a truncated understanding of what life means. "I feel I am richer for all of it," he wrote of his grandmother's final illness, "endowed with a more expansive vocabulary of body and spirit; and also a more intimate acquaintance with death, in all its mystery and terribleness."

On questions such as abortion and euthanasia, Catholics are often accused of placing abstract moral principles—sometimes called absolute moral truths—before the complexities of human life and suffering. That is often a danger. It is just as true, however, that the abandonment of moral principles in the name of compassion or tolerance also ends in inhumanity. The value of personal autonomy must be balanced against a moral responsibility to all humankind as well as to future generations. That requires that we think through how seemingly private actions can affect the larger community and subtly undermine our ideas about human dignity. In reminding us that we are inescapably social creatures— that we find our true identity in community, not apart from it—Catholic social teaching is an invaluable corrective to the individualistic ethos that pervades American culture.

JUSTICE FOR JEWS

THE EDITORS

The Commonweal firmly associates itself with the great mass action of public opinion which is shocked by and which utterly condemns the anti-Semitism of the Hitler government. We unite whatever measure of influence we possess with the expression of that public opinion. It is certainly quite true that many deliberate lies and grossly exaggerated charges have been circulated in connection with this matter. It is also true that many Jews have suffered not precisely because they were Jews, but also, or chiefly, because they were Communists, or Socialists, or pacifists, at the hands of a triumphant anti-Communist and antidemocratic dictatorship imposed by a militaristic and ultranationalistic revolution. Nevertheless, no matter how much what really has happened—and which will continue to happen even now that physical violence has abated, so long as Hitlerism continues to rule Germany—may have been exaggerated, no amount of official denials can conceal the fact that Jews as Jews have been subjected to a bigoted discrimination and a persecution wholly unjust and abhorrent to all believers in the human rights of personal liberty, equal justice under the protection of law, and cultural and religious freedom and equality of status.

The anti-Jewish movement in Germany is far more than a tempest of prejudice stirred up in the lower depths of mob emotion by a demagogue. It is part and parcel of a strongly developed racial nationalism, with its own passionate, even fanatical philosophy of Teutonism, the spearhead of which is nothing other than the same dangerous, almost insane Prussianism which was glorified before 1914, and which the world too naively thought to have been overthrown, and discarded by the German people themselves, but which now is violently seeking to reestablish its predominance. To such a religion of racial pride and brutal power, the purging of the people obsessed by its spirit from what is considered to be the alien and corrupting taint of the Jewish element, seems a clear and certain duty. Alarmed, for reasons of expediency, by the universal abhorrence and condemnation provoked by the violence of the first five days of the Nazi revolution, the Hitler government already has taken measures to check the cruder manifestations of anti-Semitism, but nothing other than the overthrow of Hitlerism by the German people itself will bring justice to the Jews, and to other oppressed minorities, including the Catholics. The German Catholic bishops have condemned the ultra-nationalism of the Nazi party, and that condemnation still stands, even although the Center party has been forced to vote for its own suppression. That very large minority of democratic Germans which is temporarily deprived of power, aided by elements of the Hitler majority which will return to their senses as the first, contagious delirium of the revolution subsides, can alone prevent the continuation of anti-Semitism in Germany. The democratic elements in Germany are at present impotent, crushed between the opposing forces of Hitlerism and communism; but to those elements, which alone possess the true principles of Western civilization, and of which the Catholic Center is the only stable core, the enlightened public opinion of the United States, Great Britain, France, Belgium, Holland, and the Scandinavian nations should display true sympathy, patient consideration, and the full support of its moral cooperation.

CHRISTMAS AT DACHAU

ALFRED WERNER

The Commonweal *in its Christmas issue wishes to remember the Jewish race, privileged and selected, in which the Son of God took human flesh. We publish therefore this account of contemporary Jewish (and Christian) agony and humiliation, awed before that suffering as we are awed before the redoubtable and mysterious responsibility of those who inflict it. We ask our readers to see in the action we have taken no hatred for the persecutor, nor any incitement to hatred, but only pity and terror before the evil of our world.*—THE EDITORS

Herr Gruenewald, *Standartenfuehrer* and commander of the concentration camp, had a tall Christmas tree erected in the center of Dachau, on the parade ground, a week before Christmas. The tree was more than fifteen feet high and lighted with hundreds of bulbs, shining at night strangely through the ghastly darkness.

It was, of course, designed for the Gentile guests, who were as numerous as the Jews—mostly political opponents of nazism: Communists, social democrats, liberals, Catholics, monarchists, conscientious objectors. We Jews had been taken there as hostages for the murder of Herr vom Rath in Paris.

The tree itself was neither "unto the Jews a stumbling block" nor "unto the Gentiles a foolishness." On the contrary, all of us agreed that it was rather a blasphemy on Herr Gruenewald's part—the representative of a party which had declared: "We do not require Jesus as leader"— to place this symbol of love and peace on such a spot. But perhaps we wronged the commander, since for the modern German the Christmas festival, like the Yule festival of the ancient Teutons, is in fact "the solemn acknowledgment of Strength, that Strength which apart from transcendental theories hides within itself redemption from the eternal sin of the

---

ALFRED WERNER, an Austrian writer, graduated from the University of Vienna.

weak." Indeed Nazi teachers tell the children at Christmas, or rather at the "festival of the winter solstice," that it is idle to look for the star of Bethlehem or the wondrous birth, since "in every newborn child God still comes into the world."

Yet in the evenings when, after an exhausting drill, we were forced to stand at attention for two or three hours at a stretch, to contemplate the Christmas tree, most of us were too weak and too frozen to enjoy the beauties of its symbolism. Storm troopers silently moved through our rows, cycling through the deep snow, ready to strike if a man dared even to turn his head away.

All of us had been looking forward to the holidays. There was a rumor of a coming amnesty which would include the Jews. "Good God," we prayed, "allow us to go home." We planned then to leave our beloved native country as fast as we knew how, leaving behind everything that remained of our belongings. On December 22, we were ordered to clear the camp of snow and ice. Snow sweeping is a chore in Berlin as well as in Vienna, in New York as well as in Moscow, but in Dachau all work had to be done at the "doublequick," with not a minute's rest, under the kind eye of the storm troopers, who kicked all those people who should slip or collapse from strain. I remember an elderly man whose loaded wheelbarrow skidded into the water where we had to dump the snow. The Nazi guard kicked him into the icy water, too. He remained there until after Christmas day.

December 24 came—but no reprieve. All work, however, was stopped in the afternoon. This was not done for the benefit of the prisoners, but for the sake of the Nazi guards, who really deserved a few days' vacation and recreation in Munich after such exhausting work as vexing the elderly people among us. The Gentile prisoners were allowed to receive little Christmas packages from their relatives, except for members of the Exegetist sect, which had opposed National Socialism from the first, as these people had felt it was contrary to the moral thought of the Bible. The Jews, of course, were not permitted to receive any little Christmas packages from their relatives since Herr Gruenewald respected the traditions of the Orthodox and did not want to offend their feelings. And we cannot blame him for not knowing that by giving little presents we Jews celebrate "Chanukkah," the "Feast of Lights," at the same time as Christmas.

Anyway, we could expect to get a little rest; we would be awakened an hour later in the morning, and, above all, would be spared those dreaded visits of the supervising storm trooper—or so we were told by our "trusty." And he knew the conditions at Dachau fairly well, since he had been imprisoned in 1933 and had a number below 300, whereas mine was above 30,000. He was a former Social Democratic leader, a stickler for custom himself, a veteran who had spent his Christmas there five times and knew well that Gruenewald would not leave any part of the ceremony out.

For him and the five other Gentile prisoners who were in charge of our batch of some 800 Jews, we prepared in the "dining room" of our department as nice a Christmas dinner as we could manage. There was no turkey, of course, but we bought some corned beef at the camp canteen, and instead of pies and tarts we furnished the Christmas table with cookies and jars of jam and marmalade. Our trusties were not allowed to visit their Christian friends in the Gentile camp, so they were to have as good a time as prisoners can prepare for their co-prisoners.

We had in our particular batch several converted Jews, one of whom, a man of fifty, had been baptized as a child and brought up in a monastery. According to the Nuremberg laws he was nevertheless regarded a Jew. He was a bit queer, lean, and had a high voice, yet he was very friendly, enduring and tolerant, having made friends even with our Orthodox Jews. He had been a bookkeeper, was unmarried, had no relatives or friends, nobody who would help him regain his liberty, and he did not even make use of the opportunity of writing letters to people, given every fortnight or so.

In the late afternoon, while we could hear the chimes of the church of Dachau village proclaiming, "Glory to God in the highest, and on earth peace to men of good will," Herr Suendermann (that was the convert's name) suddenly rose to address us all. "Do you know," he asked his surprised audience, "for whom we prepare our meal? For Jesus Christ! He himself is to visit our hut tonight." Now our supervisor, though a good Christian and a bright man, made the grave mistake of not taking him seriously: "No, my friend," he laughed, "the storm troopers will not let him in!" But the orator, filled with prophetic fury, shouted: "That is a blasphemy—none can stop the Lord! I myself will go to the gate to receive him when he comes."

We felt rather uneasy, so seriously and gravely did he utter his pronouncement. We knew of a man who had escaped from the hut in a fit one evening and had gone to the gate and had tried to pass as Herr Gruenewald himself. He was taken to the hospital for his pains. We tried to quiet our prophet, to divert his attention by talking about the weather. But he kept to his fixed idea that Jesus would come in person and that we all should meet him at the gate.

So, for his sake and for our own safety, we thought it best to bind and gag him; but when we approached him, he saw our intention and roared in a stentorian voice: "Jesus Christ, come and help me against these infidels!"

We knew that the few guards left in the camp must have heard the cry. And in a moment an unfamiliar guard entered the room. When he had heard the story from our supervisor, he knew how to cure the prophet, who lay exhaustedly on the floor, white foam flecking his lips. He dragged Herr Suendermann to the door and pushed him out, putting his face into the snow to "cool him off." Quietly he waited for some twenty minutes. Then he ordered the prisoner to get up. "Now, what have you to say about Jesus Christ?"

"Our Lord Jesus Christ will forgive you," the convert quietly said.

"What, you damned Jew," the enraged Nazi cried, and beat the poor man with his fists. Two of our men were ordered to carry Herr Suendermann, who was bleeding incessantly, to the Nazi barracks. The others should have their fun with that damned queer Jew.

But before leaving our hut, the guard looked at the Christmas table, heaped with good things. And with a sudden kick he overthrew the table so that the marmalade and the cookies and the corned beef splashed over the floor and the wall, and the tin plates rolled into the corners and under the stove.

On Christmas Eve, 1938, we lay down in our plain straw very early.

JUSTIFYING TORTURE

GORDON MARINO

For years now the Israeli security forces have been using torture as a method of interrogation and, thanks to the lack of space in Israeli jails, as an alternative to prison sentences. Last month, a United Nations committee condemned Israel for permitting such methods. According to human-rights groups, between 1988 and 1994 Israeli security forces detained over 100,000 Palestinian suspects, one-third of whom were violently interrogated and often severely beaten. To put flesh on these statistics, one repentant Israeli officer reports going into a village, rounding up over a dozen Palestinian youths, taking them to a nearby field, and breaking their arms and legs (*see* James Ron's "Rabin's Two Legends," *Index on Censorship,* September-October 1996). Gilad Anat, a cog in the harrowing machine, recalls:

> When we were driving toward the field they said to make certain that you hit the Arabs on the kneecap, since that was the way to make sure the leg would break. When it was over the Palestinians were left lying in the field, and the soldiers drove off in silence. I was surprised that none of the soldiers protested.

Security personnel report that, when they are instructed to try and beat the truth or spirit out of someone, the only restrictions they are given is, "Don't kill them," or at least not their bodies, for as Elaine Scarry showed in her minor classic, *The Body in Pain,* torture can kill the spirit. When people are brought to a pitch of pain where they are willing to do anything to be released, including turning their loved ones over to their torturers, the body may endure but henceforth, "all is but toys; renown and grace are dead."

GORDON MARINO (1952–) is a philosopher and the director of the Howard V. and Edna H. Hong Kierkegaard Library at Saint Olaf College in Northfield, Minnesota.

In a recent highly publicized case the Israelis did kill the body of a suspect, which prompted the Israeli High Court to place an injunction against the use of physical pressure as a method of interrogation. A day later the court acceded to a request from the legal counsel for the security forces to suspend the injunction, so that they could put the screws to someone whom they claimed to suspect of planning a terrorist action.

Whenever the issue of violent interrogation has come up in Israel, people of practical wisdom maintain that the use of force is necessary to extract information about terrorist activities that will in the end save the lives of many potential victims. In fact Andre Rosenthal, the lawyer who pressed for the suspension of the injunction, said: "No enlightened nation would agree that hundreds of people should lose their lives because of a rule saying torture is forbidden." Upon hearing that one of the High Court judges was playing Pilate and would not offer a ruling either for or against the use of physical force, Rosenthal fulminated, "That's the most immoral and extreme position I have heard in my life. A thousand people are about to be killed and you propose that we don't do anything." In the view of Rosenthal and many other Israelis, when you have someone in custody who may be able to tell you the whereabouts of a bomb that is ticking toward the loss of many innocent lives, it is the moral obligation of the state to do anything necessary to make him speak.

One would like to think that if citizens of a democracy really grasped what it was like to be beaten to the rim of death by servants of the state, they would rise up against such practices. Apparently not. Israelis know what is going on, and many of them either put their hands over their eyes or, like Rosenthal, have no qualms about the beatings.

But it is one thing not to protest and it is another legally to tolerate breaking heads. Or is it? While many Israelis are appalled by the use of violence, others argue that they are just being honest about a practice that is common to every police force in the world. Still others maintain that when the use of physical force is acknowledged by the state, it can be monitored and limited, but that when the use of hoods, prongs, and electric prods is covert, there is no mechanism to rein in professional pain makers.

One of the most popular strategies in teaching ethics courses is to prepare slides of each of the major moral paradigms, for example, divine-command theory, virtue ethics, deontological ethics, feminist ethics, or utilitarianism. With this approach, one points out the appeal and liabilities of each paradigm. For example, utilitarianism is the view that we are obligated to do whatever promotes the greatest good for the greatest number of people. As with the other moral lenses, there are a number of cracks in the utilitarian position. The most commonplace objection to utilitarianism is that it would seem to commend and command acts which we would otherwise judge to be unjust. For instance, if by routinely torturing criminal suspects one could extract information which would promote national security, then, according to the utilitarian position, we ought to torture criminal suspects.

However, most of us believe that individuals have rights which would be trammeled by a policy of torture first and ask questions later. Most of us would consider the utilitarian notion that it is permissible to torture individuals for the good of the community as an argument against utilitarianism. Indeed, we would consider anyone who floated a bill to sanction torture to be "morally challenged." Just such a bill has been drawn up by Israeli legislators, but has not yet been submitted to Parliament.

The debate over sanctioning torture, or as some would prefer to euphemize it, "the use of physical force," has been burbling for quite some time now in Israel. As the liberal Israeli magazine *Challenge* tells it, proponents of interrogation by ordeal invariably invoke the "ticking bomb scenario"—that is, the situation in which a terrorist action has been planned and a suspect is in custody who could provide the information that would stop the action. The suspect will not cooperate, and the hour and minute hands of the clock are circling, seemingly faster and faster. According to Roni Ben Efrat (*Challenge*, No. 41) and others, it does not take a ticking bomb to get either the Israeli or the even less discriminating forces of the Palestinian Authority to start shaking people's heads (a common form of violent interrogation) to the brink of death and once in a while over the brink. Just the same, Efrat argues that even in the ticking-bomb situation it is unlikely that torture will work:

> For it is a cardinal assumption of this scenario that the prisoner is one of the two or three people who know where the bomb is and when it will go off. He knows, therefore, exactly how long he has to hold out. Being dedicated he will mislead his interrogator until it's too late or until his colleagues have changed the plan.

Thus, it could be argued that torture should be prohibited not because it is inherently evil but rather because it is not efficacious. After all, some are able to remain silent even while their very ability to communicate is being melted in pain. Others will spill misleading beans of information. And heaven only knows what someone will say who lacks the information that others are trying to torture out of him. Finally, one could viably argue that, while torturing suspects may save lives in the short run, adopting a policy of torture will imbrute the whole society and eventually produce more pain than it spares. From a utilitarian perspective, whether or not violent interrogation is anathema or obligatory is an empirical question. But is the utilitarian perspective the right one?

In the intellectual badminton that occurs in ethics courses one player will inevitably serve the idea that, even if it were possible to save five people by euthanizing and harvesting the organs of a reprobate one, it would still be wrong to kill the one to save the many. The riposte is usually, "But suppose it were a million against one." At this juncture, feminists such as Nel Noddings complain that only a man would think of testing a theory by flinging far-fetched examples against it. For Noddings and others, decontextualized thought experiments are not illuminating. And yet I think those of us who believe that murder and torture are inherently wrong would have to concede that murder and torture would remain wrong even when the consequences of refraining from murder and torture are murderous. Socrates taught that, for our soul's sake, it is better for the individual himself to suffer an injustice than it is to do an injustice, better for him to be killed by a terrorist than it is to kill innocent people in an attempt to prevent being killed by terrorists. And yet this begs the utilitarian claim that notions of justice were developed by humans to serve human ends and that any course of action that leads to the inhuman consequence of putting the interests of an individual above the community is necessarily unjust.

I suspect that when the Israeli proponents of violent interrogation read that Americans find their practices morally repugnant, they will mutter words to the effect, "Americans would think differently if they had to worry about their children being killed by a bomb on the way to school!" No doubt that is true, which only goes to show that the horde of us are weak vessels who cannot help but feel and act as though the need to secure the safety of our own children trumps all other considerations—including the needs of other people to protect their children. During the first seventy years of this century, over four thousand African-Americans were lynched in the United States. When these killings took place there were, no doubt, white people who had the impulse to resist mob violence, only they resisted that impulse because they feared putting their own children in harm's way.

Though the use of torture on prisoners of war is prohibited by the Geneva Convention, Israeli advocates of the use of physical force base their claim on what they take to be their extraordinary security situation. That is, they give the impression that if matters were otherwise, if there were no cloud of terrorism hanging over their heads, they would not sue for tolerance of torture. And yet, if situation ethics is good for the Israeli it must also be good for the Palestinian. If the notion that what is hideous in one circumstance is acceptable or even commendable in another holds for people on one side of the Jordan, it must also hold for people on the other. All Israelis condemn acts of terrorism. However, by the logic of their own implicit argument, those who want the state to bless instruments of torture would have to agree that, if the Palestinians can show good reason for believing that the only way to protect their own lives and the lives of their children is to engage in acts of terrorism, then the Israelis could not condemn, with moral consistency, the planting of bombs on buses.

Indeed, so far as the Palestinians are concerned, the fact that the state of Israel is poised to give its legal blessing to acts which, if committed against a pet, would suffice to have the owner jailed, is very good reason for Palestinians to believe that in their relations with the Israelis no act should be morally proscribed. The very criterion that some Israelis invoke to sanction beating after beating after beating can also be invoked to sanctify the very acts which the beatings are intended to suppress.

THE SEARCH FOR AN ALTERNATIVE

PETER STEINFELS

I t is hard to tell whether the present impasse over abortion will be lasting. At the moment both sides are in disarray. The prochoice lobby has suffered a series of legislative and judicial setbacks, culminating in the election of a theoretically anti-abortion administration. Right-to-life groups remain effectively organized to exercise political muscle. But they are not winning the battle of public opinion; indeed, as more women undergo abortions, or know those who have done so, the difficulties of arguing for a total ban will mount. Thus any victory the anti-abortionists win may be almost as "elitist" and at least as subject to public resistance and reversal as the 1973 prochoice victory in the Supreme Court.

One would think that liberal Catholics might have a distinctive contribution to make in this painful and apparently irresolvable conflict. . . .

First, from long immersion in church-state questions liberal Catholicism forged a relatively sophisticated theory of law and morality, one that neither divorced nor equated the two. Second, while liberal Catholics refuse to treat traditional moral positions as beyond reexamination, they remain rooted in a philosophical tradition that rejects relativism and moral individualism. Morality is neither a matter of social conditioning, nor of arbitrary "personal" opinion, nor of majority vote. Liberal Catholics cannot, like the Supreme Court or the prochoice movement, slough off the issue of the moral status of fetal life as just too complicated to be considered.

In fact, liberal Catholicism has remained on the margin of the abortion controversy. Part of the explanation is historical. When the abortion issue surfaced in American politics, liberal Catholics were not only preoccupied with the war in Vietnam but also absorbed in the aftermath of

---

PETER STEINFELS (1941–), formerly editor of *Commonweal*, writes the "Beliefs" column for the *New York Times* and teaches at Georgetown University.

the Vatican Council. Though the reaction in these circles to the repeal of abortion statutes and then to *Roe v. Wade* was negative, the reaction to the bishops' plans for a right-to-life campaign was even more negative. People who were disappointed in the church's implementation of conciliar reforms, and for whom the credibility of church leadership had already been sorely tested by *Humanae vitae,* now saw the bishops embark on a course that promised to repeat many of the errors of the past. The fact that prominent segments of the nascent anti-abortion forces exhibited all the characteristics of past crusades against birth control, dirty books, and the Reds didn't help. Liberal Catholics said and wrote some extremely intelligent things about the abortion question in those early years, but already a pattern of detachment, if not embarrassment, had been established.

The fear that the right-to-life movement would harden resistance to reform and renewal in the church has been succeeded by the fear that the right-to-life movement is reinforcing political and social forces that liberal Catholics see as antilife. The wariness remains. And yet I believe it is being counterbalanced by the increasing impatience many liberal Catholics feel at the tactics and rhetoric of the prochoice representatives. It is disturbing when a grassroots anti-abortionist denounces Bella Abzug not only for being prochoice but for being "antifamily." It is equally, or even more, disturbing when a sophisticated newspaper like the *New York Times* publishes its umpteenth abortion editorial avoiding any discussion of the value of fetal life and thereby delivering its Olympian advice while begging the question at issue. Or when an article on right-to-lifers in *Mother Jones* resurrects the hoariest of nineteenth-century anti-Catholic canards, that Catholics don't really have to practice the morality they preach because they can always wipe their consciences clean in the confessional. Or when NOW and other prochoice groups raise the alarm that the anti-abortionists are out to ban birth control. One could go on.

In the end, however, the character of both the right-to-life and prochoice movements is a peripheral matter. The central issue remains the meaning of unborn human life. Can its destruction be justified? Who should decide, the individual mother or the society? As the increasing resort to abortion—one-and-a-half million a year—mocks all the hopes that this would be an exceptional last resort, limited to tragic dilemmas, liberal Catholics have had to put aside their dissatisfaction with the contending armies and return to the basic questions.

What they find upon returning is not reassuring. Abortion is surely becoming an alternative or "fall-back" form of birth control, with the statistics showing a sharp increase in repeat abortions. Rather than being isolated culturally as a "special case," abortion is now mentioned neutrally in everything from Sylvia Porter's *New Money Book for the 80s* ("How to Shop for—and Reduce the Costs of—an Abortion") to health and sex primers for teen-agers. It is just another "option."

Will the logic of abortion, as anti-abortionists have always warned, further undermine what respect and protection we currently afford other human lives when, like the fetus, they are vulnerable, unproductive, and threatening to our psychic or material resources? It is hard to tell how slippery the slope is in America. Both practically and psychologically, abortion *has* opened the way to *in vitro* fertilization and sex selection, both on a small scale. It has become the conventional wisdom that a Down's syndrome child should not be brought into the world, and cases appear to be multiplying where such children are not medically sustained *after* being brought into the world. Here the logic of abortion is indeed powerful: why hesitate to do to a newborn what one is willing to do to a well-developed fetus a few months earlier? (We can, of course, substitute the medical term "neonate" to reduce distracting emotions about this matter.)

But quite apart from worries about where the logic of abortion may lead, which depends on innumerable sociological factors, the logic itself does not withstand scrutiny. Not at least to those who morally reject infanticide. I do not introduce infanticide as a fright word. It is just that in their emphasis either on the woman's right to choose or on social, interpersonal, relational, and rational criteria for "humanness," prochoice arguments almost always deny the fetus any moral standing in such a way that, except for sheer arbitrariness (and instinctive decency, one might add), moral status should also be denied the newborn. Those familiar with philosophical literature know that, logic being logic, defenses of infanticide are no longer uncommon.

Last January, the *Christian Century* published an article that aptly illustrates why liberal Catholics may be moving away from peripheral worries to the central issue. It was not by some hawkish population controller but by the distinguished philosopher Charles Hartshorne. Hartshorne set out to refute the "fanatics against abortion" with the familiar argument that a fetus is not an "actual person" because it lacks "the quality that we have in mind when we proclaim our superior worth to the chimpanzees or dolphins. It cannot speak, reason, or judge between right and wrong. It cannot have personal relations, without which a person is not functionally a person at all." Hartshorne is too conscientious to ignore the objection that an infant does not possess these capacities either. His answer is blunt: "Of course, an infant is not fully human. . . . I have little sympathy with the idea that infanticide is just another form of murder." There may be good social or symbolic reasons for not killing infants but since the infant cannot claim equal rights with "already functioning persons," such killing is not "fully comparable to the killing of persons in the full sense." Hartshorne extends the same distinction to the killing of "a hopelessly senile person."

One can even grant this argument some plausibility. We do not think as badly of primitive societies that practice infanticide as we do of those that practice human sacrifice. We do not think as badly of societies that put their burdensome old folks on ice floes as we do of those that regularly slaughter adults in warfare. But that does not mean we want to slide merrily back to that state of things. People who are angered by glib talk of the "truly needy" cannot rest easy with the recent discovery of the distinction between the human and the "truly human."

In the light of prochoice rhetoric and prochoice principles, for many liberal Catholics the oversimplifications and insensitivities of the right-to-life movement no longer loom as large as they once did. But liberal Catholics still remain betwixt and between. On the one hand, they are "personally" opposed to almost all abortion and further reject the idea that abortion-on-demand be accepted as the social norm. On the other hand, they are unhappy with the right-to-life alternative, a constitutional amendment declaring all unborn life inviolable from conception.

If liberal Catholics are going to make a difference in the struggle over abortion, there are two steps they must take. Each involves a break with one or the other side, at least as the dispute is now constituted.

The first step is to give up the idea that this issue can be resolved without legislative restriction on abortion. I have in mind various "compromise" positions that some liberal Catholics have found attractive. In one version, for instance, abortion is to be condemned by the churches (but not too harshly) and deplored by the culture. In a second version, extensive social efforts to assure job opportunities and provide child care are added to cultural disapprobation in order to encourage the pregnant woman to carry her child. In no case is abortion finally disallowed for any woman who seeks it, nor funding for abortion denied any woman who needs it.

The psychological assumption behind these schemes is that women naturally find abortion so painful and morally ambiguous that a religious or cultural reminder—or the provision of real support for childbearing and child-rearing—will suffice to dissuade from abortion almost all but the genuinely tragic cases. This psychological assumption, I suspect, may be a projection of the moral and generative sensitivities of those who make the argument. What they assume is quite likely true of most women; what they are unwilling to face is the strong evidence that millions of women simply do not feel this way. Instinctive rejection of abortion does not prevent them from returning, perhaps with regret, though often, too, with a good deal of self-righteousness, for one, two, three abortions. And while equal life opportunities for women—and vastly strengthened social supports for child-raising—are a crying need quite apart from the abortion question, it is hard to imagine any such system that could move either the trivially motivated woman or the seriously burdened and tested one to prefer lifelong responsibilities to a clinic visit and a ten-minute procedure.

What merit there is in these schemes rests on the hope that psychological or social incentives can allow cultural disapprobation of abortion to coexist with a completely noncoercive legal treatment of it. Whether other societies have been capable of maintaining a strong disapproval of some practice without in any way institutionalizing that disapproval in law or social sanctions, I don't know. This society certainly is not. These days our pluralism itself, combined with the pressures of a homogenized national culture, results in the boundaries of morality being largely marked out by the boundaries of the law. To believe that this society can effectively insist on the value of fetal life while refusing to restrict legislatively any assault that a woman may choose on that value, is to indulge in sociological fantasy. Preachment will gradually fall in line with practice.

"Would you then use the law to *force* a woman to carry through a pregnancy to term?" That is the challenge liberal Catholics must be willing to face if they are to make any difference at all in the moral controversy. Their answer will have to be "Yes." Not for every pregnancy (we'll get to that), but for many pregnancies, yes.

Giving that answer will not be easy, especially for Catholic feminists, both male and female. They are justifiably alert to see in any legal coercion of women not the restraints that all members of a reasonable society must submit to, but an extension of the special fetters and disabilities that have historically been inflicted on women. All the more so since pregnancy is not a condition that affects men except indirectly. And sharing a struggle on so many other fronts, Catholic feminists will be loath to break with allies on this point. Nonetheless that is exactly what they will have to do if their often stated opposition to abortion-on-demand is not to equal a mere verbal protestation.

If the first step requires liberal Catholics to disagree frankly with the prochoice forces, the second step requires them to do the same with the prolife movement. Anti-abortionists may be divided on what exceptions to tolerate in a ban on abortion, but they are virtually united on insisting that conception is the decisive moment which should trigger the law's protective shield. Thus the two alternatives: *Roe v. Wade* or a constitutional amendment prohibiting abortion at every stage.

The prudential argument against such an amendment has been made—that it so far departs from public opinion as to risk nonenforcement, bringing the law into disrepute while putting abortion itself into a shadow area where grave abuses are likely to occur. The historical test case is Prohibition.

This prudential argument is impressive. . . . It is unlikely that a human life amendment would pass; if it somehow passed, it would create martyrs who would find ready public sympathy. The end result would be the certain identification of the prolife impulse with heartless coercion.

Blocking the search for another solution, however, has been the anti-abortion movement's insistence that there can be no compromise on a matter of human life. . . . To accept anything but a nearly total ban on abortion would be to surrender the very principle of human life at stake and to become complicit with an evil program of extermination. It would be like going halfway with Hitler—a Semi-Final Solution, the right-to-lifers might say bitterly.

It is at this point, I believe, that liberal Catholics must intervene. They must say quite frankly that *the moral status of the fetus in its early development is a genuinely difficult problem.* It is so *of its nature,* as a unique and boundary-line situation, and not because of the blindness or self-interest of those examining the problem.

It should be understood exactly what kind of a challenge this is, and is not, to the dominant position of the right-to-life movement. Just as the prochoice movement seems utterly oblivious to biology in discussing (when it does) the issue of "humanhood," the right-to-life movement is naively overconfident in its belief that the existence of a unique "genetic package" from conception onwards settles the abortion issue. Yes, it does prove that what is involved is a human individual and not "part of the mother's body." It does not prove that, say, a twenty-eight-day-old embryo, approximately the size of this parenthesis (—), is *then and there* a creature with the same claims to preservation and protection as a newborn or an adult.

I am *not* saying that the anti-abortion argument, with its appeal to potentiality, is untrue. In many respects, I find it persuasive. But it is much less persuasive than most anti-abortionists themselves believe. The theologians and philosophers among them have always recognized these difficulties—and fall back on taking the "safer" course in case of uncertainty.

Argument in this area always proceeds by analogy. We analogize from the end of life to the beginning of it. We analogize from the potentiality of an infant or a sleeping person or someone in a reversible coma to the potentiality of the unborn. We analogize from the physical structure and organic integrity of an adult to that of an embryo or fetus. We analogize from the uncertainty of a hunter who doesn't know whether that moving creature in the bushes is a child or a dangerous animal to the uncertainty we face contemplating the unborn life. Philosophers defending abortion have resorted to the most fantastic analogies yet—"thought experiments" involving Martians, violin players mysteriously hooked without permission to someone's circulatory system, or kittens injected with a chemical so that they develop human brains.

All of these analogies are meant to bring what is obscure and unique into the realm of the visible and more familiar (although one doubts that the last category accomplishes this). But all fall short in this effort, some much farther than others. We are left with a large area where we feel our way, relying on imagination, intuition, and a sense of appropriateness as much as on logic. Although it is not *logically* impossible, for example, to consider the great number of fertilized eggs that fail to implant themselves in the uterus as lost "human beings," a great many people find this idea totally incredible. Similarly, very early miscarriage does not usually trigger the sense of loss and grief that later miscarriage does. Can we take these instinctive responses as morally helpful?

The debate about fetal life always reminds me—I swear—of a Dr. Seuss story called *Horton Hears a Who*. The protective elephant, Horton, rescues a civilization of tiny creatures (the "Who") in a series of wild stanzas each ending with the refrain, "A person's a person no matter how small!" But the endangered creatures Horton saves are, of course, exact but minuscule versions of people—at least grown Dr. Seuss people. I have the impression that the clarity of the anti-abortionists' position rests on an image like that—a homunculus, or at least a microscopic baby, inhabiting not the head of the sperm as in medieval lore but the changing shape of the embryo and fetus. It is such an image that provides the emotional force for analogies to Herod's massacre of the innocents or Hitler's extermination of the Jews.

Such an analogy as the latter—whatever else may be said about its uses and abuses—springs from a neglect of biology as great as that of prochoice advocates who claim the fetus is "part of the mother." It is simply *not* the case that a refusal to recognize Albert Einstein and Anne Frank as human beings deserving of full legal rights is equivalent to a refusal to see the same status in a disc the size of a period or an embryo one-sixth of an inch long and with barely rudimentary features. The old theories of delayed animation and "formed" and "unformed" fetuses may have been based on bad biology. But it seems to me they were also based on a powerful intuition: that what a thing really is corresponds somehow to an overall physical configuration. Thus Dr. Maurice Mahoney of Yale's medical school, who is surely aware of the "genetic package" argument, testifies, "For me, humanness requires that some process of development has taken place which gives the embryo a human form, so that it has a nervous system, a heart and circulatory apparatus, and indications of human shape."

As a Catholic confronting this question, I am not, to be sure, an isolated moral ponderer. Popes, episcopal conferences (Belgium, Italy, Switzerland, Scandinavia, Germany, Quebec, the United States, France), and theologians have reached a remarkable consensus on the obligation to protect human life from its earliest stages. I am impressed not only with the multiple sources of this agreement but with the general moral sensitivity to related social questions that marks many of these statements. I cannot, however, expect my fellow citizens to appreciate the weight of this testimony as I might. Perhaps someday a combination of philosophical argument, moral credibility gained on other issues, and behavior that proclaims the sanctity of human life at every stage could persuade the majority of Americans to accept the current anti-abortion position. At the present time, I believe the force of differing moral intuitions should be recognized. Liberal Catholics who oppose abortion-on-demand should strive for the protection of unborn life not from conception but from that point when not one but a whole series of arguments and indicators have converged to support the "humanness" of the unborn.

The goal, in sum, should be the prohibition of abortion after eight weeks of development. At this point, when the embryo is now termed a fetus, all organs are present that will later be developed fully, the heart has been pumping for a month; the unborn individual has a distinctly human appearance, responds to stimulation of its nose or mouth, and is over an inch in size. Electrical activity in its brain is now discernible. As Jerome Lejeune noted before a Senate hearing, at this point "with a good magnifier the fingerprints could be detected. Every document is available for a national identity card."

The argument is not that this is the "magic moment" when "human life begins." The argument is rather that this is one moment when an accumulation of evidence should compel a majority, even in a pluralist society and despite whatever obscurities about early life continue to be debated, to agree that the unborn individual now deserves legal protection. After this point, abortion could be permitted only for the most serious reasons: endangerment of the mother's life or risk of her incapacitation. "Mental" illness (likelihood of suicide or institutionalization) should not be disallowed as though it were not "real," but the decision-making mechanism has to be one of assured integrity because such indications are undeniably more subjective.

Such should be the minimum national policy, established if necessary by constitutional amendment. States should have the freedom to enact stricter restrictions if they chose. Thus the debate about life from conception would not be foreclosed.

What, in practice, would such a prohibition accomplish? On the face of it, it would prevent fewer than half the current abortions. The 1977 figures showed 50 percent of abortions taking place before the end of the eighth week. Another 25 percent or so take place in the next two weeks— and the pressure of a legal time limit would probably mean many of these would be obtained earlier. Still, to those who believe, as I do, that later abortion is a greater evil and a much greater challenge to our standards of protection for human life, such a measure would make a great difference.

Such a measure would also *lead*, not follow, public opinion. It would be a decisive step back from *Roe v. Wade*, and it would put the lie to the notion that widespread abortion is an inevitable part of modern "progress." By declaring the legal inviolability of the greater part of fetal life, and by leaving open to states the possibility of defending the rest, such a prohibition would be a statement about the seriousness and moral precariousness of abortion at any stage.

Although the notion of a ban on abortion after eight weeks will be rejected and even derided by many anti-abortionists, it is not to convert them that I advance the proposal. Despite their recent gains, it is still the regime of *Roe v. Wade* that we live under. Public opinion and elite opinion-makers are still massively opposed to outlawing abortion from conception—and so fall into line, for want of a rational alternative, behind abortion-on-demand. It is to this audience that the possibility of an alternative must be presented. For liberal Catholics, that means:

- They should take every opportunity to voice, without hesitation or embarrassment, their disagreement with *Roe v. Wade* in liberal milieus, and insist on the need for an alternative that is not so blatantly neglectful of the reality of fetal life.

- If Democrats, they should lobby for the repeal of that party's platform support for abortion and its funding. At the same time, they should make it clear that they utterly reject the belief of some centrist and conservative Democrats that the party should draw back on a host of other welfare-and-human-services commitments.

- Finally, they should find a way to articulate the kind of prohibition suggested here in legal form and have it entered into the lists in Congress.

We cannot rest with the two alternatives of *Roe v. Wade* or a ban on all abortion from the time of conception; the former is morally intolerable; the latter, politically and socially impossible. Liberal Catholics cannot let the present dominance of those alternatives be an excuse for abdication.

THE PRIMACY OF CARING

DANIEL CALLAHAN

I n thinking about health priorities, we would do well to remind ourselves of a point long made, well supported, and yet routinely neglected: The most important health gains up until very recently were those that came from aiming at the health of groups, not that of individuals. The great historical improvements in life expectancy, from the seventeenth through the early twentieth centuries, first came about as a result of better nutrition, sanitation, and general living conditions. With this phase was born the idea of public health and preventive medicine. I will call that the "first phase." The next most important set of gains, from the late nineteenth through the mid-twentieth centuries, came about with the virtual conquest of infectious disease by means of vaccinations and antibiotics. This can be called the "second phase." Thereafter, as we have come to know, other improvements—surgical techniques, intensive care units, improved rehabilitation, organ transplants—have made some contribution. But this, the "third phase," has been accompanied by an increase in chronic disease and illness, particularly accompanying longer life expectancies: Cancer, heart disease, stroke, and the various dementias are the obvious examples of that. Combined with an aging population, this last cluster of conditions does not promise to give way to rapid solutions. Since they are also predominantly conditions associated with aging, they will in any case almost certainly give way to replacement illnesses, that is, to other diseases, possibly chronic also, that will in turn become the successor marks of old age.

The success of those first two phases and our difficulty with the third suggest some important lessons, of direct bearing on the case for societal priorities. One of them is that health care directed toward the welfare of large groups at risk from common, pervasive, and relatively controllable

---

DANIEL CALLAHAN (1930–), a former executive editor of *Commonweal,* is cofounder and former director of the Hastings Center.

health threats still remains the most effective and relatively inexpensive kind. A healthy environment, including the provision of sanitation and a good diet, makes the most important contribution to the good health of individuals. It is the kind of contribution, moreover, that is not addressed to the uniqueness and idiosyncrasies of individuals, but to their common features. Preventive medicine has the same feature: It is directed in general to that which promotes health for everyone, not for those at risk from some specific ailment. The techniques of the second phase—childhood immunization, on the one hand, and the use of antibiotics to cope with infections, on the other—turn out to have the same characteristics. They are directed to generic health hazards to which we are all comparatively subject, not to those less common, more idiosyncratic conditions not well or fully addressed by general public-health measures or social and environmental responses.

The health hazards that have been so effectively dealt with by such means all spring, as a rough generalization, from external, exogenous threats and conditions—for example, environment, diet, lifestyle, hostile bacteria, and viruses. They affect all individuals in relatively similar ways and pose comparable hazards to all individuals. The difficulties that we face, by contrast, with the chronic illnesses that now dominate health care—schizophrenia, Alzheimer's, cancer, heart disease, stroke, multi-organ failure—are in many important respects different. While it is true that we will not know in advance those to which we might personally be predisposed or vulnerable, they are not a general threat to all individuals, but threats much conditioned by genetic and other individually unique features. Many of them, most importantly, correlate heavily though not exclusively with aging. Our success in keeping people alive through their childhood and into their adult years means an increased risk for the chronic illnesses of later life.

What are the possible policy implications of that historical trend? Perhaps simple and ultimately inexpensive treatments (or prevention regimens) will someday be found for those diseases and conditions that most characteristically pick on individuals in their individuality. That is possible. Yet to make that kind of hope the foundation of policy and spending—to act and spend *as if* it must happen—is exceedingly unwise. It is a mistake to assume that the kinds of successes characteristic of earlier medical history will necessarily be repeated in the future. That so many of the most difficult conditions are associated with aging means also that, given human nature itself, the ragged edge of aging will most likely *always* and *necessarily* generate new debilitating and lethal conditions to replace those earlier reduced or eradicated. Even if, under the most optimistic possibility, there is an eventual "compression of morbidity" (a shorter period of illness prior to death in old age), there could still be frantic efforts at that diminishing ragged edge to extend life and defeat death. In any event, death always wins. To constantly invoke the success of the past to justify research on the remaining health agenda is not only costly, but increasingly so. There is also no certain likelihood, much less guarantee, of success. The reality of aging makes it certain, in fact, that it must sooner or later fail in some fundamental ways.

What can we conclude? When we look at health care from the perspective I have sketched here, a number of conclusions can be drawn. The first is that the greatest benefit the health-care system can bestow is to focus its efforts on those approaches that historically constituted what I have called the first two phases. That means focusing on the population as a whole, not beginning with the special needs of individuals.

The second conclusion is that the system promotes the greatest societal benefit by that focus at the lowest possible cost per person. A health-care system that provided *nothing* other than sanitation, good food, a decently clean environment, childhood immunization, antibiotics, and trauma care would already have done enough to assure that the majority of its citizens could carry out their societal roles. The more the system attends to individual needs not met by basic public-health measures and primary health care, the more it guarantees an ever-larger agenda and ever-higher costs, and especially as the curative research agenda gravitates, as it has, to conditions affecting the individual lives of the elderly. A society may move on beyond that point, but there is no compelling reason to think it must do so. A society cannot be said to owe its citizens the pursuit of every medical possibility to meet every curative need, much less when the possibilities of doing so are endless.

The third conclusion is that it is much easier to morally justify, and even demand, a strong societal role in providing that kind of basic care. It benefits in principle everyone more or less equally. . . . It has the supreme advantage that it provides a very general benefit, one in itself sufficient to meet the most important societal need for health. And it admits of limits, for we already can, at a reasonable and circumscribed cost, provide that level of health care without inherently limitless expenditures—particularly if we accept the fact that, while it will not achieve good health for all, it will achieve good health for a sufficient number to carry out the main functions of society.

Exactly the opposite is true in the quest to meet individual curative need. It will not be possible for us to meet such need, no matter how hard we try or how far research advances, or to pay the costs of such a crusade, one ever doomed to fail on one ragged edge or another. But we can, as individuals, make a solid claim for a health-care system that provides for the general health of society, of which we are a part. Our claim is simply this and no more: We cannot endure together as a people without a sufficient level of health care for the community as a whole. That claim establishes the moral foundation for a system of universal health care, while at the same time limiting our claim for individual cure.

It is striking, moreover, that the progress of the historical first phase—nutrition and sanitation, most decisive for longevity—is far more a reflection of social and living conditions than of medical conditions. It is no less striking that the second historical phase was achieved through (*a*) concern, not with individual welfare as such, but with the damage done to groups by infectious disease, especially epidemics; and (*b*) basic biological knowledge, pertinent to human beings in their common features rather than in their particularity. This is not to deny that something similar may one day turn out to be true of many chronic diseases of the third phase; it is just not as likely.

If our health-care system (and the social system of which it is a part) did nothing more than keep the conditions of the first two phases in good working order, it would ensure long and healthy lives for the majority of the population. If it only did that, and nothing more, it would be an adequate health-care system for any nation.

Yet that is likely to seem too stringent a standard, not only because a country might be able to afford more, but also because it would leave as a residue some significant problems for particular groups within the population. They fall into two categories. One of them is made up of the health problems that the advances of the first two phases do not fully respond to: accidents, genetically induced illnesses not wholly amenable to behavioral or societal eradication, mental illness, and other conditions that tend to lead to premature though not necessarily early deaths or to a high probability of a life of suffering and disability. The other category is made up of the "third-phase" chronic illnesses and disabilities, especially those that increase in incidence with age, becoming especially pronounced in old age.

What priority should we give these additional categories? My argument is that, once society has provided the baseline of preventive care and public health I have so far sketched, it has done most of what ought

morally to be required of it. With one critical exception—that of providing care (not cure) for each individual in all of his or her individuality—it may consider other health services morally optional and set them
aside, if necessary, in the name of other legitimate social goods. But to
make that case and to argue for the primacy of caring, I must now move
from the bottom up, coming back to the individual.

What kind of claim can we make as individuals in all of our individuality? A good society ought to respond to that individuality. It will be a
fearful and threatening one if it does not. We will simply be anonymous,
replaceable parts. Writ large, our mutual and shared response to the
suffering of others is what makes the difference between merely well-
functioning society and a decent and humane one. It is what is con-
ducive to the devising of a rewarding and supportive society, showing us
that our existence as identifiable persons, regardless of our economic or
societal worth to the collective whole, has a central place. Yet if we cannot guarantee the individual unlimited medical cure of disease, the
meeting of all individual curative needs, then what alternative is there to
find that central place for the individual? To get at that question, let me
see if I can bring to the surface the basic impulse that seems to lie behind
our concern for each other in our sickness and disability, and then go beyond that to the provision of health care through the government.

To be sick is to be vulnerable. If we are sick enough, we usually look
to others for help. We turn to them, they turn to us. Do we, in some
sense, owe it to our neighbor to see that he or she has access to health
care, or should we see it only as an act of charity or benevolence, not
strictly required but expressive of our moral feelings? The answer to that
question is unclear, for much will depend upon just what is being asked
of us. In a general way, however, there is an almost universal sentiment
in developed countries that there is some kind of mutual obligation to
provide care. What is its basis? It is undoubtedly our shared sense that we
cannot, alone or on our own, cope with the ravages of illness and death,
even though they are our most private of experiences. We need the help
of others, and the provision of health care can be understood as an expression of a need for solidarity in our common plight. The important
question is not only how we might justify this sense of solidarity, if we assume that justification is needed, but how we choose to articulate it and
to encompass it within the social and political systems.

What is it about the sickness of our fellow human beings that most
draws our sympathy and desire to be of help? If we can understand that,

we have a basis for both the solidarity and for its embodiment in a health-care system. I believe that it is, above all, the pain and suffering that most disturb us. This is something we can empathize with, sharing as we all do some occasions of pain. We may not know what it is like to suffer a heart attack if we have not had one, but we can understand what it is to feel pain, to experience a desperate shortage of breath, to suffer anxiety and fear. We respond most immediately and directly to that kind of pain and suffering, and it may be the most common and universal impulse behind the drive to help those who are ill. It is more difficult to appreciate so directly the thwarting of other goods and goals that sickness brings to another person—a trip thwarted, a job deferred, for instance. . . . In the case of other goods thwarted by illness, moreover, it is possible in many cases for alternatives to be found (even if a lesser choice), or for the deprivation to be adapted to and tolerated. This is rarely so possible with pain and suffering, whose insistence can be powerful, direct, and destructive of any possibilities of secular redemption.

The pain and suffering of individuals should, for all these reasons, always receive a high priority in the health-care system. They are both essentially private experiences, even though we can often observe their effects. Pain may be defined as a distressing, hurtful sensation in the body. Suffering, by contrast, is a broader, more complex idea. It may be defined, in the case of illness, as a sense of anguish, vulnerability, loss of control, and threat to the integrity of the self. There can be pain without suffering, and suffering without pain. In either case, only I can experience it, and only I can be relieved of it. Of course some degree of pain and suffering can be tolerated, and I do not mean to imply that the relief of *all* pain and suffering would be an appropriate goal for the system. It would not. I am only saying that they are forms of individual need—private, hidden, not directly sharable with others—that most merit our attention and that are most open to our help. It is the vulnerability that illness creates that most requires the response of others. I call that response one of "caring."

The term "caring" has its liabilities. It conveys, for some, sentimentality and softness, a vague ambiance of feeling rather than a systematic effort to make an effective difference. It need not and should not have those connotations. That in itself is symptomatic of the bias toward acute-care, high-technology medicine, with its comfortable presumption that it *does* something for people in contrast to merely holding their hands. Caring might also suggest acting by default; it is then taken to be what we give people if we cannot cure their disease or change their condition, a kind of consolation prize.

That is a biased understanding. Caring can best be understood as a positive emotional and supportive response to the condition and situation of another person, a response whose purpose is to affirm our commitment to their well-being, our willingness to identify with them in their pain and suffering, and our desire to do what we can to relieve their situation. . . .

The caring response can take two related forms. One of them is constituted by the attitudes and personal traits we bring to bear—our concern, sensitivity, dedication, and steadfast patience, for example. The other is the way we socially structure our response: by organizing institutional support when needed, a support oriented toward the provision of comfort and security, assisting the patient to accommodate to his or her situation in some structured way. To care for someone is to give him or her our time, attention, sympathy, and whatever social help we can muster to make the situation bearable and, if not bearable, at least one that never leads to abandonment, the greatest of all medical evils. Caring should always take priority over curing for the most obvious of reasons: There is never any certainty that our illnesses can be cured or our death averted. Eventually they will, and must, triumph. Our victories over sickness and death are always temporary, but our need for support, for caring, in the face of them is always permanent.

Is there not something anachronistic, even archaic, about urging the priority of caring over curing? Does that not undo the very point of scientific medicine, that of finding cures for illness rather than settling for care? Not at all.

The primary assurance we all require is that we will be cared for in our sickness regardless of the likelihood of cure. Of course it is important for the health-care system as a whole to know how it can prevent disease, and to know what it might do to cure it once individuals are afflicted. But above all it must be prepared to support and minister to people in their vulnerability to sickness and death, which can only be reduced, never vanquished. That is the one assurance we must all have from our fellow citizens and human beings. The greatest failure of contemporary health care is that it has tended to overlook this point, has become distracted from it by the glamour of cure and the war against illness and death.

At the center of caring should be a commitment never to avert its eyes from, or wash its hands of, someone who is in pain or is suffering, who is disabled or incompetent, who is retarded or demented; that is the most fundamental demand made upon us. It is also the one commitment a health-care system can almost always make to everyone, the one need that it can reasonably meet. When the individual need for cure is infinite in its possibilities, the need for caring is much more finite—there is always something we can do for each other. The possibilities of caring are, in that respect, far more self-contained than the possibilities of curing. That is also why their absence is inexcusable.

We might look at caring more closely by attending to the three basic human needs: the need to exist, the need to think and feel, and the need to function (to act in the world). The threat of death is the most obvious, and extreme, instance of danger to our need to exist. In most people, that threat evokes fear and dread. Even though many seem, in their dying, to be able to accept it, the passage from life to death must stand as the center of the drama of human fate. It is that passage, more than the inconceivable situation of actually being dead, that most grips the imagination, most presses us back upon and into ourselves. As the ultimate form of separation from the human community, those undergoing the passage most need the company and care of others, to keep them socially in the community until the last possible moment, to assure them that they will not be forgotten, that the death of their body will not be preceded by the death of their social self, pushed out of sight and out of mind by fearful medical workers or families. The great value of the hospice movement is its contribution to the care of the dying and to opening up, once again, the possibility of accepting illness and death in an affirmative way.

Consider also our need to think and to feel. In the most extreme cases, those suffering from severe mental illness, dementia, or retardation can seem well beyond caring, so cut off from others that they appear irrevocably trapped within themselves. Care for them can seem useless, yet because there is no clear certainty about what it means to the victim of a severe pathology of mind or emotions, their care becomes important as a way of binding them to the community, a way of treating them with dignity, of recognizing the humanity remaining, however hidden or distorted. For those with lesser conditions, burdened by anxiety, or with distortions of affect, or with mild retardation or dementia, they need the care of others to function in the world, to have it made a safe place for them.

Something similar is true for the handicapped and physically disabled, thwarted in their need to function. They require the assurance that they will not be cut off from the company of those able to move about and act in the world. They will depend upon others to act for them, to move them from place to place if they are in a wheelchair, to read to them if they are blind, to change their underclothes if they cannot do so for themselves, and, most of all, to accept them as still valuable, still cherished members of society. If they are chronically ill, they may suffer some combination of all these needs; for reassurance in the face of death, for help with the emotional stress of a drawn-out, unending illness, for assistance with the physical tasks, the movement, that may gradually come to be beyond them.

At the center of these needs is the experience of illness, disability, and loss of self-control and self-creation that ordinarily accompanies them. Illness is hostile to the integrity of the self, its sense of being at one with and in direction of itself. Sickness alienates us from ourselves first of all, from the familiar, comfortable, healthy body or mind. It sets us at odds with ourselves, and that alienation can quickly spread to a sense of alienation from others, those who remain among the healthy and the active.

To care for another is to minister to these fears, to supply love and patient fidelity to the anxiety about separation from others. It is to assure another that they remain important to others, that their illness has not deprived them of a life in the community. It is to ease their pain where possible, and then to help them live with their frailty, whether of body, mind, or function. To do this effectively requires skill and insight. The continuing failure of medical education to train students to do this well is revealing. It is surely not because the subject has never been mentioned in discussions of curriculum reform. It has been a perennial topic, but it always loses out to an emphasis on scientific knowledge and technical skills, and there is no end in sight to that bias. . . .

Caring is just not the trait that is emphasized for physicians the way medical knowledge is. The technical skills they deploy are impersonal, directed to organ and system failures, not to the particularities of individual suffering. The ability to care requires a capacity to acknowledge our own mortality and our common vulnerability, as well as to understand the privacy and hiddenness of much pain and suffering in others, an understanding that requires imagination. We are all fellow patients or potential patients, doctors and laypeople alike; that should never be forgotten. The medical educational system has fitfully tried, by rhetoric and exhortation, to bring caring back to the center of medicine. That can hardly work when the enterprise itself is so decisively oriented toward cure, toward aggressive action, toward mastery of the body. That bias pushes, and must push, care to the side. Care will only become central if, and when, medicine shifts its goals and ends.

If the center of caring is the way we respond to another as an individual person, a way of being with that person in all of his or her uniqueness, then its effective manifestation requires institutions, accommodating social structures, and a society prepared to make room for those it cannot cure or return to "productive" life. For the dying, the need may be for that of an institutional hospice, for a solid home-care program, for the kind of psychological and social counseling necessary to ease the passage from life to death—which may be true for the family as well as the dying person. The family may on occasion require legal assistance, and sometimes the help of social workers in trying to hold itself together in the face of the death of one of its members. For the mentally ill, or retarded, or the elderly demented person, institutional care will be necessary in the most severe cases, and good programs of home care for those not quite so badly off. In still milder cases, counseling of family members may be needed, and vocational help. For the functioning of the disabled, their families will need technical training and psychological counseling to understand how to do what they must do, and how to live with the enormous pressures that being a caretaker can entail. Programs of occupational therapy will be required, as well as a range of community services, most of them going well beyond the narrowly medical.

Again, I need not fill in the details of these familial and institutional needs. However intricate and elaborately structured such institutions may be, the provision of caring of that kind is within the range of finite possibility. A decent, if not perfect, job could be done. I am not claiming that it is inexpensive. It is not. I am also not claiming that it would be possible to do everything that might be imagined in the name of caring. Demand could exceed possibility there as well. I am only claiming that caring does not have about it the inherent infinity of possibilities characteristic of that medicine which aims to cure illness and to forestall death. The individual need for caring is more limited, able to be reasonably well-circumscribed in decent social programs and caring individuals.

Where the limitation of curative medicine in the name of the good of the society as a whole—which I believe necessary—courts the danger of an unfeeling utilitarianism, a simultaneous and counterbalancing focus upon individual caring can keep a concern for the individual at the center of the health-care system. Caring is the foundation stone of respect for human dignity and worth upon which everything else should be built. Its presence can be a steady and faithful one even in the inevitable absence of resources to carry forward the open-ended enterprise of cure. It is in caring that we can address the uniqueness of persons, that which makes them different from each other. It is in caring that we can respect the claims and calls of individuality, that we can most show our solidarity with each other. When all else fails, as it eventually must in the lives of all of us, a society that gives a priority to caring in its response to individuals is worthy of praise.

THE DIGNITY OF HELPLESSNESS

RAND RICHARDS COOPER

'm looking for an argument with Jack Kevorkian; or rather, for one against him. Life for Kevorkian lately has come laden with satisfying vindications. Weary prosecutors, having failed to convince three Michigan juries that Kevorkian's eagerness in assisting suicide is a crime, now seem ready to toss in their cards and go home. Once dubbed "Dr. Death" by medical school classmates for his unseemly obsession with terminal illness, the ex-pathologist stands redeemed and embraced as a pioneering American hero. "Jack's doing something that is right," says his lawyer, Geoffrey Fieger. "Everyone instinctively understands that—that's why we're winning."

Whatever you may feel about Kevorkian personally—and I admit to finding him an unlikely standard-bearer, with his smug and aggressive looniness, for a human dignity movement—you have to admire how deftly he has taken the pulse of the nation's moral reasoning. Kevorkian has put our agonized ambivalence about life-prolonging medical technologies into the rights-based framework of our political discourse, producing a case for assisted suicide that seems unassailable. Its logic goes like this: If I am afflicted, say, with inoperable cancer, and if after discussions with loved ones I decide I would rather die now, in dignity, than a year from now, why shouldn't I have this right? How does my exercising it conceivably impair the rights of any other person?

It doesn't, say the juries who keep acquitting Kevorkian; that's why the government should butt out. Whose death is it, anyway?

As a means of sparing loved ones suffering, assisted suicide expresses our most compassionate urges and motives. Nevertheless, I believe the

RAND RICHARDS COOPER (1958–) is the author of two works of fiction, *The Last to Go* (Harcourt Brace Jovanovich) and *Big As Life* (Dial Press). He has taught at Amherst and at Emerson.

notion of a "right" to die provides far too narrow a framework for discussing the widespread institutionalization of the practice. Talk about rights resonates deeply with Americans. It is our strongest political instinct; our melody and our beat. Other societies stress sacrifice or obedience, glory or passion or style or work, but we always come back to rights. And therein lies the rub. The appeal of rights is so compelling that it leaves scant room for realities and interests not easily expressed as rights. And with assisted suicide that means leaving out way too much.

Consider the predicament of the elderly. Kevorkian pledges himself to "the absolute autonomy of the individual," and insists that practitioners of "obitiatry" (as he proposes calling the new medical specialty) would administer only to those who truly *want* to die. But what exactly is the "absolute autonomy" of an elderly, ailing person convinced he or she is a burden to everyone? I remember how my grandmother, who died a few years ago at ninety-seven, used to lament being a "burden" on the rest of us. "I don't know why I'm still alive," she'd say, sighing. She didn't really mean it; but there's no doubt in my mind that the obitiatric option, had it existed, would have added an extra tinge of guilt to her last couple of years—particularly after she entered a nursing home whose costs began to eat up the savings she and my grandfather had accumulated over decades of thrift. Do we want to do that to our elderly and infirm? How will we prevent the creep toward an increased sense of burdensomeness that the very availability of assisted suicide is likely to cause?

Next, what about creeping changes in the rest of us? In a society in which assisted suicide is a ready option, how will we view those who don't choose it? I'm imagining Ben Jonson's grim sixteenth-century farce, *Volpone,* updated for our time, a circle of heirs crowding round the bedside, impatient for the obitioner. But I'm also thinking about something far subtler, that gradual habituation of mind Tocqueville called the "slow action of society upon itself." Much as we like to imagine otherwise, the truth is that our inventions and our beliefs are implacably dynamic. The things we make turn around and remake us; and just as the Pill helped transform our ideas about sexual freedom, so will the obitioner change the way we regard aging. How often in the assisted-suicide future will someone look at an elderly person and think, consciously or semiconsciously, "Gee, guess it's about time, huh?"

And do we want that?

Such questions find scant place in a discussion that focuses solely on the "autonomous" individual and his "right" to die. That's why I want to take Kevorkianism out of the discussion of individual rights and put it into a discussion of something I'll call, for want of a better phrase, the texture of civic life. By this I mean simply the thoughts we have in our heads about ourselves and one another; the shape and feel of our daily, moment-to-moment relations. Will institutionalizing assisted suicide equip us to be better human beings for each other, or will it unequip us?

When I was twenty I lived for a time in Kenya. One hot afternoon found me at a grade school in Nairobi, helping out at a fair for handicapped children. The event was understaffed, and when after games and lunch the children started having to go to the bathroom, things got hectic. A clamorous line of kids in leg braces and primitive wheelchairs formed outside the single outhouse. They needed help getting in, help going and cleaning up afterward. I did what I could, but I was young and singularly unschooled in this kind of neediness. Vividly I recall a boy of ten who walked with two crutches, dragging useless legs behind him. During the long wait he had defecated in his pants, and as I helped him to the outhouse door I retched, despite myself, at the stench and the stifling heat. Seeing my distress, another organizer, a thirtyish guy named Dennis, picked up the boy and swiftly carried him into the outhouse. I followed, watching as Dennis squatted before the boy, cleaning him with a towel, the boy looking up with a calm and patient expression.

That memory comes back to me whenever an acquaintance of mine—a man in his mid-sixties and in good health—outlines his game plan for old age. For him, goal number one is never, ever to become a helpless burden. "Once I start shitting my pants," he says, "that's it. Take me out and shoot me." I share his dread of becoming vulnerable, dependent, smelly; who doesn't? Yet at the same time I find myself looking back to that moment in the outhouse in Kenya, years ago. Helplessness was there, of course, and burden too, but beauty as well, so much so that I have never forgotten it—the helper and the helped joined in a mutual courage I could only hope some day to possess.

My point is that we experience a profound aspect of our humanity precisely in our intimate and awful knowledge of each other's physical neediness; and further, that what we draw from this knowledge constitutes not only a spiritual good but a social good. If, following the quality-of-life, take-me-out-and-shoot-me principle, we end up using assisted suicide to preempt the infirmities of old age and terminal illness, how well equipped will we be to encounter infirmity elsewhere? How to become fluent in help if we have banished helplessness from our vocabulary? I'm thinking of the way we treat people in wheelchairs, people who can't feed themselves, whose bodies don't look or work "right." Taken together with prenatal genetic testing and selective abortion, might not assisted suicide further a gradual drift toward functionalism in our attitude to life? Societies that drift in this direction, as Germany did under the Nazis, instill in their citizens a visceral sense of the handicapped as a drain or drag on the healthy body of the rest of us: a pointless deformity; an un-luck; an un-person. Such attitudes are not spontaneous manifestations of evil. You have to train people to feel this way; but if you do, they will.

A few years ago, my mother's lifelong best friend died at sixty of lung cancer. The last phase of Gretchen's life involved multiple surgeries, long hospital stays that sapped the will, and the disorienting pressures of pain and medication. For my mother, there was the anguish of watching a person she loved being overwhelmed by illness—an especially hard kind of sorrow. ("She's not there anymore," my mother would say after a bad visit.) But then came moments of joy—a visit or a phone call or a handwritten note in which, suddenly, Gretchen was there again, emerging by some grace from the fog of her illness to share with my mother an affirmation of how much they had loved and enjoyed each other through the decades of their friendship.

My mother has a bulletin board in her kitchen where she tacks up cards, favorite maxims, snapshots, and the like. But she doesn't display the last few notes she got from Gretchen. Instead, she keeps them taped to the inside of a cabinet high over the stove. I suspect they are still too highly charged for her; too much suffering and beauty attach to them.

Gretchen's illness is the kind on which Kevorkianism makes its core appeal—a remorseless, irreversible disease that steals a person from us bit by bit. Assisted suicide offers a way, in effect, to manage death so that it arrives before this insidious larceny has begun. As such it is an attempt to do people dignity—and our memories of them, too—by enabling them to go out whole. It's an option I imagine Gretchen might well have availed herself of; my mother, for her part, came away from her friend's death with a firm belief in the rightness of assisted suicide.

And yet I think about those notes in her cabinet. It's hard to say this, but I believe that part of what makes them so profoundly meaningful to my mother is that they came from such a dark and pressured place, where Gretchen was not always the "same" Gretchen she had known. Finding her way back from that place to write those notes fashioned an understanding of courage which my mother carries with her today: the last of Gretchen's many gifts to her.

One needs to tread very softly here. Taken to extremes, the notion of a vested interest in each other's suffering becomes barbaric; and I don't want anyone to think I'm questioning the correctness of relieving misery and pain. In fact, it's not assisted suicide per se I'm questioning, which in other forms has long been practiced unofficially by physicians informing the gravely ill about lethal doses, turning off ventilators to "let nature take its course," and so on. It's the institutionalizing of the practice I'm wondering about, and its effect on our relation to the *idea* of suffering. If we make assisted suicide widely available, will we end up virtually eliminating that phase of life in which people are not whole, "not there"? If so, will we be a better, richer, more humane society for having done so?

I'm aware many will consider this a pernicious basis for discussing the legality of assisted suicide. The notion that our laws should promote virtues as well as protect rights is anathema to modern American political thought. But the idea of rights alone can't capture the complexity of our connectedness to one another, and anyone who insists exclusively on them can end up sounding weirdly hollow. It is the hollowness, in fact, of Jack Kevorkian himself. I watched him not long ago on *60 Minutes*. Asked by Mike Wallace to discuss the ethics of abortion—he is vehemently prochoice—Kevorkian mulled it over for a moment, then responded in this way: "The autonomy of the fetus can never supersede the autonomy of the mother." Whatever you may think of Kevorkian, or of abortion, I think you'll agree that these are exceptionally arid terms with which to encounter complex human dilemmas. But in purest form they are the terms of rights.

Current debates about welfare reform, about drug policy, violence on TV, the legality of youth curfews and school uniforms: all suggest a growing urge in America, across the political spectrum, to move beyond *laissez-faire* liberalism—what political theorist Michael J. Sandel has called our modern "aspiration to neutrality"—toward some vision of the good. Whether you call this impulse communitarianism, republicanism, statecraft as soulcraft, or a concern for civic texture, what it means is making connections not only between laws and rights, but between laws and character—the kind and quality of citizen that laws inevitably help produce. Where does assisted suicide fit in? Is it possible that accompanying and consoling those we love through grievous terminal illness constitutes one of the core experiences we need to have? That part of us, some quality of pity and compassion and terror and love, is reachable only by taking that awful journey? And if so, does the law have a role to play? Should laws, can laws, have a stake in our complexity—in the quality of our togetherness as well as the fact of our separateness?

For the last few months of her very long life, my grandmother lay in a nursing home, floating in and out of consciousness, largely unable to eat. She wasn't in pain, but clearly she no longer possessed the active, vigorous perception which I believe institutionalizing assisted suicide may ultimately lead us to establish as the bottom-line criterion for meaningful life among the aged and the ill. For my part, I'd been fearing my visits to her, worrying that these last images of her, diminished and helpless, would later greedily elbow out other, happier memories. But this fear proved groundless. As it turns out, even those deeply unsettling moments when she looked more dead than alive and I barely recognized her, or when she unexpectedly squeezed my hand, as if sending a last, bodily message from some strange place between being and not-being—all of that forms part of the story of my grandmother that I carry with me; and I feel I am the richer for all of it, endowed with a more expansive vocabulary of body and spirit; and also a more intimate acquaintance with death, in all its mystery and terribleness.

Anyone who has accompanied someone through a terminal illness knows the solitariness of mortality—"the unknown," wrote English poet Edward Thomas shortly before his own death in World War I, "I must enter, and leave, alone." A sense of this deep privacy drives the right-to-die movement in America today. And yet to step outside the rights framework is to ask how institutionalizing assisted suicide will affect not only those who die, but those who live on; not only individuals, but society. The fact is, our deaths are both solo journeys toward an ultimate mystery and strands in the tapestries of each other's lives. Which side of this reality will we emphasize? Whose death is it, anyway? The debate about assisted suicide should begin at the place where that question ceases to be a rhetorical one.

WHY DOCTORS MUST NOT KILL

LEON R. KASS

So you want your doctor licensed to kill? Should he or she be permitted or encouraged to inject or prescribe poison? Shall the mantle of privacy that protects the doctor-patient relationship, in the service of life and wholeness, now also cloak decisions for death? Do you want *your* doctor deciding, on the basis of his own private views, when you still deserve to live and when you now deserve to die? And what about the other fellow's doctor—that shallow technician, that insensitive boor who neither asks nor listens, that unprincipled money-grubber, that doctor you used to go to until you got up the nerve to switch: do you want *him* licensed to kill? Speaking generally, shall the healing profession become also the euthanizing profession?

Common sense has always answered, "No." For more than two millennia, the reigning medical ethic, mindful that the power to cure is also the power to kill, has held as an inviolable rule, "Doctors must not kill." Yet this venerable taboo is now under attack. Proponents of euthanasia and physician-assisted suicide would have us believe that it is but an irrational vestige of religious prejudice, alien to a true ethic of medicine, which stands in the way of a rational and humane approach to suffering at the end of life. Nothing could be further from the truth. The taboo against doctors killing patients (even on request) is the very embodiment of reason and wisdom. Without it, medicine will have trouble doing its proper work; without it, medicine will have lost its claim to be an ethical and trustworthy profession; without it, all of us will suffer—yes, more than we now suffer because some of us are not soon enough released from life.

Consider first the damaging consequences for the doctor-patient relationship. The patient's trust in the doctor's wholehearted devotion to the

---

LEON R. KASS, M.D. (1939–), is Addie Clark Harding Professor for the College and the Committee on Social Thought at the University of Chicago.

patient's best interests will be hard to sustain once doctors are licensed to kill. Imagine the scene: you are old, poor, in failing health, and alone in the world; you are brought to the city hospital with fractured ribs and pneumonia. The nurse or intern enters late at night with a syringe full of yellow stuff for your intravenous drip. How soundly will you sleep? It will not matter that your doctor has never yet put anyone to death; that he is legally entitled to do so will make a world of difference.

And it will make a world of psychic difference too for conscientious physicians. How easily will they be able to care wholeheartedly for patients when it is always possible to think of killing them as a "therapeutic option"? Shall it be penicillin and a respirator one more time, or, perhaps, this time just an overdose of morphine? Physicians get tired of treating patients who are hard to cure, who resist their best efforts, who are on their way down—"gorks," "gomers," and "vegetables" are only some of the less than affectionate names they receive from the house officers. Won't it be tempting to think that death is the best "treatment" for the little old lady "dumped" again on the emergency room by the nearby nursing home?

It is naive and foolish to take comfort from the fact that the currently proposed change in the law provides "aid-in-dying" only to those who request it. For we know from long experience how difficult it is to discover what we truly want when we are suffering. Verbal "requests" made under duress rarely reveal the whole story. Often a demand for euthanasia is, in fact, an angry or anxious plea for help, born of fear of rejection or abandonment, or made in ignorance of available alternatives that could alleviate pain and suffering. Everyone knows how easy it is for those who control the information to engineer requests and to manipulate choices, especially in the vulnerable. Paint vividly a horrible prognosis, and contrast it with that "gentle, quick release": which will the depressed or frightened patient choose, especially in the face of a spiraling hospital bill or children who visit grudgingly? Yale Kamisar asks the right questions: "Is this the kind of choice, assuming that it can be made in a fixed and rational manner, that we want to offer a gravely ill person? Will we not sweep up, in the process, some who are not really tired of life, but think others are tired of them; some who do not really want to die, but who feel that they should not live on, because to do so when there looms the legal alternative of euthanasia is to do a selfish or cowardly act? Will not some feel an obligation to have themselves 'eliminated' in order that funds allocated for their terminal care might be better used by their families or, financial worries aside, in order to relieve their families of the emotional strain involved?"

Euthanasia, once legalized, will not remain confined to those who freely and knowingly elect it—and the most energetic backers of euthanasia do not really want it thus restricted. Why? Because the vast majority of candidates who merit mercy killing cannot request it for themselves: adults with persistent vegetative state or severe depression or senility or aphasia or mental illness or Alzheimer's disease; infants who are deformed; and children who are retarded or dying. All incapable of requesting death, they will thus be denied our new humane "assistance-in-dying." But not to worry. The lawyers and the doctors (and the cost-containers) will soon rectify this injustice. The enactment of a law legalizing mercy killing (or assisted suicide) on voluntary request will certainly be challenged in the courts under the equal-protection clause of the Fourteenth Amendment. Why, it will be argued, should the comatose or the demented be denied the right to such a "dignified death" or such a "treatment" just because they cannot claim it for themselves? With the aid of court-appointed proxy consenters, we will quickly erase the distinction between the right to choose one's own death and the right to request someone else's—as we have already done in the termination-of-treatment cases.

Clever doctors and relatives will not need to wait for such changes in the law. Who will be around to notice when the elderly, poor, crippled, weak, powerless, retarded, uneducated, demented, or gullible are mercifully released from the lives their doctors, nurses, and next of kin deem no longer worth living? In Holland, for example, a 1989 survey of 300 physicians (conducted by an author who supports euthanasia) disclosed that over 40 percent had performed euthanasia *without the patient's request,* and over 10 percent had done so in more than five cases. According to the 1991 *Report of the Dutch Government,* over one thousand patients were directly killed by doctors in the previous year, *without their knowledge or consent,* including more than one hundred persons who were fully competent mentally. Is there any reason to believe that the average American physician is, in his private heart, more committed than his Dutch counterpart to the equal worth and dignity of every life under his care? Do we really want to find out what he is like, once the taboo is broken?

Even the most humane and conscientious physician psychologically needs protection against himself and his weaknesses, if he is to care fully for those who entrust themselves to him. A physician-friend who worked many years in a hospice caring for dying patients explained it to me most convincingly: "Only because I knew that I could not and would not kill my patients was I able to enter most fully and intimately into caring for them as they lay dying." The psychological burden of the license to kill (not to speak of the brutalization of the physician-killers) could very well be an intolerably high price to pay for the physician-assisted euthanasia.

The point, however, is not merely psychological: it is also moral and essential. My friend's horror at the thought that he might be tempted to kill his patients, were he not enjoined from doing so, embodies a deep understanding of the medical ethic and its intrinsic limits. We move from assessing consequences to looking at medicine itself.

The beginning of ethics regarding the use of power generally lies in nay-saying. The wise setting of limits on the use of power is based on discerning the excesses to which the power, unrestrained, is prone. Applied to the professions, this principle would establish strict outer boundaries—indeed, inviolable taboos—against those "occupational hazards" to which each profession is especially prone. *Within* these outer limits, no fixed rules of conduct apply; instead, prudence—the wise judgment of the man-on-the-spot—finds and adopts the best course of action in the light of the circumstances. But the outer limits themselves are fixed, firm, and non-negotiable.

What are those limits for medicine? At least three are set forth in the venerable Hippocratic Oath: no breach of confidentiality; no sexual relations with patients; no dispensing of deadly drugs. These unqualified, self-imposed restrictions are readily understood in terms of the temptations to which the physician is most vulnerable, temptations in each case regarding an area of vulnerability and exposure that the practice of medicine requires of patients. Patients necessarily divulge and reveal private and intimate details of their personal lives; patients necessarily expose their naked bodies to the physician's objectifying gaze and investigating hands; patients necessarily expose and entrust the care of their very lives to the physician's skill, technique, and judgment. The exposure is, in all cases, one-sided and asymmetric: the doctor does not reveal his intimacies, display his nakedness, offer up his embodied life to the patient. Mindful of the meaning of such nonmutual exposure, the physician voluntarily sets limits on his own conduct, pledging not to take advantage of or to violate the patient's intimacies, naked sexuality, or life itself.

The prohibition against killing patients, the first negative promise of self-restraint sworn to in the Hippocratic Oath, stands as medicine's first and most abiding taboo: "I will neither give a deadly drug to anybody if asked for it, nor will I make a suggestion to this effect. . . . In purity and holiness I will guard my life and my art." In forswearing the giving of poison, the physician recognizes and restrains a god-like power he wields over patients, mindful that his drugs can both cure and kill. But in forswearing the giving of poison, *when asked for it*, the Hippocratic physician rejects the view that the patient's choice for death can make killing him—or assisting his suicide—right. For the physician, at least, human life in living bodies commands respect and reverence—*by its very nature.* As its respectability does not depend upon human agreement or patient consent, revocation of one's consent to live does not deprive one's living body of respectability. The deepest ethical principle restraining the physician's power is not the autonomy or freedom of the patient; neither is it his own compassion or good intention. Rather, it is the dignity and mysterious power of human life itself, and, therefore, also what the oath calls the purity and holiness of the life and art to which he has sworn devotion. A person can choose to be a physician, but he cannot simply choose what physicianship means.

The central meaning of physicianship derives not from medicine's powers but from its goal, not from its means but from its end: to benefit the sick by the activity of healing. The physician as physician serves only the sick. He does not serve the relatives or the hospital or the national debt inflated due to Medicare costs. Thus he will never sacrifice the well-being of the sick to the convenience or pocketbook or feelings of the relatives or society. Moreover, the physician serves the sick not because they have rights or wants or claims, but because they are sick. The healer works with and for those who need to be healed, in order to help make them whole. Despite enormous changes in medical technique and institutional practice, despite enormous changes in nosology and therapeutics, the center of medicine has not changed: it is as true today as it was in the days of Hippocrates that the ill desire to be whole; that wholeness means a certain well-working of the enlivened body and its unimpaired powers to sense, think, feel, desire, move, and maintain itself; and that the relationship between the healer and the ill is constituted, essentially even if only tacitly, around the desire of both to promote the wholeness of the one who is ailing.

Can wholeness and healing ever be compatible with intentionally killing the patient? Can one benefit the patient as a whole by making him dead? There is, of course, a logical difficulty: how can any good exist for a being that is not? But the error is more than logical: to intend and to act for someone's good requires his continued existence to receive the benefit.

To be sure, certain attempts to benefit may in fact turn out, unintentionally, to be lethal. Giving adequate morphine to control pain might induce respiratory depression leading to death. But the intent to relieve the pain of the living presupposes that the living still live to be relieved. This must be the starting point in discussing all medical benefits: no benefit without a beneficiary.

Against this view, someone will surely bring forth the hard cases: patients so ill-served by their bodies that they can no longer bear to live, bodies riddled with cancer and racked with pain, against which their "owners" protest in horror and from which they insist on being released. Cannot the person "in the body" speak up against the rest, and request death for "personal" reasons?

However sympathetically we listen to such requests, we must see them as incoherent. Such person-body dualism cannot be sustained. "Personhood" is manifest on earth only in living bodies; our highest mental functions are held up by, and are inseparable from, lowly metabolism, respiration, circulation, excretion. There may be blood without consciousness, but there is never consciousness without blood. Thus one who calls for death in the service of personhood is like a tree seeking to cut its roots for the sake of growing its highest fruit. No physician, devoted to the benefit of the sick, can serve the patient as person by denying and thwarting his personal embodiment.

To say it plainly, to bring nothingness is incompatible with serving wholeness: one cannot heal—or comfort—by making nil. The healer cannot annihilate if he is truly to heal. The physician-euthanizer is a deadly self-contradiction.

But we must acknowledge a difficulty. The central goal of medicine—health—is, in each case, a perishable good: inevitably, patients get irreversibly sick, patients degenerate, patients die. Healing the sick is *in principle* a project that must at some point fail. And here is where all the trouble begins: How does one deal with "medical failure"? What does one seek when restoration of wholeness—or "much" wholeness—is by and large out of the question?

Contrary to the propaganda of the euthanasia movement, there is, in fact, much that can be done. Indeed, by recognizing finitude yet knowing that we will not kill, we are empowered to focus on easing and enhancing the *lives* of those who are dying. First of all, medicine can follow the lead of the hospice movement and—abandoning decades of shameful mismanagement—provide truly adequate (and now technically feasible) relief of pain and discomfort. Second, physicians (and patients and families) can continue to learn how to withhold or withdraw those technical interventions that are, in truth, merely burdensome or medical additions to the unhappy end of a life—including, frequently, hospitalization itself. Ceasing treatment and allowing death to occur when (and if) it will seem to be quite compatible with the respect life itself commands for itself. Doctors may and must allow to die, even if they must not intentionally kill.

Ceasing medical intervention, allowing nature to take its course, differs fundamentally from mercy killing. For one thing, death does not necessarily follow the discontinuance of treatment; Karen Ann Quinlan lived more than ten years after the court allowed the "life-sustaining" respirator to be removed. Not the physician, but the underlying fatal illness becomes the true cause of death. More important morally, in ceasing treatment the physician need not *intend* the death of the patient, even when the death follows as a result of his omission. His intention should be to avoid useless and degrading medical *additions* to the already sad end of a life. In contrast, in active, direct mercy killing the physician must, necessarily and indubitably, intend *primarily* that the patient be made dead. And he must knowingly and indubitably cast himself in the role of the agent of death. This remains true even if he is merely an assistant in suicide. A physician who provides the pills or lets the patient plunge the syringe after he leaves the room is *morally* no different from one who does the deed himself. "I will neither give a deadly drug to anybody if asked for it, nor will I make a suggestion to this effect."

Once we refuse the technical fix, physicians and the rest of us can also rise to the occasion: we can learn to act humanly in the presence of finitude. Far more than adequate morphine and the removal of burdensome machinery, the dying need our presence and our encouragement. Dying people are all too easily reduced ahead of time to "thinghood" by those who cannot bear to deal with the suffering or disability of those they love. Withdrawal of contact, affection, and care is the greatest single cause of the dehumanization of dying. Not the alleged humaneness of an elixir of death, but the humanness of connected living-while-dying is what medicine—and the rest of us—most owe the dying. The treatment of choice is company and care.

The euthanasia movement would have us believe that the physician's refusal to assist in suicide or perform euthanasia constitutes an affront to human dignity. Yet one of their favorite arguments seems to me rather to prove the reverse. Why, it is argued, do we put animals out of their misery but insist on compelling fellow human beings to suffer to the bitter end? Why, if it is not a contradiction for the veterinarian, does the medical ethic absolutely rule out mercy killing? Is this not simply inhumane?

Perhaps *inhumane*, but not thereby *inhuman*. On the contrary, it is precisely because animals are not human that we must treat them (merely) humanely. We put dumb animals to sleep because they do not know that they are dying, because they can make nothing of their misery or mortality, and, therefore, because they cannot live deliberately—that is, humanly—in the face of their own suffering and dying. They cannot live out a fitting end. Compassion for their weakness and dumbness is our only appropriate emotion, and given our responsibility for their care and well-being, we do the only humane thing we can. But when a conscious human being asks us for death, by that very action he displays the presence of something that precludes our regarding him as a dumb animal. Humanity is owed humanity, not humaneness. Humanity is owed the bolstering of the human, even or especially in its dying moments, in resistance to the temptation to ignore its presence in the sight of suffering.

What humanity needs most in the face of evils is courage, the ability to stand against fear and pain and thoughts of nothingness. The deaths we most admire are those of people who, knowing that they are dying, face the fact frontally and act accordingly: they set their affairs in order, they arrange what could be final meetings with their loved ones, and yet, with strength of soul and a small reservoir of hope, they continue to live and work and love as much as they can for as long as they can. Because such conclusions of life require courage, they call for our encouragement—and for the many small speeches and deeds that shore up the human spirit against despair and defeat.

Many doctors are in fact rather poor at this sort of encouragement. They tend to regard every dying or incurable patient as a failure, as if an earlier diagnosis or a more vigorous intervention might have avoided what is, in truth, an inevitable collapse. The enormous successes of medicine these past fifty years have made both doctors and laymen less prepared than ever to accept the fact of finitude. Doctors behave, not without some reason, as if they have godlike powers to revive the moribund; laymen expect an endless string of medical miracles. Physicians today are not likely to be agents of encouragement once their technique begins to fail.

It is, of course, partly for these reasons that doctors will be pressed to kill—and many of them will, alas, be willing. Having adopted a largely technical approach to healing, having medicalized so much of the end of life, doctors are being asked—often with thinly veiled anger—to provide a final technical solution for the evil of human finitude and for their own technical failure: If you cannot cure me, kill me. The last gasp of autonomy or cry for dignity is asserted against a medicalization and institutionalization of the end of life that robs the old and the incurable of most of their autonomy and dignity: intubated and electrified, with bizarre mechanical companions, once proud and independent people find themselves cast in the roles of passive, obedient, highly disciplined children. People who care for autonomy and dignity should try to reverse this dehumanization of the last stages of life, instead of giving dehumanization its final triumph by welcoming the desperate goodbye-to-all-that contained in one final plea for poison.

The present crisis that leads some to press for active euthanasia is really an opportunity to learn the limits of the medicalization of life and death and to recover an appreciation of living with and against mortality. It is an opportunity for physicians to recover an understanding that there remains a residual human wholeness—however precarious—that can be cared for even in the face of incurable and terminal illness. Should doctors cave in, should doctors become technical dispensers of death, they will not only be abandoning their posts, their patients, and their duty to care; they will set the worst sort of example for the community at large—teaching technicism and so-called humaneness where encouragement and humanity are both required and sorely lacking. On the other hand, should physicians hold fast, should doctors learn that finitude is no disgrace and that human wholeness can be cared for to the very end, medicine may serve not only the good of its patients, but also, by example, the failing moral health of modern times.

THIS MAN HAS EXPIRED

ROBERT JOHNSON

The death penalty has made a comeback in recent years. In the late sixties and through most of the seventies, such a thing seemed impossible. There was a moratorium on executions in the United States, backed by the authority of the Supreme Court. The hiatus lasted roughly a decade. Coming on the heels of a gradual but persistent decline in the use of the death penalty in the Western world, it appeared to some that executions would pass from the American scene. Nothing could have been further from the truth.

The execution of Gary Gilmore in 1977 marked the resurrection of the modern death penalty and was big news. It was commemorated in a best-selling tome by Norman Mailer, *The Executioner's Song.* The title was deceptive. Like others who have examined the death penalty, Mailer told us a great deal about the condemned but very little about the executioners. Indeed, if we dwell on Mailer's account, the executioner's story is not only unsung; it is distorted.

Gilmore's execution was quite atypical. His was an instance of state-assisted suicide accompanied by an element of romance and played out against a backdrop of media fanfare. Unrepentant and unafraid, Gilmore refused to appeal his conviction. He dared the state of Utah to take his life, and the media repeated the challenge until it became a taunt that may well have goaded officials to action. A failed suicide pact with his lover staged only days before the execution, using drugs she delivered to him in a visit marked by unusual intimacy, added a hint of melodrama to the proceedings. Gilmore's final words, "Let's do it," seemed to invite the lethal hail of bullets from the firing squad. The nonchalant phrase, at once fatalistic and brazenly rebellious, became Gilmore's epitaph. It

---

ROBERT JOHNSON (1948–) is professor of justice, law, and society at the American University, Washington, D.C.

clinched his outlaw-hero image, and found its way onto tee shirts that confirmed his celebrity status.

Gilmore's execution generally, like his parting fête, was decidedly out of step with the tenor of the modern death penalty. Most condemned prisoners fight to save their lives, not to have them taken. They . . . remain anonymous to the public and even to their keepers. They are very much alone at the end.

In contrast to Mailer's account, the focus of the research I have conducted is on the executioners themselves as they carry out typical executions. In my experience executioners—not unlike Mailer himself—can be quite voluble, and sometimes quite moving, in expressing themselves. I shall draw upon their words to describe the death work they carry out in our name.

Executioners are not a popular subject of social research, let alone conversation at the dinner table or cocktail party. We simply don't give the subject much thought. When we think of executioners at all, the imagery runs to individual men of disreputable, or at least questionable, character who work stealthily behind the scenes to carry out their grim labors.

This image of the executioner as a sinister and often solitary character is today misleading. To be sure, a few states hire free-lance executioners and traffic in macabre theatrics. Executioners may be picked up under cover of darkness and some may still wear black hoods. But today, executions are generally the work of a highly disciplined and efficient team of correctional officers.

Broadly speaking, the execution process as it is now practiced starts with the prisoner's confinement on death row, an oppressive prison-within-a-prison where the condemned are housed, sometimes for years, awaiting execution. Death work gains momentum when an execution date draws near and the prisoner is moved to the death house, a short walk from the death chamber. Finally, the process culminates in the death watch, a twenty-four-hour period that ends when the prisoner has been executed.

This final period, the death watch, is generally undertaken by correctional officers who work as a team and report directly to the prison warden. The warden or his representative, in turn, must by law preside over the execution. In many states, it is a member of the death watch or execution team, acting under the warden's authority, who in fact plays the formal role of executioner. Though this officer may technically work alone, his teammates view the execution as a shared responsibility. As one officer on the death watch told me in no uncertain terms: "We all take part in it; we all play 100 percent in it, too. That takes the load off this one individual [who pulls the switch]." The formal executioner concurred. "Everyone on the team can do it, and nobody will tell you I did it. I know my team." I found nothing in my research to dispute these claims.

The officers of these death-watch teams are our modern executioners. As part of a larger study of the death-work process, I studied one such group. This team, comprised of nine seasoned officers of varying ranks, had carried out five electrocutions at the time I began my research. I interviewed each officer on the team after the fifth execution, then served as an official witness at a sixth electrocution. Later, I served as a behind-the-scenes observer during their seventh execution. The results of this phase of my research form the substance of this essay.

The death-watch or execution-team members refer to themselves, with evident pride, as simply "the team." This pride is shared by other correctional officials. The warden at the institution I was observing praised members of the team as solid citizens—in his words, country boys. These country boys, he assured me, could be counted on to do the job and do it well. As a fellow administrator put it, "an execution is something [that] needs to be done and good people, dedicated people who believe in the American system, should do it. And there's a certain amount of feeling, probably one to another, that they're part of that— that when they have to hang tough, they can do it, and they can do it right. And that it's just the right thing to do."

The official view is that an execution is a job that has to be done, and done right. The death penalty is, after all, the law of the land. In this context, the phrase "done right" means that an execution should be a proper, professional, dignified undertaking. In the words of a prison administrator, "We had to be sure that we did it properly, professionally, and [that] we gave as much dignity to the person as we possibly could in the process. . . . If you've gotta do it, it might just as well be done the way it's supposed to be done—without any sensation."

In the language of the prison officials, "proper" refers to procedures that go off smoothly; "professional" means without personal feelings that intrude on the procedures in any way. The desire for executions that take place "without any sensation" no doubt refers to the absence of media sensationalism, particularly if there should be an embarrassing and undignified hitch in the procedures. Still, I can't help but note that this may be a revealing slip of the tongue. For executions are indeed meant to go off without any human feeling, without any sensation. A profound absence of feeling would seem to capture the bureaucratic ideal embodied in the modern execution.

The view of executions held by the execution team members parallels that of correctional administrators but is somewhat more restrained. The officers of the team are closer to the killing and dying, and are less apt to wax abstract or eloquent in describing the process. Listen to one man's observations:

"It's a job. I don't take it personally. You know, I don't take it like I'm having a grudge against this person and this person has done something to me. I'm just carrying out a job, doing what I was asked to do. . . . This man has been sentenced to death in the courts. This is the law and he broke this law, and he has to suffer the consequences. And one of the consequences is to put him to death."

I found that few members of the execution team support the death penalty outright or without reservation. Having seen executions close up, many of them have lingering doubts about the justice or wisdom of this sanction. As one officer put it:

"I'm not sure the death penalty is the right way. I don't know if there is a right answer. So I look at it like this: if it's gotta be done, at least it can be done in a humane way, if there is such a word for it. . . . The only way it should be done, I feel, is the way we do it. It's done professionally; it's not no horseplaying. Everything is done by documentation. On time. By the book."

Arranging executions that occur "without any sensation" and that go "by the book" is no mean task, but it is a task that is undertaken in earnest by the execution team. The tone of the enterprise is set by the team leader, a man who takes a hard-boiled, no-nonsense approach to correctional work in general and death work in particular. "My style," he says, "is this: if it's a job to do, get it done. Do it and that's it." He seeks out kindred spirits, men who see killing condemned prisoners as a job— a dirty job one does reluctantly, perhaps, but above all a job one carries out dispassionately and in the line of duty.

To make sure that line of duty is a straight and accurate one, the death-watch team has been carefully drilled by the team leader in the mechanics of execution. The process has been broken down into simple, discrete tasks and practiced repeatedly. The team leader describes the division of labor in the following exchange:

The execution team is a nine-officer team and each one has certain things to do. When I would train you, maybe you'd buckle a belt, that might be all you'd have to do. . . . And you'd be expected to do one thing and that's all you'd be expected to do. And if everybody does what they were taught, or what they were trained to do, at the end the man would be put in the chair and everything would be complete. It's all come together now.

So it's broken down into very small steps. . . .

Very small, yes. Each person has *one* thing to do.

I see. What's the purpose of breaking it down into such small steps?

So people won't get confused. I've learned it's kind of a tense time. When you're executin' a person, killing a person—you call it killin', executin', whatever you want—the man dies anyway. I find the less you got on your mind, why, the better you'll carry it out. So it's just very simple things. And so far, you know, it's all come together; we haven't had any problems.

This division of labor allows each man on the execution team to become a specialist, a technician with a sense of pride in his work. Said one man, "My assignment is the leg piece. Right leg. I roll his pants leg up, place a piece [electrode] on his leg, strap his leg in. . . . I've got all the moves down pat. We train from different posts; I can do any of them. But that's my main post."

The implication is not that the officers are incapable of performing multiple or complex tasks, but simply that it is more efficient to focus each officer's efforts on one easy task.

An essential part of the training is practice. Practice is meant to produce a confident group, capable of fast and accurate performance under pressure. The rewards of practice are reaped in improved performance. Executions take place with increasing efficiency, and eventually occur with precision. "The first one was grisly," a team member confided to me. He explained that there was a certain amount of fumbling, which made the execution seem interminable. There were technical problems as well: The generator was set too high so the body was badly burned. But that is the past, the officer assured me. "The ones now, we know what we're doing. It's just like clockwork."

The death-watch team is deployed during the last twenty-four hours before an execution. In the state under study, the death watch starts at 11 o'clock the night before the execution and ends at 11 o'clock the next night when the execution takes place. At least two officers would be with the prisoner at any given time during that period. Their objective is to keep the prisoner alive and "on schedule." That is, to move him through a series of critical and cumulatively demoralizing junctures that begin with his last meal and end with his last walk. When the time comes, they must deliver the prisoner up for execution as quickly and unobtrusively as possible.

Broadly speaking, the job of the death-watch officer, as one man put it, "is to sit and keep the inmate calm for the last twenty-four hours—and get the man ready to go." Keeping a condemned prisoner calm means, in part, serving his immediate needs. It seems paradoxical to think of the death watch officers as providing services to the condemned, but the logistics of the job make service a central obligation of the officers. Here's how one officer made this point:

"Well, you can't help but be involved with many of the things that he's involved with. Because if he wants to make a call to his family, well, you'll have to dial the number. And you keep records of whatever calls he makes. If he wants a cigarette, well he's not allowed to keep matches so you light it for him. You've got to pour his coffee, too. So you're aware what he's doing. It's not like you can just ignore him. You've gotta just be with him whether he wants it or not, and cater to his needs."

Officers cater to the condemned because contented inmates are easier to keep under control. To a man, the officers say this is so. But one can never trust even a contented, condemned prisoner.

The death-watch officers see condemned prisoners as men with explosive personalities. "You don't know what, what a man's gonna do," noted one officer. "He's liable to snap, he's liable to pass out. We watch him all the time to prevent him from committing suicide. You've got to be ready—he's liable to do anything." The prisoner is never out of at least one officer's sight. Thus surveillance is constant, and control, for all intents and purposes, is total.

Relations between the officers and their charges during the death watch can be quite intense. Watching and being watched are central to this enterprise, and these are always engaging activities, particularly when the stakes are life and death. These relations are, nevertheless, utterly impersonal; there are no grudges but neither is there compassion or fellow-feeling. Officers are civil but cool; they keep an emotional distance from the men they are about to kill. To do otherwise, they maintain, would make it harder to execute condemned prisoners. The attitude of the officers is that the prisoners arrive as strangers and are easier to kill if they stay that way.

During the last five or six hours, two specific team officers are assigned to guard the prisoner. Unlike their more taciturn and aloof colleagues on earlier shifts, these officers make a conscious effort to talk with the prisoner. In one officer's words, "We just keep them right there and keep talking to them—about anything except the chair." The point of these conversations is not merely to pass time; it is to keep tabs on the prisoner's state of mind, and to steer him away from subjects that might depress, anger, or otherwise upset him. Sociability, in other words, quite explicitly serves as a source of social control. Relationships, such as they are, serve purely manipulative ends. This is impersonality at its worst, masquerading as concern for the strangers one hopes to execute with as little trouble as possible.

Generally speaking, as the execution moves closer, the mood becomes more somber and subdued. There is a last meal. Prisoners can order pretty much what they want, but most eat little or nothing at all. At this point, the prisoners may steadfastly maintain that their executions will be stayed. Such bravado is belied by their loss of appetite. "You can see them going down," said one officer. "Food is the last thing they got on their minds."

Next the prisoners must box their meager worldly goods. These are inventoried by the staff, recorded on a one-page checklist form, and marked for disposition to family or friends. Prisoners are visibly saddened, even moved to tears, by this procedure, which at once summarizes their lives and highlights the imminence of death. At this point, said one of the officers, "I really get into him; I watch him real close." The execution schedule, the officer pointed out, is "picking up momentum, and we don't want to lose control of the situation."

This momentum is not lost on the condemned prisoner. Critical milestones have been passed. The prisoner moves in a limbo existence devoid of food or possessions; he has seen the last of such things, unless he receives a stay of execution and rejoins the living. His identity is expropriated as well. The critical juncture in this regard is the shaving of the man's head (including facial hair) and right leg. Hair is shaved to facilitate the electrocution; it reduces physical resistance to electricity and minimizes singeing and burning. But the process has obvious psychological significance as well, adding greatly to the momentum of the execution. . . . [H]e is then made to shower and don a fresh set of clothes for the execution. The clothes are unremarkable in appearance, except that velcro replaces buttons and zippers, to reduce the chance of burning the body. The main significance of the clothes is symbolic: they mark the prisoner as a man who is ready for execution. Now physically "prepped," to quote one team member, the prisoner is placed in an empty tomblike cell, the death cell. All that is left is the wait. During this fateful period, the prisoner is more like an object "without any sensation" than like a flesh-and-blood person on the threshold of death.

For condemned prisoners, like Gilmore, who come to accept and even to relish their impending deaths, a genuine calm seems to prevail. It is as if they can transcend the dehumanizing forces at work around them and go to their deaths in peace. For most condemned prisoners, however, numb resignation rather than peaceful acceptance is the norm. By the accounts of the death-watch officers, these more typical prisoners are beaten men. Listen to the officers' accounts:

"A lot of 'em die in their minds before they go to that chair. I've never known of one or heard of one putting up a fight. . . . By the time they walk to the chair they've completely faced it. Such a reality most people can't understand. 'Cause they don't fight it. They don't seem to have anything to say. It's just something like 'Get it over with.' They may be numb, sort of in a trance."

"They go through stages. And, at this stage, they're real humble. Humblest bunch of people I ever seen. Most all of 'em is real, real weak. Most of the time you'd only need one or two people to carry out an execution, as weak and as humble as they are."

These men seem barely human and alive to their keepers. They wait meekly to be escorted to their deaths. The people who come for them are the warden and the remainder of the death-watch team, flanked by high-ranking correctional officials. The warden reads the court order, known popularly as a death warrant. This is, as one officer said, "the real deal," and nobody misses its significance. The condemned prisoners then go to their deaths compliantly, captives of the inexorable, irresistible momentum of the situation. As one officer put it, "There's no struggle. . . . They just walk right on in there." So, too, do the staff "just walk right on in there," following a routine they have come to know well. Both the condemned and the executioners, it would seem, find a relief of sorts in mindless mechanical conformity to the modern execution drill.

As the team and administrators prepare to commence the good fight, as they might say, another group, the official witnesses, are also preparing themselves for their role in the execution. Numbering between six and twelve for any given execution, the official witnesses are disinterested citizens in good standing drawn from a cross-section of the state's population. If you will, they are every good or decent person, called upon to represent the community and use their good offices to testify to the propriety of the execution. I served as an official witness at the execution of an inmate.

At eight in the evening, about the time the prisoner is shaved in preparation for the execution, the witnesses are assembled. Eleven in all, we included three newspaper and two television reporters, a state trooper, two police officers, a magistrate, a businessman, and myself. We were picked up in the parking lot behind the main office of the corrections department. There was nothing unusual or even memorable about any of this. Gothic touches were notable by their absence. It wasn't a dark and stormy night; no one emerged from the shadows to lead us to the prison gates.

Mundane considerations prevailed. The van sent for us was missing a few rows of seats so there wasn't enough room for all of us. Obliging prison officials volunteered their cars. Our rather ordinary cavalcade reached the prison but only after getting lost. Once within the prison's walls, we were sequestered for some two hours, in a bare and almost shabby administrative conference room. A public information officer was assigned to accompany us and answer our questions. We grilled this official about the prisoner and the execution procedure he would undergo shortly, but little information was to be had. The man confessed ignorance on the most basic points. Disgruntled at this and increasingly anxious, we made small talk and drank coffee.

At 10:40 P.M., roughly two-and-a-half hours after we were assembled and only twenty minutes before the execution was scheduled to occur, the witnesses were taken to the basement of the prison's administrative building, frisked, then led down an alleyway that ran along the exterior of the building. We entered a neighboring cell block and were admitted to a vestibule adjoining the death chamber. Each of us signed a log, and was then led off to the witness area. To our left, around a corner some thirty feet away, the prisoner sat in the condemned cell. He couldn't see us, but I'm quite certain he could hear us. It occurred to me that our arrival was a fateful reminder for the prisoner. The next group would be led by the warden, and it would be coming for him.

We entered the witness area, a room within the death chamber, and took our seats. A picture window covering the front wall of the witness room offered a clear view of the electric chair, which was about twelve feet away from us and well illuminated. The chair, a large, high-back solid oak structure with imposing black straps, dominated the death chamber. Behind it, on the back wall, was an open panel full of coils and lights. Peeling paint hung from the ceiling and walls; water stains from persistent leaks were everywhere in evidence.

Two officers, one a hulking figure weighing some 400 pounds, stood alongside the electric chair. Each had his hands crossed at the lap and wore a forbidding, blank expression on his face. The witnesses gazed at them and the chair, most of us scribbling notes furiously. We did this, I suppose, as much to record the experience as to have a distraction from the growing tension. A correctional officer entered the witness room and announced that a trial run of the machinery would be undertaken. Seconds later, lights flashed on the control panel behind the chair indicating that the chair was in working order. A white curtain, opened for the test, separated the chair and the witness area. After the test, the curtain was drawn. More tests were performed behind the curtain. Afterwards, the curtain was reopened, and would be left open until the execution was over. Then it would be closed to allow the officers to remove the body.

A handful of high-level correctional officials were present in the death chamber, standing just outside the witness area. There were two regional administrators, the director of the Department of Corrections, and the prison warden. The prisoner's chaplain and lawyer were also present. Other than the chaplain's black religious garb, subdued grey pinstripes and bland correctional uniforms prevailed. All parties were quite solemn.

At 10:58 the prisoner entered the death chamber. He was, I knew from my research, a man with a checkered, tragic past. He had been grossly abused as a child, and went on to become grossly abusive of others. . . . The prisoner walked quickly and silently toward the chair, an escort of officers in tow. His eyes were turned downward, his expression a bit glazed. Like many before him, the prisoner had threatened to stage a last stand. But that was lifetimes ago, on death row. In the death house, he joined the humble bunch and kept to the executioner's schedule. He appeared to have given up on life before he died in the chair.

En route to the chair, the prisoner stumbled slightly, as if the momentum of the event had overtaken him. Were he not held securely by two officers, one at each elbow, he might have fallen. Were the routine to be broken in this or indeed any other way, the officers believe, the prisoner might faint or panic or become violent, and have to be forcibly placed in the chair. Perhaps as a precaution, when the prisoner reached the chair he did not turn on his own but rather was turned, firmly but without malice by the officers in his escort. These included the two men at his elbows, and four others who followed behind him. Once the prisoner was seated, again with help, the officers strapped him into the chair.

The execution team worked with machine precision. Like a disciplined swarm, they enveloped him. Arms, legs, stomach, chest, and head were secured in a matter of seconds. Electrodes were attached to the cap holding his head and to the strap holding his exposed right leg. A leather mask was placed over his face. The last officer mopped the prisoner's brow, then touched his hand in a gesture of farewell.

During the brief procession to the electric chair, the prisoner was attended by a chaplain. As the execution team worked feverishly to secure the condemned man's body, the chaplain, who appeared to be upset, leaned over him and placed his forehead in contact with the prisoner's, whispering urgently. The priest might have been praying, but I had the impression he was consoling the man, perhaps assuring him that a forgiving God awaited him in the next life. If he heard the chaplain, I doubt the man comprehended his message. He didn't seem comforted. Rather, he looked stricken and appeared to be in shock. Perhaps the priest's urgent ministrations betrayed his doubts that the prisoner could hold himself together. The chaplain then withdrew at the warden's request, allowing the officers to affix the death mask.

The strapped and masked figure sat before us, utterly alone, waiting to be killed. The cap and mask dominated his face. The cap was nothing more than a sponge encased in a leather shell with a metal piece at the top to accept an electrode. It looked decrepit and resembled a cheap, ill-fitting toupee. The mask, made entirely of leather, appeared soiled and worn. It had two parts. The bottom part covered the chin and mouth, the top the eyes and lower forehead. Only the nose was exposed. The effect of a rigidly restrained body, together with the bizarre cap and the protruding nose, was nothing short of grotesque. A faceless man breathed before us in a tragicomic trance, waiting for a blast of electricity that would extinguish his life. Endless seconds passed. His last act was to swallow, nervously, pathetically, with his Adam's apple bobbing. I was struck by that simple movement then, and can't forget it even now. It told me, as nothing else did, that in the prisoner's restrained body, behind that mask, lurked a fellow human being who, at some level, however primitive, knew or sensed himself to be moments from death.

The condemned man sat perfectly still for what seemed an eternity but was in fact no more than thirty seconds. Finally the electricity hit him. His body stiffened spasmodically, though only briefly. A thin swirl of smoke trailed away from his head and then dissipated quickly. The body remained taut, with the right foot raised slightly at the heel, seemingly frozen there. A brief pause, then another minute of shock. When it was over, the body was flaccid and inert.

Three minutes passed while the officials let the body cool. (Immediately after the execution, I'm told, the body would be too hot to touch and would blister anyone who did.) All eyes were riveted to the chair; I felt trapped in my witness seat, at once transfixed and yet eager for release. I can't recall any clear thoughts from that moment. One of the death-watch officers later volunteered that he shared this experience of staring blankly at the execution scene. Had the prisoner's mind been mercifully blank before the end? I hoped so.

An officer walked up to the body, opened the shirt at chest level, then continued on to get the physician from an adjoining room. The physician listened for a heartbeat. Hearing none, he turned to the warden and said, "This man has expired." The warden, speaking to the director, solemnly intoned: "Mr. Director, the court order has been fulfilled." The curtain was then drawn and the witnesses filed out.

As the team prepared the body for the morgue, the witnesses were led to the front door of the prison. On the way, we passed a number of cell blocks. We could hear the normal sounds of prison life, including the occasional catcall and lewd comment hurled at uninvited guests like ourselves. But no trouble came in the wake of the execution. Small protests were going on outside the walls, we were told, but we could not hear them. Soon the media would be gone; the protesters would disperse and head for their homes. The prisoners, already home, had been indifferent to the proceedings, as they always are unless the condemned prisoner had been a figure of some consequence in the convict community. Then there might be tension and maybe even a modest disturbance on a prison tier or two. But few convict luminaries are executed, and the dead man had not been one of them. Our escort officer offered a sad tribute to the prisoner: "The inmates, they didn't care about this guy."

I couldn't help but think they weren't alone in this. The executioners went home and set about their lives. Having taken life, they would savor a bit of life themselves. They showered, ate, made love, slept, then took a day or two off. For some, the prisoner's image would linger for that night. The men who strapped him in remembered what it was like to touch him; they showered as soon as they got home to wash off the feel and smell of death. One official sat up picturing how the prisoner looked at the end. (I had a few drinks myself that night with that same image for company.) There was some talk about delayed reactions to the stress of carrying out executions. Though such concerns seemed remote that evening, I learned later that problems would surface for some of the officers. But no one on the team, then or later, was haunted by the executed man's memory, nor would anyone grieve for him. "When I go home after one of these things," said one man, "I sleep like a rock." His may or may not be the sleep of the just, but one can only marvel at such a thing, and perhaps envy such a man.

MARRIAGE: THE LAY VOICE

MICHAEL NOVAK

In almost any Catholic bookstore, one can find perhaps a dozen books on how to be happy in marriage, written by priests. How can it be that laymen are silent on what they know best? No doubt, here as in other matters, the clergy have a head start in expressing themselves on what the faith implies. Moreover, the layman seems intimidated by the difference between the daily reality of marital love, which he knows, and the images presented by priests; he then hesitates to speak for fear of violating orthodoxy. Add to this the confusions in philosophical and theological theory generated by the controversies and empirical discoveries of our century; add also the reticence about sex inculcated in the Christian environment, and the natural hesitance to speak in a realistic vein which might seem to reveal one's own personal life. It is easy to understand, then, why the inhibitions blocking speech are very strong.

The layman's strong point in discussing marital questions is that he alone has a connatural, empirical grasp of the nature of Catholic marriage. His weak point is that he has been silent for so long that he lacks a language for expressing himself. When, in frustration, he finally does blurt out his views on what Catholic marriage is, he often ends up playing not from his strong side, his grasp of the empirical evidence, but from his weak side, a terminology and conception of the issues which has little to do with marriage as he knows it. He begins arguing about "natural law," or "primary and secondary ends of marriage," and "faculty and act." But these terms, as used in recent centuries at least, are not proper to marriage as experienced by ordinary laymen, but to marriage as codified by canon lawyers. . . .

MICHAEL NOVAK (1933–), a former contributing editor of *Commonweal*, is a fellow of the American Enterprise Institute. His books include *The Spirit of Democratic Capitalism*.

The layman makes a mistake, then, by arguing in a language not congenial to him and not expressive of his purposes or needs. . . . What the layman can usefully do is to think carefully and hard, choosing his words as well as he can, in order to express what the experience of Catholic married life is like. Out of this relatively new effort, of significant empirical value, new insights might possibly arise.

From the layman's point of view, for example, the use of marital sex does not first pose itself as a problem of abstinence and control. The acts of marital love, even for the man but particularly for his wife, are far more complex than the reading of theology would give one to believe. The very wellsprings of one's psychological life are at issue, and actions or attitudes of certain kinds on the part of each partner are capable of having the most surprising effects on the other. The woman may require a very long preparation, not only for each exchange of love, but also for reaching that maturity and relaxation in love which allows her to be at peace. In some instances, it would not be an exaggeration to say that many hours of a woman's day revolve around the moments of love. Biological or emotional movements, once aroused, require a long time to resolve themselves.

The early and continuing moral problems the layman faces in the use of marital sex are, therefore, primarily those of responding well to another person. But three misconceptions about sexuality obscure the moral imperatives the layman feels. Each of the three is a variety of romanticism; each has a different source. Only after the three are set aside do the realities of the situation begin to emerge.

The first of these we may call the virginal misconception. Those inexperienced in sexual matters, male or female, tend to think of the sexual act as mysterious, passionate, and immediate. They tend to think that the sexual impulse, once stimulated, is simple and strong. The image of water held in check by a dam, or horses reined in by a driver, would not jar their sensibilities; in their minds, the conflict between indulgence and abstinence can seem of primary significance. Between married persons, however, mystery and passion are not primary realities. Commenting on Denis de Rougement's *Love in the Western World,* for example, John Updike took some pains to show how easily and regularly passion is absent from marriage. The old saying that marriage cannot be based on passion has another side: the use of sex in marriage is not generally passionate and ecstatic, but calm and ordinary. Deep, affective love can keep the coals of passion strong; those who prefer momentary bursts of flame to the steadiness of that affective commitment misjudge matrimony.

The second misconception is the mystique of sex. This mystique has a masculine and a feminine side. On the one hand, sex is viewed as direct, simple, neat: a tension to be discharged. On the other, sex is viewed as pure communion, total unselfishness, the supreme fulfillment of the personality. The temptation here is to begin distinguishing biological values and interpersonal values, lust and love, conquest and submission. One has only to read prominent women's magazines concomitantly with *True* or *Playboy* to see how the two sides of the mystique are built up. Fuse them together with the idea of "fulfillment," and the two lines of fantasy feed one another. Each side must bend only enough to protect the fantasy of the other: women must go along with male drive, while men must speak in circumlocutions to avoid a shock to feminine sensibilities.

The third misconception is more theoretical. In *The Second Sex,* Simone de Beauvoir works out in painstaking detail a philosophy of cultivated sexual egotism. In reaction against the drab puritan sexual life of the factory towns of our civilization, D. H. Lawrence tried to rediscover the joy and spontaneity of natural sexuality. In so doing, he helped to feed the cult of sex for sex's sake that was already gaining momentum under the impact of important psychological discoveries. Once it was seen that sexuality is central to the development of human personality, it became easy in the intellectual as well as in the popular mind to center one's personality upon sex. "They will say of our generation," Albert Camus wrote, "they fornicated and they read the papers." Mary McCarthy once described our time as one in which men and women try to do as much to each other's genitals as possible. Proper and religious people frequently fail to understand the depths of these cultural characteristics; they sometimes speak as if the major problem is that advertising, swimming suits, and the movies are encouraging a lapse into wantonness and lack of self-control. It is rather that even serious people have come to believe that sexuality is the high road to fulfillment as a human person.

It seems obvious, however, that sexuality will not carry the immense weight our society places upon it. Even a brief foray into the literature of our century reveals the inadequacy of sex as a pillar of human aspiration, or of the use of sex as the necessary and sufficient path of development as a mature human being. So intimately is sexuality involved in the structure of the human psyche that it seems reasonable to regard a man's or a woman's sexual orientation as the groundwork of his development as a person. But development as a human person is not a simple, uncomplicated process, nor does it follow a single line. In discussions of the centrality of sexuality in the process of human development, it turns out that "sexuality" is used in an increasingly broader sense. In Norman Mailer's *The Naked and the Dead,* for example, perhaps twenty marital and extramarital love relationships are described, of which only a few seemed even to Mailer right and satisfying. Presumably, it was not the sexual factors, narrowly construed, which were at fault. In authentic love, interpersonal values and biological values are integral.

The informed layman knows, therefore, that the pursuit of sex for the sake of sex, or the high road to human fulfillment, is the pursuit of an abstraction, a passion without reference to the conditions of human life. Sexuality is inextricably wound up with the growth and expression of personality; but it is on the broader, concrete context of personality rather than on the narrower, more abstract concept of sexuality that emphasis is wisely placed. When the layman argues that in ordinary daily marital life the exchanges of love between him and his wife, which occur with whatever regularity, are of more concrete significance than much theology seems to recognize, he is far from aligning himself with such theorists about sex as Simone de Beauvoir. He is trying to express his experience.

In response to the mystical misconceptions about sex, the layman will wish to respect the ordinary, imperfect, stumbling ways proper to most things human. In practice, fully satisfactory exchanges of love in marriage are by no means always achieved. Hemingway, in one of his more exalted moments, speaks somewhere of "three" perfect exchanges allotted to fortunate men in a lifetime. The countless details in the lovemaking situation are enough in themselves to free from mystical views, were not the passion for the unreal so tenacious. The acts of lovemaking are many and delicate; too much haste, or lassitude, or preoccupation with other concerns, can easily mar them and offend. The layman's ordinary education about the birds and the bees probably taught him very little about either the physically or the psychologically graceful moves that are expected of him. There are a great many details, even about simple biological matters, which he must know; there is an almost inexhaustible and still hardly understood wealth in the psychology of love. The number of books offering help in these matters should be a hint to theologians that achieving good, even mutually unharmful, sexual relations is quite difficult in our society.

It must be one of God's favorite jokes, C. S. Lewis remarks in his splendid little book *The Four Loves,* to observe the hilarious, complex method he gave his married creatures for expressing their love for one another. On the one hand, the use of sex is an art which must be learned; far from being an escape from the complexities involved in life, the wise use of sexuality calls for knowledge, care, and sensitivity. It requires time to learn well. On the other hand, far from needing more constraint and more self-consciousness in their use of sex, men and women of our society seem to need more "naturalness," easy spirits, playfulness, and humor. One of the layman's moral struggles is to achieve a degree of honesty and ease which makes the natural use of sex possible.

In response to the virgin's misconceptions about sex, finally, the layman will wish to insist that concepts like indulgence and self-control have little direct application to his moral concerns in the use of sex. Acts of love are not direct and automatic; they are lingering and complex, especially for the woman. Marriage counselors are well aware that it may take the young wife as much as a year or even two years before responding naturally. If, in the meantime, she is caught up in a series of pregnancies, she may never have a chance to develop a sense of peace in having given and received love as she wished; in that case, she may well feel like "a baby machine." Ignorance of sexual matters is widespread; even among educated women the frequency of those who do not know how to attain climax appears to be high.

Meanwhile, the husband's own feelings and actions are affected by those of his wife. The husband's role is sometimes pictured as simple and direct; male novelists, and sometimes theologians, certainly make it appear that way. But marital love is primarily a communion; the actual physical release fades in importance among the goods and demands of that communion. At its given moment release comes and is climactic, but much else comes before and after. Furthermore, those surrounding matters, by subtle laws of biology and psychology, turn out to have been quite important, even for the climax itself. Since interpersonal and biological values are integral, both man and wife can be most pleased when the climax of both is full. Playfulness and the giving of pleasure become part of the moral requirement of their love.

In the abstract, of course, the use of sexual intercourse is not essential to marriage; even in the concrete, a few married couples may be able to live as brother and sister for long periods of time without injuring their mutual love. Moreover, among ordinary married couples, it is not certain that all, asked to choose which among the many goods of marriage they could not do without, would rank intercourse as one of the indispensables. Some might rather have the steady friendship, the concern for one another in illness or need, or other goods. But in the concrete these goods are not readily separated from intercourse; intercourse is to married love as speech to thought. It is necessary to deflate the extreme claims which are sometimes made in the name of sex; but in actuality one hardly does well to separate marital love too far from its natural expressive sign.

Finally, it is probably important to remark the number of ordinary daily matters which influence the exchange of love. The couple's relative maturity, past history, recent relationship, present mood, each alter the conditions of successive exchange. Moreover, fatigue, routine, annoyance, conflicting schedules, disqualify many moments as unfitting. Sometimes the couple prefers to talk, or sleep, or merely to be together, without going on to intercourse. Again, it sometimes happens that there are very few moments of peace for the leisure, calm, and quiet affection which the exchange of love between persons requires. Sometimes, on days of special joy or conflict, or on an anniversary or festive occasion, the couple is especially stirred to expressiveness. Such matters seem to be among the rhythms of nature.

It is perhaps not too fanciful to draw an analogy between the importance to married persons of the moments of love and the importance to religious of moments of prolonged prayer. In each case what is at issue is personal communion, with one another or with God; this communion gives Saint Paul the base for his analogy between the life of marriage and the life of the church. Laymen live in the ordinary human state, the state which the Son of God condescended to redeem; priests, and religious live in an eschatalogical state, the state in which all shall live after the last day. Laymen witness to the ordinariness of redemption, priests and religious to its extraordinary, ultimate significance. The church suffers when it emphasizes either one of these poles to the diminishing of the other. Those in either vocation suffer when they forget the witness of the other. The religious gains the freedom possible to the single and the unattached, but at a serious emotional risk; it is not easy to mature sexually in a state removed from normal ways of men and the normal processes of maturation. Thus praise is traditionally given to virgins and celibates for leading extraordinary, heroic lives. The layman leads a more ordinary life, but in the light of the same redemption and by the same charity.

Once the layman has tried to thread his way through the many misconceptions about sexuality, he can make a beginning in expressing his dilemmas about responsible parenthood. The most significant recent historical change he feels in his moral obligations concerning childbirth are the higher standards of nurture and above all of education with which he must provide his children. Another change lies in the greater expenditure of time and effort required of him to master a professional field than obtained some years ago; and another lies in the expectations which a higher degree of education has inspired in his wife. Thus, from an empirical point of view, a married couple of today feels many new pressures upon their exchange of love. Not every time that they exchange the sign of their love are they desirous of having a child; not every time are they psychologically, physically, or financially able to care for another child. They recognize their obligation as members of the race to have children, in the natural course of their marriage. Many come to see that they must be able to decide when they should have these children, as much as lies in their power.

In the first fervor of the lay Catholic renaissance in the United States, in the decade after World War II, a good number of the most devout Catholic laymen took to heart the theme of several prominent books, and in spite of the professional obligations of one or both parents threw themselves into the arms of Providence. A decade later, with seven, eight, or nine children, some of these parents are quite convinced that theirs was not the only, or even the best, Catholic way. For themselves, they and their families are quite happy; it would be inconceivable, in the concrete, to look Paul or Mary in the eye and say, "You are the one we would not have had, had we made the choice." No professional achievement would have been, to these parents, worth the sacrifice of any one of their children.

On the other hand, some of these same parents are among the first to insist that their way need not, and perhaps should not, be emulated. As professional people, they recognize clearly the sacrifice of quality or quantity in their professional work which the responsibilities of a large family entailed. They are acutely aware of other values than those they have chosen, and well disposed toward seeing other Catholics make another kind of choice when their vocation so demands. But if a Catholic couple finds that the method of rhythm is not successful in planning how to meet their responsibilities, there does not seem to be at present any other recommendation a pastor can urge but abstinence.

In itself, the problem of abstinence does not seem to be an insuperable one; the church does not promise that it is easy or normal, only that if one is correspondingly more devoted to prayer and to the sacraments the compensations of grace will make up for the losses of nature. On the other hand, in the concrete, abstinence cannot be the ordinary way. It is difficult to see why married people should be asked, today nearly as a matter of course and in a vast number of instances, to live for long periods as though they were not married. They are asked to live as celibates, in an extraordinary vocation, not in the ordinary one to which they believed themselves called.

It is amidst these conflicting moral imperatives that the dilemma of married laymen arises. The question does not appear to him as one of indulgence versus self-denial. It appears to him as a conflict between the ordinary expressive sign of his vocational commitment, his desire to plan the coming of his children in some responsible fashion, and the professional, financial, or medical situation in which he and his family find themselves. His dilemma is that many moral demands, of seemingly equal weight, are made on him at once. It is not aberrant will but frustrated good will which sometimes fatigues him and introduces him to bitterness.

Perhaps the most grievous moral harm which laymen suffer in marriage questions is that of an enforced dishonesty. In the first place, laymen do not speak openly enough in public or in forums where their testimony would count; their private conversations, on the other hand, are spirited and full of conviction. Again, as the Belgian woman wrote to Pope John, urging him to turn to the question of birth control: "God will not be deceived." That is to say, those many Catholic parents who positively do not want another child at a given time, but are nevertheless obliged through the risks of the rhythm method to act as if they do, are not fooling God. But they themselves feel the contradiction in what they do. Finally, a significant number of Catholic laymen, and not only among the more educated, find it difficult to convince themselves in their own conscience that Catholic teaching in this matter has not suffered by want of sufficient alertness and attention. These persons are then faced with the dilemma either of accepting on authority what they do not accept in their own mind, or of following their own conscience despite an authority they have all their lives respected and obeyed. Very little in their Catholic training prepares them for such a dilemma.

Catholic laymen, it seems, would do well to begin breaking through the vicious circles of most public discussions of these questions, by speaking as frankly and as clearly as they can of what Catholic marriage is as they have come to know it. If every Christian state has its own proper charisma, then it is laymen who should be writing the authentic and prophetic books on the sacrament of marriage as it is lived.

THE ENCYCLICAL CRISIS

BERNARD HÄRING

No papal teaching document has ever caused such an earthquake in the church as the encyclical *Humanae vitae*. Reactions around the world—in the Italian and American press, for example—are just as sharp as they were at the time of the *Syllabus of Errors* of Pius IX, perhaps even sharper. There is the difference, of course, that this time anti-Catholic feelings have been rarely expressed. The storm has broken over the heads of the curial advisors of the pope and often of the pope himself. The document is regarded as a great victory by those groups who opposed the Council from beginning to end. The conservative magazine *Triumph* is a typical example of the mentality of the far right: of priests who do not believe what the encyclical declares, it demands that they be honest and leave the church since they are automatically schismatics if they do not accept the words of the pope. The day after the encyclical appeared, a doctor in consultation said: "Your church has lost two members; both of my Catholic colleagues here have declared that they are leaving the church, since they find this whole mentality of the pope unbelievable." The same day a priest came with the question whether he should not in honesty to his conscience give up his priestly ministry; he could not act in accordance with the encyclical. This traumatic experience, with the great danger of a mass departure from the church, drove theologians to emphasize strongly the fallible character of the encyclical and to take a courageous stand.

If the pope deserves admiration for the courage to follow his conscience and to do the most unpopular thing, all responsible men and women must show forth similar honesty and courage of conscience. I am convinced that the subjective and conscious motive of the pope was love

---

BERNARD HÄRING, C.SS.R. (1912–98), was a member of the Papal Birth Control Commission and the author of the three-volume *Law of Christ*.

for the church. Those who contradict him must do it also out of love for the whole church, out of love for those whose faith is endangered. This also can and must be a service of love for the successor of Saint Peter.

Monsignor Lambruschini, the curia official appointed by the Vatican to explain the encyclical to the press, emphasized that it was not an infallible statement, and that the possibility of a revised statement, if new data appeared, could not be excluded. However, the tone of the encyclical seems to leave little hope that this will happen in Pope Paul's lifetime—little hope, that is, unless the reaction of the whole church immediately makes him realize that he has chosen the wrong advisors and that the arguments which these men have recommended as highly suitable for modern thought are simply unacceptable.

Noninfallible but very authoritative statements of popes were in the past officially corrected only after a relatively long delay. Even when they were strongly criticized within the church, this criticism became known only slowly. But the radical change which rapid communication has brought about in the modern world has created a totally new situation for authoritative church statements which are not infallible. The dialogue with the rest of the church, which formerly took decades to unfold, takes place now in a matter of days or weeks. No significant theologian can write or express his opinion on an important issue without its being known almost the same day by anyone in the world with enough curiosity to learn about it.

In the past things were different. It took centuries before the extraordinarily dangerous "teaching" of the direct power of the pope over all temporal matters was rejected. It demanded courage for Friedrich von Spee finally to speak out openly and forcefully against the persecution, torture, and burning of witches, a practice which had been recommended and doctrinally justified by a very authoritative encyclical of Innocent IV. For a long time the moralists did not dare to explain that the castration of the Vatican choir boys was immoral, since it had strong papal approval. The Council of Vienna explained in 1311 that theologians who tried in any way to justify usury were to be "imprisoned in iron chains" for the rest of their lives. And as late as the eighteenth century, moral theology textbooks published in Italy had to print that warning. Pius IX's *Syllabus* lay undigested in the church's stomach and in her relationship to the world until the Second Vatican Council's *Declaration on Religious Liberty* and the *Constitution on the Church in the Modern World*. The immorality of torture, which was justified for so many centuries by the popes, and practiced in their name, was condemned by a papal statement only after a long period of time. Pius XII declared unequivocally that it was against the natural law. The "Holy Inquisition" and "holy wars" could have been wiped out from the picture of the church if the prophetic spirit and the courage to speak out openly with Christian freedom had been more highly valued in the church. When the popes and their curial theologians so frequently and so emphatically defended temporal power and the Vatican States as a divinely commissioned right and a spiritual necessity, this critical Christian frankness should have been more in evidence.

In discussing *Humanae vitae* and the developments of the last two years, the question, when all is said and done, is really, "When you have come to yourself, you must lend strength to your brothers" (Lk. 22:31). What is needed is an enlightened understanding of the spiritual office of the successor of Saint Peter, as it appeared so remarkably in Pope John, against the most bitter opposition of that curial group which at the moment is triumphant, a group which, despite the era of internationalization in which we live, was powerfully strengthened at the last consistory by the appointment of twelve Italian cardinals. What is needed is the liberation for this ecumenical era of the papacy in the direction in which Pope Paul VI himself has already made such giant strides. Call to mind the visit on two occasions of Paul to the Patriarch Athenagoras, before Paul ventured to invite him to a visit in Rome. That was a sensitive and delicate touch, a special sign of humility of Paul with the Patriarch.

What is needed now is for all men in the church to speak out unequivocally and openly against these reactionary forces. This alone can prevent the reactionary forces from pushing the pope in the opposite direction, back to that worldly narrowness exemplified in the *Syllabus* and the church prohibition of Italians from voting in their own country which lasted from 1870 to 1929.

Despite this many will say: in this question it is not a matter of power; it is simply a matter of understanding Christian marriage. At first sight this may seem to be so, but if one looks more closely, it is clear that an outmoded understanding of curial power is the real issue, and, in conjunction with it, the issue of noncollegial exercise of the teaching office, and the inadequately explored issues of how the pope teaches.

Whether or not this was his intention, Pope Paul contributed greatly to the rapid development of the birth-control issue. Among large groups in the church, among lay people, theologians and bishops, and most of all among confessors, who suffered enormously under the old norms, Pope John had aroused fresh hope that the birth-control question would finally be thought out anew. The prospects did not seem good. The Holy Office unhesitatingly issued condemnatory warnings to those who spoke openly. We must have a precise picture of this aspect of the problem if we want to understand the historical developments which led to *Humanae vitae*. The subcommission of the council preparatory commission, which was to prepare a draft document on marriage, was completely dominated by the men of the Holy Office. When, through the insistence of certain persons, I was finally invited to the subcommission as a consultor, I received from officials on all levels of the Holy Office unequivocal instructions and warnings that I was to keep precisely within the framework of *Casti connubii*. However, efforts to restrain freedom of speech were only partially successful.

If my judgment of the situation is correct—although I may be mistaken on this point—the reason Pope John set up a small commission of theologians for a leisurely study of this issue was in order to open up discussions; the membership of the preconciliar and, at the start, of the conciliar subcommission on marriage questions was dominated by the inflexible men of the Holy Office. At the insistence of leading men among the council fathers, Pope Paul enlarged the special independent commission which John had formed. When he announced the membership of that commission in June 1964—it was still relatively unrepresentative—he asked for a kind of a moratorium on discussion in the church until the commission had made its statement. He immediately gave assurances that there was not much hope that the commission would change anything in what had been taught up to that time on the matter, and he was convinced that the commission would very quickly arrive at his conclusion. In the atmosphere of the council the pope's announcement occasioned a breakthrough of frankness and outspokenness in thinking and speaking.

The papal commission now stood at about sixty-five members; all the human probabilities, as far as the composition of the group permitted, were that the result of discussions would be a basic confirmation of *Casti connubii*— possibly with significant changes in the pastoral approach. At the start, only about three or four of the theologians were in favor of a new theological approach; the rest were known for their faithfulness to *Casti connubii*. When one of these more conservative theologians was named to a significant post (Qualificator) in the Holy Office, I heard from several men of the Holy Office itself that this was recognition for his orthodox stand in the commission. However, developments in the council, the absolute honesty of thought in the commission, and especially the presence of lay people, who were now assured that they could think and speak frankly, changed the situation, especially toward the end of the council and right after it was over. . . .

In June of 1966 the papal commission came to its well-known conclusions. Paul VI had taken a step toward collegial representation of the bishops. The final report was to be presented to a small commission of cardinals: on this commission again was a considerable number of men whose conservative attitude seemed beyond doubt, along with men like Cardinals Suenens and Döpfner. The overwhelming majority of the commission of theologians and lay people and a sufficient majority of the bishops' commission approved the majority report, which argued that the choice of methods of birth regulation be left to the discretion of the married couple, within the guidelines given in the *Constitution on the Church in the Modern World.* In this council document, married couples are asked to act in a manner commensurate with married unity and self-giving and with the preservation of a genuine atmosphere of married love, within which life might responsibly be handed on and the children properly reared. The biological norm, or, to put it in other words, the absolute sacredness of the biological rhythm was explicitly rejected. Biology is one part of man; but man should not be simply subject to and determined by biological functions any more than by psychological processes. Even less, in fact. An interference with psychological patterns can in some circumstances be a much more serious matter than biological interference. An example of this would be an overly fearful and anxious following of the rhythm method with all its fussy complications, especially at times when a new pregnancy simply has to be avoided.

The new papal encyclical does not really deal with the arguments of the commission, but simply states, "the conclusions at which the commission arrived could not be considered as definite . . . above all because certain criteria of solutions had emerged which departed from the moral teaching on marriage proposed with constant firmness by the teaching authority of the church" (paragraph 6). This seems to be saying: the commission did not come to the conclusion it had to in order to maintain human traditions in the teaching church. The commission had to come to the conclusion that nothing in *Casti connubii* or its mentality can be basically changed. Would it not have been the best solution to publish the report of both groups of the commission, the majority and the minority, and invite everyone to stay within the limits of both positions, without issuing any declarations of the official teaching authority?

Pope Paul said in his audience of July 31, 1968, that the struggle involved in making this decision had caused him no small suffering. We believe that completely. But everyone asks: why then did he exclude this decision from the agenda of the bishops' synod in the fall of 1967? Would not a collegial decision have had much greater weight than an emphatically noncollegial decision against the majority of a papal commission of bishops, theologians, sociologists, psychologists, marriage counselors, men and women? The World Congress for the Lay Apostolate, which surely gave strong representation to the more conservative and docile elements of the Catholic laity, spoke out along the lines of the majority report of the papal commission. A sharp papal warning and correction, and even sharper action from the Vatican followed with the speed of lightning. Were these voices the "noisy voices of public opinion" which Pope Paul spoke of in his audience of July 31 and against which he armed himself with stout Christian courage?

The proclamation of the doctrine of the absolute sacredness of biological laws in the marriage act came at the time of the 1968 Lambeth Conference. Furthermore, this circumstance was explicitly called to attention by Monsignor Lambruschini, the official spokesman of the pope, with an attack by him on the Anglicans. Pius XI directed *Casti connubii* as a sharp and unmistakable answer to the Lambeth Conference of 1930, which had for the first time approved by majority vote the responsible use of means to regulate births.

Patriarch Maximus IV had appealed to the pope during the council to make use of the knowledge and experience of Christians of other churches. The text of *Humanae vitae* proves that the attitude of other churches had no positive influence on the making of this decision. I frequently heard from the man who worked on *Humanae vitae* the argument that it was impossible the Anglicans could be right. That would dishonor the Catholic church.

The encyclical *Humanae vitae* explicitly reconfirms the main thesis of *Casti connubii,* namely, that every use of marriage, each individual marriage act, must remain open for the possibility of procreation and that the two meanings of the conjugal act, the unitive meaning and the procreative meaning, must remain *unconditionally* bound together in each act. Then it goes on to say, "We believe that the men of our day are particularly capable of seizing the deeply reasonable and human character of this fundamental principle."

This is simply a question of fact. Public opinion within the church, and even more so outside the church, is rather unanimous in its view that modern man, to put it mildly, has very special difficulties with this way of thinking. The truth of facts, whether they are pleasing or not, must be respected if we wish people to believe us. That is one characteristic of modern thought. It begins precisely with a search for the facts, so that it can then further develop its research.

On the one hand the encyclical is quite optimistic about the force of the arguments it proposes and the information provided by the pope's advisors, so that "the magisterium could give adequate reply to the expectation not only of the faithful, but also of world opinion." Nevertheless, when the pope speaks to "his own children" and to his "sons, the priests," optimism about the force of the arguments diminishes somewhat. He asks for "loyal internal and external obedience to the teaching authority of the church" and then adds: "That obedience, as you well know, obliges not only because of the reason adduced, but rather because of the light of the Holy Spirit, which is given in a particular way to the pastors of the church in order that they may illustrate the truth." There can be no doubt that our obedience of faith to the church rests on the confidence that the church enjoys the special assistance of the Holy Spirit in the explanation of the gospel and the guidance of the church. But it is not possible to make the Holy Spirit responsible for everything which in past centuries was loudly asserted in an authoritative tone by men of the church. However, in *Humanae vitae* the central argument is clearly and unambiguously a thesis of the natural moral law, and therefore a truth which is to be proven from human experiences and arguments of reason.

If the Holy Spirit gives a very special grace in the composition and promulgation of this document, then one may legitimately expect that this grace will manifest itself in the way the question itself is handled. That means in the solid presentation of proofs from human experience and with good arguments. In my opinion, that is not true in the present instance. Therefore, it is no insult at all to the Holy Spirit if we continue to express our doubts. . . .

The argumentation of *Humanae vitae* rests mainly on two points. The first is the constant teaching of the church; the second is the absolute sacredness and inviolability of the biological functions in every use of marriage, so that every act must remain open for procreation, whether or not procreation can at this moment responsibly be undertaken.

Humanae vitae differs from *Casti connubii* by no longer making the effort to base the teaching of the church in this matter on Genesis 38. It no longer tries to base its proof on Scripture. For every layman knows today that the intention of that text was to insist on the obligation to raise up children from the wife of one's dead brother, an obligation which is now forbidden by the church. The text is not dealing with the absolute sacredness of the sperm.

So the only argument which remains is the fact that the church has always taught this doctrine ("constant firmness by the teaching authority of the church"). In a chapter on tradition in one of my books I have attempted to show that the tradition is not so unequivocal as many think. Attention must also be given to the historical context in which the teaching was presented. But if the argument from tradition is to play so important a role, we must call to mind Jesus' struggle against the important role assigned to human traditions. "He also said to them, 'How well you set aside the commandment of God in order to maintain your tradition'" (Mk. 7:9). When the legalists asked the Lord, "Why do your disciples break the old-established tradition?" Jesus answered, "Why do you break God's commandment in the interest of your tradition?" (Mt. 15:24).

The second argument is the biological understanding of the inviolable laws of nature. In the "hierarchy of values," the biological seems to rate very high on the scale. The whole purpose of the act in its "metaphysical structure" is directed, so the argument goes, toward procreation and therefore every act must remain open to procreation, even in cases in which it would be absolutely meaningless and irresponsible to bring new life into being. "In relation to the biological processes, responsible parenthood means the knowledge and respect of their functions; human intellect discovers in the power of giving life biological laws which are a part of the human person." I believe that biological functions are one part of man; but these biological functions are often upset; and the art of healing is possible only if man is a responsible steward of these functions and can intervene. It has not been proven that the biological functions connected with the power of procreation are absolutely untouchable and sacred, especially since they are often upset and, even according to the teaching of the church, measures to restore health may be undertaken. The biological functions must be subordinated to the good of the whole person and marriage itself. This is, if I am not mistaken, by far the most common opinion in the church.

Pope Paul's advisors hold to an absolutely biological understanding of the natural law. They have not even progressed from a very materialistic style of medicine to man-centered medicine, which views medicine not as the art of restoring biological functions, but of serving the whole person.

Pope Paul asserts that an intervention in the biological process necessarily destroys married love. This assertion has no more proof to back it up than the assertion of *Casti connubii* that it is necessarily against the dignity of a woman for her to have some occupation outside the home.

The Second Vatican Council, following scientific developments in the field of moral theology, strongly developed the issue of responsible parenthood. There it is clear that birth control is evaluated quite differently in different circumstances. It is one thing if it is practiced as the result of a conscientious decision that new life cannot responsibly be brought into being here and now; it is quite another if it is a simple rejection of the parental vocation. Since Pope Paul makes the analysis of the act his starting point, this fundamental distinction does not appear. The evil seems to consist exclusively, or at least principally, in the violation of sacred biological functions. The encyclical also fails to see that abortion is a much greater problem than the methods of birth control. In the encyclical, abortion is rejected only in passing; the council put its principal emphasis on a condemnation of abortion. So the encyclical, from a pedagogical standpoint, is rather confusing.

Pope Paul's encyclical gives an extraordinarily great significance to the rhythm between fertile and infertile periods. "God has wisely disposed natural laws and rhythms of fecundity which, of themselves, cause a separation in the succession of births." Practically the only method permitted for responsible birth control is periodic continence. "It is then licit to take into account the natural rhythms immanent in the generative functions, for the use of marriage in the infecund periods only."

Here is the problem of the present teaching: women whose periods are regular, who can use all the necessary means, including the possibility of an undisturbed temperature reading and, if necessary, seven doctors at their disposal, can live in accordance with the teaching of the church. What about the poor, the uneducated, when their periods are irregular, or when, because of their level of culture, they are simply incapable of understanding these methods? What happens if these methods not only fail biologically, but lead to severe psychological disturbances?

Over the years I have received at least fifty letters which present cases in which the unsuccessful use of rhythm has led to psychoses for these women and required treatment for them in mental institutions. Just a week before the encyclical appeared, an English doctor wrote me that the confessor of a woman for whom he had prescribed the pill had refused her absolution when she had been released from a half-year of treatment in a mental institution after a pregnancy psychosis. And the superioress of an American hospital told me that the chaplain refused absolution to a severely ill woman who had taken the progesteron pill for the most valid reasons. He refused because she was not prepared to promise that she would take no more after her convalescence.

The encyclical *Humanae vitae* is so apodictic and absolute that no exceptions of any kind may be permitted for objective reasons. The appeal for merciful consideration for the sinner can only be interpreted, it seems, to mean that one can be gentle only when one opposes the evil, that is, when the poor sinner has promised to amend.

In former years, even in the papal commission, 1 Cor. 7:1–5 was often cited ("The husband must give the wife what is due to her, and the wife must give the husband his due. . . . Do not deny yourselves to one another, except when you agree upon a temporary abstinence in order to devote yourselves to prayer. . . ."). It is the only biblical text that has the least connection with our problem. Paul warns energetically against a long period of continence, since it can turn out to the devil's advantage. This need not mean adultery. The devil has already gained a great deal if husband and wife are irritable and hostile. Psychologists and concrete research, whose results were presented to the Holy Father (from Mr. and Mrs. Crowley and others) show that by far the majority of couples who were questioned said that the practice of periodic continence over a long period had notably upset the harmony of married life. All psychologists say also that total abstinence from intercourse for a long period, especially when forced on one of the partners, can be very dangerous.

Relying on this psychological knowledge, and following Paul's line of thinking in 1 Cor. 7, the council gave this warning: "Where the intimacy of married life is broken off, it is not rare for its faithfulness to be imperiled and its quality of fruitfulness ruined. For then the upbringing of the children and the courage to accept new ones are both endangered" (*Constitution on the Church in the Modern World*, Section 51).

The question has been asked: Does the encyclical bind all Catholics in conscience? The pope seems to answer this question unambiguously. Nevertheless I believe that one must give the pope credit for not abrogating or denying the general principles for forming a right conscience (*The Church in the Modern World*, Section 16). My answer along these lines is this: (1) those who can accept the encyclical with an honest conscience must do so, with all the consequences; (2) those who doubt whether they can, must study it thoroughly and also make use of further information in order to form a clear conscience; (3) those who, with an honest conscience, cannot accept the teaching and requirements of *Humanae vitae,* must follow their honest conscience. When married couples, then, for good reasons and with a good conscience use methods of birth regulation which in their minds are the most suitable—abortion is obviously excluded—they need not mention it in confession; (4) priests must instruct the faithful clearly about the pope's teaching. However, I do not see how they can be denied the right to speak out their own opinion with equal honesty.

On one occasion in the presence of Auxiliary Bishop Colombo the suggestion was made (by him or by someone else who was present) that the pope should simply forbid under pain of disobedience all methods except periodic or total abstinence, without giving any reasons, I answered vigorously, "That would be the best method to destroy the authority of the pope."

The pope did not follow that advice; he tried, with the help of his close associates, to give reasons. Some questions, of course, he simply did not put to himself, perhaps with the intention of doing it at a later date. But it is really remarkable that in the long time they had, his advisors found no better reasons than those presented in the encyclical. The conclusion was settled. They had to find the premises to back it up. May others be more successful. But it seems that the conclusion doesn't stand very solidly.

However, what is most important at this time is that the authority of the church not be destroyed. What must be destroyed is everything which is an obstacle to the reunion of Christians and spiritual leadership. When this situation has arrived, the church as a whole and especially the

Holy Father must find ways out of this impasse. More than that, they must come to a style of authority that can move effectively, inspire confidence and belief. The general direction must be toward collegiality and internationalization. But in this question collegiality must also be a sharing in the whole experience of the laity, especially of married couples and married counselors.

MARRIAGE VERSUS JUST LIVING TOGETHER

JO McGOWAN

Some months ago we had a beautiful young woman from India (my husband is also from India) staying with us. At dinner, the conversation turned to the question of marriage versus simply living together. Smita, the Indian woman, maintained that marriage was nothing more than a convenience, a way to avoid the censure of society; that if two people were willing to commit their lives to each other, then marriage was an unnecessary formality, signifying nothing.

To engage in the kind of discussion that followed is to risk sounding foolish. One talks of "marriage" as an institution and yet it is apparent that one is talking out of personal experience that cannot help but be narrow and unimposing compared to the subject itself. Having been married not very long myself, I realized how presumptuous it is to say almost anything (even at the dinner table, let alone in print) about marriage in general. But when will it become not presumptuous—after five years, ten, twenty, fifty? The more years pass, I also realize, the more changes in social and cultural conditions will separate me from those entering marriage then, and so perhaps my reflections would take on a presumptuousness of a different sort. In any case, the discussion that evening was so enlightening to me that I decided to risk my dignity and write down some of the thoughts that emerged.

Apart from anything else, marriage is simply a very practical institution. It is an institution which recognizes and makes allowances for human failings. Since constancy is a virtue that very few of us possess at all times, it is important that we see marriage as something beyond ourselves. The very nature of marriage insists that we see it so: when we marry, we create new life; we go beyond ourselves. We create responsi-

---

Jo McGowan (1958–), an American who lives in India, is founder of Karuna Vihar, a school for children with special needs, in Dehra Doon.

bilities, the weight of which our marriages must be strong enough to bear. Marriage is one of those peculiar things (like God!) which makes immense demands of us while simultaneously giving us the strength to meet those demands. It is precisely because marriage is so difficult that we must see it as permanent. It is precisely because we are so likely to give it up that we must promise—at the outset, when everything is wonderful—that we are in it for life. (This is one reason, then, why the extreme prevalence of divorce is so troubling. It not only destroys the marriages of those individuals who choose to separate, but it erodes the *concept* of the permanence of marriage. It makes it that much easier for the next couple to give up.)

Simply living together, without "benefit of marriage," does not provide the security of knowing that this is forever. But if you need that security, our friend Smita says, then the relationship can't be that strong to begin with. Smita and I are both in our early twenties, still young enough to believe in the power of love to overcome all odds. And I do believe that. What I don't believe is that a wife and husband always love each other enough to stay married. There are times when love fails, and in those times, many people just take a deep breath and stay married because they *are* married. And when they come through to the other side, their marriages are stronger and more firmly rooted in love.

Smita grew up in India where divorce is practically unheard of—I grew up in an America where marriage is practically unheard of. She can perhaps afford to take marriage for granted. I can't. I have seen far too many of my friends—and even my parents' friends—divorce. I have taken care of too many children whose parents are separated. I have seen the scars that divorce inevitably leaves—the pain and near-despair in grownups; the bewilderment and insecurity in the children. I'm not saying that these couples didn't have problems; I'm sure they did. But no human relation is without problems. And if one enters into marriage, one should do it knowing full well that this is the case and that *in spite of it,* the marriage is forever. Living together does not carry with it the weight of a centuries-old tradition. The content of the relationship—a woman and a man living together sexually—contains all the elements that are present in a marriage, but without its form. It is like taking on all that is difficult in a marriage without taking the helps that marriage can offer. Simply knowing that one is married, that one has promised—before God and the human community—that this is forever, puts a different light on the inevitable problems that one faces. One is more likely (given, of course, a belief in the permanence of marriage) to slog through, to get past whatever it is in the way, to stay together.

Constancy, of course, is not limited to those couples who are formally married. Many of my friends are living together. They have made serious commitments to each other, they have children and, for all practical purposes, they might as well be married. Indeed, several of them have relationships that I consider to be closer to the ideal of marriage than most of the married couples I know. But that, I think, is more a function of the kind of people they are, and not of the form of their living arrangements. They are extraordinary people who would probably make a success of any relationship.

Even so, there is, it seems to me, something missing. I wouldn't presume to judge what goes on between two people who have committed themselves to each other—in whatever form they have chosen. I can only look at their relationship as it is perceived by the rest of the human community. It is here, I think, that the strongest argument for marriage as opposed to living together can be made.

Let us assume two couples: one married, one living together. Both have promised a lifetime commitment, both have children, both are trying to live with each other as lovingly, gently, and nonviolently as they can. What is the difference?

The difference, as Ravi and I pieced it together that night with Smita, is this: one is a community-building act from the very beginning and the other is not.

To marry, to celebrate a love and a commitment publicly, in the presence of family and friends, is to say that the meaning of one's life can only be found in the context of a community. It is to acknowledge one's part in the human family, to recognize that one's life is more than one's own, that one's actions affect more than oneself. It is to proclaim that marriage is more than a private affair between one woman and one man.

To live together seems to me to imply that the central relationship of one's life is nobody's business but one's own. To live together is a decision reached privately and put into motion alone. There is no community blessing or celebration of the decision.

And what the community does not bless, it does not feel responsible for. Couples who are living together often find themselves quite alone when problems arise in their relationships. Their community may quite properly feel that such problems are none of its business. It was not asked for advice, or even congratulations, at the outset; why should it feel any responsibility now that things are going badly? On the other hand, a community which is asked to witness and bless the beginning of a marriage is far more likely to feel a sense of responsibility to the couple as their marriage grows and develops. I grant that most couples who do actually marry do not ask this of their community. Indeed, most couples think of the people at their wedding simply as guests who have to be fed, and not as participants in a community celebration. More on that in a bit.

The need for privacy, for individualism, looms extraordinarily large in American culture. We have been brought up to believe that it is a sign of weakness to admit that we need others. We have made a virtue of going it alone. Our ideal family is composed of a mother, a father, and one or two children. Grandparents, aunts, uncles, and cousins are all kept at a safe distance, and even neighbors are required, by zoning laws, to be at least an acre away. That this should be reflected in young people's choosing to live together, an essentially private choice, is not surprising. What *is* perhaps surprising is the extent to which most *marriages* are also quite private affairs, all the while purporting to be community events.

Most weddings say very little about the two individuals marrying—or about the community witnessing the union. Most weddings say something about the amount of money the participants have to throw about. They say something about fashion. They say something about respect for authority, in the form of the state, which issues the license, for a fee.

Most wedding ceremonies take place on an altar—so far from the guests who, theoretically, are there to witness the union of these two, that no one but the priest can hear the vows they exchange.

Most weddings are the occasion for bitter arguments: over relatives one cannot abide but invites anyway, seating arrangements at the reception, who pays for what, how many guests each family is allowed. . . . It goes on and on until many couples wish they *had* just decided to live together and skip all the hassle.

What is most telling, though, is the fact that so many weddings do not welcome children. Indeed, many outright discourage them. The phrase "No children, please" can be found frequently on wedding invitations and hard are the judgments passed on parents who dare to bring them anyway. Children, the hope and the future of any community, are an interruption, a noisy distraction, an additional and unnecessary expense—they take away from what is really important.

And what is really important, apparently, is that two grownups want to live together, but before they can, they have to get married.

This alienation of the community from the wedding ceremony, this lack of identification with the bride and groom—who seem more like actors playing pre-arranged roles than two people expressing their love for each other—serves to depersonalize the celebration. There is a boring sameness to weddings—one goes because one has to, because it is expected. The community is not asked to take part, and it does not. And the wedding sets the tone for the community's role in the marriage itself. The message is clear: It should limit its involvement to making appearances at the appropriate times, giving gifts on the appropriate occasions. Nothing more.

When Ravi and I married, we wanted a community celebration, one involving as many of our friends and families as possible. We wanted our wedding to reflect our religious (Catholic/Hindu) and cultural backgrounds, as well as our social and political concerns; we wanted our wedding to be a celebration of our love, naturally, but also for the community who had come to share our joy.

And it was. What a diversity of talents went into that day—from the wedding invitations and programs we designed, Ravi's side in Hindi and mine in English, to the wedding clothes made by Ravi's cousin and the wedding cake made by my father and a close friend. Ravi's mother performed the Hindu wedding ceremony, two priest friends witnessed the Catholic ceremony. Ravi and I wrote our own vows and selected the readings (from the Hindu and Christian scriptures) that friends and relatives read at the ceremony. Two nuns who had taught me in high school provided their oceanside convent for the day. The vegetarian banquet (both Indian and American foods) was entirely prepared by friends who arrived a few days early to cook. . . . And best of all were the children everywhere, behaving exactly as children should behave, especially at a wedding.

It seemed to us then, and it seems even more so now, that our wedding was a symbol of the way we want to live our lives: surrounded by family and friends; giving and receiving the gifts of time, laughter, advice, and help; sharing food, work, prayer, and celebration; creating a world where children are free and full of joy.

But marriage is a community event. It expresses, in its ideal form, a belief in the goodness of community, a belief in the beauty of two people who love each other coming together to live in communion, a belief in the wonder of human life, a belief so strong that it expresses itself in the creation of new human life.

If two people who say they want to marry do not believe this, then perhaps they should not marry. If they want to "join America"—to live in the suburbs with themselves and their 1.7 genetically screened children, exactly one acre from the nearest neighbor—then perhaps what they want is not marriage but just to live with each other.

If they want to be part of the human community, to start building the kingdom of God here on earth, then marriage is probably what they are seeking. And if it is, then the wedding itself, which is the beginning of marriage, should be an expression of their belief in community.

AGAINST GAY MARRIAGE

JEAN BETHKE ELSHTAIN

very society embraces an image of a body politic. This complex symbolism incorporates visions and reflections on who is inside and who is outside; on what counts as order and disorder; on what is cherished and what is despised. This imagery is fluid but not, I will argue, entirely up for grabs. For without some continuity in our imagery and concern, we confront a deepening nihilism. In a world of ever more transgressive enthusiasms, the individual—the self—is more, not less, in thrall to whatever may be the reigning ethos. Ours is a culture whose reigning ethic is surely individualism and freedom. Great and good things have come from this stress on freedom and from the insistence that there are things that cannot and must not be done for me and to me in the name of some overarching collective. It is, therefore, unsurprising that anything that comes before us in the name of "rights" and "freedom" enjoys a *prima facie* power, something akin to political grace.

But perhaps we have reached the breaking point. When Madonna proclaims, in all sincerity, that mock masturbation before tens of thousands is "freedom of expression" on a par, presumably, with the right to petition, assemble, and protest, something seems a bit out of whack—distorted, quirky, not-quite-right. I thought about this sort of thing a lot when I listened to the stories of the "Mothers of the Disappeared" in Argentina and to their invocation of the language of "human rights" as a fundamental immunity—the right not to be tortured and "disappeared." I don't believe there is a slippery slope from queasiness at, if not repudiation of, public sexual acts for profit, orchestrated masturbation, say, and putting free speech as a fundamental right of free citizens in peril. I don't

---

JEAN BETHKE ELSHTAIN (1941–), political theorist and teacher, is the Laura Spelman Rockefeller Professor of Social and Political Ethics at the University of Chicago and the author of *Real Politics: At the Center of Everyday Life,* among other works.

think the body politic has to be nude and sexually voracious—getting, consuming, demanding pleasure. That is a symbolism that courts nihilism and privatism (however publicly it may be trumpeted) because it repudiates intergenerational, familial, and communal contexts and believes history and tradition are useful only to be trashed. Our culture panders to what social critic John O'Neill calls the "libidinal body," the body that titillates and ravishes and is best embodied as young, thin, antimaternal, calculating, and disconnected. Make no mistake about it: much of the move to imagery of the entitled self and the aspirations to which it gives rise are specifically, deeply, and troublingly antinatal— hostile to the regenerative female body and to the symbolism of social regeneration to which this body is necessarily linked and has, historically, given rise.

Don't get me wrong: not every female body must be a regenerative body. At stake here is not mandating and coercing the lives of individuals but pondering the fate of a society that, more and more, repudiates generativity as an animating image in favor of aspiration without limit of the contractual and "wanting" self. One symbol and reality of the latter is the search for intrusive intervention in human reproducing coming from those able to command the resources of genetic engineers and medical reproduction experts, also, therefore, those who have more clout over what gets lifted up as our culture's dominant sense of itself. One finds more and more the demand that babies can and must be made whenever the want is there. This demandingness, this transformation of human procreation into a technical operation, promotes a project Oliver O'Donovan calls "scientific self-transcendence." The technologizing of birth is antiregenerative, linked as it is to a refusal to accept any natural limits. What technology "can do," and the law permits, we seem ready to embrace. Our ethics rushes to catch up with the rampant rush of our forged and incited desires.

These brief reflections are needed to frame my equally brief comments on the legality, or not, of homosexual marriage. I have long favored domestic partnership possibilities—ways to regularize and stabilize commitments and relationships. But marriage is not, and never has been, primarily about two people—it is and always has been about the possibility of generativity. Although in any given instance, a marriage might not have led to the raising of a family, whether through choice or often unhappy recognition of, and final reconciliation to, the infertility of one or another spouse, the symbolism of marriage-family as social regenesis is fused in our centuries-old experience with marriage ritual, regulation, and persistence.

The point of criticism and contention runs: in defending the family as framed within a horizon of intergenerationality, one privileges a restrictive ideal of sexual and intimate relations. There are within our society, as I already noted, those who believe this society can and should stay equally open to all alternative arrangements, treating "lifestyles" as so many identical peas in a pod. To be sure, families in modernity coexist with those who live another way, whether heterosexual and homosexual unions that are by choice or by definition childless; communalists who diminish individual parental authority in favor of the preeminence of the group; and so on.

But the recognition and acceptance of plural possibilities does not mean each alternative is equal to every other with reference to specific social goods. No social order has ever existed that did not endorse certain activities and practices as preferable to others. Ethically responsible challenges to our terms of exclusion and inclusion push toward a loosening but not a wholesale negation in our normative endorsement of intergenerational family life. Those excluded by, or who exclude themselves from, the familial intergenerational ideal, should not be denied social space for their own practices. And it is possible that if what were at stake were, say, seeking out and identifying those creations of self that enhance an aesthetic construction of life and sensibility, the romantic bohemian or rebel would get higher marks than the Smith family of Remont, Nebraska. Nevertheless, we should be cautious about going too far in the direction of a wholly untrammeled pluralism lest we become so vapid that we are no longer capable of distinguishing between the moral weightiness of, say, polishing one's Porsche and sitting up all night with an ill child. The intergenerational family, as symbolism of social regenesis, as tough and compelling reality, as defining moral norm, remains central and critical in nurturing recognitions of human frailty, mortality, and finitude and in inculcating moral limits and constraints. To resolve the untidiness of our public and private relations by either reaffirming unambiguously a set of unitary, authoritative norms or eliminating all such norms as arbitrary is to jeopardize the social goods that democratic and familial authority, paradoxical in relation to one another, promise— to men and women as parents and citizens and to their children.

WHY I CHANGED MY MIND

SIDNEY CALLAHAN

Last month I came out of the closet and confessed at an evening lecture that I believed that homosexuals should be allowed to marry. The morning after I had second thoughts, but I'm afraid my reconsiderations were mostly the result of cowardice and churlishness.

First the cowardice. Yes, I undoubtedly dread getting into arguments, especially with people I admire. I'm also distinctly uneager to be harassed by true believers playing punitive hardball, whether on the right or the left. Already I've been denounced and disinvited for being a feminist, and been greeted by banners unfurled to protest my acceptance of birth control, this while delivering a prolife speech at a Catholic conference. Yet in other venues I've been picketed, booed, hissed, and raged at by abortion advocates. (At least the latter episodes have the excitement of being thrown to the lions in the arena.) Still, do I need to get into one more religious and cultural donnybrook?

As for churlishness, I must say that as much as I hate being disliked, I loathe even more being approved of by certain groups. Who wants to end up on the same side with aggressively secular ideologues? And how unappetizing to aid and abet militant gay groups who engage in gross anti-Catholic tactics. Most of all I hate agreeing with those mindless religious types (I have my little list) who regularly seem to sell out their Christian birthright, along with the lives of the unborn, for a mess of PC pottage.

Unfortunately, flailing about and grinding one's teeth availeth naught, it gets you nowhere. The only way out of moral paralysis is to forget extrinsic political considerations and enter into the necessary struggle. If we want to bring forth a Christworthy, coherent sexual ethic

---

SIDNEY CALLAHAN (1933–) is a regular *Commonweal* columnist. Her books include *With All Our Heart and Mind* and *Parents Forever*.

for the twenty-first century then we must all think hard, pray hard, and seek God's Spirit of Love and Truth. Where? In all the familiar places: in Scripture, in tradition, in natural law reasoning, and in the signs and sciences of the times. So what is the gospel truth regarding homosexuality?

At this point I've read thousands of pages written by assorted experts and theologians giving their views on what constitutes an adequate moral, legal, scientific, and/or scriptural-theological approach to homosexuality (including recent *Commonweal* exchanges). But since I'm in the confessional mode let me own up to the fact that I also try to decide difficult moral dilemmas by praying, meditating, and naively imagining what Christ would have done and wants now. If the mind of Christ is in us, we must be transformed rather than being conformed to the world.

As I try to draw all these various strands of thought, imagination, and prayer into some order, I find myself diverging from official Vatican teaching. Yes, we are all told to look upon homosexuals as equal children of God who must be protected from assault, bigotry, and infringement of their civil rights. Indeed, Christ loves and includes the gay in his kingdom. And almost everyone on all sides agrees that homosexuality is not freely chosen but a given condition. So, too, all acknowledge that personal qualities and the call to holiness are not determined by sexual orientation. So far, so good.

But why is it intrinsically disordered for homosexuals and lesbians to act on their sexual orientation, even if they would fulfill all the same moral conditions required of heterosexual marital activity, such as commitment, love, and lifelong fidelity? After all, some heterosexual marriages need not, nor can be biologically procreative. I just cannot imagine Christ asking such an unequal sacrifice from homosexual persons with beloved partners who have not been called to vowed celibacy.

Those who do assign this burden in Christ's name describe the deprivation as morally and religiously necessary. They speak of maintaining the family for the common good, of how gender complementarity is necessary for marital bonding across genders, of the importance of embodiment and being a part of the ongoing procreative narrative. The pope denounces "the false families" of homosexuals and lesbians. Well, of course, I agree that a viable society must support and privilege procreative families, but I don't see why this positive support necessitates barring the marriage of gay couples.

Good Catholic parents of adult children I know welcome their gay children's lifelong partners as "in-laws," who are part of their family.

Doesn't it seem a confirmation of the Christian teaching on the goodness of monogamous marriage that gay couples eschew promiscuity and desire to regularize and ritualize their loving commitment to one another?

Assertions about the complementarity of the two genders appear to be false to new psychological insights on the range of gender variability and overlapping similarities, as well as to the Christian call to transcend gender in Christian unity where "there is neither male nor female." If the symbol of Christ as male bridegroom in union with the church is used too literally as the form for marriage, then could only females (as brides) be church members? (Rigid overestimation of gender is also the fallacy that bans women from ordination.)

Any two persons must struggle to obtain loving unity, but when you take into account the multitude of inevitable differences in temperament, intelligence, taste, talents, and moral maturity, gender can be a minor consideration.

Affirming embodiment and respect for the symbolic language of the body is important, but I'd say the grammar book includes a wider range of syntax and idiom than is officially published. In fact I've come (finally) to see the rejection of loving gay erotic expression as a rejection of embodiment, and another form of resistance to the goodness of sexual desire and pleasure. For most persons, gay or straight, chaste friendships and general charity cannot produce the same intense intimacy, bodily confirmation, mutual sanctification, and fulfilling happiness that come from making love with a faithful partner. (The inability of some celibates to accept the importance of freely expressing sexual and erotic marital love has produced the birth control impasse.)

Other rejections of the body also may be surfacing when whatever homosexuals do together is considered especially revolting and repugnant. Our stringent toilet, cleanliness, and touch taboos enforced in infancy can linger on in the feeling that certain parts or functions of the body are intrinsically disgusting. Some of the antigay articles I've been dutifully perusing are revealing. They begin with warnings against the "gay conspiracy" and "homosexual cult" that aims "to seduce our children" into its diseased and perverted "clutches." Then follow references to "debased," "mutual self-gratifications," "through what very definitely and clearly is nothing but deathhole . . . it yields only dead matter." Lesbians are absent from these phallocentric fulminations, presumably because they possess no "life giving or sharing organ" to end up in the wrong orifice.

Well, it has taken centuries to get over the ancient convictions that menstruating females are unclean and ritually pollute the altar. If, that is, we have gotten over it. When you see some of the heated resistance to women's ordination, one wonders. Oh Christ, if we could only take your words to heart and learn what defiles a person and what doesn't.

Beliefs

Explaining how he was drawn to Catholicism, English novelist Graham Greene wrote of his youthful curiosity concerning the "subtle distinctions of an unbelievable theology." Much to his own surprise, Greene became convinced of the intellectual case for the existence of God and of the truth of Catholicism's historical and sacramental claims after taking religious instruction. He candidly admitted that his initial, hard-won intellectual assent was eventually supplanted by a much harder to articulate sense of God's mysterious presence and of faith as a "turbulent sea" whose tide would bear him away to places he could not foresee.

"Faith seeking understanding" is the classic definition of theology, and as Greene's experience suggests, the assent to religious truth is rarely won once and for all. Rather, it is a challenge that must be taken up again and again throughout one's life, just as the church itself has refined its doctrines and practices over the course of two millennia. In that process, Catholicism has developed a tradition of intellectually rigorous theological discourse. That tradition has been vigorously engaged in the pages of *Commonweal* on two of the most pressing issues of the day, the role of women and the compatibility of faith and science, by Elizabeth Johnson and John Polkinghorne. Johnson argued that the church has betrayed its truest heritage and tradition by marginalizing the contributions of women. The neglect of female imagery for God, she notes, has for too long allowed the church to discriminate against women. Moreover, the embrace of feminine symbols in the language we use to talk about God can expand and revivify our understanding of the divine mystery. Polkinghorne, too, wants to turn what has too long been an antagonistic relationship—that between science and religion—into a mutually supportive one. A physicist himself, Polkinghorne tells us that what we have learned about particle physics suggests that theistic—rather than atheistic or naturalistic—assumptions about the origins and nature of the physical world can lead to more comprehensive and persuasive explanations of material reality. "The elusive, unpicturable quantum world is found to obey a different kind of logic," he wrote. "May the same not also be true of encounter with divine reality?"

The emergence of feminist theology and the engagement of the church with modern science are in large part the result of efforts to open the church to the world that spring from Vatican Council II (1962–65). The council reforms have left a mixed legacy, however, especially concerning church unity and the coherence of Catholic doctrine and practice. George Lindbeck, a Lutheran observer at the council, astutely described the crisis of authority that has characterized the post–Vatican II church as the inevitable result of the "radical and fundamental ambiguities" of the council's own documents. Vatican II embraced principles that justified sweeping reforms while at the same time affirming the authoritarian structures and doctrinal formulations of the past. At the deepest level, the council was "equivocal" about these issues, thus undermining the implementation of any reform. "The crisis," Lindbeck concluded, "cannot be solved, not even by a new pope, but only lived through."

Commonweal editor Margaret O'Brien Steinfels agreed. She argued that religious communion, in the best sense of the term, necessarily implies the sort of dissent that now exists within the church. "During the Second Vatican Council, American Catholics made our positive experience of the First Amendment a gift to the whole church, which has now adopted a policy of religious freedom and defense of the rights of conscience." The results are messy, but a return to more authoritarian ways is insupportable because the laity can be "reached only by voluntary compliance and not by ecclesial penalties." Within the church, said Steinfels, Catholics now need to learn and "practice a pedagogy and politics of persuasion." It will take time.

Asked by *Commonweal's* editors to offer his assessment of American Catholicism, the eminent theologian Reinhold Niebuhr rehearsed Protestant concerns about Catholicism's support of the concept of separation of church and state. The Catholic commitment to moral truth, he noted, does not sit easily with democracy's willingness to "take a chance with error rather than give anyone the absolute authority to define the truth." At the same time, Niebuhr admitted that Protestants "underestimate the resources of Catholicism for preserving justice and stability in a free society."

Uncovering those resources, rooted as they are in the deepest beliefs Catholics hold about God and the purpose of life, remains an ongoing political and theological task for *Commonweal.*

ON BECOMING A CATHOLIC

GRAHAM GREENE

Vivien was a Roman Catholic, but to me religion went no deeper than the sentimental hymns in the school chapel. "Lord Dismiss Us with Thy Blessing" represented the occasional mercy of God, and I enjoyed the luxurious melancholy of "Abide with Me." The only prize I had ever won at school was a special prize for an "imaginative composition," given by an elderly master in memory of his son killed in the First World War. It was the first time the prize had been awarded, and being a deeply religious man he was grieved that it should go to a story about an old senile Jehovah who had been left alone in a deserted heaven.

I met the girl I was to marry after finding a note from her at the porter's lodge in Balliol protesting against my inaccuracy in writing, during the course of a film review, of the "worship" Roman Catholics gave to the Virgin Mary, when I should have used the term "hyperdulia." I was interested that anyone took these subtle distinctions of an unbelievable theology seriously, and we became acquainted. Now it occurred to me, during the long empty mornings, that if I were to marry a Catholic I ought at least to learn the nature and limits of the beliefs she held. It was only fair, since she knew what I believed—in nothing supernatural. Besides, I thought, it would kill the time.

One day I took Paddy for a walk to the sooty neo-Gothic cathedral— it possessed for me a certain gloomy power because it represented the inconceivable and the incredible. There was a wooden box for inquiries and I dropped into it a note asking for instruction. Then I went back to my high tea of tinned salmon and Paddy was sick again. I had no intention of being received into the church. For such a thing to happen I would need to be convinced of its truth and that was not even a remote possibility.

GRAHAM GREENE (1904–91), the British novelist, was the author of *The Power and the Glory, The Heart of the Matter, Our Man in Havana, A Sort of Life,* and many other works.

The impossibility seemed even more pronounced a week later when I returned to the cathedral and met Father Trollope. I was to grow fond of Trollope in the weeks which followed, but at the first sight he was all I detested most in my private image of the church. A very tall and very fat man with big smooth jowls which looked as though they had never needed a razor, he resembled closely a character in one of those nineteenth-century paintings to be seen in art shops on the wrong side of Piccadilly—monks and cardinals enjoying their Friday abstinence by dismembering enormous lobsters and pouring great goblets of wine. Poor Trollope, his appearance maligned him. He led a very ascetic life, and one of his worst privations was the rule which, at that period, forbade him to visit the theater, for he had been an actor in the West End— not a star, but one of those useful reliable actors who are nearly always in demand for secondary roles. First he had become converted to Catholicism (Dr. Fray, that former ogre of Berkhamsted, had persuaded his family, who lived in Lincoln under the shadow of the deanery, to oppose his conversion), and then he was driven further by some inner compulsion to the priesthood. There were many plays on his shelves among the theological books—reading them was the nearest he could get to the footlights.

It was some weeks before he told me his story, and it came like a warning hand placed on my shoulder. "See the danger of going too far," that was the menace his story contained. "Be very careful. Keep well within your depth. There are dangerous currents out at sea which could sweep you anywhere." Father Trollope had been swept a very long way out, but the turbulent sea had not finished with him yet. He held a high position in the Catholic Nottingham world: he was administrator of the cathedral, well placed to rise into a hierarchy where men of business ability are valued, but he was deeply dissatisfied with any future which could be represented as success—he hadn't yet sacrificed enough, and a few years after I left Nottingham he wrote to tell me that he was entering an order, an order which was to my mind the least attractive of any, the Redemptorist. What had these monks, with an obligation to dwell in all their sermons and retreats on the reality of hell, in common with this stout cheerful man who loved the smell of grease paint and the applause at a curtain fall? Perhaps nothing except the desire to drown. A few years later he was dead of cancer.

It was quite a while before I realized that my first impression was totally false and that I was facing the challenge of an inexplicable goodness.

I would see Trollope once or twice a week for an hour's instruction, and to my own surprise I came to look forward to these occasions, so that I was disappointed when by reason of his work they were canceled. Sometimes the place of instruction was an odd one—we began our lesson, perhaps, with a discussion on the date of the Gospels on the upper deck of a tram swaying out to some Nottingham suburb where he had business to do and concluded it with the significance of Josephus in the pious pitch pine parlor of a convent.

I had cheated him from the first, not telling him of my motive in receiving instruction or that I was engaged to marry a Roman Catholic. At the beginning I thought that if I disclosed the truth he would consider me too easy game, and later I began to fear that he would distrust the genuineness of my conversion if it so happened that I chose to be received, for after a few weeks of serious argument that "if" was becoming less and less improbable. Bishop Gore in his great book on religious belief wrote that his own primary difficulty was to believe in the love of God; my primary difficulty was to believe in a God at all. The date of the Gospels, the historical evidence for the existence of the man Jesus Christ: these were interesting subjects which came nowhere near the core of my disbelief. I didn't disbelieve in Christ—I disbelieved in God. If I were ever to be convinced in even the remote possibility of a supreme, omnipotent, and omniscient power I realized that nothing afterwards could seem impossible. It was on the ground of a dogmatic atheism that I fought and fought hard. It was like a fight for personal survival.

My friend Antonia White many years later told me how, when she was attending the funeral of her father, an old priest who had known her as a child tried to persuade her to return to the church. At last—to please him more than for any other reason—she said, "Well then, Father, remind me of the arguments for the existence of God." After a long hesitation he admitted to her, "I knew them once, but I have forgotten them." I have suffered the same loss of memory. I can only remember that in January 1926 I became convinced of the probable existence of something we call God, though now I dislike the word with all its anthropomorphic associations and prefer Chardin's "noosphere," and my belief never came by way of those unconvincing philosophical arguments which I derided in a short story called "A Visit to Morin."

"Oh," it may be said, "a young man is no match for a trained priest," but in fact, at twenty-two, fresh from Oxford and its intellectual exercises, I was more capable of arguing an abstract issue or debating a historical point than I am today. The experience of a long life may possibly increase one's intuition of human character, but the mass of memories and associations which we drag around with us like an overfull suitcase on our interminable journey would weary me now at the start with all such arguments as we indulged in then. I cannot be bothered to remember—I accept. With the approach of death I care less and less about religious truth. One hasn't long to wait for revelation or darkness.

Although I was not received till early February 1926, I must have made my decision some weeks before, for I wrote flippantly to my mother in January, in the course of a letter full of other concerns, "I expect you have guessed that I am embracing the Scarlet Woman." The flippancy was fictitious: the fun of the intellectual exercise was over. I had reached the limit of the land and there the sea waited, if I didn't turn back. I was laughing to keep my courage up.

The first general confession, which precedes conditional baptism and which covers the whole of man's previous life, is a humiliating ordeal. Later we may become hardened to the formulas of confession and skeptical about ourselves: we may only half intend to keep the promises we make, until continual failure or the circumstances of our private life finally make it impossible to make any promises at all and many of us abandon confession and Communion to join the foreign legion of the church and fight for a city of which we are no longer full citizens. But in the first confession a convert really believes in his own promises. I carried mine down with me like heavy stones into an empty corner of the cathedral, dark already in the early afternoon, and the only witness of my baptism was a woman who had been dusting the chairs. I took the name of Thomas—after Saint Thomas the doubter and not Thomas Aquinas—and then I went on to the *Nottingham Journal* office and football results and the evening of potato chips.

I remember very clearly the nature of my emotion as I walked away from the cathedral: there was no joy in it at all, only a somber apprehension. I had made the first move with a view to my future marriage, but now the land had given way under my feet and I was afraid of where the tide would take me. Even my marriage seemed uncertain to me now. Suppose I discovered in myself what Father Trollope had once discovered, the desire to be a priest? At that moment it seemed by no means impossible. Only now after more than forty years I am able to smile at the unreality of my fear and feel at the same time a sad nostalgia for it, since I lost more than I gained when the fear belonged irrevocably to the past.

ON THE HOLY MOUNTAIN

JOHN ALDEN WILLIAMS

For more than a thousand years, Athos, the Holy Mountain, has owed much of its peculiar character to its isolation, and even in an era of rapid communication, it is able to preserve something of its aloofness. After the traveler has presented a letter of recommendation from his consulate to the Greek foreign ministry, and secured another letter commending him to the Sacred Kinotis, the government of the monk-republic, he must travel the better part of a day by country bus from Thessalonica, through the prosperous countryside of Chalkidike and the village of Stagira, where Aristotle was born, to a fishing town from whence the next morning he can get a fishing boat to the Mountain—the easternmost of the three fingers of the Chalkidike peninsula. Disembarking at one of the monasteries, or at the port village of Daphne, one can walk or hire a mule for the two-hour climb up to Karyes, the capital. Here is the seat of the Kinotis, a twenty-man Senate of representatives from the twenty "great cloisters" and the residence of the official who represents Greece, the protecting power. Here also one receives in exchange for the documents the *diamonitirion,* which alone entitles him to the hospitality of the Holy Mountain.

The still undeforested mountains, with their fountains and streams, the magnificent Aegean blues and greens, the marble cliffs of Athos itself, form, with the castellated monasteries, an un-Greek and even romantic landscape. In the clearings are the herds of steers and wethers that provide the little meat eaten here; the only exceptions to the ancient ban on "every female creature" today are cats—since it has been equally impracticable to prohibit female rodents' residence on Athos—and in one or two monasteries, as an innovation, hens. The otherwise strictly observed law is taken from the reform of the Basilian Rule of Saint Theodore, the ninth-century defender of the holy icons and of papal rights in Con-

---

JOHN ALDEN WILLIAMS was a writer and traveler with an interest in monasticism.

stantinople. The saintly abbot of Studion forbade the keeping of animals in pairs, lest the sight of their coupling offend the eyes and the consciences of his monks. And it is many centuries since any woman has set foot here, in "The country where no one is ever born."

This curious designation, still employed with striking pride by the monks, is one of the several insistent reminders that here one is dealing with a type of spirituality and of monasticism which is much closer to the Desert Fathers than anything which has survived in the West. This is a land where it is a matter of lively debate as to whether "deviation from the Julian calendar may not endanger one's salvation," where the carrier of a tiny statue of Our Lady is likely to be told—as was one of my companions, a Rhineland Byzantinist—that "the representation of Holy Persons in the round is heretical," and where the devil is looked upon as so real a personal enemy that his frescoed representations are scratched and spat upon, just as the icons are devoutly kissed, for as at least some monks will assure you, "the clawing of the devil's picture gives him great anguish."

It is a land where marvels and legends are the small talk of the day, and where every cloister is a Byzantine fortress, built to keep out not only sea robbers but all the raids of "the world"—here not an abstract term, but a place which lies on the other side of the borders.

Although every guest is welcomed with great courtesy and hospitality, and his origins learned with friendly and insistent curiosity, the monks evince little curiosity as to the happenings in "the world." One excellent old monk told me how, after a stay at his cloister, a visitor had sent him a year's subscription to a famous newspaper. "Now, what was I supposed to do with that?" he asked in evident mystification. An exception was an old monk who promised to remember me in his prayers if I would send him "some pictures of New York, and the buildings."

And there are few countries where money is more useless than the Holy Mountain. It can be used for transportation by mule or fishing boat, but outside Karyes and Daphne, the two "secular" villages inhabited by workmen, police, customs officials, and charcoal burners, only the *diamonitirion* gives one the right to the necessities of life.

If it was the intellectual task of the West to bind together the supernatural and the natural in a rational system of thought, it was the concern of the East to set in stable formulae the definitions of orthodoxy, and then to follow them with single-minded "spiritual athleticism." Thus the monks, the spiritual athletes, have been the guardians of "orthodoxy," coming out of their retreats to guide the religious policy of the empire and the Eastern church—as for instance in the late period of Byzantium, when emperor and patriarch were seeking to heal the schism with Rome, the determined opposition of the Holy Mountain and the moral influence of the monks on the laity forbade any union with the Latin "nonyeasters."

More than the distrusted secular clergy, more even than the patriarch of Constantinople, who as chief priest of the imperial cult became merely an important member of the Byzantine bureaucracy, the monks have been the center of gravity of the Eastern church. Fallmerayer, the nineteenth-century German scholar who traveled here, referred to Mt. Athos, not without reason, as "*das Anti-Vatikan.*" Germany's foremost Byzantinist, Franz Dölger, states: "The Eastern church knows no scholasticism in the proper sense; she is the church of *Mystery*"; and only once, on Athos, has this statement been even temporarily challenged. In 1743, influenced partly by echoes of the Enlightenment, a seminary arose under the patronage of Constantinople where some of the greatest Greek scholars of the time sought to revive the remnants of the Byzantine humanistic tradition. But the monks, perhaps frightened by rumors of the intellectual revolution taking place in Europe, knew no rest until they had made its continued existence impossible. When it was closed, they celebrated their triumph by looting and destroying the buildings.

Every monastery has, of course, its library. The libraries are filled with a priceless splendor of illuminated Greek codexes, the majority of which have not been copied or microfilmed. But very few of the monks can read the archaic language, and usually one finds the libraries ill-cared for and poorly ordered. Within living memory several books have either disappeared completely or disintegrated. The monks not unnaturally fear theft, and we soon found out that often the best way to view them—as well as the many magnificent reliquaries and the oldest icons—is not to express too much curiosity concerning them. But it is pleasant to note that there are two or three librarians who have carefully rebound, catalogued, and housed the books in their care, and show them with great interest and pride.

What inevitably strikes the visitor is the scarcity of monks under middle or old age. There are only about 2,500 monks on the mountain today, and the average "great cloister" has around forty monks. Although the huge monasteries have housed many times more, whole wings today are abandoned. When we spoke of this to one of the older monks, he replied, smiling complacently, "yes, it is *dissolving* now."

Unlike the Benedictines of the West, work is not a necessary part of the day's routine. Most of the work of food-producing and maintenance is done by hired laborers who come to spend a year or so on the mountain in return for food, lodging, and a daily wage of about sixty-five cents. Some monks work to support themselves; others, hermits, rent a hermitage and a field from one of the monasteries and raise their own food.

By losing our way, a companion and I stumbled onto one of these— who left us with one of our strongest impressions of the mountain. A little, white-bearded man whose robe hung in greasy tatters, he met us with easy courtesy and showed us his hermitage: a tiny chapel with a few icons, a kitchen-storeroom, and a sleeping cell with a bed of planks on two trestles. He served us a glass of brandy of his own making, and guided us at least two miles by a shortcut to the monastery we were seeking. His whole bearing was warm, intelligent, and independent, well disposed to and interested in his fellowmen—but without any need for their company. He sees them once a week, he said, when he goes to Sunday Mass at the monastery, and fetches home his weekly ration of bread, oil, and wine. Other than this ration, he eats "what the earth gives me."

For those monks who live in cloister, a large part of the day—properly about eight hours—is spent in recitation of the office and liturgical prayers. This begins at two or three o'clock in the morning, announced by wooden clappers, and culminates at six o'clock with Mass. In the afternoon there is more recitation and vespers. In some monasteries, however, the prayers are shortened, and the beautiful Byzantine liturgy hurried through at great rate. The responses are sung by one or two cantors, while the other monks chat in a corner, wander in and out of the church, or sleep in their stalls. I remarked to an Orthodox seminarian who was spending the summer in one of the monasteries that I had found participation in village congregations more devout. He shrugged his shoulders. "What do you expect?" he asked. "The monks do this every day. They are tired."

The rest of the day is more or less at the monk's disposal. He may work, meditate, or sleep in his cell. A good deal of time is spent in leisurely conversation under the trees in the courtyard.

Although Mass is offered daily, daily Communion is not practiced. In some cases, the monk communicates only the four times a year prescribed, on great feasts. The three-days pre-Communion fast from all animal food and oil, and seven-days fast from flesh prescribed for laity is a factor here, for only enough monks are ordained in major orders to fill the liturgical needs of the cloister.

The monasteries are divided into two classes: the *idiorrhythmic,* where each monk cares for himself, and only prayers are said in community, and the *cenobitic* cloisters of the common life. In the nine idiorrhythmic cloisters, each monk receives a weekly ration of bread, oil, wine, and sardines. The rest of his food, and its preparation, he must provide for himself. Hence, most of the monks work for the cloister as paid cantors, night-watchmen, servants for a richer monk, or—if educated—as clerks handling the correspondence and accounts of the monastery. Some of the older monks carve or paint icons which are eagerly bought in the Orthodox world, but these crafts have declined greatly in the last few decades. Some of the monks are so poor as to have great difficulty in providing for even their limited necessities.

There are also the richer monks—with an income from "the world." They can rent from the cloister one of the tiny houses built into the walls, furnish it as they please, and hire one or two of the other monks to work for them. A well-set table can be found here, and the owner can have such amenities as rugs, upholstered furniture, and habits of black silk.

The monks elect a provisional abbot yearly, who has little real power. The eleven cenobitic cloisters owe their origin to Saint Athanasios of Trebizond—the friend and counselor of the Emperor Nicephorus Phocas—who in the tenth century first gathered together some of the hermits of Athos and gave them a rule, based on that of Saint Theodore of Studion.

Rather ironically, the cloister which he founded and where he is buried, the Great Lavra, is today idiorrhythmic, but at one time every monastery was cenobitic. The cenobites own everything in common, tasks are divided, and the usual monk's fare of black bread, vegetables dressed with oil, wine, and occasional fish, is taken twice daily in the refectory, while a lector reads. No meat is served here. The abbot is elected for life, and has supreme authority in all but economic matters. These are the poorest cloisters, but where there is a strong abbot one finds the services carefully and reverently performed, Communion frequent, the state of maintenance high, the welcome of strangers especially warm, and the monks generally well-kempt and contented.

In the Western church, since the early Middle Ages at least, the idea has developed that the act of becoming a monk is for the purpose of serving God, but also of serving humanity, either by work or by prayer. The monk becomes a monk not because he hates the world, but because he loves it, and he prays for it by bringing as sacrifice his own worldliness and his self-will. In the East, however, it is the hermit who is the monk par excellence—and the idiorrhythmic cloisters, which may strike one as laden with abuses, began in the fourteenth century as an effort to return to a hermit-like existence, a private meditation free of the authority of rule or abbot. The ideal Athos monk seeks, in the words of the liturgy, "a blameless life, and a good defense before the dread judgment seat of Christ." By fleeing the world, by cutting every possible tie with it, by wrestling with his personal adversary, the devil, he seeks to become "like the angels," a citizen not of this world, but of the next.

A THEOLOGICAL CASE FOR GOD-SHE

ELIZABETH A. JOHNSON

A remarkable thing is happening in contemporary theology. God is moving back to the center of attention, accompanied by vigorous debate over the right way to speak about the divine mystery.

This situation is not entirely new. In the late fourth century Saint Gregory of Nyssa recorded how his contemporaries, high and low, seriously engaged the question of how to speak about God. Their issue, in a culture awash with Greek philosophical notions, was whether Jesus Christ was truly divine or simply a creature subordinate to God the Father. The question engaged not only theologians or bishops but just about everybody. "Even the baker," wrote Gregory, "does not cease from discussing this, for if you ask the price of bread he will tell you that the Father is greater and the Son subject to him."

In our day interest in how to address and speak about God is alive and well again thanks to a sizable company of bakers, namely, women who throughout history have borne responsibility for lighting the cooking fires and feeding the world. The women's movement in civil society and the church has spotlighted the exclusion of women from public discourse and decision making, and their resulting absence from the formation of cultural and theological symbols. This exclusion has had a decided effect on how we do—and do not—speak about God.

While theology has consistently acknowledged that God is Spirit, and thus beyond gender identification, the church's daily vocabulary for preaching, worship, catechesis, and evangelization broadcasts a different message: God is male, or at least more like a man than a woman, and "he" is more fittingly addressed as male than as female.

ELIZABETH A. JOHNSON, C.S.J. (1941–), teaches systematic theology at Fordham University. She is the author of *She Who Is: The Mystery of God in Feminist Theological Discourse* and *Friends of God and Prophets*.

Today, women and men in a variety of settings are questioning our exclusive reliance on male metaphors for God. In prayer and study they are rediscovering female imagery for God long hidden in Scripture and tradition. Feminist artists, poets, composers, and theologians are fashioning new images and idioms for God out of women's embodied experience. Language about God is expanding, even to the point of addressing divine mystery as "she." In this essay I would like to make a theological case for such language and argue that its development is of the highest religious significance.

The starting point for this case is a discerning attention to women's experience of themselves and of God, today occurring around the world in a new way. Struggling to reject sexism with its limits on their self-worth and self-identity, women are affirming their own identity, not as nonpersons or half persons or "deficient males," but as genuine human persons. This rebirth, moreover, brings in its wake a positive judgment about women's ways of being in the world. Female bodiliness, passion, modes of thought, love of connectedness, friendship, and a host of other historical characteristics are revalued as good rather than deficient or evil. Given the ingrained negative assessment of women's humanity under patriarchy, women's experience of themselves in this way is a powerful event, the coming into maturity of suppressed selves. In a religious sense, it is the experience of conversion of heart and mind.

Insofar as the experience of self is profoundly intertwined with the experience of God, growth or diminishment in one conditioning the other, women's awakening to their own human worth is a new event in the religious history of humankind. It occasions an experience of God as beneficent toward the female and an ally of women's flourishing. Great images of the divine, Martin Buber observed, come into being not simply as a projection of the imagination but as an awakening from the deep abyss of human existence in real encounter with divine power and glory. Images with the capacity to evoke the divine are given in encounters that, at the same time, bring persons to birth as persons, as Thous, in reciprocal relation with the Eternal Thou. Far from being silly, superficial, or faddish, language about holy mystery in female symbol emerges gracefully, powerfully, and necessarily from women's encounter with divine presence in the depths of their own blessed selves. Women's reality forms part of the treasury of created excellences that can be used to refer to God.

Christian feminism expresses this by claiming the fullness of Christian identity for women as well as men. Women are equally created in the image and likeness of God, redeemed by Christ, graced by the Spirit, called to mission in this world, and destined for life in glory. They are, furthermore, not only *imago Dei* but also *imago Christi,* reborn through baptism into the one body of Christ and transformed into icons of Christ through the power of the Spirit. It is a mistake akin to heresy to locate the *imago Christi* in sexual similarity to the human male Jesus. Being conformed to Christ is not a sex-specific gift. It consists rather in embodying Jesus' compassionate, liberating manner of life and the paradox of his dying and rising through the power of the Spirit. Using a physical metaphor, Paul recognizes how this same Spirit shapes individuals into members of the body of Christ who, together with their head, form the whole Christ. The lives of all the baptized are so transformed into Christ's image (2 Cor. 3:18) that traditionally they have been called other Christs. The historical form of Christ may be male or female, *christa* or *christus.* Theologically the capacity of women and men to be images of Christ is identical. The recognition of women's human dignity as *imago Dei, imago Christi,* justifies the use of female symbols when speaking about God. Since women are theomorphic and christomorphic, their humanity offers excellent metaphors for speaking about divine mystery, *who* remains always ever greater.

The first step in the case for God-She has attended to the conversion experience of vast numbers of women in our day and the theological insight that sees this experience revealing new symbols and language for God. This theological case gains strength from a second step, consulting the basic resources of Scripture.

Numerous biblical texts offer potent female images of the living God: God as a woman in labor, giving birth, midwifing, nursing, and carrying a child; God as an angry mother bear robbed of her cubs; God knitting, baking, washing up, searching for her money; God as Woman Wisdom creating, ordering, and saving the world. The figure of Wisdom provides one of the earliest interpretive frameworks for Christology, Jesus even being called the Wisdom of God. In a special place is the symbol of the Spirit, God's moving presence and activity in the world, often presented in female metaphors. When Scripture is read with a feminist hermeneutic, such images provide a treasure trove of new yet ancient ways to speak about God.

For some literal-minded believers, however, the Christian community is not free to expand its language about God. They argue that Jesus himself spoke to and about God as father (*abba*) and that he taught his disciples to do likewise. Such an argument sets its sights too narrowly. Jesus' language about God, far from being exclusive, is diverse and colorful, as can be seen in the imaginative parables he created. A woman searching for her lost coin, a shepherd looking for his lost sheep, a baker-woman kneading dough, a traveling businessman, the wind that blows where it wills, the birth experience that delivers persons into new life, an employer offending workers by his generosity: Jesus used these and many other human and cosmic metaphors for divine mystery, in addition to the good and loving things that fathers do.

In the light of Jesus' own usage, the difficulty with restricting our language about God to "father" alone is readily apparent. Speech that was originally pluriform, subtle, and subversive gets pressed into an exclusive, literal, and patriarchal mold. This does not do justice to Jesus' own language nor to his understanding of God. Furthermore, it fails to examine the deleterious effect that relying almost exclusively on the father symbol has had in Christian history. Diverse images of God, including female ones, are not only plausible; they are necessary, and scripturally justifiable.

Retrieving biblical female symbols of God requires another critical move. Since even these symbols are embedded within a text, a culture, and a tradition shaped by sexism, they cannot be merely lifted and plunked down whole like the prophet Habakkuk. They must first pass through the fire of feminist hermeneutics and be used by a community struggling to be a community of the discipleship of equals. Otherwise they will remain supplementary, subordinate, and stereotyped symbols within a traditionally dualistic male-female framework.

Turning to Catholic classical theology is a third step in this argument. While limited by its androcentric anthropology, this tradition nevertheless contains salutary insights that further our case. These include God's hiddenness or incomprehensibility; the play of analogy in speech about God; and the consequent need for a plurality of ways to address God. All are positive factors that open the door to inclusive speech.

In essence, God's unlikeness to the finite world of matter and spirit is total. Human beings simply cannot understand God. No human concept, word, or image can ever circumscribe the divine reality. Nor can any human construct express with any measure of adequacy the mystery of God who is ineffable. As Augustine says, "If you have understood, then what you have understood is not God." This applies even to the language of revelation. Rather than remove divine mystery, the love of God poured out in Jesus Christ deepens it, moving it far beyond any philosophical notion of incomprehensibility.

Speech about God, therefore, can never be literal but is always analogical. This means that images and concepts are taken from the created world and said about God indirectly. In a threefold movement of the mind they are affirmed, negated, and reaffirmed in a transcending movement: God is good; God is not good in the limited way creatures are good; God is good in an excellent way as source of all good. Saying this, the human spirit passes from light into darkness and thence into brighter darkness, intuiting an unspeakably rich and vivifying reality while God, nonetheless, remains hidden. Words about God, therefore, point rather than enclose. As Aquinas noted, "All affirmations we can make about God are not such that our minds may rest in them, nor of such sort that we may suppose God does not transcend them."

This being so, we must use many words to speak of God. Since God created the world by giving it a share in being, every created perfection points to the One who is the source of it all. Every fragment of beauty, goodness, and truth in the human and natural world reflects the Creator. None of these alone, or even all taken together, exhausts the reality of divine mystery. But our speech about God is less inadequate the more we include a variety of created excellences as starting points.

There is always the danger of forgetting the nature of speech about the hidden God, and absolutizing particular expressions. Introducing female symbols has the effect of purifying God-talk of its direct, even if unintentional, masculine literalism. Used inclusively, these symbols create a greater sense of the mystery of God who is beyond all telling; restore our understanding of analogy; and add a wealth of created excellence from the lives of women to our storehouse of the names of God. Not only is the theological tradition open to the use of God-She, but the tradition itself is better served by doing so.

A final step in the case for female symbols of God comes when we consider the existential and practical effects of God language on the church. A faith community's imagery of God is its lodestar. This imagery helps it interpret and understand life, experience, the world. The way a faith community speaks about God indicates what it considers the highest good, the profoundest truth, the most appealing beauty. This language, in turn, molds the community's corporate identity and behavior as well as the individual self-understanding of its members.

A religion, for example, that speaks about its God as a warrior and extols the way he smashes his enemies to bits would likely promote among its adherents aggressive group behavior. On the other hand, images of a beneficent, loving God who forgives offenses have the power to turn a faith community toward care for one's neighbor and mutual forgiveness. The symbol of God functions. It is neither abstract in content nor neutral in effect, but expresses a community's bedrock convictions.

This being so, the fact that the Christian community ordinarily speaks about God in the image of a ruling man is a problematic practice. For reformist feminist theology, which includes a remarkable spectrum of diverse theological opinion, the difficulty does not lie in the fact that male metaphors are used. Men as well as women are created in the image of God and may serve as points of reference to God. The problem, however, is that these male images are used almost exclusively, which results in their being taken rather literally. Furthermore, the specific male images used reflect a patriarchal arrangement of the world, casting God into the mold of an omnipotent, even if benevolent, monarch.

This exclusivity and patriarchy are apparent in concrete images and abstract concepts. Recall Michelangelo's Sistine Chapel painting of God as an elderly, Caucasian gentleman with a flowing white beard calling into life a single younger man in "his" own image. Historically in the West, metaphysical descriptions of the divine nature and attributes have betrayed a similar bias. With implicit stress on solitariness, superiority, and omnipotent power, they present the divine mystery as an isolated, privileged male who is set off from and above others.

The exclusive use of patriarchal images and concepts of God has a two-fold negative effect. First, it reduces the divine mystery to a single, reified metaphor of a ruling male. Once reified, a symbol no longer points beyond itself to ultimate truth. Instead it becomes an idol, eclipsing the mystery of God. Second, images and concepts of God modeled exclusively on ruling men (fathers, lords, kings) support and justify the dominance of this one group over those who by sex, race, or class are not part of their privileged group. In particular they prevent women from identifying themselves as *imago Dei,* the image of God, which profoundly affects their personal and religious identity.

In sum, exclusive use of male God language is both religiously idolatrous and socially oppressive. It does damage to the truth of the living God and to the dignity of women made in her image. Given the lodestar quality of a community's image of God, it results in a community bent out of shape by the relations of patriarchy. What is at stake in this question is not only the truth about God but the identity and mission of the Christian faith community itself.

One remedy used by a number of contemporary scholars and liturgists is to speak about and address God simply as "God." This has produced some positive results but is, in the end, unsatisfactory. The persistent use of the term "God" clouds over the personal or transpersonal character of divine mystery. It hampers not only the sense of personal presence but also the insights that might occur were female symbols of God allowed to guide our thought. In a serious way it papers over an assumption that needs explicit scrutiny, namely, that women's reality is fundamentally inadequate to represent God.

I would argue, to the contrary, that women, created in the image and likeness of God, bear excellences that reflect the being of their Creator. Using female imagery of God has many advantages. It effectively points to the personal character of holy mystery. In doing so it challenges the literal-mindedness that clings to exclusively male images, thus making us mindful of the mystery of God. Demonstrating a profound respect for the humanity of women, it calls into question their marginalization within patriarchy. Finally, it suggests an understanding of community characterized by relationships of mutuality and reciprocity rather than by the sacralized dominance of one group over another.

If the experience of God in our day is summoning up female symbols; if Scripture and tradition are open to this development; and if there are negative effects from not using inclusive language and positive effects from so doing, how shall we proceed? For Christian theology, speaking about God involves reflection on the one triune God made known in creation, incarnation, and grace. Female symbols act as a corrective not only for sexist distortions of God-talk in general, but for Trinitarian symbols in particular. To wit: the Spirit is virtually forgotten in the West, being faceless, with no proper name; the Christ is distorted through assimilation to the framework of male dominance; and God's maternal relation to the world is eclipsed through concentration on the paternal metaphor: "You forgot the God who gave you birth" (Deut. 32:18).

Incorporating female patterns of speech puts all of these notions back in play. We speak about the vivifying Spirit, forever drawing near and passing by. She is the giver of life who pervades the cosmos like a mother bird hovering over the primordial chaos (Gen. 1:2). She shelters those in difficulty under the protective shadow of her wings (Ps. 17:8), and bears up the enslaved on her great wings toward freedom (Ex. 19:4). Other images deepen our understanding of the Spirit's work: like a woman she knits new life together in the womb (Ps. 139:13); like a midwife she works deftly with those in pain to bring about the new creation (Ps. 22:9–10); like a washerwoman she scrubs away at bloody stains till the people be like new (Ps. 51:7).

We can also speak about Jesus-Sophia, Wisdom made flesh in a particular history. Writing of Wisdom Augustine noted, "But she was sent in one way that she might be with human beings [as Spirit]; and she has been sent in another way that she herself might be a human being [as incarnate in Christ]." Not only does the use of this female symbol remove the male emphasis in Christology that so quickly turns to androcentrism, but it evokes Sophia's gracious goodness, her life-giving creativity, and her passion for justice, all key elements in understanding the person, ministry, death, and Resurrection of Jesus.

We can also speak about God as the Origin without an origin, the Mother Creator of all that is seen and unseen. Since it is women whose bodies bear, nourish, and deliver new persons into life and who, as society is traditionally structured, most often carry out the responsibility of raising children into maturity, language about God's maternity is easily assimilated. In her, as once literally in our own mother, we live and move and have our being, as some of our poets now say (see Acts 17:28).

We can also speak of the Trinitarian mystery itself in female images. The mystery of mutually related, radically equal "persons" in a community of diversity can be named as unoriginate Mother, her beloved Child, and the Spirit of their mutual love; or as Wisdom's self-reference, her personal Word, and her overflowing Energy, moving in an encircling embrace. This language is analogical and indirect. It depicts the threefold character of the one God hidden in the fullness of her power, eternally uttering the distinct word of herself, and pouring forth her personal love.

What is modeled in these and other such symbols is the exuberant, life-giving dignity and power of women, applied analogically to the divine persons. The eternal friendship that is the triune mystery opens to encompass the whole broken world, awakening in those who are willing the experience of her compassion and freedom. Modeling the triune symbol on relations of women's loving and speaking of it in Wisdom metaphors offers a promising antidote to the exclusive male imagery of the classical model and the hierarchic patterns of relationship that attend it.

Such symbols are but modest starting points for a more inclusive God-talk. As the history of theology shows, there is no "timeless" speech about God. Rather, symbols of God are cultural constructs, entwined with the changing cultural situation of the faith community that uses them. Developing these symbols today is a theologically central task for the whole church.

In the *Summa Theologiae* Thomas Aquinas dealt with the legitimacy of such historical development. He noted that since Scripture does not use the term "person" to refer to God, some had objected that we should not use the term either. But, Aquinas argued, "person" can be used with confidence about God since the perfections the word signifies, namely, being, intelligence, etc., are in fact frequently attributed to God in Scripture. Furthermore, if our speech about God were limited to the very terms of Scripture, we could speak about God only in the original languages of Hebrew and Greek. Aquinas defended the use of extra-biblical language on grounds of historical need: "The urgency of confuting heretics made it necessary to find new words to express the ancient faith about God." Finally, he exhorted his readers to value these new expressions: "Nor is such a kind of novelty to be shunned; since it is by no means profane, for it does not lead us astray from the sense of Scripture."

Aquinas's arguments provide a useful framework for evaluating new patterns of speaking about God in female symbols. In light of the longevity and pervasiveness of sexism in culture and religion, it is imperative to find more adequate ways of expressing the ancient good news. The present ferment about imaging, naming, and conceptualizing God in female symbols is a contemporary manifestation of the fact that, as in every epoch before us, we as a faith community are involved in an open-ended history of faith seeking understanding that is not yet finished.

No language will ever adequately encompass the unquenchable mystery toward which we make limited but necessary gestures. But the living God and the vitality of the faith community require that a more inclusive way of speaking about and to divine mystery be developed. God-She can breathe new life into religious language and symbols that bear the ancient responsibility of conveying what is most holy, loving, merciful, just, and wise.

THE TRAGEDY

JOHN COGLEY

A s time passes I come more and more to realize that for the adult the past swiftly grows dim. Two years ago, ten years ago, the wartime years in the Army are covered with mist. Yet it is possible to evoke the years from six to sixteen with immediate clarity.

I thought I had forgotten about my four years as a pupil at Our Lady of the Angels School in Chicago. Then those searing headlines which described one of the great tragedies of modern history appeared, and memories rushed back like a flood. The very church building where I was baptized, later turned into a school, was the scene of such horror as is rarely visited on Americans.

Here I first attended Mass. Here I received confirmation. Here, like the eighty-seven children who lost their lives, I was taught my first lessons by devoted nuns like the three who lost their lives in the fire.

Our Lady of the Angels in my day was a very ordinary parochial school, practically indistinguishable from hundreds like it in the Archdiocese of Chicago. Like the others, it did its work so quietly it was barely known beyond the confines of the city and the order of sisters which administered it. But as I write, there are pictures of the building which has been familiar to me all my life, in newspapers all over the world. And I suppose that there are people like me, some of them perhaps scattered over the globe, who feel an extraordinary sense of personal identification with the tragedy because long ago that plain church building was the center of their small lives.

Just about a year ago I happened to be in Chicago and made a lonely

JOHN COGLEY (1916–76) was a *Commonweal* editor from 1949 to 1955, and a columnist until 1964. Later he served as an editor at the *New York Times,* as a presidential campaign adviser for John F. Kennedy and Eugene McCarthy, and as founding editor of the *Center Magazine.*

sentimental journey to the parish which I left so many years ago. There were many changes; a much larger, grander church had taken the place of the modest building we knew, and the old church had been remodeled to serve as a school building. Yet everything was very much as I remembered it. I recall thinking at the time that though I had changed a great deal and had enjoyed experiences such as I never dreamed of as a child, I was forever tied to this place. In the formative years it had been my San Pietro, my Notre Dame, my Santa Sophia, my Holy Sepulcher. Here, I reminded myself, hundreds of us from the bleak streets of Chicago were first introduced to the glory and beauty of Catholicism: here we were incorporated into the great Western tradition that stretches back, back, back to the saints and prophets of old, so that in later years when I was fortunate enough to visit Rome, Paris, Istanbul, and Jerusalem, it was not wholly as a stranger but as one coming home that I knelt before their altars.

I remember thinking this at the time I stood again outside Our Lady of the Angels. I remember wondering about the kids who now sat in the familiar classrooms under the tutelage of a new generation of nuns, some of whom—it struck me sharply—were years younger than I. I wondered whether life would be as good to these youngsters as it has been to me and whether in time their world too would broaden out from the parochial limits of Our Lady of the Angels to undreamed of horizons. Watching them playing around the school, I saw myself when I was their age and I sighed a little over the passing of innocence and the death of dreams, as the middle-aging are wont to do when they return to the places of their past.

Then I turned around and forgot about Our Lady of the Angels and the kids playing outside until the day the terrible thing happened.

There are no words for the kind of tragedy that lifted Our Lady of the Angels out of obscurity; attempts to find soothing words of consolation or to draw morals from it strike me as a kind of impiety. One's heart goes out to the stricken parents, the valiant nuns, the children who have survived—but words are too cheap to offer them. They have been called upon to face up to mystery, actually the most terrible mystery of all, and facing mystery is something that everyone must do for himself. In the face of such a disaster one must fall back on faith or find only bitter meaninglessness in the universe. To my mind, this is the greatest challenge faith offers—to believe that the hand of God has not been withdrawn from the world when such things happen. It is human to look for meaning, some immediate, recognizable meaning, so that one can say the children did not die in vain—but to do that is to avoid mystery, not to face it.

In the presence of the grief of those who were stricken by the tragedy one can only ask that they be strengthened in faith, nurtured in hope, and that they grow in charity. Remembering the boundless faith of parochial school children from my own days at Our Lady of the Angels, I think I can say that this harsh wisdom comes easily only to those who are as innocent as the ones who perished. As we grow older, all of us may find it easier to express such wisdom—but, God help us, how much harder it is to hold onto it.

Most of us go through life unburdened by its demands. It is part of the mystery, however, that those who are called upon to accept it with finality are specially blessed. What a dreadful thing love is, said Father Zossima. And yet love is the beginning and the end of Christianity.

SO FINELY TUNED A UNIVERSE

JOHN POLKINGHORNE

I have spent most of my working life as a theoretical physicist and all of my consciously remembered life as part of the worshiping and believing community of the church. I want to take absolutely seriously the possibility of religious belief in a scientific age. I believe that science and religion are friends and not foes. To see that, we must recognize two things:

1. We must take account of what science has to tell us about the pattern and history of the physical world. Of course, science itself can no more dictate to religion what it is to believe than religion can prescribe for science what the outcome of its inquiry is to be. The two disciplines are concerned with the exploration of different aspects of human experience: in the one case, our impersonal encounter with a physical world that we transcend; in the other, our personal encounter with the One who transcends us. They use different methods: in the one case, the experimental procedure of putting matters to the test; in the other, the commitment of trust which must underlie all personal encounter, whether among ourselves or with the reality of God. They ask different questions: in the one case, how things happen, by what process? In the other: why things happen, to what purpose?

Though these are two different questions the ways we answer them must bear some consonant relationship to each other. The fact that we now know that the universe did not spring into being ready-made a few thousand years ago but that it has evolved over a period of 15 billion years from its fiery origin in the Big Bang, does not abolish Christian talk of the world as God's creation, but it certainly modifies certain aspects of that discourse.

JOHN POLKINGHORNE (1930–), president emeritus of Queens College, the University of Cambridge, is a priest in the Church of England. His works include *The Faith of a Physicist*.

2. We must understand that religious belief, just like scientific belief, is *motivated* understanding of the ways things are. Of course, a religious stance involves faith, just as a scientific investigation starts by commitment to the interrogation of the physical world from a chosen point of view. But faith is not a question of shutting one's eyes, gritting one's teeth, and believing the impossible. It involves a leap, but a leap into the light rather than the dark. It is open to the possibility of correction, as God's ways and will become more clearly known.

Scientists do not ask "Is that reasonable?" as if we knew beforehand what the world is going to be like. They know that when we move into regimes far away from everyday experience, all sorts of surprising things can happen. Common sense will not be the measure of all things. We are not clever enough to see very far ahead. Therefore, the scientific question is "What makes you think this might be the case?" That is a different question from "Is that reasonable?" and a question that is open to the possibility of enlarging our understanding of how things are.

Let me give an example of the surprises that the physical world has proved to have in store for us. If I were to say, "Bill is at home and he is either drunk or sober," you would expect either to find Bill at home drunk or to find him at home sober. It seems trivial and obvious; the learned would say that you have used the distributive law of logic. Oddly enough, the corresponding argument applied to a quantum entity like an electron does not work. The elusive, unpicturable quantum world is found to obey a different kind of logic. May the same not also be true of encounter with divine reality?

My Christian belief in this age of science has to be motivated belief, based on evidence that I can point to. The center of my faith lies in my encounter with the figure of Jesus Christ, as I meet him in the Gospels, in the witness of the church, and in the sacraments. That is the heart of my Christian faith and hope. Yet, at a subsidiary but supportive level, there are also hints of God's presence which arise from our scientific knowledge. The actual way we answer the question "How?" points on to the question "Why?" so that science by itself is found not to be sufficiently intellectually satisfying. I want to sketch out these encouragements to religion.

A characteristic of scientific thought is the drive for synthesis. We want to have as unified an understanding as we possibly can. That is the drive behind the present activity in particle physics, which is looking for a grand unified theory—a GUT, as scientists say in our acronymic way.

So, it's the instinct of a scientist to seek as economic and as extensive an understanding of the world as possible.

I believe that the grandest unified theory that you could ever conceivably reach is a theological understanding of the world. Theology is the drive to find the most profound and comprehensive understanding of our encounter with reality.

If we're going to look for such a total theory, there are basically two alternative strategies, for if we are looking for a total explanation we won't get it for nothing. Every explanation depends upon certain basic unexplained assumptions. *Ex nihilo nihil fit,* nothing comes from nothing. That's true intellectually. Any theory of the world proceeds from some set of basic assumptions. One way to look at the world is to take the brute fact of the physical world as your starting point. That's how somebody like David Hume would proceed. Start with the brute fact of matter as your unexplained basis. But another way to proceed is to start with the brute fact (if that's the word to use) of God. In other words, one can appeal to the will of an agent, the purpose of a Creator, as the basic unexplained starting point for understanding the world.

The first approach is the strategy of atheism. The second approach is the strategy of theism. I want to defend the second strategy and to explain why I believe that, if we are driven by the desire to have as comprehensive and unified an understanding as possible, we shall find it in a scheme of things that has a place for belief in God.

If we were to start with the brute fact of the physical world, that world is described for us at least in part by the laws of science. But if we take the laws of nature as discerned by science seriously, and if we look at them carefully, we will find that they are not sufficiently intellectually satisfying in themselves. In fact, they seem to have a certain character which actually points beyond themselves. In other words, out of the scientific understanding of the world arise questions which seem to direct us beyond science itself to a deeper level of intelligibility. Here are two examples.

The first example is a fact about the physical world which is very familiar to us, a fact indeed that makes science possible. It is simply this: that we can understand the physical world, that it is intelligible to us in its rational transparency. Not only is that so, but it is mathematics which is the key to the understanding of the basic structure of the physical world. Moreover, we look for theories in physics which in their mathematical expression are economic and elegant. In other words, we seek theories which have about them an unmistakable character of mathematical beauty. It is our expectation that it is precisely theories characterized by mathematical beauty which will describe the structure of the world.

When we use mathematics as a key to unlock the secrets of the universe, something very peculiar is happening. Mathematics is the free exploration of the human mind. Our mathematical friends sit in their studies, and out of their heads they dream up the beautiful patterns of mathematics. Inexplicably, some of the most beautiful patterns thought up by the mathematicians are found actually to occur in the structure of the physical world. In other words, there is some deep-seated relationship between the reason within (the rationality of our minds—in this case mathematics) and the reason without (the rational order and structure of the physical world around us). The two fit together like a pair of gloves. That is a rather significant fact about the world, or so thought Einstein. Einstein once said, "The only incomprehensible thing about the universe is that it is comprehensible." Why, we should ask, are our minds so perfectly shaped to understand the deep patterns of the world around us?

You can always just shrug your shoulders and say, "Well, that's just the way it happens to be, and a bit of good luck for you chaps who are good at mathematics." But my instincts as a scientist, as someone who is searching for understanding, is not to be as intellectually lazy as that. A famous theoretical physicist, Eugene Wigner, once asked: "Why is mathematics so unreasonably effective in understanding the physical world?" One popular answer is that evolutionary biology explains it all. If our minds didn't fit the world around us, we just wouldn't have survived in the struggle for existence. That is obviously true, but it's only true up to a point. It's true about our experience of the everyday world of rocks and trees where we have to dodge the rocks and miss the trees. It's also true of our mathematical thinking of that world, which I suppose amounts to a little elementary arithmetic and a little elementary Euclidean geometry.

But the power of mathematics to illuminate and give understanding of the physical world is not just confined to the everyday world. For example, mathematics also describes the counter-intuitive, unpicturable quantum world. That is a world that we can't visualize, but we can understand it using very abstract mathematics, ultimately the mathematics of spontaneously broken, gauge-field theories. The theoretical physicist Paul Dirac discovered something called quantum field theory which is fundamental to our understanding of the physical world. I can't believe Dirac's ability to discover that theory, or Einstein's ability to discover the general theory of relativity, is a sort of spin-off from our ancestors having to dodge saber-toothed tigers. Something much more profound, much more mysterious, is going on. Why do the reason within and the reason without fit together at a deep level? Religious belief provides an entirely rational and entirely satisfying explanation of that fact. It says that the reason within and the reason without have a common origin in that deeper rationality which is the reason of the Creator, whose will is the ground of both my mental and my physical experience. Theology has the power to answer a question, namely the intelligibility of the world, that arises from science but goes beyond science's ability to answer. Remember, science simply assumes the intelligibility of the world. Theology can take that striking fact and make it profoundly comprehensible.

When we look at the rational order and transparent beauty of the physical world, revealed through physical science, we see a world shot through with signs of mind. To a religious believer, it is the mind of the Creator that is being discerned in that way.

Let me give another example, a scientific discovery of a more specific character that's been made in the last thirty or forty years. We live in a universe that started about 15 billion years ago and it started extremely simple. One of the reasons why cosmologists can talk with great confidence about the very early universe is that the very early universe was so simple, just an expanding ball of energy. Yet, the world that started so simple has become very rich and complex through its evolving history, with human life being the most interesting consequences of that history. Human beings are the most complicated physical systems that we have encountered in our explorations of the world. The history of the universe has been astonishingly fruitful, and we understand many steps in that evolving, fruitful process. When we think about those steps and our understanding of them, we reach a very surprising conclusion.

Scientists play intellectual games, and they play those games with a serious intent. The sort of game they play is this: when we think of the universe we live in, it is characterized by certain types of scientific laws and certain types of basic forces that go with those laws. For example, we live in a universe which has gravity in it; not just any old gravity, but gravity of a particular type and a particular strength. There is an intrinsic strength to the force of gravity built into the fabric of our universe, into the specification of what sort of world we live in. In fact, gravity is a very weak force. That might surprise you if you have ever walked out of a second-story window, but the force of gravity is intrinsically very weak. We can play intellectual games and say, "I wonder what the universe would be like, and what its history would have been like, if gravity had been a bit different—if it had been much stronger, or even a little bit weaker than it is." And we can play similar games with all the other fundamental forces of nature. We can take electromagnetism, the force that holds matter together. We can sit on our chairs because electromagnetism holds them together, and it holds us together as well! We can again say, "What would the universe be like if electromagnetism were weaker, or if it were stronger?" We can play these intellectual games and, when we do that, a very surprising conclusion follows: Unless the fundamental physical laws were more or less precisely what they actually are, the universe would have had a very boring and sterile history. In other words, it's only a very special universe, a finely tuned universe, a universe in a trillion, you might say, which is capable of having had the amazingly fruitful history that has turned a ball of energy into a world containing human life. This insight is called the anthropic principle: a world capable of producing *anthropoi* (complicated "consequences" comparable to men and women) is a very special finely tuned universe. That's a very surprising discovery!

Let me illustrate why. If you are to have a fruitful universe, one of the things you've got to have in it are stars. And, you've got to have stars of the right sort. The stars have two jobs that are absolutely indispensable to the fruitful history of the universe. One is, they have to act as long-term, steady energy sources. Essentially all energy here on earth comes from the sun, either directly or indirectly through fossil fuels. The sun has been burning steadily for about 5 billion years and it will continue to burn steadily for about another 5 billion years more. Long-term energy sources are indispensable because it takes billions of years for life to develop, and you must have what physicists call main sequence stars which are steadily-burning, long-lived stars.

We understand what makes stars burn in that sort of way. Basically it's the balance between the force of gravity and the electromagnetic forces. If you were to alter either of those forces, you would put the stars out of kilter. You'd have stars that either burned up very rapidly, that lived just for millions of years rather than billions of years, or you'd have stars that were very turbulent and unstable and flared up and died down, and that would be disastrous. No life could develop in a universe of that character. It is difficult to design a fruitful universe. You've got to get the right balance between gravity and electromagnetism to make the stars act as acceptable energy sources for life.

But that's only part of the story, because the stars have another tremendously important thing to do. The nuclear furnaces that burn inside the stars are the source of the chemical elements which are the raw materials of life. The early universe was very simple, and because the early universe was very simple it produced only very simple consequences. In fact, the very early universe made only the two simplest chemical elements, hydrogen and helium. And they are just not rich enough in their chemistry to make life possible. For life you need a much more complicated chemistry than hydrogen and helium by themselves could sustain. In particular, you need the chemistry of carbon, which has the ability to make those immensely complicated macro-molecules which are the basis of the possibility of life.

Every atom of carbon inside your body was once inside a star. We're all made from the ashes of dead stars. The only place you can make those heavier elements is inside the right sort of stars, and it's pretty difficult to make the stars do that. First, you've got to make carbon by making three helium nuclei stick together. That's actually quite hard to do and it depends upon very delicate aspects of the nuclear forces. Now, suppose you've figured out how to do that. You can't sit back and feel satisfied, because carbon is not enough. You've got to make lots more elements. You've got to make oxygen for example. That means making another helium nucleus stick to the carbon you already made and turn the carbon into oxygen. But, wait a minute. You've got to do that, but you must not overdo it. You mustn't turn all the carbon into oxygen; otherwise you've lost the carbon. So, you've got to get all these balances right, and so on, and so on, up to iron. If you can just tune the nuclear forces right, you can make all the elements up to iron inside the stars, but iron is the most stable of all the nuclear species and you can't get beyond iron inside the stars. You've still got two problems left that you've got to solve. One is you'll need to make some of the heavier elements beyond iron, and you also have to make accessible for life the elements you've already made. It's no good making carbon, oxygen, and all that, and leaving them locked up, useless, inside the cooling core of a dying star. You'll have made the elements, but they won't be of any use to bring about life. You've got to make sure that your stars are such that when they come to the end of their natural life, which is about 10 billion years, some of them will explode as supernovae and so will scatter out into the environment those chemical elements that they've made. If you're made from stardust, there's got to be some dust from stars around for you to be made of. You've got to have stellar explosions. And, if you're very clever, you can arrange in the explosion that the neutrinos, as they blow off the outer layer of the star, then make those heavier elements like zinc and so on that you couldn't make inside the star itself.

I hope I've given some idea of how making elements is a very complicated process, which depends for its fruitfulness on a very delicate, fine-tuned balance between the nuclear forces that control these processes. If those nuclear forces were in any way slightly different from the way they actually are, the stars would be incapable of making the elements of which you and I are composed.

What are we to make of all this? What do we make of the fact that the world we live in is fruitful only because its basic scientific constitution is of a very special, very finely tuned character? Once again, you can shrug your shoulders and say, "Well, that's just the way it happens to be. We're here because we're here and that's it." That doesn't seem to me to be a very rational approach to this issue. John Leslie, a philosopher at Guelf University in Canada, writes about these questions. He has written the best book about the anthropic principle, called *Universes*. He's a beguiling philosopher because he does his philosophy by telling stories, which is a very accessible way for those of us who are not professionally trained in philosophy to get the hang of it. He tells the following story. You are about to be executed. Your eyes are bandaged and you are tied to the stake. Twelve highly-trained sharpshooters have their rifles leveled at your heart. They pull the trigger, the shots ring out—you've survived! What do you do? Do you shrug your shoulders and say, "Well, that's the way it is. No need to seek an explanation of this. That's just the way it is." Leslie rightly says that's surely not a rational response to what's going on. He suggests that there are only two rational explanations of that amazing incident. One is that many, many, many executions are taking place today and just by luck you happen to be the one in which they all miss. That's a rational explanation. The other explanation is, of course, that the sharpshooters are on your side and they missed by choice. In other words there was a purpose at work of which you were unaware.

That parable translates well into thinking about a finely tuned and fruitful universe. One possibility is that maybe there are lots and lots of different universes, all with different given physical laws and circumstances. If there are lots and lots of them (and there would really have to be rather a lot) then just by chance, in one of them, the laws and circumstances will be such as to permit the development of carbon-based life. But, of course, that's the one in which we live, because we couldn't appear anywhere else. It's a possible explanation and in fact it's called the "many-universes" interpretation. The other possibility is that there is more going on than has met the eye and the sharpshooters are on our side. That translates into the idea that this is not just any old universe. Rather it is a universe which is a creation which has been endowed by its creator with just those finely tuned given laws and circumstances that will make its history fruitful. Our world and our lives are the fulfillment of a purpose.

Leslie says in relation to the anthropic principle that there is an even-handed choice between the many-universes and the anthropic theories. By itself, I think that is correct. Let me emphasize that both are metaphysical explanations. We have no adequate, scientific motivation for thinking of any other universe but the universe of our direct experience. So the speculation that there are many, many other universes is a metaphysical speculation. I'm not against metaphysics. In fact, you can't live without it. But the many-universes interpretation is a metaphysical speculation just as positing the existence of a creator is a metaphysical speculation. Of course, if you think there are other reasons, as indeed I do, for believing that there is a God whose will and purpose lie behind the universe, then that second explanation, that the world is fruitful because it is a creation, becomes the more economic and persuasive explanation.

In both the intelligibility of the world and the finely tuned fruitfulness of the world, we see insights arising from science, but calling for some explanation and understanding which, by its very nature, will go beyond what science itself can provide. I think that suggests the insufficiency of a merely scientific view of the world. In fact, I think we're living in an age where there is a great revival of natural theology taking place. That revival of natural theology is taking place, not on the whole among the theologians, who have rather lost their nerve in that area, but among the scientists. And not just among pious scientists like myself, but among scientists who have no particular time for, or understanding of, conventional religion. Nevertheless, many agnostic scientists feel that the rational beauty and the finely tuned fruitfulness of the world suggest that there is some intelligence or purpose behind the universe.

That revived natural theology is also revised in the sense that it is more modest in its ambitions. Unlike either the natural theology of the late Middle Ages or the eighteenth century, it doesn't claim to talk about proofs of God. We're in an area of discourse where knock-down argument or proof is not available. Rather, we're looking for insights which are intellectually satisfying.

Theology offers science a deeper, more comprehensive understanding than would be obtained from itself alone. But there is traffic across the border in both directions. The gift that science gives to theology is rather different—for it is to tell theology what the physical world is actually like in its structure and in its history. That raises issues to which theology has to address itself.

The classic interaction between science and theology concerns the question of origins. How did things begin? Actually I don't think that's a very important subject. People wrongly think that the theological doctrine of Creation is concerned with how things began. Who lit the blue touch paper of the big bang? The biblical doctrine of Creation isn't about that. It's not concerned with temporal origin, but with ontological origin. It answers the question, why do things exist at all? God is as much the Creator today as he was 15 billion years ago. Thus, though big-bang cosmology is very interesting scientifically, theologically it is insignificant. In *A Brief History of Time,* my friend and former colleague, Steve Hawking, says that if you think about quantum cosmology and how quantum mechanics fuzzed out the very early universe, then, though the universe has a finite age, it has no dateable beginning. Now that's a very interesting scientific speculation, but there's no particular theological mileage in it. Hawking says, "If there is no beginning, what place then for a Creator?" It is theologically naive to answer other than by, "Every place, as the Sustainer of the universe in Being." God is not a God of the edges, with a vested interest in beginnings. God is the God of all times and all places.

It is in sustaining the fruitful process of the world that God is at work as the Creator. Two insights about the process of the world come to us from science. The first is the very fertile process which turned a ball of energy into a world containing you and me. The second question is: Given we've got a universe with fine-tuning (given we've got the right ground rules), how does it actually come about that the world makes itself? How does it realize its in-built fruitfulness, its in-built potentiality? We understand many bits of that process quite well. All those bits we do understand seem to realize that fruitfulness through an interplay between two opposing tendencies which we could describe as "chance" and "necessity." Those are slippery words. By "chance," I mean simply happenstance—just the way things happen to be. When the universe was about a billion years old, there just happened to be a little bit more matter here than there. That was chance—happenstance—getting things going. That happenstance produced something lasting through the operation of "necessity," or lawful regularity. Because there was a little bit more matter here than there that matter exerted a little bit stronger gravitational pull, and draws more matter to itself in a sort of snowballing process. That's how scientists picture the universe: it started so uniform and began to get a bit grainy and lumpy. You've got to have the stars and you've got to have the galaxies that contain the stars. A fruitful universe has to become lumpy at some stage. That begins through chance, happenstance, and develops through necessity, snowballing through the attractive force of gravity. And, it seems that the interplay between those two tendencies, chance as the origin of novelty, and necessity as the sifter and preserver of the novelty thus produced, is the prime way in which the fruitfulness of the universe is realized.

A more familiar example of this process is provided by biological evolution. Mutations occur through happenstance. That produces some new possibility for life, which is then sifted and preserved in the lawfully regular environment which is necessary for the operation of natural selection. In every stage of the fruitful history of the universe there is an interplay between chance and necessity. What do we make of that?

Jacques Monod, a great French biochemist, wrote a famous book in the early 1970s called *Chance and Necessity*. Monod argued that "Pure chance, absolutely free, but blind lies at the basis of this stupendous edifice of evolution." Of course the point where Monod puts in the knife is the word "blind." For Monod, the role of chance, of happenstance, in the evolving history of the universe subverts the religious claim that there is a purpose at work in the world. For Monod, the role of chance means that ultimately the universe is a tale told by an idiot.

Monod's is a serious challenge. Nonetheless, we can take the same scientific picture of the interplay between happenstance and regularity, but offer an alternative interpretation, a more evenhanded interpretation, which lays as much emphasis on the necessary half as upon the chance half of the process. I respectfully suggest that when God came to create the world he was faced with a dilemma. The Christian God is a God of love and the gift of love is always the gift of independence, the genuine otherness of the beloved. Parents know that. There comes a time when Johnny has to be allowed to ride his bicycle into dangerous traffic on his own. The gift of love is a gift of a true independence. A God who is loving will endow his creation with its own due freedom, its own due independence. But independence by itself can easily degenerate into license and chaos. However, God is not only loving, he is faithful. And the God who is faithful will surely endow his creation also with the gift of reliability. Yet reliability by itself can easily rigidify into a merely mechanical world. I believe that the Christian God, who is both loving and faithful, has given to his creation the twin gifts of independence and reliability, which find their reflection in the fruitful process of the universe through the interplay between happenstance and regularity, between chance and necessity.

Moreover, many people have an outdated picture of the physical world. The great triumphs of science in the eighteenth century, and the further discoveries of the nineteenth century, encouraged a mechanical, rather deterministic view of the physical world. We've always known that can't be right because we've always known that human beings have the experience of choice and responsibility. Twentieth-century science has seen the death of a merely mechanical view of the world. In part, that is due to the cloudy fitfulness of quantum theory. But more important still, it is also due to another unexpected insight of science gained in the last thirty-four years.

Even the physics of the everyday world, even the physics of Newton, is not as mechanical as Sir Isaac and his followers thought it to be. That's a very surprising discovery. Those of us who learned classical physics, learned that subject by thinking about certain tame, predictable systems, like a steadily ticking pendulum. That's a very simple robust system. If you take a pendulum and slightly disturb it, or you are slightly ignorant about how it is moving, the slight disturbance only produces slight consequences, the slight ignorance produces only slight errors in your estimation of how it will behave. We thought the everyday physical world was all like that. It was tame, it was predictable, it was controllable. Now, we've discovered that, in fact, almost all the everyday physical world is not like that at all.

Almost all of the everyday physical world is so exquisitely sensitive that the smallest disturbance produces quite uncontrollable and unpredictable consequences. This is the insight that is rather ineptly named chaotic dynamics. The discovery was first made in relation to attempts to make models of the earth's weather systems. In the trade it is sometimes called the butterfly effect: that the great weather systems of the earth are so sensitive to individual circumstance that a butterfly stirring the air with its wings in Beijing today will have consequences for the storm systems over New England in a month's time! Now, the world—that exquisitely sensitive world—is an intrinsically unpredictable world. We can't know about all those butterflies in Beijing. We've learned that the physical world, whatever it is, isn't mechanical, even at the everyday level. It is something more subtle and more supple. Modern science already presents us with a picture of the physical world that is unpredictable in detail and open to the future. That is a gain for science. Science begins to describe a world which is sufficiently flexible in its development, a world of true becoming, of which we can consider ourselves as inhabitants. The future is genuinely new, not just rearrangement of what was there in the past. In such a world of true becoming, with its open future, we can begin to understand our own powers of agency, our own powers to act and bring things about. Such a physical world is capable also of being open to God's providential interaction and his agency. Our whole picture of the physical world is much more hospitable to the presence of both humanity and divine providence than would have seemed conceivable a hundred years ago.

I'd like to conclude with a quotation which in many ways summarizes what I'm trying to do as a physicist and as a priest. I want to hold these two parts of me together, and to enjoy their friendly relationship. I believe I can do so, not without puzzles, of course, but I hope without dishonesty and without compartmentalism. I've tried to show how science and theology interact positively, how their mutual relationship is one of friendship in the search for truth and not warfare with each other. Bernard Lonergan once said, "God is the all-sufficient explanation, the eternal rapture glimpsed in every Archimedean cry of Eureka." I like that very much. The search for understanding, which is so natural to a scientist, is, in the end, the search for God. That is why science and religion must be friends.

DISSENT AND COMMUNION

MARGARET O'BRIEN STEINFELS

My title, "Dissent and Communion," joins two terms that often crop up in churchspeak but don't usually live together, much less marry. As will appear, I think that's regrettable.

Both "dissent" and "communion" have specialized meanings in formal Catholic discourse. In my use here, the word "dissent" means explicit theological expression of views that question or challenge some established Catholic teaching. The position held by many of us Catholics, that *Humanae vitae* and the present pope are tragically mistaken in considering every act of contraceptive sex by married people inherently evil, is dissent. Griping about your pastor's sermon, or refusing to give to Peter's Pence, or not helping the poor may be wrong (indeed, the latter may be a sin!), but none of them is an example of dissent, at least not unless it derives from some doctrinal position about the nature of the church or the Christian's obligations in charity.

"Communion" also takes on different meanings in the theological context. Since Vatican II, there has been a flowering of something called communion ecclesiology, an effort to define and understand the church as communion. It has many formulations: the church as community *(koinonia);* as the mystical body of Christ and the people of God; it is a notion that struggles to grapple with the church as both a visible institution and an invisible reality, as a hierarchical body and the totality of Catholic believers.

Lumen gentium speaks of the church as a sacrament—"a sign and instrument . . . of communion with God and [a sign] of unity among all men [and women]" (chapter 1). The 1985 extraordinary synod and a 1992 instruction from the Congregation for the Doctrine of the Faith also grappled with communion ecclesiology, in particular underlining the

MARGARET O'BRIEN STEINFELS (1941–) is editor of *Commonweal*.

need to maintain a place for and a consciousness of what is often deri-
sively referred to as "the institutional church." The synod put it this way:
"The ecclesiology of communion cannot be reduced to purely organiza-
tional questions or to problems which simply relate to powers." Thus
they concede a point, but then they go on: "Still, the ecclesiology of
communion is also the foundation for order in the church and especially
for a correct relationship between unity and pluriformity in the church"
(*Origins,* December 19, 1985).

What I like particularly about the idea of communion ecclesiology is
that it tries to unite, sometimes in tension, an understanding of the
church that is inclusive yet has designated boundaries, that is structured
yet interpersonal, that is human yet mystical, that is visible sign and invisible transformation. . . .

It may seem paradoxical, even perverse, but in my view a true *understanding of communion implies dissent, and real dissent demands communion.* To understand this, we need to think about the ways in which
dissent commonly arises. It is very seldom an exercise in pure speculation, or the self-aggrandizing acts of disobedience, rebellion, or disloy-
alty commonly portrayed. More frequently, dissent's origins are found in
painful disjunctures between pastoral experience and existing teaching.

Think of the traditional missionary going off in the early decades of
this century to a land where he finds good people, who are devotees of a
religion that in Catholic teaching was considered heretical or idolatrous,
even satanic. Coming to know these people, might he be heartbroken by
the obstacles that such a teaching erected to any sort of communion with
the church? Might he not even feel a deep rift in communion in his own
heart? Torn between the teachings of the church and the truth that he
has learned about these people he had come to serve and love, he might
well have found himself "feeling apart." The rethinking of established
teachings that he might have been led to was born out of his sense of
communion and his search for a way to restore it. It was in fact just such
missionaries, or the theologians to whom they reported their experiences, whose dissent contributed to the decision of Vatican Council II to
revise church teachings on ecumenism and non-Christian religions.

The same story could be told of many others. In most cases, they are
not called missionaries or are not ordained. But they have tried to take
Christ's message and the church's teachings into the lands of family life,
of broken marriages, of modern science and culture, of political and economic oppression, of racial minorities, of excluded women, of sexual

outcasts. They have found dissonances between the formulations of doctrine they were taught and what they have seen and experienced.

I am not, of course, arguing that every expression of dissent arising from pastoral problems or obstacles to evangelization is legitimate or helpful. I am saying that a church understanding herself as communion—not, then, as a massive, unmoving, take-it-or-leave-it repository of answers and remedies, but as a gift of love and worship that wants to destroy barriers and offer reconciliation—that church as communion will naturally be a church *semper reformanda.* It will naturally give rise to self-examination, self-criticism, self-extension, and in the process, to dissent. Indeed, it is often the warmth of feeling that communion involves, active participation and not passive subservience, that stirs the passion, the outspokenness, the commitment, the stubbornness in which dissent sometimes cloaks itself.

If one doubts whether real communion implies dissent, imagine a church where dissent had been rendered unthinkable, impermissible, or inexpressible. Would such a church be likely to resemble the interpersonal, vital, ever-deepening, always outstretching encounter of hearts and minds that is communion? Or would it be more likely to resemble the bureaucracy of a government, the conformity of a corporation, the discipline of an army, or even the ideological unanimity of a totalitarian political movement?

But if real communion implies dissent, then real dissent demands communion. I mean nothing more than this: disagreement can only be meaningful when it takes place within a framework of agreement. One cannot really feel apart unless at some level one still feels joined. One can feel estranged from a family member, but not from a casual vacation acquaintance made twenty years ago.

To the extent that communion is attenuated, dissent becomes less significant. When advocates of women's ordination insist that the witness of historical Christianity is irredeemably distorted by patriarchy, or when they reconceive the role of the priest so as to resemble that of the imam, then their dissent over ordination becomes a good deal less compelling. Dissent is possible only when it acknowledges accountability to something outside itself—to a teaching, an authority, a tradition, a history, a people, a revelation.

Now I take it for granted that somewhere a line must be drawn between the dissent that is an inevitable and healthy aspect of communion and the dissent that is no longer compatible with communion. I do not question the efforts of bishops and theologians (it is important to include both) to resolve where, exactly, that line should be drawn in principle. But I do want to argue—and this is my second major point—that in the practical, everyday life of the church, the question of distinguishing between responsible and irresponsible dissent, between dissent in the service of communion and dissent destructive of it, is less than we often suppose a matter of intellectual propositions, and more often a matter of conduct, of attitude, of affection, and of heart.

When liberation theology was flying very high, I often heard the expression "orthopraxis" (right conduct) contrasted to "orthodoxy" (right teaching). I would like to yank orthopraxis from that context and apply it here. Is there an orthopraxis of dissent? An orthopraxis of dissent and communion? An orthopraxis, if you will, of maintaining a dynamic orthodoxy?

I am not suggesting that the church can do without the conceptual apparatus of magisterium and ordinary and extraordinary magisterium and papal ordinary magisterium and solemn definition and infallible and irreformable doctrine and probabilism and equiprobabilism and all the other categories developed over the centuries and used to identify the settled or unsettled state of the church's mind on important issues.

But frankly all this paraphernalia has always mattered (and I believe will continue to matter) far more in the relatively small, closed, and institutionally accessible world of the clergy than in the world of the laity—a laity whose role in the church, I remind you, has been reasserted by the Second Vatican Council and is assured at least in the United States by the demography of the priesthood and women's religious communities, a laity who can be reached only by voluntary compliance and not by ecclesial penalties.

What is needed is at least as much attention to the manner of dissent as to the matter. Is it articulated with respect, or with derision? Does it acknowledge its accountability to the tradition? Does it root itself in the sources of the faith? Is it expressed with both humility and rigor, including rigorous faithfulness in representing, not caricaturing, the existing teaching? Does it admit qualifications, or does it traffic in slogans? Does it consciously exploit and ride piggyback on the cultural fashions of the day, or does it deliberately strive to guard against such exploitation? Is it sensitive to pastoral problems, to the cost of conflict and the temptations of partisanship and factionalism?

There is a danger today of a kind of established dissent, dissent as a way of life, dissent as the primary stance some take toward the church. Beyond diversity, beyond clashes of ideas, beyond differences in pastoral practice, beyond the disarray that simply comes with life in such a large and human church, there is something we might want to call dissent of the heart—a state in which one's own spirit stands pridefully apart from community.

Concern about the manner as well as the matter of dissent is in fact already part of our tradition. "Dissent, in the form of carefully orchestrated protests and polemics carried on in the media, is opposed to ecclesial communion and to a correct understanding of the hierarchical constitution of the people of God." So writes John Paul II in *Veritatis splendor.*

So far I seem to have suggested that the orthopraxis of dissent and communion is entirely the responsibility of the dissenter. In fact, I think communion demands a certain kind of conduct on the part of the authorities who represent established teachings as well.

Unfortunately there is a version of communion ecclesiology sometimes articulated in the Vatican that comes close to reasserting the pre–Vatican II understanding of the church as institution, as "perfect society," but now garbed with the rhetoric of mystical communion. Communion becomes the rhetorical armor of an essentially juridical, clerical, and centralized understanding of the church, rather than a richer balance and a corrective to such an understanding.

Currently the American bishops and college and university presidents are struggling to write ordinances that would put into terms of concrete obligations the conditions for preserving the Catholic identity of Catholic colleges and universities, in keeping with the papal document *Ex corde ecclesiae.* This whole effort has run aground on the question of whether members of Catholic theology departments must seek a mandate to teach from local bishops, a measure that Vatican officials consider essential to quelling what they see as dissent, but which many Catholic educators see as an outside intervention in the affairs of the university incompatible with academic freedom and autonomy. The possibility of confrontation and alienation between bishops and educators is very real. In this way, a very serious concern about the religious identity of Catholic higher education and the danger of a drift toward secularization may end, in counterproductive fashion, by actually encouraging that drift.

This impasse, I believe, reflects a misplaced focus on dissent. Imagine

Catholic colleges and universities with theology departments where no one ever said or wrote a word that raised an eyebrow in Rome. Students might dutifully take two semesters of required courses from those teachers, but otherwise encounter little or nothing of the Catholic tradition— and of the questions that have preoccupied it in their history, philosophy, literature, social or natural science courses, in their extracurricular activities, and in conversations between faculty members and students. The little dissent-free enclave of a theology department is surely not going to communicate Catholic identity, indeed it may strangle it, especially if it is established and maintained in ways that convince most academics that the church and its teachings are hostile to genuinely free inquiry.

So to sum up: Beware the notion that dissent is the single most important factor in the American church's many current difficulties, and the companion idea that by quelling dissent we will be home free. It remains to examine the context . . . in which this complex relationship between dissent and communion is affected by the realities of contemporary America.

The first of these realities that comes to mind is that we are a First Amendment culture. Freedom of religion, separation of church and state, and free speech are our deservedly prized achievements. Like other valuable things, these achievements can be idolized, but, looking around the world, one sees why we prize them. During the Second Vatican Council, American Catholics made our positive experience of the First Amendment a gift to the whole church, which has now adopted a policy of religious freedom and defense of the rights of conscience, becoming in the past thirty years a champion of human rights in lands less blessed than our own.

American Catholics live in a country born in dissent and sustained by it. In one way that creates a problem for communion. But in another sense the American conviction that religious faith must be personal, voluntary, free of coercion, and subject to all the pressures and crosscurrents of free speech and open debate is a declaration of what communion must be about. . . .

Second, and less happily, our First Amendment culture is also, and not coincidentally, an individualist culture. We view and organize society in terms of individual rights and personal choices, which seem to trump all social bonds and social responsibilities. We are more *pluribus* than *unum*. This mindset makes a sense of community and concern for the common good fragile and vulnerable. It affects not only our civic community but reaches into the realm of religion, raising obstacles to communion. It is not just that we love underdogs, naysayers, people who thumb their noses at established authority. No, our individualism leads us to believe that religious faith needs no community. . . .

The healthy, practical-minded, live-and-let-live form of tolerance that individualism also encourages can easily slide into a shallow relativism. If everyone has his or her own opinion, and if everyone's opinion is as good as everyone else's, then there is no real reason to reexamine, grapple, rethink. Both dissent and communion are trivialized, treated almost as matters of happenstance that can be worn lightly and shed as easily.

All this is reinforced by a dominant market economy and consumer culture. We exercise our judgment simply by abandoning one product or label for another. The ultimate in such selective ease is TV channel-surfing, and baby boomers are said to be religion-surfing, moving from church to church on the basis of whatever satisfies their immediate needs, from a twelve-step program or a child-care center to their special taste in music.

This consumer culture has given us terms like cafeteria Catholicism, supermarket Catholicism, pick-and-choose or mix-and-match Catholicism. I think such images are an insult to those Catholics who have made conscientious decisions after serious prayer, reflection, and anguish that a specific church teaching does not deserve their adherence. But I also think that such terms do name a reality, and one that is obviously at odds with both communion and serious dissent. . . .

How do we bridge all of these chasms between dissent and communion, some of our own making, some of the culture's? The best starting point is our most common and direct experience of communion, the Sunday liturgy. In the Eucharist not only is the bread and wine transformed into the body and blood of Christ, but in that transformation, the people too are transformed, our work given meaning, our sorrows blessed, our lives reordered and reoriented, our hearts turned from stone to living flesh.

And then we are sent forth in the name of the Lord . . . to do mischief, be an annoyance, to live our faith in this world, this United States with all of the ambiguities, conflicts, and tensions inherent in our kind of culture. We Catholics, all of us, need to become smarter about how we deal with them and live with them. We need to practice a pedagogy and politics of persuasion.

A PROTESTANT LOOKS AT CATHOLICS

REINHOLD NIEBUHR

Though the Catholic may find the practice dubious, every discussion of the Catholic church, at least in America, is bound to begin with the issue of the relation of the church to a "free society." Such a discussion almost always contains more-or-less prejudiced views of the resources and defects of the Catholic church for the achievement and preservation of "democracy." The Catholic may find this American habit dubious because it probably involves an idolatrous estimate of democracy, which lifts a democratic society into the position of an ultimate criterion of value and truth.

Although I share these misgivings, I shall start this non-Catholic estimate of American Catholicism in the same way, first because I regard the preservation of a free society as important, and secondly because all the judgments about the church by outsiders have, as a matter of fact, this implied or explicit yardstick.

A sympathetic critic of the church would be bound to begin with this theme, if for no other reason than because he is bound to dispel misconceptions general among his fellow-Americans about the relation of the church to democracy. The church is thought to be antidemocratic, partly because it is authoritarian, and partly because its religious unity appears, at least from the perspective of the multicolored Protestant and secular life, to be politically monolithic.

Partly the misconception rests on stereotypes which identify Catholicism with the political structure of Spain, let us say, rather than with France or the German Rhineland. I must admit that these misconceptions have the one grain of truth that they prove that forces other than

---

REINHOLD NIEBUHR (1892–1971), eminent American Protestant theologian and educator, was the author of *Moral Man and Immoral Society, The Nature and Destiny of Man,* and other works.

those in the church operated to transmute medieval social structures into modern ones. But they are misconceptions nevertheless because they underestimate the resources of Catholicism for preserving justice and stability in a free society, once established. They are misconceptions because they do not do justice to the role of Catholicism in the free societies in America, France, Germany, and Western Europe. They do not realize, for instance, what a contribution the Catholic conception of the superiority of political authority over the economic process made in avoiding the aberrations of both doctrinaire "free enterprise" economics and contrasting Marxist aberrations. Nor do these criticisms take account of the practical effects of the church's ability to qualify the class antagonisms in an industrial society by holding the loyalty of the industrial classes and allowing their viewpoints to color the political positions of Catholic political parties. It was this achievement, together with a Christian check on extreme nationalism, which gave Catholicism such a stabilizing influence in an otherwise unstable Weimar Republic, and which determines the creative force of the Catholic parties in modern France and Western Germany.

I say this, though I am grateful that Anglo-Saxon democracy has avoided religious parties, and grateful that Catholic viewpoints have expressed themselves in American life in the voices of such men as the late Philip Murray and the present secretary of labor, without the organization of a Catholic party. I believe, in short, that American non-Catholics do not appreciate the tremendous difference between the church in an unreconstructed medieval social setting and the church finding a creative place in the moral and political reconstruction of a modern industrial society.

An appreciation of this creative role does not eliminate some of the difficulties which even a friendly critic must experience with the role of the church in modern society. The Catholic belief that error does not have the same right as the truth, and its consequent impatience with those democratic practices which seem to arbitrate matters of truth and value by counting noses, is a point of friction between the church and a democratic society. It can be partly resolved if a distinction is made between matters of truth and morals and between matters of detailed application and the technical details involved in the application of moral principles.

I frankly cannot find, in some modern Catholic theory, an adequate consideration of Aquinas's warning that matters of application become increasingly hazardous the further they are removed from principle and involved in adjustment to historical contingency. In this, modern Catholic theory seems to me comparable to modern social science, which does not heed Aristotle's warning that a field of inquiry embodying the historically contingent is not a proper realm for *nous* [the mind] but rather for *phronesis* or "practical wisdom."

Beyond these possible misunderstandings between Catholicism and the ethos of a democracy, there remains the profound difference that democracy, while not determining the truth by the count of noses, is of course relativist in the sense that it would take a chance with error rather than give anyone the absolute authority to define the truth. I think this tension could be overcome if it were understood that no democratic political authority can challenge the authority of the church to define the ultimate truth in its sphere while it was also understood that the state, that is the democratic state, was at least provisionally relativist in not permitting any definition of the truth to infringe upon the "rule of the majority."

Some of us are frankly a little puzzled to know why it was thought necessary, in such books as Ryan and Boland's *Catholic Principles of Politics,* to disavow the early position expounded by the late Cardinal Gibbons and the late Archbishop Ireland, which came to terms with our practical democratic presuppositions, and to insist instead that it was the duty of the state to teach not only religion but the "true religion." This position seems to threaten our nation with the prospects of an established religion, though the fears of non-Catholics are probably unrealistic in view of the qualifications in the Catholic theory.

Some of us hope that the theory will gain ground in the Catholic church that the state is responsible for the general welfare but not for the salvation of souls. We don't know how respectable or orthodox it is, though it has good parentage. It would eliminate a point of friction between the church and the traditions of our nation without sacrificing any important claims of the church.

Next to the problem of the relation of the church to the state, the problem of the relation of Catholicism to the Protestant churches is of great moment to us. I am not anxious to apportion degrees of guilt for a deplorable situation for which the blame must probably be divided fairly evenly; but the relations between Catholics and Protestants in this country are a scandal and an offense against Christian charity.

Last year I was visited by a German Lutheran pastor from the

Rhineland, here on a study tour to acquaint himself with our life. The presupposition of the visit was that the victors could instruct the vanquished in every aspect of "democratic" life, including the relations of the various religious groups. The German visitor was amazed to find the Catholic-Protestant relations were on the level of professional "love feasts" in which members of the various traditions exhorted a common audience in the values of cooperation and of mutual tolerance. But there was nowhere an honest and searching interchange of thought either on questions which have traditionally separated Catholics and Protestants or on current issues which are sore points between them in practical politics.

The German pastor contrasted this condition with the community which existed between Protestants and Catholics in the Rhineland, where he had only recently attended a joint retreat under the leadership of the Bishop of Mainz. He was naturally somewhat amused by the assumption that he could learn from American ecumenical practices, which seemed from his perspective to be "primitive." The fact is that there is very much mutual mistrust and fear between the two groups, partly derived from general causes and partly from conditions which are uniquely American.

It should be recognized on both Protestant and Catholic sides that religion can be a complicating factor in ethnic and racial rivalries. An ethnically heterogeneous nation, such as our own, will therefore be impatient with religious prejudices which aggravate ordinary points of tension. The tension between Catholicism and Protestantism is largely a tension between the Irish and the Anglo-Saxons in Boston, and between earlier and later migrations in the rest of the country, or sometimes between the Nordic and the Slav or Latin. Our religious institutions can assuage, rather than aggravate, these tensions only if there is knowledge of the peculiar force of the religious factor; and commerce rather than hostility between the religious communities.

Beyond this obvious cause there are other points of friction between us. To the Protestant the Catholic church will seem to be a political power rather than a religious community; and to the Catholic the Protestant churches will seem to be Christianity in various states of dissolution into secularism rather than as related to Christian communities. There is no full justice in either impression, but these impressions are bound to grow in a situation of hostility. Naturally one wonders why we could not establish methods of intercourse through which Protestants might learn to appreciate the Catholic church as a religious community with a treasure of graces of the spirit, and Catholics might know Protestant churches as religious communities with a common treasury of faith rather than merely as rival political groups.

While the blame for a deplorable condition must be assessed fairly evenly between the two sides, I feel that Catholicism has a special blame on at least one point of friction between us. This point has to do with the effort to apply the standards of natural law to the life of the community. There is something ironic in the fact that the concept of natural law is regarded by Catholics as a meeting ground for Catholics and non-Catholics, and for Christians and non-Christians, whereas, as a matter of fact, it is really a source of tension between the Catholics and non-Catholics. Marital and family standards, on questions both of divorce and birth control, are the chief points at issue.

I remember participating in one of those formal symposia between Catholics, Jews, and Protestants which pass for serious discussion in America in which the Catholic speaker blandly made the Reformation responsible for the moral relativism and nihilism which ends in "modern sexual promiscuity." It is one of the hazards of Catholic-Protestant relations (which require much more frank discussion to eliminate) that those of us who believe that rigid natural-law concepts represent the intrusion of stoic or Aristotelian rationalism into the more dynamic ethic of Biblical religion are unqualifiedly accused of "moral relativism" or even moral nihilism: our motives in rejecting the thesis that a rigid legalism is the only cure for relativism are impugned; and we are given no credit for wrestling with the moral problems of such historical creatures as human beings who exhibit both a basic structure and endlessly unique elaborations of that structure. This in our opinion makes a rigid rational formula inapplicable while there is no situation in which the double love commandment is not applicable.

In regard to the problem of divorce, we do not, of course, challenge the right of the church to preserve the scriptural standard of the indissolubility of marriage in its community. But we believe it unwise to enforce this standard upon a semi-pagan or semi-secular community by law, when as a matter of fact the preservation of marriage requires real grace and not merely the force of law. We believe that the secular state must do what Moses did "because of the hardness of your hearts," and we do not find the marital records of nations which prohibit divorce rigorously too impressive. They contain too many instances of clandestine arrangements outside of marriage.

The prohibition of birth control becomes a problem among us when bishops threaten long-established "Community Chest" forms of communal cooperation because one of the charities included in the Chest may happen to harbor a birth-control clinic. The prohibition of contraception is regarded by some of us as an illustration of the fact that the Christian abhorrence of naturalism does not prevent "natural law" theories in this instance from sinking to a naturalistic dimension. Nothing is more obvious than the assertion that "nature" intends the end of procreation in sexual relations; but we believe also that the freedom of the human person rises indeterminately above the primary ends of nature. We believe that the temptation to abuse the new freedom which contraception makes possible is in no different category than the temptations and abuses in the whole of modern technical civilization.

The problem of religious education in our nation is a potent source of friction and misunderstanding between the church on the one hand and Protestantism and the general community on the other. Catholics may well be aggrieved to find Protestants and secularists making common cause on this issue and doing so upon the basis of a rigorous interpretation of the historic principle of the separation of church and state which allegedly prohibits even the granting of auxiliary services such as luncheons and bus rides to Catholic children.

Catholics know, and others ought to know, that this conception of an "absolute wall of separation" is not a *sine qua non* of democracy as their opponents claim, because some very healthy democracies in Europe do not observe a principle which our American "liberals" profess to regard as the cornerstone of democracy. Catholics have accepted the situation which forces them to pay double for their children's education with fairly good grace, knowing that whatever may be the traditions in other nations, the "secular" universal public school is a unique American institution which cannot be successfully challenged, not only because hallowed national traditions have a special potency but because the religious pluralism of our nation would make any other solution impossible. They are naturally baffled, and sometimes alarmed, when a nation which extols freedom endlessly seems to envisage the possibility of coercing attendance at the public school in the interest of national unity.

While causes of friction on this issue would seem to lie primarily on the Protestant side, and the Catholics rightly feel the force of a secularist-Protestant alliance against them, they probably do not appreciate the fact that their criticism of the secular character of the secular school is resented, particularly in view of the fact that they could not, in the light of their own principles, support a general religious instruction in the public schools. This resentment is hardly justified, however, since there could not be religious instruction in the public schools even without this complication.

Some of us who would like to see the state grant auxiliary services to Catholic children feel that the failure of Catholics to assure the nation that such a grant would not mean the opening wedge for further claims upon the state for support of parochial schools, has a tendency to stiffen opposition to policies which seem to Catholics to represent simple justice. But our expectation of such promises are probably unreasonable, and indeed the promises might prove ineffective in dissipating Protestant opposition to such measures.

I must apologize for considering the problem of Catholic-Protestant relations in this article rather than the exact theme which the editor assigned to me. This was done because of a pressing personal concern about the absence of any genuine community between us, and the conviction that the inevitable frictions between religious groups and churches will breed mistrust, fear, and even hatred if there is no effort to eliminate misunderstandings.

We owe it to our common Lord to heal the breach between us and to eliminate the scandal of our enmities, which threaten the common decencies and the good order of our country. We would be well advised to remember that the secularism which we pretend to abhor has at least one resource necessary for the health of a democratic community. It knows how to make pragmatic compromises in order to achieve harmony between seemingly incompatible positions, and Christian charity would accomplish the same end if Christians were humble enough to achieve the necessary charity.

THE CATHOLIC CRISIS

GEORGE A. LINDBECK

I n what now seems the distant past before the council ended, I published an article suggesting that the relationship of Catholic and Protestant is rather like that between an occupied country and exiled freedom movements. In this case, however, the freedom forces have forgotten that the reason for their existence is to return to their homeland, a liberated homeland. Instead, they have tried to reestablish their native country abroad, alienated from the depths and continuities of culture and tradition from which they sprang.

This is not a modest view. It is no more modest, though I hope more self-critical, than de Gaulle's attitude toward Vichy France. Nevertheless, as could be expected, a good many of my fellow Protestants thought that it manifested an inordinate lack of self-esteem. They did not, and do not, like to think of Catholicism as having anything which we lack. As a group, we Protestant theologians have little feel for what Paul Tillich called "catholic substance." We tend to talk as if all that is needed is the "protestant principle" with its anti-absolutism, antitraditionalism, iconoclasm, secularism, and liberationism. We are inclined to forget that this principle is essentially a corrective which becomes destructive rather than purifying when it has nothing substantial on which to act.

Given this starting point, a Protestant like myself can't help but be ambivalent about the last ten years of Roman Catholic history. My instinctive sympathies are with Catholic reformers like Hans Küng for whom the chief villains in the present turmoil are the church authorities. They could have saved the church from crisis if only they had not been gradualists or reactionaries. Very little is wrong that would not have been cured by jettisoning ancient rigidities on such matters as birth control and clerical celibacy. "It is best not," Küng concludes one essay, "to flip

---

GEORGE A. LINDBECK (1923–), Lutheran theologian and professor emeritus of the Yale Divinity School, served as a Protestant observer at the Second Vatican Council.

an omelette step by step," and "one has to jump a stream if one wants to avoid getting wet feet." Now, as an heir of the Reformation, my natural inclination is to want the bishops and pope to do even more than Hans Küng asks, but I am increasingly skeptical that this would diminish the crisis.

Almost against my will, I find myself in part persuaded by such "romantic conservatives" (I don't know what else to call them) as James Hitchcock and Garry Wills. It seems to me, as it does to them, that many of those who claim the progressive name have misused the council as a cloak for innovative ego-tripping. They have appealed to the council to justify their own loss of faith, their mindless capitulation to *modernitas*, their devious and unacknowledged departures from what is essential, not only to the Roman tradition, but to Christianity itself. Even the more responsible among them, even the council fathers have done great damage, even if unintentionally. In their search for contemporary relevance or for Christian faithfulness, they have undermined that popular, traditional, cultural Catholicism which, however oppressive and obscurantist it may seem to the upwardly mobile, the educated elite, and the biblical purists, is still the source of meaning and life to multitudes.

The Catholic ghetto provided the masses with group and individual identity, a sense of community, the dignity of belonging someplace amidst the anonymity of postindustrial civilization. It gave them access to glimpses of transcendence, apprehensions of the sacred, awareness of ultimate significance. Perhaps their lives were bedeviled with primitive taboos and superstitions, but the terror and beauty of the primitive are vastly preferable to the flat, moralistic reasonableness of liberal religion, or the mechanical triviality, superficiality, and sensuality of commercialized American secularism. Thus in attacking traditionalism, the *avant garde* has often proved to be, not the proponent of Christian renewal, but simply the accomplice of contemporary Western liberalism and its elitist adherents.

When looked at in this way, the Catholic crisis appears, not as an isolated phenomenon, but as an acute form of a malaise common to all the historic Christian traditions. That, indeed, is my reason as a Protestant for being concerned about it. The Catholic problem is also a non-Catholic problem. The strength also of Protestant churches rests on particular forms of traditional cultural Christianity. They also are in need of both updating and of a return to the sources, of greater relevance and greater faithfulness to revelation, of *modernitas* and *Christianitas*. Otherwise the traditions will continue to decline, increasingly unable to serve either the human needs of their members and of the larger society, or the imperatives of Christian faith.

Yet the difficulties are immense. Most of the Christian faith and vitality which persists is deeply embedded in ever more archaic traditional forms. Nine-tenths of the church members in America whether Protestant or Catholic are, in Gordon Allport's terminology, "extrinsically religious." They use their religion chiefly as a security blanket, a legitimation and support for the way they already live, for the so-called values of an often reactionary version of the American Way of Life. As a result they are more prejudiced against blacks and Jews than the majority of non-churchgoers. Yet there is also a minority of men and women who are intrinsically religious, largely consisting, so the sociologists surprisingly report, of those who go to church and pray and read Scripture most often. For them, substantially more frequently than for the mass of church members, religion is an often uncomfortable transforming power, freeing them in statistically reportable ways from the standard prejudices of their milieu.

There are, to be sure, innumerable exceptions. The ranks of the pious contain the worst hypocrites—namely, the self-deceived ones—as well as men and women of faith. What we need to remember is that the latter have, in most cases, personally interiorized the faith, not apart from their traditions, but in and through them. They have developed their transforming loyalty to the God and Father of the Lord Jesus Christ *via* some specific traditional interpretation of the Christian story, whether Catholic or Protestant, not by unmediated leaps into transcendence or into mystical or romantic interiority, nor even by jumping directly back to the Bible. Therein lies the problem. The destruction of these traditions, whether of fundamentalist revivalism or of Marian devotion, whether by modernization or by insistence on chemically pure Christianity, is also the destruction of the seedbeds of most of the genuine Christian vitality and authentic Christian faith which still lives in our world. To paraphrase what Luther said about the Bible: traditional religion, though often extrinsic and perverted, is the cradle of Christ.

This, then, is the perspective from which my thinking about Catholicism starts. I think first of the people, the religion of the masses, for that is where the strength of any church lies. As long as they retain a strong sense of Catholic identity, institutional and theological collapse can be survived without mortal damage.

Now it seems that the erosion of traditional piety is proceeding faster in American Catholic than in Protestant circles. Its sociological base in the immigrant subcultures is disappearing as Catholics move upwards and outwards in the social, economic, and educational spheres. The devotional practices which were its emotional-experiential core have swiftly disappeared or been downgraded since the council. Younger Catholics even from devout traditional backgrounds know little or nothing of the novenas, benedictions, recitations of the rosary, and cults of the saints which were the major affective components in their parents' religion. The reformed liturgy does not seem to serve as an adequate substitute, in part, as Aidan Kavanaugh and many others have said, because it is in its essential structure a celebration of the intimate communion of believers with Christ and with one another, and simply does not fit in large parish settings. Thus, like the old Mass, the new liturgy is for most Catholics a duty rather than an experience; and now the Counter-Reformation sense of discipline is itself weakening.

Thus, articulated convictions seem to be draining out of popular Catholicism much as they have out of liberal Protestantism, and this is rather more dangerous for the Catholics because they have no remaining, coherently organized mass of traditionalists to recruit from as liberal Protestant denominations have recruited and may expect to continue to recruit from conservative ones.

It is this which makes the institutional crisis, the crisis of authority, so agonizing. I find myself worrying about this crisis precisely because of its effects on the people. They are without a shepherd. Catholic consensus-building mechanisms are in greater disarray than in most other churches.

Current Catholic difficulties involve a special problem of legitimacy. It is true that all institutions are under attack these days, but what has happened in Roman Catholicism is that the church authorities have unwittingly delegitimized themselves. This has happened in a rather precise, almost juridically precise way. What might be called a constitutional crisis has erupted. There are radical and fundamental ambiguities in the most authoritative of recent formulations, those of the Second Vatican Council. Comparable equivocity would be a recipe for disaster in any large and highly organized society. When the supreme law of the land directly authorizes rival, perhaps contradictory, positions and provides no way of settling the disputes, conflict becomes inevitable and, unless changes are made in the supreme law, irresolvable.

The ambiguities which I have in mind can be easily illustrated. Principles were laid down by Vatican II which theologically justify sweeping reforms in the structures, procedures, and goals of the church. At the same time that these revolutionary principles were enunciated, however, the old formulations were also repeated. What the First Vatican Council said a hundred years ago about the papacy, for example, were simply re-iterated, inserted without modification or re-interpretation in what is a radically different vision of both church and world. Similarly, individu-alistic other-worldliness is juxtaposed rather than joined with a cosmic and communal eschatology which makes the humanization of social and cultural structures a primary Christian duty. Thus biblicists, moderniz-ers, traditionalists, and papalists can all appeal quite consistently to this or that aspect of the council's teaching, and can argue that the features they choose as primary provide the hermeneutical key for the interpreta-tion of the whole. The Berrigans and their supporters can point to the conciliar social and political interpretations of the commandment of Christian love as authorization for their opposition to Vietnam, while their opponents can argue that tradition forbids, and the council never specifically approves, the kind of civil disobedience in which the Berri-gans engage. Hans Küng can insist that the council's emphasis on the Bible demands a thorough review of the doctrine of infallibility, while his critics reply that the biblical emphasis must be understood in the light of tradition, especially the tradition of Vatican I, rather than the other way around. There is no publicly persuasive way of showing who is the faithful Catholic, simply because the council is equivocal on these and a whole range of other questions.

At the time of the council, most of us who were observers thought of these equivocations as politically necessary, but of no great practical mo-ment. The ambiguities would give the pope and bishops greater freedom in interpreting and implementing the conciliar decrees, but the Catholic clergy, religious, and faithful would remain obedient. We could not have been more mistaken. Many in the lower ranks remained obedient, per-haps, but not so much to the current directives of the church leaders as to what they regard as even more authoritative, namely, the spirit and the letter of the council.

As a consequence, non-Catholic church leaders, oddly enough, are now less likely to be attacked than Catholic ones. Their authority is more clearly legitimated. The Eastern Orthodox, when challenged, can take refuge in tradition, and the Protestants in past or future general conven-tions. "If you don't like what we do," they can generally say, "then get the next assembly to vote on your side." The Roman Catholic hierarchy has no such recourse. It still has, of course, tremendous power. It controls appointments and the purse, makes and unmakes rules, and determines policy. But illegitimate power is perceived as *tyranny*, and at point after point the bishops can't help but act tyrannically because they contradict what many in the church sincerely believe to be the import of the council.

The difficulty, to repeat, cannot be resolved. A pope who agreed theologically with Hans Küng, for example, might well have every whit as difficult a time as Paul VI, except that now the opposition would shift. People like Bill Buckley make it clear that conservatives also are able to refer to council, church, tradition, and even the Bible against the pope or bishops whenever it suits their purposes.

If this general view of what is happening has any validity, then the crisis cannot be solved, not even by a new pope, but only lived through. Another council will in all likelihood eventually settle the constitutional question, that is, the question of how to interpret Vatican II, just as the Council of Constantinople quieted the storms raised by Nicea, and Chalcedon by Ephesus. This settlement, however, cannot be rushed. It would be disastrous to try in the near future to remove the ambiguities of Vatican II. A basic consensus ranging from the people through the clergy and theologians to the bishops has not yet been forged. When it is, perhaps Catholics will have come to think that the solution of their constitutional crisis is inseparable from the question of Christian unity. They may have come to believe, for example, that the full symbolic, even if not canonical, ecumenicity of a council requires the participation of all interested Christian bodies, not just of the Roman communion. If so, perhaps decades will pass before the basic institutional problem is finally resolved.

This is an appalling prospect, yet it does not, in my view, justify the predictions of a Malachi Martin, for example, that the Roman church as we have known it will disappear before the end of the century. No church, not even the Roman, is fundamentally its hierarchy. Even total institutional collapse on the highest levels is likely to be transitory. For the foreseeable future, there will be millions and millions of people throughout the world who take pride in thinking of themselves as Catholic Christians as did their fathers and fathers' fathers back, in some cases, to the sixtieth generation. If a great schism were to occur, as happened in the Middle Ages, they would be most unhappy. A precious part of their identity would be threatened. They would have difficulty in thinking of themselves as Catholic because there would no longer be an agreed-upon successor to the bishops of Rome with whom they could be in visible communion, along with Asians and Africans and Europeans. This would generate an enormous and lasting popular pressure on the leaders—who would be leaders of nothing without the people—to settle the disputes. Eventually, in all likelihood, there would be another council like that of Constance in the fifteenth century, and the schism would be healed. This is simple elementary social psychology. It is also, I would suppose, elementary Catholic theology, now that the council has made clear that the church is, first of all, not the institution of salvation, but the people of God. The Roman church does not endure first of all because of the papacy, but the papacy endures because its symbolization of universality and continuity exerts a powerful attraction on the imagination and emotions, wills and minds, of multitudes of human beings.

Further, in long-range terms, it seems to me possible to be moderately optimistic about popular piety also. Given a generation or two, the liturgical reforms may well be the source of a renewed and far more biblical spirituality. It took that long or longer, in some regions, so historians tell us, for the Reformation's changes in worship to shape a new piety among the people. Especially in view of the structural intimacy of the new liturgy, this will be the more likely to occur to the degree that the church declines in numbers and becomes a diaspora, a scattered minority, in the world.

As we come now to the end of this analysis, I am acutely aware of a great gap. Crisis spells, not only threat, but opportunity. I have said scarcely anything of the immense vitality and creativity of contemporary Catholicism. I have said not a word about what Archbishop Camara represents in Brazil, nor about the exhilarating conflict in Spain, nor the depressing one in Holland, nor about developments in Africa—to mention just four points which may prove decisive to world Catholicism and therefore also for the United States. The major excitement in the church these days is on the Catholic, not the Protestant side. Nothing in the non-Catholic world remotely compares in tragedy and comedy, both high and low, to the scene sketched in last spring's *Time* magazine cover story on the Jesuits. A half-filled Catholic seminary is in my experience often much more lively, as well as chaotic and frustrating, than a full Protestant one. This liveliness is both pastoral and theological, extending both to the struggle for the personal reality of faith and for its intellectual formulation and understanding. Catholics at this moment in history may rarely feel this way, but my impression is that the future of Christianity as a whole, to the degree that it has a future, is now bursting forth in a thousand often absurdly unexpected forms within the Roman church. Most of the innovations will and should perish, but some contain the seeds of what is to come. The losses and confusion are great, but so is the hope.

THE CHURCH UNDER HITLER

GORDON C. ZAHN

I n one sense it might be said that the church has come upon unfriendly times. Despite all the favorable attention earned . . . at Vatican II, it finds itself the object of a continuing (and increasingly critical) review which has at times verged upon an outright indictment for complicity—at least by silence—in the criminal acts of Adolf Hitler and his Third Reich.

A new breed of German historians and journalists, including some outstanding Catholics, have played a significant part in this revisionist study. The most widely publicized, though perhaps least meritorious in terms of scholarship, has been the contribution of Rolf Hochhuth and the worldwide controversy it has stirred. He, it will be remembered, did not content himself with chronicling the sad failure of German Catholicism to recognize a gross moral evil and oppose it effectively and in time; instead, he chose to indict the leader of the universal church with a personal, and major, share of responsibility for the atrocity of the "Final Solution."

Now we have yet another treatment of this general theme, *The Catholic Church and Nazi Germany,* written by Guenter Lewy (McGraw-Hill). It is undoubtedly the best. Professor Lewy's analysis is different from the others in the range of issues it covers, in the probing thoroughness of its analysis, and in the authoritative quality of his sources. It is unlikely that its preeminence will be challenged until (if even then?) the Vatican archives for this tragic period are finally made available to scholars for free and independent research. One suspects that the materials made available to this author in the various diocesan archives he visited in Germany are a reliable foreshadowing of what the Vatican deposits will reveal.

GORDON C. ZAHN (1918–), professor emeritus of sociology at the University of Massachusetts–Boston, is the author of *German Catholics and Hitler's Wars* and *In Solitary Witness: The Life and Death of Franz Jägerstätter.*

It will be interesting to see how this work will be received by that hardy band of apologists who regard it as their sacred duty to denounce anyone who would dare voice even the slightest hint of criticism concerning the Catholic record in Nazi Germany. Lewy has closed most, if not all, doors of escape for them. On the one hand, he presents evidence that is so brutally clear and shocking that one wonders how it has been overlooked until now. At the same time, he presents it in a tone of restrained scholarly detachment that makes it possible for him to so control his personal disapproval of the story he tells that his work never crosses the line separating scholarly analysis from indictment.

The first section sets the stage by reviewing the "prehistory" of the encounter between the Catholic church and National Socialism. It begins with a survey of the early pattern of firm and open opposition and ends with the "great reconciliation" which took place once what had been an objectionable political movement became "legitimate authority." The negotiations which brought the surprisingly speedy conclusion of a Concordat in 1933 are discussed in careful detail with the result that the author's interpretation, placing a greater measure of responsibility for this development upon the Catholic parties than is usually the case, becomes quite convincing.

The heart of the work, however, is the extensive review of the *modus vivendi* issuing from that Concordat. Whether he surveys the suppression of Catholic organizations and press, the harassment of confessional schools, or the areas of church support for Nazi foreign policies and the war to which these led, the pattern held. None of the repeated violations of the Concordat on the part of the state, none of the offenses against human values initiated by the Nazi leaders, were ever allowed to provoke a final break or even the serious threat of such a break as far as the official Catholic leadership was concerned. Protests there could be, of course; but they were always voiced in a tone of sorrow or indignation derived from the fact that the unshaken loyalty and compliance shown by the church and its members were not being given proper recognition by the secular authority. Even the one outstanding exception, the firm opposition to the sterilization and euthanasia programs, is weakened by the fact that, in the case of the former at least, theological lines were being drawn to permit confessors to spare individual Catholics the "conflict of conscience" or the personal risk that a rigid conversion of general moral principle to individual moral obligation might have provoked.

Other troubling findings concern the endemic strains of anti-Semitism in German Catholic thought and practice and the implications they obviously held for the absence of effective opposition to even the earliest stages of Hitler's persecution of the Jews. Similarly, the discussion of the attitudes concerning support for, or participation in, the Resistance movement forces the reader to question the official praise and honor that has since been lavished upon the Delps, the Rupert Mayrs, the Lichtenbergs, and all the others who did "redeem the day" by taking some kind of stand in opposition to an evil regime and its immoral policies. It is quite clear that they took that stand alone and with no significant encouragement from their spiritual superiors.

The book concludes with Lewy's rather brief statement and discussion of what he, a political scientist, sees as the three basic dimensions of "Catholic political ideology."

The criticisms are not new. Once again the point is made that the church has only recently, and with some reluctance, come to recognize the virtues of democracy; that the frequently proclaimed indifference to the various forms of government, coupled with its own authoritarian and autocratic structure, has rendered its members too susceptible to the appeals of totalitarianism; that it is perhaps too reticent about stressing sociopolitical applications of moral principles when doing so would seem to present some threat to institutional security. What is new is the terribly compelling force these familiar criticisms gain in the context of this most tragic historical example of the failure these tendencies can produce.

There are so many important lessons to be drawn from a book like this that one despairs of making an adequate choice. There is, first of all, what one might term the "boomerang effect" of the myth of total church opposition to Nazism that was so carefully created after the war and is, even today, so fervently (if hopelessly) maintained in some quarters. It is now quite clear—and should have been frankly admitted all along—that the general support given the Hitler regime as "legitimate authority" outweighed whatever opposition was mounted by any of the major religious communities of Germany and that even this opposition was generally restricted to limited ecclesiastical concerns. Had there been an honest admission of this fact at the time of the collapse of the Third Reich, the religious communities—and this holds particularly true for the Catholic community—could still have claimed a significant measure of respect and honor if only by virtue of the fact that, however restricted it was, they constituted virtually the only center of any open opposition to the regime.

Unfortunately, this was not enough. With the eager acquiescence of the Western occupation authorities, the apologists set to work and brought forth an overly idealized portrait of a suffering but still unbending church rallying its loyal supporters to heroic resistance against the Nazis. To accomplish this dubious success, some of these writers did not even stop short of tampering with the carefully selected documentation they offered to support their case. What had to happen has now happened: objective scholarly research has zipped away the veils of this carefully manufactured mythology.

The tragedy is that now the record which would have looked so good in comparison with what other groups in Germany had been able to do has to look extremely bad because it is compared instead with the false picture that was so laboriously engineered. Even so respected a figure as Cardinal Faulhaber loses much of the luster that was rightfully his, simply because of the misguided attempt to elaborate upon his record and present him as a far more open and forthright defender of the Jews than the cold facts now show him to have been.

A second lesson relates more to the substance of the record described in that it forces us to consider the extent to which the actions of the official church were marked by a particularistic, rather than universal, concern. Instead of voicing open protest whenever the rights of any individuals or groups were being trampled, the responsible Catholic spokesmen apparently saw their proper range of concern limited to those of their own household. In fact, there were instances in which the violations of the rights of others were condoned or even applauded.

Thus we have the almost eager willingness to accept and praise the Nazi suppression of Socialist organizations and press followed by indignant shrieks of protest when the same violations of rights were directed against their Catholic counterparts. . . .

The sharpest illustration of the shameful effects of such particularistic thinking is the record of silence in the face of the persecution of the Jews. Long before the transports took off for the journey to the extermination camps, there were occasions demanding appropriate and effective protest. Certainly one may hold that, had the excesses of *Krystallnacht* in November 1938 and the officially proclaimed boycott of the Jews which followed been greeted by a firm episcopal statement advising Catholics not to support so patently unjust a policy, it is very likely that "the Hochhuth problem" would have been nipped in its earliest bud. But, once again, these actions were directed against those not of "our household" with the result that, however much personal sympathy they might have stirred, the course of "prudent" silence ruled the day. . . .

This kind of particularist thinking was at least linked to an awareness of religious identification. Another, and in some respects even more scandalous, kind relates to the excessively nationalistic commitment evidenced by German Catholics from the highest ranking prelate to the ordinary man in the pew. Once again we are faced with irrefutable evidence of how this factor can work to distort and block moral judgment in such a way as to support the contention that nationalism should be recognized as the "characteristic heresy of our day."

The record of the efforts made by the German bishops of the Saar to assure as unanimous a vote as possible favoring return to Germany in the 1936 plebiscite—and this despite the fact that the Nazi regime had already given evidence of its hostility to the Catholic church in Germany—has to be read in full detail to be believed. Yet they were not alone in this. The German bishops themselves (with the ardently anti-Nazi Galen playing a leading part) issued a proclamation calling for the return of the Saar, a proclamation which included an order that three Lord's Prayers and *Ave Marias* be added to all Sunday Masses on the day of the vote so that this outcome might be assured.

In such a context we are no longer surprised at the exaggerated nationalism following the "success" of the vote, nor should it be surprising that, once Hitler's foreign policies reached their logical culmination in a series of clearly aggressive wars, German Catholics were more than ready to do "their Christian duty" in support of those wars.

Thus, just as a circle was drawn to limit the moral concern of the official church to Catholics within the national community, another set of boundaries limited its moral concerns to that same national community as against the rest of the world. It is difficult to imagine a more persuasive case for the kind of separation of church and state which will protect the religious community against the temptation of ever again reducing itself to an instrumentality of a warring secular power.

Lewy's careful work should be for us a beginning. It should prompt us to reevaluate the adequacy and validity of the ethical principles which have come to dominate Catholic political philosophy and its application in the real political order. If it is quite clear in retrospect that they were not adequate and certainly not valid as they operated to govern the relationship between the Catholic church and the Third Reich, it might be most prudent to work on the admittedly pessimistic assumption that the same would be true with respect to the relationships that obtain between the church and any modern state.

MISREMEMBERED

THE EDITORS

Eleven years in the writing, "We Remember: A Reflection on the Shoah," released last month by the Vatican's Commission for Religious Relations with the Jews, will not and should not satisfy those on any side of the tortuous debate about the church's responsibility for anti-Semitism and possible complicity in the Nazi extermination of 6 million Jews. Although the sincerity of the statement's desire for genuine reconciliation between Christians and Jews cannot be second-guessed, the document as a whole is a grievous disappointment.

Most notably, some Jewish leaders have expressed sharp exception to, and even anger at, the Vatican's defense of Pius XII's failure to condemn Nazi atrocities in explicit terms. That reaction is understandable, although in fairness to the Vatican it should be said that Pius's alleged moral insensibility is not as self-evident as many—thanks largely to the distortions of Rolf Hochhuth's 1963 play, *The Deputy*—assume. Similarly, the pope's power "To Save Jews From Nazis" (as a recent *New York Times* headline put it) continues to be much exaggerated, even as the church's actual efforts to help hundreds of thousands of Jews are too easily dismissed. Nonetheless, calls for the opening of the Vatican's diplomatic archives to independent scholars should be heeded. Although it is not likely that Pius's moral culpability will be greatly clarified in the process, there is no chance that Pius will be dealt with fairly until all relevant documents are made public.

Other Jewish spokespersons have commended the Vatican statement for its unequivocal condemnation of anti-Semitism, and of past Christian persecution and violence against Jews. The document's embrace of the religious heritage and aspirations shared by Jews and Catholics is another reason for commendation. For many involved in the ongoing Catholic-Jewish dialogue, "We Remember" is rightly seen as an incremental step in a long journey, in this regard resembling *Nostra aetate* (1965), Vatican II's groundbreaking repudiation of the idea of collective Jewish guilt for Christ's death and affirmation of God's continuing covenant with the Jews. No one familiar with these issues can expect two thousand years of misunderstanding and worse to be set straight in a few decades.

Or without missteps along the way. In that regard, certain aspects of "We Remember" will need revising. Most unsatisfactory is the statement's refusal to attribute any fault or error for anti-Semitism to the church itself. "Erroneous and unjust interpretations of the New Testament regarding the Jewish people," Christian teachings that engendered "feelings of hostility," are acknowledged. But "the church as such," according to the Vatican, was never responsible. "The Catholic church desires to express her deep sorrow for the failures of her sons and daughters in every age," but never, it seems, does the church as a responsible entity have anything to repent for.

Catholics familiar with the traditional theological distinction that places the "church as such" over and above its fallible human members will understand how this kind of language is being used. The tradition holds that any suggestion of error on the part of Christ's mystical body is a theological oxymoron. But that very subtle distinction, expressing as it does a valid understanding of the church's unique access to religious truth, will certainly be lost on most readers of "We Remember." More likely, this assertion of the church's metaphysical reliability will be read, with reason, as the worst kind of this-worldly moral evasion. If over the course of centuries anti-Semitism was rarely if ever condemned but rather ignored, tolerated, even encouraged; if it infected not only the laity but priests and bishops; if church councils promulgated laws segregating and discriminating against Jews; if until very recent times anti-Semitism was given vivid expression in the Good Friday liturgy (the "perfidious Jews") and in religious art; and if this led to pogroms, to the terrors of the Inquisition—if, in short, anti-Semitism suffused much of Catholic culture for nineteen centuries, it is hard to see how "the church as such" can be held guiltless.

However one wants to understand the relationship between the mystical and the visible elements of the church, the incontrovertible historical record attests to the fact that "the church," and not just its members, taught erroneously, even perniciously, about Judaism and the Jews. If the Vatican statement means only that no pope or ecumenical council or curial body ever elevated anti-Semitism to the level of formal doctrine, that is not so large a claim and will not, in the eyes of most people of any faith or none, absolve "the church as such" of responsibility for policies, attitudes, and actions that taught as clearly as any encyclical.

Sad to say, "We Remember" is also tendentious and unpersuasive in its analysis of the nature of Nazi anti-Semitism and its relationship to what the document calls historic Christian anti-Judaism. Nazi racial anti-Semitism is attributed to "a false and exacerbated nationalism . . . essentially more sociological and political than religious." The document insists that the Holocaust had "its roots outside of Christianity" as the "work of a thoroughly modern neo-pagan regime."

To be sure, there are important distinctions to be made between Christian anti-Semitism and Nazi race hatred. The Vatican is right to remind the world that the church condemned the "idolatry of race and of the state." Although it proved to be a woefully ineffective obstacle to the Nazis, and millions of Catholics rallied to the Nazi cause, the Catholic church did not in any sense perpetrate the Holocaust. However, to argue that there was no connection between nearly 2,000 years of church-inspired anti-Semitism and the Nazi assault on European Jewry is utterly fallacious and offensive. Similarly, for "We Remember" to rehearse the political history of the nineteenth and twentieth centuries and not acknowledge how the church's opposition to liberalism and democracy weakened the forces best able to deter fascism is equally disingenuous.

Nazi totalitarianism was, as the document argues, an unprecedented modern horror whose unique evil was difficult for all but the most prescient to grasp at first. But Nazism did not spring full grown from the atheistic brow of the modern world. It had obvious roots in Europe's near and ancient Christian past.

How the church can repent or correct the manifest errors of its past if it cannot honestly admit to any errors at all is, to say the least, something of a problem. This is brought home again when "We Remember" calls Western democracies to account for their failure to give refuge to Jews seeking asylum from the Nazis. That failure to act placed a "heavy burden of conscience on the authorities in question," judges the Vatican. Fair enough. But is no similar burden to be placed on the shoulders of church authorities who failed to act in their own sphere?

Various contemporary challenges to Catholic teaching seem to make the appeal to church inerrancy an increasing temptation on the part of the Vatican. But as "We Remember" exemplifies, the doctrine of inerrancy errantly applied is no real help to authority in the end.

THE EVERLASTING DILEMMA

PAUL ELIE

I't's something I do whenever I go to church, part of the ritual before the ritual, the liturgical pregame. I claim my six feet of pew, shuck my coat, check my watch, and make a nodding attempt to woo solemnity. Then I size up the crowd. Anybody else young here? There's a couple whose matching madras shorts declare them JUST MARRIED. A girl wearing a Cardinal Hayes sweatshirt twists a finger through her brilliant red hair. A Columbia University student, Opus Dei division, is bent over in the stylized prostration of a fresco saint. I take an interior leap, joining them in that most inclusive of groups, the generation. Our generation. What brings us together? What do we share? How do we believe? What are we doing here, today?

If you cast the net wide and claim as "young Catholics" all of the people between the ages of twenty and thirty-five who at least "retain residual loyalties to and identification" with the church, we are a crowd (40 percent of adult Catholics are younger than thirty-five, according to one study). Having grown up in the shadow of Vatican II, during a period of phenomenal social change, we share a compelling experience. Yet our religious character is felt to be limp and shallowly rooted; perhaps we aren't authentically Catholic. Older Catholics have found it hard to get a handle on us—a problem compounded by our lack of a collective identity, and by our seeming reluctance, or inability, to articulate our religious beliefs and act on them.

Of course, concerns about passing on the faith are endemic to Catholicism, and to religion in general. In this country the alarm seems to sound every other papacy or so, as the church feels The World aggressively courting the faithful's hearts and minds and attention spans. Re-

PAUL ELIE (1965–), an editor for a New York publishing house, graduated from Fordham University and Columbia University's Graduate Writing Division. He is the editor of *A Tremor of Bliss: Contemporary Writers on the Saints*.

sponses to the alarm have been various. After the Third Plenary Council a century ago, the parochial school system tried walling the world out in order to nurture God's children within; a generation ago the church as a whole took the opposite tack, practically redefining itself as God's people in order to go out into the world along with those children.

Like those efforts, the present discussions about young Catholics have the split personality of a saving act, with everyday pessimism under-girded by the hopefulness of a redeemed people. There are important differences this time around, however. Most striking, to me, is the extent to which these discussions about young Catholics are grounded in Vati-can II's understanding of the church as the people of God. If what I've gleaned from paperback religious history is sound, previous reclamation efforts focused on saving souls, with the church's continued eminence taken for granted. In contrast, the present discussions about young Catholics suggest that Catholic leaders are less concerned with our wel-fare than with the well-being of the church generally. This is a natural consequence of the council's revised understanding of the church, and its corresponding revision of the nature of salvation. If you see the church chiefly as the body of its people, and not chiefly as, say, a divine agency appointed by God to do his saving work on earth, your in-house evan-gelizing efforts will be less menacing but also somewhat less compelling. Since you see young Catholics as responsible adults and not as God's children in need of divine protection, at most you can strongly encour-age them to be open to the life of faith. Your sense that Catholicism isn't taking hold on the younger end leads you to think not of souls lost for eternity, but of the church losing its vigor in the here and now. Because you can't get all that worked up about young people going to hell, you mostly worry that if you fail to sponsor a Catholic identity in them, the religion you've known will go out of this corner of the world, and the kids will have missed out on something grand.

Protest though you may, if you are an American church leader today, deep down you see Catholicism as necessary in our culture but optional for this or that person. This is realistic, right-thinking, open-minded, a balm for the soul in tough times—but it lowers the stakes of your enter-prise, and ushers in a spirit of contradiction and self-doubt right from the start.

How or why should young adults continue as bearers of the Catholic tradition? Earnestly, older Catholics try to understand our relationships with the church—our tendency to pick and choose from church teachings, our relative ignorance of Christian history and doctrine, our way of measuring the church by our own experience, our willingness to keep religion at the margins of our lives, and our basically good intentions despite it all. Robert Egan has summed up these concerns: "How do we hand on anything we love or care about? How do we hand on the inspirations for our committed service and the causes of our joy? How do we hand on an intellectual tradition, a symbolic and sacramental tradition, a prophetic and politically engaged tradition, a tradition of valuing community, in a culture like our own?"

It is a formidable challenge in any era. The problem, many say, is that young Catholics are in the church but not of it. We belong to parishes, attend services, marry other Catholics, and hope to raise our children Catholic, whatever that might mean. We keep abreast of the most visible church activities and controversies, let our thoughts tend Christward when time permits, have vague spiritual experiences and ethical criteria, mean well. Okay, we are Catholics—and yet we lack a moral and religious vocabulary, an informed awareness of tradition, an acceptance of duty, an understanding of obedience, a respect for a hierarchy of values, a sense of the church's absoluteness. In short, many say, we lack the essential traits of Catholicism as it has been passed down from age to age.

Such a view enables church leaders to identify much that is true about young Catholics today, as well as to address absences or failures of the spirit that they feel in the church themselves. Yet in the end the in-the-church-but-not-of-it interpretation obscures as much as it clarifies. Why? It puts the emphasis in the wrong place, presents the paradox upside down. More than we are in the church but not of it, my experience suggests, young Catholics today are of the church but not in it: Though we will describe ourselves as Catholic, we balk at calling ourselves Catholics, wary of the belonging the stronger noun form connotes. The differences are subtle, but crucial. I think the church's recognition of this might encourage young Catholics to stop sliding down the slippery slope and get on with our ascent.

How are young Catholics "of the church"? First of all—as the experts' statistics make clear—we consider ourselves Catholic. We share the "Catholic sensibility" and "sacramental imagination" identified by Eugene Kennedy and David Tracy. We measure our lives, and the church's, by Christ's teachings in the Gospels. We feel the influence of this or that priest, nun, or lay person (often a parent). We take a familial, proprietary interest in the doings of Governor Mario Cuomo or Father Bruce Ritter or the "20/20" exorcist. Even if we don't know our way around the *Summa* or read the encyclicals the day they come out, we seek wholeness, harmony, and radiance, a sense of order and a rule of life, a body of values and images that will locate transcendence in the day to day. We have misgivings as we strive for "worldly" success, and feel uneasy as we attain it. Pursuing our own ends, we try to be unselfish and attentive to other people's needs and suffering. We want to live Christian lives and then go to heaven—and yet we are (most of us, most of the time) wary of full-blown belonging, the sort of commitment that, Catholic leaders contend, would regenerate Catholicism and American culture as well.

In what ways are we not quite "in the church"? The most talked-about indicator, of course, is that few of us consider ourselves called to serve the church as priests or religious. As much as this has to do with the demands of professed religious vocations (celibacy, tests of orthodoxy, long hours, low pay), it has more to do with a deeper impulse: namely, that so many of us are willing to let our Catholicism rest at the level of "residual loyalties and affiliation." This impulse shakes out for us in all sorts of ways. We might check "Catholic" on a census form or Lilly questionnaire, but we often check our Catholicism at the door of the top-flight graduate school or big corporation; conversely, we too often leave our skills as thinkers or workers at home when we go to church, consigning the dirty work to the priests and veterans and fanatics. Rather than seriously challenging church positions to which we might object—sexuality, the role of women, capitalism, war—we disregard them, or else confine our dissent to our kitchens and bedrooms. We partake of the sacraments as if they're performed for us as a public service, without feeling compelled to serve in our own ways. Though we feel misgivings about success, we stay on the ladder; though we want to be unselfish, we don't go out of our way to be. While the surveys count us as "young Catholics," for us church membership is usually a secondary affiliation—mainly we're bankers or teachers or students or feminists or Deadheads or New Yorkers or Giants fans. The church has always been there for us, and so, we assume, it always will be, regardless of whether we play active roles in it. After all, it's not our church; sure, we belong to it—but not really. Someone else will assume the day-to-day responsibility; somebody else will take charge.

Most of these traits have been noted. But interpreting them as signs that we are Catholic more than we are Catholics, and not the other way round, might yield the solutions about how to revive us and the church.

It might explain a number of phenomena: Why the polls say the churches are full of young people, while the priests' eyes say the young laborers are few—being "of the church" always and everywhere, we don't need to confirm it by being in the church on any particular day. Why young Catholics, so stealthy and somnolent when we are in church, are so animated by the God-talk in Woody Allen's films or Bill Moyers's PBS chats with Joseph Campbell: glib and elliptical as they are, those people discuss life and death, history and eternity, in the sort of frank, learned language that rarely issues from the pulpits of suburbia. Why our collective identity is so slippery and vague: without the shared liturgy and community that come with being in the church, our of-the-churchness makes itself felt in more varied and ambiguous ways. Why there is a definite "twice-born" sensibility among those young Catholics, especially the better-educated ones, who are learned in and committed to a life of faith: since so little is expected of us by now beyond residual loyalties and affiliation, real religious experience comes upon us like the hand of God. Why attendance at campus chapels usually tops that in the average parish: there, far more than elsewhere, young Catholics are encouraged to believe that this is our church, that we are not junior members or summer associates or novices in formation but the thing itself—Catholics, worshiping our God, taking part in the rites of our religion, practicing our faith.

Perhaps most important, seeing young Catholics as of the church more than in it might explain why people thirty-five years old, fully adult by any other standard, can still be considered "young Catholics." If solid, informed, public commitment is Catholic leaders' measure of religious maturity, it follows that so many of us, uncommitted less because of age than because of disposition, nonetheless seem so young to them, so reluctant to come into our inheritance, with all its demands and rewards.

Such a measure of religious maturity is a fundamental reason why so many of us will never get there. For the of-the-church outlook I've described is a religion of sensibility; and sensibility, as the *New Republic*'s Andrew Sullivan has noted, "is a paltry substitute for revealed truth," a shadow of the spiritual promise that Jesus announced and urged us toward. Sensibility is not the stuff of commitment. It alone cannot regenerate any church or transform any culture, and a generation of Catholics who consider themselves merely "of the church" won't invigorate their religion, much less usher in any kingdom of God.

How might young Catholics' religion of sensibility be fleshed out and made whole? Clearly our acceptance or rejection of this religion is ultimately our own responsibility. But older Catholics clearly have much to offer us as we come to terms with Christ and the church—if they are willing. Ironically, many such leaders, having done everything in their power to bring us up in the church, now would keep us out of it because we aren't Catholic enough, with their sense of our difference from them undermining their efforts to share a faith with us. Not only is this sense of our difference a self-fulfilling prophecy; it also obscures what we all share—our Americanness, for example, and our place on this side of Vatican II. Today's older American Catholics are the first to have lived in rapprochement with the modern world, bodying forth the outward-looking church the council called for in a setting where modernity is particularly aggressive and enchanting. As such they have a great deal in common with young Catholics, whether they think so or not.

As far as church leaders' responsibilities go, then, the first step toward young Catholics' fleshy wholeness is fairly simple. Passive and uninformed as our faith may seem to be, older Catholics should regard it as continuous with their own faith and the one handed down by the Apostles, hoping that keener faith will follow. Is this a deal with the devil? Arguably. Will it "work"? Maybe.

But how? How might sensibility be developed, prompting the church's younger members to come more fully into the fold? *Commonweal*'s editors have suggested that most observers "too readily credit the council for a generation gap and overlook the powerful pull of American culture in absorbing young Catholics into the mainstream." Powerful as the influence of American culture upon young Catholics is, in my view the influence of Vatican II upon us cannot be stressed enough. And in the analyses of the council's effects, the key one is often underplayed. This is our sense that there are two churches—the church as it is now and the church as it was before Vatican II. From what I've seen, young people striving for a mature understanding of Catholic faith feel that we must come to terms not only with the present church, but with another, older one. Largely through legend and anecdote and outdated depictions in the media and the arts, that church lingers just over the horizon as the church we never knew—an evil empire, a land of milk and honey, the repressive regime, the real thing, a straw man, the body of Christ, the source of life or of our parents' compulsions and our neuroses. Young Catholics may act as if we're unaware of, or uninterested in, Catholic tradition—but we're grappling with that old church, its Latin Masses and catechisms and Friday fasts and seeming certitudes and its way of affecting those who did know it. Making our peace with that church is often a necessary step toward making our peace with the present one.

Here a snapshot of my own spiritual gropings might help to illustrate the point. The outlines of it are the kind that Catholic leaders have held up as ideals. A Catholic upbringing that imparted a sense of God's presence and the church's importance, in a family that offered the constancies of faith, hope, and love. After public high school, a Jesuit university education, which provided all the elements of "Catholic identity": the instruments for navigating in the Christian heritage, a number of exemplary teachers and priests, a sense of the church's intellectual resources past and present, and a life among Catholic believers of all sorts, in a setting where religion was actively practiced and intelligently discussed—a school of, with, and for faith, to put it simply. Later, graduate work at a university on the frontiers of multiculturalism, which prompted me to explore and assert my own cultural heritage, if only to set myself apart the way everybody else was doing.

With all due gratitude to everyone, however, I must say that in understanding Catholicism I came to feel that I was on my own. Regardless of whether this was true, it was made so by my sense that it was, and enforced by the fact that my religious flare-ups came during the summers, when I was out of school and pretty much alone. As an aspiring writer, I naturally looked to books; as a typically literal-minded young person, I longed for a synthesis that would interpret Catholicism for me and answer all the big questions: What brings us together? What do we share? How do we believe? What are we doing here, today?

In my pursuit of synthetic truth, I ran smack up against Vatican II. The old medieval and Tridentine syntheses seemed tainted, since I assumed that their essentials had been revised or reversed by the council. Though the broadest of the newer books (such as Rahner's and Küng's) seemed shorn of Catholic language and history, they presupposed the very knowledge of Catholic tradition that I sought from them. Sure, these were shallow impressions—but thus deterred, I never read any of those books through.

Instead, while I waited to discover the big book that would make sense of it all, I read little ones of all sorts—old and new, Orbis and Ignatius, Penguin and Paulist, skeptical and devotional, from Augustine to Chesterton to Copleston to Berrigan to Pelikan to all sorts of "Catholic"

fiction—Waugh's, Endo's, David Lodge's *How Far Can You Go?* And
then, of course, there were the Gospels and Epistles, bound pocket-size
or in massive study versions with their involuted commentaries and tiny
notes. Of all these books, the ones I found most congenial and moving
were those by Newman, Merton, and Flannery O'Connor—the greatest
hits of the preconciliar era, I know now. Each of these writers became my
companion in faith for a while, as I tried to fully enter into his or her
outlook. But my efforts were thwarted, again, by Vatican II. Reading
these writers required an ongoing act of translation, as I compared the
church they described with the one I encountered, which seemed to give
the lie to so much of what they set forth—whether Newman's idea of the
church as "a supereminent prodigious power sent upon earth to encounter and master a giant evil," or O'Connor's praise of its "absolute
values," or Merton's evocation of a Sunday when the priests were young
and the church was full and the sermon was "clear and solid," carrying
"the full force not only of Scripture but of centuries of a unified and
continuous and consistent tradition." What did that church have in
common with the shifty and self-doubting church I knew—its values
uncertain, its everyday tradition going back to 1955 or so, its sermons inspired by M. Scott Peck and Phil Donahue? And which church was the
one, holy, catholic, apostolic one? As a young Catholic, had I been dis-
inherited by the council, or given the keys to the kingdom?

Of course, the two churches had much in common—namely, God
and Christ and the workings of the Spirit in a fallen world. And what
Merton and Newman and O'Connor conveyed, as no synthesis could
have, was the urgency and necessity with which the church can represent
those workings to the individual soul. Even as they gave me a sense of
Catholicism's essentials, those writers made clear that this is a "multiform
Communion" (Newman), with the believer apprehending shared truths
through his or her own disposition and obsessions. Even as they conveyed the tenor of an earlier era's Catholicism, they exploded my view, a
common one among young Catholics, that a monolithic and changeless
church preceded Vatican II. Most important, my ongoing "translation"
of those writers compelled me to actively engage this religion, past and
present, and as a result to see ways in which the old church and the new
church are one church after all—Newman's principle of doctrinal development laying the groundwork for the council, or Merton's life joining
monastic contemplation to contemporary social justice efforts, or
O'Connor's Catholic vision focusing on characters who are practically

unchurched, and so must grapple toward God through a terrible alone-
ness.

Is my experience unique? Perhaps, and yet I think that it is representative. For example, most young Catholics are painfully aware of the distance between the church here and the church in Europe, historically
and currently. The distance between Saint Peter's Basilica and the
poured-concrete structure down the road; between the soaring, abstruse
language of the *Confessions* and the easy slang of Catholic self-help
books; between the pope's absolute statements on his world tours and Father So-and-So's utter uncertainty about whether to give today's homily
with or without a microphone—for us these are constant and bewilder-
ing. While older Catholics, recalling the preconciliar church and what it
taught them, seem able to make their own judgments and adjustments,
many young Catholics simply find the distances absurd, and leave it at
that.

Partly as a result, among the church's younger members, Catholic
guilt has been supplanted by Catholic *shame*—a deep embarrassment
about our church and its presence in the culture. In part we are ashamed
for the reasons that Christians have always felt ashamed: we associate
faith with childhood and are eager to throw off childish ways; we disap-
prove of the church's doings; we appraise the church by its own standards
and it doesn't measure up; or we appraise ourselves and realize that we
don't live up to what Christ and the church demand of us.

Mostly, though, we are ashamed because we lack the resources of
Catholic tradition that might enable us to reconcile seeming opposites
and make sense of the absurdity we confront. Tradition can tell us that
poured concrete reflects postwar America just as gilt and statuary did
Baroque-era Rome; that Augustine's intimate first-person address to God
was pretty slangy for its time; and that the pope's triumphal junkets and
So-and-So's mike-anxiety both reflect the contemporary priest's dilemma
whether he should speak as a leader over his people or just go out and try
to be one of them. And tradition can remind us that the church is by its
nature less than perfect, with doubt, dissent, and contradiction always as
crucial to its project as the celebrated virtues of certainty and authority.

Absurd-seeming, shame-inducing—often the Catholic church in
America doesn't seem like the way to God. Catholics, young and old,
sense this, so there are diminished expectations on both ends, grounded
in a fear that this religion can't be efficacious, much less necessary. And
in day-to-day Catholic life there is far too little that suggests otherwise.

For older Catholics, in their embrace of Vatican II, have in many cases forfeited the resources of the larger tradition, and as a result often seem to be making things up as they go along. In reversing this trend, a reacquaintance with the Catholic tradition seems especially promising. For all of its anachronisms and complications, our heritage is a treasure house of the kingdom of necessity—full of riches, from the patristic writings to the purposeful wanderings of a David Toolan, that testify to the urgency and fruitfulness of an encounter with the God who came to earth.

Of course, calling for a reacquaintance with the Catholic tradition is neither a modest proposal nor a novel one. No doubt many Catholic leaders have been trying to bring such a reacquaintance about, with disappointing results. How might such efforts be made more compelling? Perhaps we all could learn from the liberation movements to which the church often seems outwardly opposed. Lacking authorized, institutionalized examples of their own heritage, women, blacks, and homosexuals, for example, are reconsidering history with a fervor that can seem alarming. What alarms, perhaps, is that in doing so they have not set aside their contemporary urgency; rather, they have unabashedly brought it to their appraisal of history, so that they might bring the past to bear on their current concerns, which, however forward-looking, need a longer perspective to inform, guide, and inspire.

For the church, too, a reacquaintance with the past is necessary, not optional. Too often Catholics try to pass on tradition untranslated, handing off *The Long Loneliness* or *The Everlasting Man* as if its ability to speak without commentary is a mark of its timelessness. Or we look to the unifying forces of sociology or core curricula, supposing that once the general outlines are in place we can set about passing on the tradition. In doing so, we invoke the one element of Catholic tradition that is unlikely to return any time soon, or to be of much use to us: the sense that the church's chief note is its internal coherence, which will answer all questions and dispel all doubts.

Our concerns about how the church should share the Catholic faith with its younger members are with us to stay, and they are necessarily many-sided and discursive. Recognizing this, we should resist simplifying them in order to make the going easier. Tradition alone cannot answer our questions for us; nor can modernity. We must consult Saints Thomas and Teresa along with the social sciences, look at *The Idea of a University* as well as the academic-freedom guidelines, drawing on each as we translate the other. There will be conflicts—but conflicts, as our tradition tells us, can be the grounds for faith as well as obstacles to it. Ask Saint Paul.

In the short term, getting reacquainted with the Catholic tradition would enable us—all of us—to see the present concerns about "Catholic identity" against a transcendent background. History can remind us that the challenges of passing on faith are abiding ones, thus disallowing us the modern solipsism which exalts the present as a time unequaled in its despair and sense of loss. Scripture can let us say, with the psalmist, that to "dwell in the house of the Lord" is "to inquire in his temple," and, with Peter in council, that "we believe we are saved in the same way as they are: through the grace of the Lord Jesus." Doctrine can help us to understand today's dilemmas—the Fall testifying that the impulse to see the present as inferior to the past is at the core of our nature, or infant baptism showing that the church, confident of "growth in faith," has long been willing to regard the most nascent believer as Catholic, no doubt about it. And the act of passing on tradition, with the act of translation this requires, can spur us to try bridging all the familiar gaps—between younger Catholics and older ones, between the present and the past, between mortality and eternity, and so on.

In saying this, I don't mean to underestimate the realness of generational differences or the sense among church leaders that what constitutes Catholicism for the church's younger members often barely resembles the faith they know. I don't mean to romanticize the Catholic past, just to say that it's back there, either to enrich us or to haunt us. And I don't mean to chastise the Catholic leaders whose intelligence and compassion have so animated their discussions of young Catholics and our religious identity. I mean only to suggest that the best way for older Catholics to minister to "young Catholics," and vice-versa, is for all of us to renounce such a distinction as limiting and divisive, choosing instead to emphasize what we share—our common faith and our long and complex tradition and our contemporary American situation and our bonds to one another.

WHEN A CHILD DIES

JOHN GARVEY

The church I serve is a small one, and in some ways the commonly heard idea that the church should be like a family is a reality here, for better or worse. Just as in a family at its best, people frequently bear one another's burdens and accept people in their complexities; and just as in families at their worst, there are sometimes long-standing arguments, old grudges, and generalizations ("He was always like that . . .") that freeze people into their places. For the most part, it is a warm, closely knit community, and people work together well.

When a tragedy hits at this level, it shows how deep the reality of the church-as-family can be. A few weeks ago a little girl, two years and four months old, died suddenly. She choked on a grape as she played with her brothers, and when her mother saw her falling it was too late. The grief of Anna's parents is bottomless. The rest of us remembered her from the previous Sunday, running around, singing—she was a lively, delightful girl—and everyone has been mourning. Parents wonder how they can explain this to children who think often of Anna; everyone asks "why?" And of course there is no answer.

It is the great sin of some religious people to think that there is a satisfactory answer to a tragedy of this sort, and to tell the afflicted parents such dreadful things as, "At least you have the other two," or "God must have needed her," or "She's in heaven now," or "It must have been her time." Some people are more patient than I am with the intentions of these people; they only want to console, they mean well. I know that. But their words can go in like knives, and it seems to me that there is a kind of sentimental rudeness here, at least, and a terrible insensitivity.

I was fifteen when my sister Grace died suddenly. She was eighteen

JOHN GARVEY (1944–), an Orthodox priest and the author of *Saints for a Confused Time,* has been a *Commonweal* columnist since 1976.

months old and had just begun to walk, and one of our favorite photographs was of this little girl crossing a room carrying a copy of a book called *Understanding Language*. Her death was devastating. When people said stupid and banal things to my parents, or to me, I was furious. The morning after her death I thought the sun shouldn't shine, water shouldn't flow, the world shouldn't work in the pleasant, indifferent way it usually does.

Nothing can console you after a loss like this, and there were no answers to the question, "How can a child die before her parents? What can make this all right, what can square this with the belief that God is good?" What answer could make you say, "Oh, then—*that* makes it all right!" We hope for resurrection, for reunion with those we love, but the reality now is that we are not with them, and their loss is close to unbearable. The death of a child is a sign that the world, as it is, is not all right, that because of sin, death reigns here, and it is not supposed to be that way. The only way to avoid the pain of living in a world like this is to refuse to love at all.

The morning of Anna's funeral I spent some time with the Book of Job. I realize that there are some scholars who see the end of the Book of Job as a tacked-on thing, an attempt to wrap everything up, and I have to admit that I agree with the reaction of a Jewish friend who said of the fact that Job had a second fortune and new children, "Big deal!" That really doesn't work—you'd reject it in fiction, and it sure doesn't work in life. But what is most important here is God's rebuke to Job's comforters, the people who tell him that his afflictions came about because of his sinfulness, or because the happiness of the just is always short-lived, or because God was testing his faith. But God says, "I burn with anger against you and your two friends, for not having spoken correctly about me as my servant Job has done." God commands Job to pray for his friends, while they are commanded to sacrifice in atonement for what amounts to dishonesty with God.

But what was Job's "correct speaking"? Although God's answer to Job is in some sense not an answer—God says, in effect, "I know what I am doing and you do not and cannot"—it is a response to Job's anguished "Why?" It is essential for us to ask this question; we would be inhuman if we did not. And it will not be answered. Job, confronted with God, says, "Before, I knew you only by hearsay but now, having seen you with my own eyes, I retract what I have said, and repent in dust and ashes." It is essential for us to ask why the innocent suffer, and essential for us to understand that we will not understand. This is what makes Job justified before God and it is false consolation and simplification that make God "burn with anger" against Job's friends.

A tragedy of this depth forces us to confront the mystery of the cross, which exists because the world is not at all what it is meant to be. In this world there can be no satisfactory answer to the question, "Why do the innocent suffer?" Any satisfactory answer would literally be obscene, whose root meaning is "in the wrong place." Here we do not have the possibility of answering the question. As Christians we know there is one who suffers with us, we have the hope of resurrection, and we have nothing else.

Art

The Church of Rome was a great patron of the arts for much of its history. The explicit religious nature of medieval and Renaissance art, the intimate involvement of church and state, and the generous (and often heavy-handed) patronage of ecclesiastical officeholders made for a remarkable collaboration between artists and the institution. In modern times, artist-church relations have been marked more frequently by mutual alienation and suspicion, if not outspoken antagonism. From its inception, *Commonweal* has described itself as a review of religion, politics, literature, and the arts. Like its efforts to forge common ground between Catholicism and American democracy, the magazine's coverage of books, plays, movies, and other cultural forms is based on a conviction that spiritual and aesthetic values both reflect and draw their power from transcendent reality. As Willa Cather wrote, "Religion and art spring from the same root and are close kin."

Admittedly, the all-too-common Catholic demand to find something morally uplifting—or at least to avoid anything morally disreputable—in a book or movie has often clashed with the freedom of expression rightly prized by the modern artist. As Evelyn Waugh observed, too many Catholics expect the Catholic writer to "produce only advertising brochures setting out in attractive terms the advantages of church membership." According to Walter Kerr, in the heyday of Hollywood's Production Code, the heavy hand of Catholic censors was responsible for "elevating bad taste to the level of a virtue." But in choosing the saccharine or merely pious over human complexity and aesthetic value on its own terms, Kerr argued, we betray the great Catholic intellectual tradition itself, with its profound understanding of our tragic and fallen nature. "I am not sure that God is well served by any . . . distortion of the world he made—not even that distortion which enables us to 'take the children,'" warned Kerr.

The French Catholic philosopher Jacques Maritain observed that art is its own form of knowledge. Art says things that cannot be said in any other way, revealing an aspect of reality otherwise inaccessible to us. The true artist creates something that has never existed before, and in doing so he or she can be said to share in God's own creative power. In that light, *Commonweal* writers have been willing to judge books or movies on their own terms, trying neither to reduce art to morality nor to ignore the morality of art. This respect for the autonomy of the artist is evident in Richard Alleva's description of the heroic protagonist of *Schindler's List* as the "saint of the sybarites," in Thomas Molnar's defense of Vladimir Nabokov's *Lolita,* and in Rand Richards Cooper's assessment of National Book Award novelist Alice McDermott. If God writes straight with crooked lines, Walter Kerr reminded us, so must the artist.

ESCAPISM

WILLA CATHER

My dear Mr. Williams:

You were asking me what I thought about a new term in criticism: the art of "escape." Isn't the phrase tautological? What has art ever been but escape? To be sure, this definition is for the moment used in a derogatory sense, implying an evasion of duty, something like the behavior of a poltroon. When the world is in a bad way, we are told, it is the business of the composer and the poet to devote himself to propaganda and fan the flames of indignation.

But the world has a habit of being in a bad way from time to time, and art has never contributed anything to help matters—except escape. Hundreds of years ago, before European civilization had touched this continent, the Indian women in the old rock-perched pueblos of the Southwest were painting geometrical patterns on the jars in which they carried water up from the streams. Why did they take the trouble? These people lived under the perpetual threat of drought and famine; they often shaped their graceful cooking pots when they had nothing to cook in them. Anyone who looks over a collection of prehistoric Indian pottery dug up from old burial mounds knows at once that the potters experimented with form and color to gratify something that had no concern with food and shelter. The major arts (poetry, painting, architecture, sculpture, music) have a pedigree all their own. They did not come into being as a means of increasing the game supply or promoting tribal security. They sprang from an unaccountable predilection of the one unaccountable thing in man.

At the moment, we hear the same cry which went up during the French Revolution: the one really important thing for every individual is his citizenship, his loyalty to a cause—which, of course, always means his loyalty to a party. The composer should be Citizen Beethoven, the

---

WILLA CATHER (1873–1947) was the author of *Death Comes for the Archbishop, Shadows on the Rock, My Ántonia,* and other works.

painter Citizen Rembrandt, the poet Citizen Shelley, and they should step into line and speed their pen or brush in helping to solve the economic problems which confront society. There have been generous and bold spirits among the artists: Courbet tried to kick down the Vendôme Column and got himself exiled, Citizen Shelley stepped into line and drove his pen—but he was not very useful to the reforms which fired his imagination. He was "useful" if you like that word, only as all true poets are, because they refresh and recharge the spirit of those who can read their language.

"Face the stern realities, you skulking escapist!" the radical editor cries. Yes, but usually the poor escapist has so little cleverness when he struggles with stern realities. Schubert could easily write a dozen songs a day, but he couldn't keep himself in shirts. Suppose the radical editor, or the head of the Works Project, had to write a dozen songs a day? I can't believe that if Tolstoy and Goethe and Viollet-le-Duc and Descartes and Sir Isaac Newton were brought together and induced to work with a will, their opinions, voiced in their various special languages and formulae, would materially help Mayor LaGuardia to better living conditions in New York City. Nearly all the escapists in the long past have managed their own budget and their social relations so unsuccessfully that I wouldn't want them for my landlords, or my bankers, or my neighbors. They were valuable, like powerful stimulants, only when they were left out of the social and industrial routine which goes on every day all over the world. Industrial life has to work out its own problems.

Give the people a new word, and they think they have a new fact. The pretentious-sounding noun, escapist, isn't even new. Just now, it is applied to writers with more acrimony than to composers or sculptors. Since poets and novelists do not speak in symbols or a special language, but in the plain speech which all men use and all men may, after some fashion, read, they are told that their first concern should be to cry out against social injustice. This, of course, writers have always done. The Hebrew prophets and the Greek dramatists went much deeper; they considered the greed and selfishness innate in every individual; the valor which leads to power, and the tyranny which power begets. They even cried out against the seeming original injustice that creatures so splendidly aspiring should be inexorably doomed to fail; the unfairness of the contest in which beings whose realest life is in thought or endeavor are kept always under the shackles of their physical body, and are, as Ulysses said, "the slaves of the belly." Since no patriarchal family was without its hatreds and jealousies and treacheries, the old poets could not see how a great number of families brought together into a state could be much better. This seems to be the writer's natural way of looking at the suffering of the world. Seventy-five years ago Dostoevski was the idol of the revolutionary party; but who could now consider his novels propaganda? Certainly they are very unlike the product of the young man who goes to spend a year in a factory town and writes a novel on the abuses of factory labor.

The revolt against individualism naturally calls artists severely to account, because the artist is of all men the most individual: those who were not have been long forgotten. The condition every art requires is, not so much freedom from restriction, as freedom from adulteration and from the intrusion of foreign matter; considerations and purposes which have nothing to do with spontaneous invention. The great body of Russian literature was produced when the censorship was at its strictest. The art of Italy flowered when the painters were confined almost entirely to religious subjects. In the great age of Gothic architecture sculptors and stone-cutters told the same stories (with infinite variety and fresh invention) over and over, on the faces of all the cathedrals and churches of Europe. How many clumsy experiments in government, futile revolutions and reforms, those buildings have looked down upon without losing a shadow of their dignity and power—of their importance. Religion and art spring from the same root and are close kin. Economics and art are strangers.

The literary radicals tell us there must be a new kind of poetry. There will be, whenever there is a new poet—a genuine one. The thesis that no one can ever write a noble sonnet on a noble theme without repeating Wordsworth, or a mysteriously lovely lyric without repeating Shelley, is an evasion. As well argue that because so many thumbprints have already been taken, there must be a new method of identification. No fine poet can ever write like another. His poetry is simply his individuality. And the themes of true poetry, of great poetry, will be the same until all the values of human life have changed and all the strongest emotional responses have become different—which can hardly occur until the physical body itself has fundamentally changed.

Now, my dear Mr. Williams, I have already said much too much about a fleeting fashion which perhaps is not to be taken seriously at all. As Mary Colum remarked in the *Yale Review:* "The people who talk about the art of escape simply know nothing about art at all." *At all*, I echo!

CATHOLICS AND HOLLYWOOD

WALTER KERR

Bad taste is not one of the seven deadly sins, and nobody is going to hell for having preferred *Quo Vadis* over *God Needs Men*. But neither is there any wisdom in elevating bad taste to the level of a virtue, or in confusing it with virtue itself. And it does seem to me that American Catholic criticism of the popular arts—especially the sort of criticism which is generally meted out to the motion picture—is rapidly driving itself into just such an unattractive, and philosophically untenable, corner.

However inadvertently, and with whatever genuine concern for the moral health of its membership, the church in this country has permitted itself to become identified with the well-meaning second-rate. In effect, it has seemed to say: "I don't care what the quality of the art work is, so long as its content is innocuous, or perhaps favorably disposed in our direction."

In the most publicized Catholic art award of 1952, the Christophers selected *Quo Vadis*. This essay in calculated vulgarity represents, we are told, "creative work of enduring significance." It is "outstanding," not merely because it throws a certain number of Christians to a certain number of lions, but because it lives up to the highest esthetic "standards." The truth, of course, slips out; in presenting the award, Father Keller immediately launches into praise of the film for showing "how a handful of human beings, fired with the love and truth of Christ, were able to overcome the might of Pagan Rome." The esthetic norm is clearly the proselytizing content, if, with a little effort of the imagination, *Quo Vadis* can be considered as really having proselytizing content.

But this avowal—that Christians ought to like *Quo Vadis* because

---

WALTER KERR (1915–96) taught in the drama department at the Catholic University and served as drama critic for *Commonweal* (1950–52), the *New York Herald Tribune*, and the *New York Times*.

Quo Vadis likes Christians—is not a frank one. There is the additional insistence that the film's special pleading, its fairly dim and remote hoeing of the Catholic row, be equated with artistic merit. Because Saint Peter has been given a certain amount of footage in this production, this form of logic demands that therefore the movie in question be praised for its craftsmanship.

The intention is virtuous; the execution must therefore not be called into question, must indeed be lauded as supremely desirable. The makers of motion pictures are explicitly urged to go on in the same vein, with the assurance that they will thereby arrive at unparalleled esthetic glories. The *Christopher News Notes* announces that "outstanding personalities in the entertainment and literary fields predict that if similar Christopher Awards are made for the next three or four years, they may do more to stimulate high quality work in these spheres of influence than any other single factor."

The sort of judgment which at best reveals an alarming innocence of the possibilities, of the very texture of art, and which at worst smacks suspiciously of cant, has pretty much become rule-of-thumb for the American Catholic moviegoer. A film featuring a saint is a film of majestic technical excellence. A film showing a nun driving a jeep is a superbly made comedy. A film embracing a jolly priest, a self-sacrificing Catholic mother, and an anti-Communist message must be defended in the diocesan press from those irresponsible esthetes and conspiratorial leftists—and even worse, those maverick Catholics—who have had the meanness and the malice to question it.

When there is no recent film of obviously Catholic sympathies—no priest in the pulpit, no nun in the backfield, no early-Christian Deborah Kerr in the jaws of a Technicolor lion—the next-best bet, in the current practice of Catholic criticism, is to play it safe. An earlier Christopher Award—I am not really out after the Christophers; they got out there by themselves—went to *The Father of the Bride.* Now *The Father of the Bride* was a pleasant little film, certainly a harmless little film. That it represented the peak of creative achievement, of imaginative artistry, in its given year is, however, fairly doubtful. But it was a film which was kind to babies, kind to parents, generally optimistic about the domestic scene. It was therefore qualified for praise on the highest level of esthetic achievement.

The identification of good will with good work is commonplace in the Catholic press. Unfortunately, the sort of art which Catholics are urged to admire is commonplace, too—and the power which Catholic spokesmen have come to wield over the motion picture has helped make the motion picture even more commonplace than it need have been.

The penalties of this inverted esthetic—the notion that what is pure is also necessarily perfect—have thus been double. Catholic taste in motion pictures has been frozen at the "unobjectionable," or purity-with-popcorn level, a level which if pursued down the ages, would have called into question nearly every literary or dramatic masterpiece ever produced. (We need not think of such rowdy samples as *Volpone* or *Tartuffe*; a *Phèdre* or a *Hamlet* will do.) And the American film has, through the rigid circumscriptions of the production code and the terrors of an unfavorable Legion of Decency rating, been dissuaded from attempting anything complex enough in the way of human behavior to serve as the basis for a new masterpiece.

The first of these penalties—the petrifaction of taste—cannot seem of much moment to men whose urgent concern is the saving of souls. Yet it has far more serious consequences than many an honest moralist realizes: it discredits the entire Catholic intellectual tradition. The man who has been to see *Quo Vadis,* and who has then read the Christopher citation, reaches certain conclusions: that the "Catholic" concept of art is a decidedly primitive one; that it probably rests on similarly primitive philosophical principles; that the church, when its true colors are showing, is essentially antipathetic to the creative spirit, essentially in league with the vulgar.

The fact that each of these assumptions is thoroughly false, and would seem strange indeed to an Augustine, an Aquinas, or a Newman, is nothing for which the contemporary observer can be held responsible; the impression is thrust upon him, paraded before him, drummed in his ears by the most vocal Catholic spokesmen in the field.

And this conviction that bad taste among Catholics is due to an ineradicable defect deep down in the Catholic philosophical mind leads to new damage: it tends to shut off Catholic intellectual influence altogether. We hear a great deal about the "influence" which Catholicism has had on the American screen. We forget that this influence has been wholly of one kind: the influence of the pressure group. The Legion of Decency is an economic weapon; the Production Code was written under the standing fear of boycott. Neither represents an intellectual victory in the sense that an esthetic principle has been stated with such clarity and force as to bring about free assent. The only persuasiveness we have been able to whip up is the persuasiveness of the dollar.

The barbed-wire barriers of the Production Code may be up; but the lines of communication are down. The theatergoer, the critic, or the creative artist who stands outside the church looking in sees only a forbidding tangle of precaution and proscription, over which hovers a halo of bad taste. He does not notice much lively discussion of esthetic value; indeed, he will quickly discover that "esthetic" is a bad word in vast areas of the Catholic press. He does not notice much effort to liberalize parochial taste; indeed, he will quickly find most such effort labeled "art-for-art's-sakeism." He will nowhere run across any frank recognition of home truths—such as that a work of art may be perfectly clean and perfectly terrible. That he should feel vaguely uncomfortable in this environment is understandable. That he should reject it is perhaps inevitable. That he should feel, in rejecting it, that he is thereby rejecting the whole body of Catholic thought on the arts, the central content of Catholic philosophy itself, is tragic. Yet by stubbornly praising what is safely banal, by strenuously encouraging a low level of taste, we are fostering such an impression.

Our fear that any recognition of the claims of the "esthetic" may undermine the Catholic accomplishment to date, our reluctance to encourage any study of the nature of art as art, our insistence that the Catholic contribution stop dead at the cautionary level, have also brought about the second penalty mentioned above: the discouragement of the creative filmmaker pursuing the ultimate possibilities of his craft.

Again this is going to seem no serious matter to the man whose whole concern is prudence. The motion picture, this man may tell himself, is probably never going to amount to much, anyway; the dangers of Hollywood indiscretion are greater than the possible damage that may be done to an exceptional film here and there; was Hollywood ever very "esthetic" in the first place?

To anyone who remembers the standard MGM scenario shortly before the Legion of Decency came into existence—Joan Crawford is Clark Gable's mistress for six reels and triumphantly marries him in the seventh—this attitude may yet evoke a twinge of sympathy, a shrug of endorsement. But cynicism is no friend of truth, despair no incentive to achievement. It is never enough to substitute one vulgarity for another.

Unless one makes an esthetically informed and basically sympathetic approach to a medium, there is a likelihood of replacing one sort of error with another sort; even the "prudent" make mistakes. In the case of the Production Code, the failure to balance prudence with knowledge

would seem to have resulted in some curious philosophical construc-
tions. The notion, for instance, that sin is always, and very precisely,
punished in this life would not appear to be Catholic dogma; yet it is at
Catholic insistence that the screen echoes and reechoes the concept.

A few years ago Warners remade the old Maugham story, *The Letter.*
In the original, as I remember it, the heroine's infidelity (and her subsequent murder of her lover) was ironically paid off by the prospect of an
eternal hell in the company of a husband who now knew the truth. In
the remake, under the code, it was necessary to dispatch the adulteress by
having a handy native girl slip a knife into her. The new ending was logically improbable, esthetically ambiguous. It was also, it seems to me,
morally simple-minded, reflecting a remarkable primitive understanding
of the ways of God and men. (It might be mentioned that it was now
also necessary to kill off the native girl, instituting a chain of blood
vengeance unknown since the *Oresteia.*) There are more subtle, and
more terrifying, punishments than the code quite envisions. There are
also more "Catholic" ones.

To take another example more or less at random, the recent filming of
A Streetcar Named Desire found Stella Kowalski leaving her loutish husband. There was sound enough reason for leaving this man, even apart
from his table manners: he had dishonored his wife's sister. But the code
which demanded this climax was written under Catholic influence, with
the guidance of Catholic spokesmen: is it actually the Catholic position
that a wife must leave her husband for infidelity? And what, in this eye-
for-an-eye, tooth-for-a-tooth world, has become of the virtue of charity?

Much more importantly, what has become of that profound little
maxim Paul Claudel has quoted: "God writes straight with crooked
lines"? This is pretty much the crux of the matter, so far as the making of
films, or the creation of any sort of art, is concerned. The great artist, be
he Claudel or Tolstoy, Racine or Shakespeare, follows the bent of human
nature honestly through its aberrant as well as its generous impulses,
through its virtues and vices alike, until all fall into place in a complex,
but truthful, pattern. The lines are crooked, the ultimate vision straight.
What is both wrong and foolish about the present Production Code is
that it insists that God write straight with straight lines, that he attend
strictly to business as the business is conceived by an either-or, black-
and-white, pay-as-you-go mentality.

Art without crooked lines is unnatural art—inevitably inferior art. And
in its production not only the creative mind is betrayed; the Catholic

mind, in its fullness, in its scope, in its centricity, is betrayed as well. Because we are terrified that any admission of the legitimate claims of art will send us all dancing off into the perilous realms of "art for art's sake"—though there are a dozen intermediate esthetic positions—we are moving closer and closer to the sort of stand which might well be described as "vulgarity for God's sake." I am not sure that God is well served by any dishonesty, by any distortion of the world he made—not even that distortion which enables us to "take the children."

None of this is meant to say that the motion picture, or any other art form, should be exempted from legitimate criticism. Nor is it meant to say that the motion picture should be exempted from such criticism as may be considered specifically Catholic, specifically drawn from that body of wisdom which the church has nurtured through the ages. I am not suggesting that a Catholic has no right to raise his voice or even to make use of such pressure tactics as a democratic society actually grants him. I do not really mean to hold out the hope that the Hollywood we know is a seething ferment of crushed genius which will, the moment the code is liberalized or the Legion relaxed, burst forth with a hundred magnificent films.

It is rather to say—as Catholics are so often and so honorably heard to say—that every right involves a responsibility. We have loudly asserted our rights where the screen is concerned; I am not sure that we have accepted, or even realized, our responsibilities, that we have behaved with full justice toward that gift of God which is known as "art," toward the artist himself, toward the central tradition of Catholic thought, or even, sometimes, toward the working intellect itself. We have, for instance, talked ourselves into a corner, and into a code, which would automatically prohibit filming certain works of Mauriac, Claudel, Bernanos, or Greene. Perversely, we have as Catholics made it difficult for the most distinguished—and the most influential—Catholic creative voices of our time to gain access to this particular medium.

FELIX CULPA?

EVELYN WAUGH

O f Mr. Graham Greene alone among contemporary writers one can say without affectation that his breaking silence with a new serious novel is a literary "event." It is eight years since the publication of *The Power and the Glory.* During that time he has remained inconspicuous and his reputation has grown huge. We have had leisure to reread his earlier books and to appreciate the gravity and intensity which underlie their severe modern surface. More than this, the spirit of the time has begun to catch up with them.

The artist, however aloof he holds himself, is always and specially the creature of the *zeitgeist;* however formally antique his tastes, he is in spite of himself in the advance guard. Men of affairs stumble far behind.

In the last twenty-five years the artist's interest has moved from sociology to eschatology. Out of hearing, out of sight, politicians and journalists and popular preachers exhort him to sing the splendors of high wages and sanitation. His eyes are on the Four Last Things, and so mountainous are the disappointments of recent history that there are already signs of a popular breakaway to join him, of a stampede to the heights.

I find the question most commonly asked by the agnostic is not: "Do you believe in the authenticity of the Holy House at Loreto?" or "Do you think an individual can justly inherit a right to the labor of another?" but "Do you believe in hell?"

Mr. Greene has long shown an absorbing curiosity in the subject. In *Brighton Rock* he ingeniously gave life to a theological abstraction. We are often told: "The church does not teach that any man is damned. We only know that hell exists for those who deserve it. Perhaps it is now empty and will remain so for all eternity." This was not the sentiment of

---

EVELYN WAUGH (1903–66), English novelist and essayist, was the author of *Decline and Fall, The Loved One, Brideshead Revisited, Officers and Gentlemen,* and other works.

earlier and healthier ages. The Last Judgment above the medieval door showed the lost and the saved as fairly equally divided; the path to salvation as exceedingly narrow and beset with booby traps; the reek of brimstone was everywhere. Mr. Greene challenged the soft modern mood by creating a completely damnable youth. Pinkie of *Brighton Rock* is the ideal examinee for entry to hell. He gets a pure *alpha* on every paper. His story is a brilliant and appalling imaginative achievement but falls short of the real hell-fire sermon by its very completeness. We leave our seats edified but smug. However vile we are, we are better than Pinkie. The warning of the preacher was that one unrepented slip obliterated the accumulated merits of a lifetime's struggle to be good. *Brighton Rock* might be taken to mean that one has to be as wicked as Pinkie before one runs into serious danger.

Mr. Greene's latest book, *The Heart of the Matter,* should be read as the complement of *Brighton Rock.* It poses a vastly more subtle problem. Its hero speaks of the church as "knowing all the answers," but his life and death comprise a problem to which the answer is in the mind of God alone, the reconciliation of perfect justice with perfect mercy. It is a book which only a Catholic could write and only a Catholic can understand. I mean that only a Catholic can understand the nature of the problem. Many Catholics, I am sure, will gravely misunderstand it, particularly in the United States of America, where its selection as the Book of the Month will bring it to a much larger public than can profitably read it. There are loyal Catholics here and in America who think it the function of the Catholic writer to produce only advertising brochures setting out in attractive terms the advantages of church membership. To them this profoundly reverent book will seem a scandal. For it not only portrays Catholics as unlikable human beings but shows them as tortured by their faith. It will be the object of controversy and perhaps even of condemnation. Thousands of heathens will read it with innocent excitement, quite unaware that they are intruding among the innermost mysteries of faith. There is a third class who will see what this book intends and yet be troubled by doubt of its theological propriety.

Mr. Greene divides his fiction into "novels" and "entertainments." Superficially there is no great difference between the two categories. There is no Ruth Draper switch from comic to pathetic. "Novels" and "entertainments" are both written in the same grim style, both deal mainly with charmless characters, both have a structure of sound, exciting plot. You cannot tell from the skeleton whether the man was baptized or not.

And that is the difference; the "novels" have been baptized, held deep under in the waters of life. The author has said: "These characters are not my creation but God's. They have an eternal destiny. They are not merely playing a part for the reader's amusement. They are souls whom Christ died to save." This, I think, explains his preoccupation with the charmless. The children of Adam are not a race of noble savages who need only a divine spark to perfect them. They are aboriginally corrupt. Their tiny relative advantages of intelligence and taste and good looks and good manners are quite insignificant. The compassion and condescension of the Word becoming flesh are glorified in the depths.

As I have said above, the style of writing is grim. It is not a specifically literary style at all. The words are functional, devoid of sensuous attraction, of ancestry and of independent life. Literary stylists regard language as intrinsically precious and its proper use as a worthy and pleasant task. A polyglot could read Mr. Greene, lay him aside, retain a sharp memory of all he said and yet, I think, entirely forget what tongue he was using. The words are simply mathematical signs for his thought. Moreover, no relation is established between writer and reader. The reader has not had a conversation with a third party such as he enjoys with Sterne or Thackeray. Nor is there within the structure of the story an observer through whom the events are recorded and the emotions transmitted. It is as though, out of an infinite length of film, sequences had been cut which, assembled, comprise an experience which is the reader's alone, without any correspondence to the experience of the protagonists. The writer has become director and producer. Indeed, the affinity to the film is everywhere apparent. It is the camera's eye which moves from the hotel balcony to the street below, picks out the policeman, follows him to his office, moves about the room from the handcuffs on the wall to the broken rosary in the drawer, recording significant detail. It is the modern way of telling a story. In Elizabethan drama one can usually discern an artistic sense formed on the dumb-show and the masque. In Henry James's novels, scene after scene evolves as though on the stage of a drawing-room comedy. Now it is the cinema which has taught a new habit of narrative. Perhaps it is the only contribution the cinema is destined to make to the arts.

There is no technical trick about good storytelling in this or any other manner. All depends on the natural qualities of the narrator's mind, whether or no he sees events in a necessary sequence. Mr. Greene is a storyteller of genius. Born in another age, he would still be spinning yarns. His particular habits are accidental. The plot of *The Heart of the Matter* might well have been used by M. Simenon or Mr. Somerset Maugham.

The scene is a West African port in war time. It has affinities with the Brighton of *Brighton Rock,* parasitic, cosmopolitan, corrupt. The population are all strangers, British officials, detribalized natives, immigrant West Indian Negroes, Asiatics, Syrians. There are poisonous gossip at the club and voodoo bottles on the wharf, intrigues for administrative posts, intrigues to monopolize the illicit diamond trade. The hero, Scobie, is deputy-commissioner of police, one of the oldest inhabitants among the white officials; he has a compassionate liking for the place and the people. He is honest and unpopular and, when the story begins, he has been passed over for promotion. His wife Louise is also unpopular, for other reasons. She is neurotic and pretentious. Their only child died at school in England. Both are Catholic. His failure to get made commissioner is the final humiliation. She whines and nags to escape to South Africa. Two hundred pounds are needed to send her. Husband and wife are found together in the depths of distress.

The illegal export of diamonds is prevalent, both as industrial stones for the benefit of the enemy and gems for private investment. Scobie's police are entirely ineffective in stopping it, although it is notorious that two Syrians, Tallit and Yusef, are competitors for the monopoly. A police spy is sent from England to investigate. He falls in love with Louise. Scobie, in order to fulfil his promise to get Louise out of the country, borrows money from Yusef. As a result of this association he is involved in an attempt to "frame" Tallit. The police spy animated by hate and jealousy is on his heels. Meanwhile survivors from a torpedoed ship are brought across from French territory, among them an English bride widowed in the sinking. She and Scobie fall in love and she becomes his mistress. Yusef secures evidence of the intrigue and blackmails Scobie into definitely criminal participation in his trade. His association with Yusef culminates in the murder of Ali, Scobie's supposedly devoted native servant, whom he now suspects of giving information to the police spy. Louise returns. Unable to abandon either woman, inextricably involved in crime, hunted by his enemy, Scobie takes poison; his women become listlessly acquiescent to other suitors.

These are the bare bones of the story, the ground plan on which almost any kind of building might be erected. The art of storytelling has little to do with the choice of plot. One can imagine the dreariest kind of film—(Miss Bacall's pretty head lolling on the stretcher)—accurately constructed to these specifications. Mr. Greene, as his admirers would expect, makes of his material a precise and plausible drama. His technical mastery has never been better manifested than in his statement of the scene—the sweat and infection, the ill-built town which is beautiful for a few minutes at sundown, the brothel where all men are equal, the vultures, the priest who, when he laughed, "swung his great empty-sounding bell to and fro, Ho ho, ho, like a leper proclaiming his misery," the snobbery of the second-class public schools, the law which all can evade, the ever-present haunting underworld of gossip, spying, bribery, violence, and betrayal. There are incidents of the highest imaginative power—Scobie at the bedside of a dying child, improvising his tale of the Bantus. It is so well done that one forgets the doer. The characters are real people whose moral and spiritual predicament is our own because they are part of our personal experience.

As I have suggested above, Scobie is the complement of Pinkie. Both believe in damnation and believe themselves damned. Both die in mortal sin as defined by moral theologians. The conclusion of the book is the reflection that no one knows the secrets of the human heart or the nature of God's mercy. It is improper to speculate on another's damnation. Nevertheless the reader is haunted by the question: Is Scobie damned? One does not really worry very much about whether Becky Sharp or Fagin is damned. It is the central question of *The Heart of the Matter.* I believe that Mr. Greene thinks him a saint. Perhaps I am wrong in this, but in any case Mr. Greene's opinion on that matter is of no more value than the reader's. Scobie is not Mr. Greene's creature, devised to illustrate a thesis. He is a man of independent soul. Can one separate his moral from his spiritual state? Both are complex and ambiguous.

First, there is his professional delinquency. In the first pages he appears as an Aristides, disliked for his rectitude; by the end of the book he has become a criminal. There is nothing inevitable in his decline. He compromises himself first in order to get his wife's passage money. She is in a deplorable nervous condition; perhaps, even, her reason is in danger. He is full of compassion. But she is making his own life intolerable; he wants her out of the way for his own peace. As things turn out the trip to South Africa was quite unnecessary. Providence had its own cure ready if he had only waited. He gets the commissionership in the end, which was ostensibly all that Louise wanted. But behind that again lies the deeper cause of her melancholy, that Scobie no longer loves her in the way that would gratify her vanity. And behind the betrayal of his official trust lies the futility of his official position. The law he administers has little connection with morals or justice. It is all a matter of regulations— a Portuguese sea captain's right to correspond with his daughter in Germany, the right of a tenant to divide and sublet her hut, the right of a merchant to provide out of his own property for the security of his family. He knows that his subordinates are corrupt and can do nothing about it. Whom or what has he in fact betrayed, except his own pride?

Secondly, there is his adultery. His affection for the waif cast up on the beach is at first compassionate and protective; it becomes carnal. Why? He is an elderly man long schooled in chastity. There is another suitor of Helen Rolt, Bagster the Air Force philanderer. It is Bagster's prowling round the bungalow which precipitates the change of relationship. It is Bagster in the background who makes him persevere in adultery when his wife's return affords a convenient occasion for parting. Bagster is a promiscuous cad. Helen must be saved from Bagster. Why? Scobie arrogates to himself the prerogations of providence. He presumes that an illicit relation with himself is better than an illicit relation with Bagster. But why, in fact, need it have been illicit? She might marry Bagster.

Thirdly, there is the murder of Ali. We do not know whether Ali was betraying him. If he had not been a smuggler and an adulterer there would have been nothing to betray. Ali dies to emphasize the culpability of these sins.

Fourthly, there are the sacrilegious communions which Louise forces upon him; and fifthly, his suicide, a restatement of that blasphemy in other terms. He dies believing himself damned but also in an obscure way—at least in a way that is obscure to me—believing that he is offering his damnation as a loving sacrifice for others.

We are told that he is actuated throughout by the love of God. A love, it is true, that falls short of trust, but a love, we must suppose, which sanctifies his sins. That is the heart of the matter. Is such a sacrifice feasible? To me the idea is totally unintelligible, but it is not unfamiliar. Did the Quietists not speak in something like these terms? I ask in all humility whether nowadays logical rule-of-thumb Catholics are not a little too humble toward the mystics. We are inclined to say: "Ah, that is mysticism. I'm quite out of my depth there," as though the subject were higher mathematics, while in fact our whole faith is essentially mystical.

We may well fight shy of discussing ecstatic states of prayer with which we have no acquaintance, but sacrilege and suicide are acts of which we are perfectly capable.

To me the idea of willing my own damnation for the love of God is either a very loose poetical expression or a mad blasphemy, for the God who accepted that sacrifice could be neither just nor lovable.

MATTER-OF-FACT CONFESSION OF A NON-PENITENT

THOMAS MOLNAR

There may yet develop, in literary and legal circles, a *"Lolita* case," as there has been a case of *Ulysses* and of *Lady Chatterley's Lover.* This does not mean that Nabokov's book reminds me of either; if similarities are to be searched for, I would think of the eighteenth-century *Les Liaisons dangereuses* by Choderlos de Laclos, and, nearer to us, Thomas Mann's *Confessions of Felix Krull.*

Lolita is a confession too, although certainly not of a penitent. It is far less matter-of-fact than Laclos's novel which is, like *Lolita,* the narrative of two systematically planned seductions by an older man, one of his victims being a sixteen-year-old girl, conquered under the eyes of her young fiancé.

Lolita's originality is that it speaks of the unspeakable in such a manner that it becomes credible, understandable, almost normal. As Lionel Trilling says, the reader simply cannot work up sufficient indignation; instead, he remains an amused observer, a sophisticated peeping Tom. Austere censors may, of course, warn him of the sensuous atmosphere in which the story is immersed, the quasi-incestuous relationship between Humbert Humbert, a scholarly, analytical-minded, very good looking "big hunk of a man," and his twelve-year-old stepdaughter, the boyish-girlish "nymphet," Lolita. The censor's case is even better when he points out that this rapport borders on the horrifying since Humbert marries Lolita's mother in order to be closer to the child, and becomes the involuntary cause of his wife's death which gives him access to the nymphet's—no longer innocent—bed.

More than one bed, many beds. The last two-thirds of the novel is a fantastic journey through the forty-eight states, through motels, hotels, lodges, and rented homes, the dreary, uniform scenes of desperate love-

---

THOMAS MOLNAR (1921–) is the author of *The Pagan Temptation, Politics and the State,* and other works.

makings and furtive side-glances at suspicious innkeepers, hotel guests, and chambermaids. In an epilogue Nabokov relates that some twenty years ago he had developed the basic plot in a short story. One can easily imagine that in such a form, appropriately pointed, the theme may have been morbid and obscene, with the hero, like Dostoevski's Svidrigailov, a grim seducer of children. But in a book of more than three hundred pages, *Lolita's* narrator cannot remain such a figure.

Humbert is a featherweight intellectual, with his point of gravity situated below the belt; but he becomes a tragic—although at the same time comic—character in his pursuit of an impossible happiness for the morsels of which he pays an ever higher price of self-debasement, humiliation, and remorse. The depth of his personal inferno is aptly measured by two episodes: the moment when Lolita, still unaware of her mother's death, finds her new stepfather in her own bed, intent like a lover, fearful and humble like a dog waiting to be patted; then that other moment, this time one of painful reminiscence, when Humbert recalls the picture of himself, having just possessed Lolita and now adoring in her the suffering, debauched child, but with lust again rising in him, imperious, demanding submission.

The central question the reader ought to ask of himself is whether he feels pity for the girl. Our ethical ideal would require that we look at Lolita as a sacrificial lamb, that we become, in imagination, her knight-protector. Yet this is impossible for two reasons. One is very simple: before yielding to Humbert, the girl had had a nasty little affair with a nasty little thirteen-year-old in an expensive summer camp. Besides, she is a spoiled subteenager with a foul mouth, a self-offered target for lechers, movie-magazine editors, and corrupt classmates. The second reason is that throughout their not-quite-sentimental journey, Lolita remains as unknown to us as to Humbert himself, seen only in bed or in the car, existing only through the lustful gaze of her stepfather. She remains an object, perhaps even to herself, and only at the very end, as a teenage mother, married to a simpleton and comically serious in her vulgarity, does she become human, no longer a corrupt little animal, and no longer a nymphet.

Yet both she and Humbert, her mother and friends, the many people we pass by in the lust-and-anguish-driven car, form a fantastic, wonderful cavalcade of humanity, described, analyzed, judged with incomparable virtuosity. It has been said that this book has a high literary value; it has much more; a style, an individuality, a brilliance which may yet create a tradition in American letters.

This is because Nabokov's writing has the rare quality of dominating the reader, body and mind, his curiosity and fears, his capacity for pity, amusement, tears, and laughter. The author rides with him up hill and down vale, enmeshes him in the marvels of a description, or entertains him, as a veritable mental juggler, with the urbane tricks of a cultured conversationalist.

Mr. Nabokov complains in the epilogue that he had to abandon his wonderfully rich, flexible, and docile Russian for an English in which he can be no better than second rate. Never have I heard of such false, although likable, modesty! Mr. Nabokov's English is beautiful and immensely suggestive, espousing with the greatest ease the mood of men, the color of landscapes, the ambiance of motels, girls' schools, and small towns. It is an ocean of a language, now calm, limpid, transparent, then turning into a roar, with waves upon waves of scintillating metaphors, images, innovations, allusions. The author swims in this ocean like a smooth-bodied fish, leaving the pursuer-reader amidst a thousand delights.

CORRESPONDENCE: *LOLITA*

I am writing to protest the extravagantly laudatory review by Mr. Thomas Molnar of Vladimir Nabokov's *Lolita*. This is, I believe, only the second time in more than ten years that I have bothered a busy editor with such protest, and I write with the more diffidence because I feel that it is a particularly risky thing for one professional book reviewer to criticize another adversely. I recognize also that a priest-reviewer is often discounted when he discusses the moral aspects of a novel, or when he criticizes another's review of a book that poses grave moral problems.

Although I have often differed in book reviewing matters with Father Harold Gardiner, S.J., the literary editor of *America*, I would quite willingly make my own his words in the August 30 issue of that journal, to the effect that "this book is, without the slightest doubt in my mind, the most obscene lucubration to disgrace U.S. publishing in many a decade." Father Gardiner speaks further of "the evasions, subterfuges, and plain double-talk to which a good number of critics have resorted to whitewash this decadent book." I would accept these words as covering such judgments of Mr. Molnar as these:

"Yet both [Lolita] and Humbert, her mother and friends, the many people we pass by in the lust-and-anguish-driven car, form a fantastic, wonderful cavalcade of humanity, described, analyzed, judged with incomparable virtuosity. . . . this book has a high literary value; it has much more: a style, an individuality, a brilliance which may yet create a tradition in American letters." Or these: "Mr. Nabokov's writing has the rare quality of dominating the reader, body and mind, his curiosity and fears, his capacity for pity, amusement, tears, and laughter."

About his ability to dominate the curiosity of a certain type of reader, I have no doubt; the rest is highly debatable. Mr. Molnar further speaks of the book's leaving the reader "amidst a thousand delights"; about this, positing a certain type of reader and a certain kind of dubious delight, I am willing to agree.

I have a theory about *Lolita* and its success which is probably depressingly *simpliste,* and it is this: that with the wide acceptance in novelistic circles of the Kinsey report and in the light of the kind of writing that followed immediately on many once-taboo themes of illicit love and perversion, a certain type of writer was hard-pressed to find a new formula that would titillate in a really original manner. The little girl/middle-aged man combination rather neatly fills the bill, and Mr. Molnar is probably right in saying that the foundation has been laid for a *Lolita* tradition, and a good many modern reviewers are trying hard to help it along. Only a few months have elapsed since many prominent reviewers and even serious critics made collective fools of themselves over *By Love Possessed,* and there is a depressing sameness about their reactions to *Lolita,* though I would admit that as a stylist and word-trickster Mr. Nabokov far surpasses Cozzens.

I would further suggest that the carrying of such a review by *Commonweal* may well have two unfortunate consequences: (1) Those Catholics who criticize *Commonweal* for being "too liberal" or an example of the dangers of lay Catholic journalism will have additional ammunition. (2) The Catholic who suspects all intellectuals will have ammunition, too. If, he may well reason, an intellectual—for I assume Mr. Molnar would wish to be so classified—can be so easily taken in as to see what is simply not there to the degree to which Mr. Molnar has seen it, and can at the same time dispose condescendingly of the "austere censors" who would condemn the work, then what is the point in wishing to be or in respecting the intellectual? Finally, I would suggest that one would be on safe ground in suspecting the critical credentials of a reviewer who can write that "*Lolita*'s originality is that it speaks of the unspeakable in such a manner that it becomes credible, understandable, almost normal." Frankly, I find none of these adjectives applicable to Mr. Molnar's review.

(Dom) D. Bernard Theall, O.S.B.
The Catholic University of America

Reply

As I have predicted in my review, there is now a "*Lolita* case," even though of miniature proportions. As it happens, the accused is not so much the book (it is simply the devil's work), as the reviewer. What is my crime? Agreeing with T. S. Eliot that "the 'greatness' of literature cannot

be determined solely by literary standards, [but] that whether it is literature or not can be determined only by literary standards," I neglected to
saddle my shoulders with a censor who would pull my hair each time I
found enjoyment in a brilliant passage, a humorous description, a piece
of deft sarcasm directed at people, institutions—or Humbert himself.

In my critic's view this enjoyment is scandalous on two accounts:
primo, I seem to condone Humbert's immorality; *secundo,* I display poor
taste as a literary reviewer.

Dom Bernard will be, no doubt, surprised to read that I too deplore
the Kinsey report, the publicity around it, and the fact that it aims at elevating mere (and questionable) statistical data to the rank of a moral
norm. The fact that something *is,* does not mean that it *ought to be.*
Lolita, however, is not a report on the sexual habits of the human male,
it does not aspire to the rank of a universal truth, and it does not intend
to set a moral standard. It is the confession of a self-admitted civic and
moral outcast who suffers more from, than delights in, his predicament.
"I perceive what is Good and approve it," Saint Augustine said, "yet I follow evil." In his own way, Humbert repeats these words many times
while he spirals down, ever faster, on the serpentine road of corruption.

But again, a literary work cannot be praised or blamed on moral
grounds *alone.* It has (or has not) other qualities which recommend it to
the reader. I tried to convey some of *Lolita's* qualities as it can be read in
the first passage quoted by Dom Bernard, where, it will be observed,
there is no trace of moral endorsement, no trace of approval, no trace of
a recommendation that we all follow Humbert's example. And elsewhere
I also stated something which appeared to me crucial: that we cannot
leap to the defense of the girl *because* (if I may quote myself) "Lolita remains unknown to us . . . existing only through the lustful gaze of her
stepfather. She remains an object, perhaps even to herself, and only at the
very end, as a teenage mother, married to a simpleton and comically serious in her vulgarity, does she become human, no longer a corrupt little
animal, and no longer a nymphet."

At the risk of appearing immodest, I consider the above passage *literary* criticism. To put it another way: if Lolita had been my neighbor, I
would have called the police upon learning what was going on between
her and her stepfather; as the reviewer of a work of *imagination,* I shall
neither call the police, nor put dynamite under the publisher's desk; I
shall appraise the work according to my own lights on the writer's craft.

It is not my task to defend *Commonweal.* But I accept no lesson from

Dom Bernard as to the tasks of intellectuals, among which the most important is not to be intimidated either by the reader "who suspects all intellectuals," or by censors, for that matter. As to the issue of literary criticism to which Dom Bernard, a professional book reviewer (as he tells us), ought to have given at least some attention, I hope that the reader, while not "taken in" by reviewers, will equally refuse to be taken in by the censors. At least until such time as the censors will not limit themselves to the expression of moral indignation, but condescend to speak of literature when literature is debated.

Thomas Molnar

A GUIDE TO HATCHET JOBS

WILFRID SHEED

I t may be merely a natural response to an insipid cultural scene, or it may be that we of the bland, cool, silent generation have been taunted beyond endurance by our rough, hot, noisy elders. But whatever the reason, there seems to have been a definite increase in critical ferocity lately—especially as measured by that howl from the depths known as the hatchet job.

By the hatchet job is meant here, not just a few surly growls about a particular book, but a calculated attempt to demolish the author, to blow him out of the water, to plant his career with salt. A good hatchet job leaves its subject looking stunted, emotionally malformed, altogether pathetic—and yet overweening and pretentious too, so that even sympathy is denied him.

The executioner starts out each time with at least one formidable advantage. People have a superstitious reverence for print, so that opinion registers almost automatically as fact. If you say that so-and-so writes badly and is emotionally starved, nobody will stop to ask how *your* emotions are, that you should be making such statements. They will just take your word for the whole thing.

In view of this very good start, it is surprising how many sloppy hatchet jobs seem to be going around these days. Again and again, the critic dissipates his natural advantages, and sometimes winds up stabbing himself as well. No hatchet job is ever a complete failure of course; however inexpertly performed, the victim never completely recovers. The reader will always feel vaguely that he has heard something discreditable about him.

WILFRID SHEED (1930–), *Commonweal's* stage critic (1964–67) and literary editor (1967–69), is the author of *A Middle Class Education, The Hack, Frank and Maisie,* and other works.

But smoother, more satisfying demolitions could surely be guaranteed, if certain simple rules were observed. These, for instance:

1. Hatchet jobs should never run an inch longer than the victim merits. Three sentences are always better than twelve—the length being in itself a form of comment.

The critic who goes on swinging after the tree is down draws attention to himself; he becomes overexposed. After all, perhaps he isn't such a hot writer either. Once the reader's own sadism has been slaked, the executioner is likely to make him a bit uneasy anyway: "Supposing that was me out there," he thinks. Prodigious amounts of reader-flattery and I-thou are needed after that to keep him from turning on the critic with an underdog snarl of his own.

2. The complete opposite of rule 1. It is a mistake to depend too much on short aphoristic dismissals unless your taste in them is absolutely infallible. Length gives at least an impression of lumbering documentation. A bad joke, a heavy-handed insult, give you nothing. The contradictoriness of these first two rules may serve as a warning. Hatcheting is not as easy as it looks.

3. Almost any quoted matter, encapsulated in sneers, will do—provided you deploy it with a little caution. The reader will assume at first that if you say a quotation is silly, it is silly. But this trust can be abused. Four or five quotations in a row which really have nothing wrong with them at all will break the spell.

Recently I came across an attempt to prove that Truman Capote writes bad prose. This was daring (*see* rule 5), but it might have worked with slightly shrewder quoting. Unfortunately it so happened that, while the passages chosen were certainly far from distinguished, they were not really horrifying either. As an average catty reader, I felt that they were written in slightly better prose than the review itself.

It is worth remembering in this connection that when dreadful examples are offered, they will be assumed to be the worst that can be found. A nimble but overworked counterdevice is to claim that you plucked your samples at random, on a five-minute thumb-through. But even then, they should either be pretty bad, or so inconclusive that the author's good qualities have no chance of coming through.

4. On the other hand, two or three short quotes, however well chosen, are barely enough. A make-believe massacre requires an appearance, at least, of massive forces.

Perhaps the best way to achieve this is to quote two or three bits for clumsiness, two or three for inconsistency, etc. This will give you a thoughtful looking page, with stacks of indented matter: and there is no author living or dead who has not made enough genuine blunders to fill it for you. (Besides, the constant changing of subject will keep the reader from noticing any innocuousness in the quotes.)

5. Don't overreach yourself. Readers will swallow almost anything in the way of exposé, but there are limits. I remember reading in a copy of *Scrutiny* a gallant attempt to demonstrate that Cyril Connolly had a bad prose style. This is akin to Vince Lombardi's football strategy of going straight for the other man's strength—but Lombardi has a very good football team to do it with. Since this demonstration had to be made in prose, it would have been wiser not to spot Mr. Connolly so glaring an advantage. (Rules 1 through 6: those who take the sword will perish by the sword.)

The dedicated hatchetman, intoxicated as he is by the prospect of annihilating some wretched author once and for all, and of sending him reeling into permanent oblivion, will begrudge every merit he is obliged to concede on the way; and yet if he concedes none at all, a certain mean-spiritedness and hysteria may show in his own work. Calling Mary McCarthy stupid, or Salinger a bad craftsman (or even Henry James immature), is exhilarating for reader and writer alike. But when sanity returns, it is the writer who has to pay. (The counter to this one is obvious: amused tolerance. "Miss McCarthy is, of course, clever. Perhaps that's the whole trouble." That kind of thing.)

6. There is such a thing as being *too* cruel. Authors may seem from a distance as unreal as circus clowns, who can flail each other all day without anyone getting hurt. But even clowns must draw the line somewhere, and too much realism will sicken the toughest audience.

This line is a fine one. People are delighted by the sight of literary blood and a good hatchet job draws as much excited attention as a good book any day. But if there is any slaughterhouse stench about it, they are likely to get squeamish and the whole effect is spoiled. Last year's Leavis-Snow rumble was a case in point. After a while, in these affairs, you begin to sympathize with the victim; and by the end you are sympathizing with the executioner too.

Since the last thing a hatchetman wants is sympathy, the thing to aim at is a hairline cut, almost invisible until the victim moves and his head topples off. An angry letter from him is equivalent (change metaphors there) to the death lunge of the brave bull. Three or four lines in riposte will sever his aorta for good.

If all this sounds bloodthirsty, it is not by inadvertence. The arts are, and should be, a rough game ("What was a man with a paper skull doing in Garrity's saloon in the first place?" to quote a quote from William Shannon's *The American Irish*); pugnacity and a thick skin are a part of every artist's stock-in-trade, and are also essential to the survival of standards in general.

But one has also seen criticism of such wanton and gratuitous brutality that it transcends all usefulness and can only be compared with something on the lines of bearbaiting or pulling the wings off flies. The victim is helpless; the executioner appears to function in an exalted, fanatic trance, where feelings no longer exist; the crowd loves it—up to a point.

For in one respect the old hatchetman is like the old gunfighter in the movies; there are always plenty of young hatchetmen waiting to chop him down in his turn. The reviews of Dwight Macdonald's latest book should be a warning to them; the end of the old hatchetman (Mr. Macdonald is far from his end of course, but a perfect analogy is hard to find these days) is unwept and unmourned. The crowd, which has indulged itself in his performance for so long, likes nothing better than to see the bully get his lumps in the end.

FLANNERY O'CONNOR: 1925–64

LEONARD MAYHEW

" 'Yes'm,' The Misfit said as if he agreed. 'Jesus thrown everything off balance.'" Into this taut sentence from her short story "A Good Man Is Hard to Find" Flannery O'Connor crammed the major preoccupations of her rich and brilliant fiction. There is her concern for the South—what today's jargon calls the Old South—with its uncomprehending and pathetic resistance to change, its colorful dialect, its apocalyptic religion. There is her hearty sense of the ironic. And, above all, there is the one "preoccupation" (that was her word) which outweighs all others: Christ and the still partial penetration of redemption into a lopsided world. In her note to the second edition of *Wise Blood,* she gently rebuked those who had missed the point of her "comic novel": "That belief in Christ is to some a matter of life and death has been a stumbling block for readers who would prefer to think it a matter of no great consequence."

The critical mistake that most bedeviled her published work was to misread it as some neo-Gothic/neo–Virginia Woolf hybrid. Writing was difficult for her, she often confessed. It meant finding and following what "every story needs—a character who can do anything credibly." As a result, her "heroes" are grotesque and off-balance, precariously perched on the brink of hysteria. Her stories and her people are authentic and universal, not because she realistically describes the outward experiences of herself and her community, but because she pierces ruthlessly through this exterior shell to a common ground of human need, pain, and expectation. She caught the sights and sounds of her world with breathtaking accuracy and vitality. But they have meaning only because she was able to transform them by her artistry.

The theme of Flannery O'Connor's fiction is free will. To her, this meant a struggle for identity, a conflict with the turmoil that has made itself at home in an unredeemed world and, above all, in the part of our-

LEONARD MAYHEW (1932–) was a friend of Flannery O'Connor in Georgia.

selves that has stubbornly resisted redemption. "Free will does not mean one will, but many wills conflicting in one man. Freedom cannot be conceived simply. It is a mystery and one which a novel . . . can only be asked to deepen." Tarwater's compulsion, in *The Violent Bear It Away,* to baptize the idiot child and to preach in the city "the terrible speed of mercy" is neither false nor unfree. Its energy is grace and love. The violence, the grotesque imbalance, is in the "dark city where the children of God lay sleeping."

She compared her approach to reality and fiction to what the medieval doctors called the anagogical sense of Scripture, the real and intended significance embedded beneath the literal and empirical sense. Within this improbable-appearing world of her own creation, she wrote with the most delicate subtlety. Without a word of warning—and with no explicit reference to the theological insight which frames her thought—she withdraws us absolutely from the everyday world and we neither resist nor avert to the strenuous demands of the transfer. She leads us willingly into the otherwise incredible categories of her private Apocalypse. Under their façade of normalcy, she unveils the structure and relationships of daily experience as off-center and grotesque and violence-breeding. Caroline Gordon wrote of Flannery O'Connor's characters: "They are 'off-center,' out of place, because they are victims of a rejection of the scheme of redemption. They are lost in that abyss which opens for man when he sets up as God."

Flannery O'Connor was widely held to be a "Catholic novelist," a term she professed not to understand. She prided herself on being "congenitally innocent of theory." In a very real and special sense, however, she was precisely a "Catholic" novelist. She was very much aware of the presently effective currents in the church. The title of her forthcoming collection of stories is from Teilhard de Chardin, "Everything that rises must converge." Her writing is profoundly marked by a highly individual synthesis of her Catholic philosophy with sympathy for the sometimes bizarre evangelism of the rural South. The religious mentality of freewheeling preachers, self-anointed prophets, and crucified lambs contained for her a kind of truncated sacramentalism. It sees the presence of the divine—of grace, if you will—immediately beyond the empirical and prosaic. Sunday supplements have made serpent handling, rolling, shouting, and the mass hysteria of river baptism familiar. In this world the very experience of religious exaltation and ecstasy becomes a sacrament. Flannery O'Connor saw the people of this mentality as spiritual *émigrés* of the Old Testament, furiously digging and searching for real and operative sacraments. The outward signs they have at hand are recalcitrant and must be forced to reveal the salvation they contain. Only the violent may bear it away. Such souls are fertile ground, in her view, for divine mercy.

In addition, she was a Bible Belt Catholic, a member of a tiny minority. She felt the tension between loyalty to conviction and heritage on one hand, and the sense of alienation, of being irrevocably foreign and different, on the other. The priest in "The Displaced Person" is a naturally foreign figure in her world as well as a telling symbol for the purpose of the story.

The vision and mission of the prophet and seer are a staple of Flannery O'Connor's writing. Her characters' eyes are the symbol of that fearful vision: Tarwater's great-uncle has "silver protruding eyes . . . like two fish straining to get out of a net of red threads"; Hazel Motes, vanquished, burns out his eyes. Truth—the living God—is a terrifying vision, to be faced only by the stout of heart. Flannery O'Connor was such a seer, of stout heart and hope. From her loss we salvage the memory of a "stranger from that violent country where the silence is never broken except to shout the truth." May she rest.

CHARMING ALICE

RAND RICHARDS COOPER

One of the pleasures of going back to a talented writer's early work is finding the promising failure, the intriguingly bad book.

Alice McDermott's first novel, *A Bigamist's Daughter* (1982), told the story of a Manhattan vanity press editor romantically involved with one of her luckless writers. Burdened with backstory, plot contrivances, and stilted dialogue ("Some love goes even beyond the lover himself. . . . Love that's like a spiritual life, like pure faith. . . ."), the novel was a classic case of a writer fighting her own strengths. It was bad in the way some clothing is bad: it just didn't fit. Bent on a single point-of-view protagonist, McDermott restrained a powerful story-telling impulse and ended up making her characters speak her own themes. She used awkward plot moves to steer the novel toward what she really wanted to write about, namely, not her heroine's present but her past—a child's perception of the physical world and the stubborn mysteries of adulthood. *A Bigamist's Daughter* was ostensibly a smart eighties novel about a woman finding her strength. But trapped inside it was a very different book, less breezy and ironic, more lyrical and backward-looking, and far less narratively conventional.

McDermott's subsequent career has been a matter of setting this trapped book free. *That Night* (1987), a sparkling, swooning evocation of a lost era, related the events of a summer evening in a 1960s Long Island suburb, when a gang of hot-rodding town toughs, attempting to steal away their leader's girlfriend, does battle with the fathers of the neighborhood. The story is told, retrospectively, by a nameless narrator who watched the rumble as a ten-year-old, and whose own adult identity is subordinated to her role as witness to the past—in effect, a stand-in om-

RAND RICHARDS COOPER (1958–) is the author of two works of fiction, *The Last to Go* and *Big as Life*. He has taught at Amherst and Emerson.

niscient narrator, telling the story and its ramifications from all angles. The close focus on one event enabled McDermott to range widely through time, and in and out of the various characters as well, creating the novel's blend of tight control with lyrical expansiveness, and giving vent to a sensibility at once rapturous and haunted.

If *That Night* discovered its author's preoccupations—memory and the world of the child, the character of community, the power of desire, the evanescence and permanence of time, the ironies of fate—*At Weddings and Wakes* (1992) pushed them further. The novel studies an Irish-Catholic family in New York, *circa* 1960, through the eyes of two girls and a boy brought on weekly visits from their home on Long Island to their grandmother's apartment in Brooklyn, where through endless afternoons the children's mother and three aunts pour out decades of pent-up disappointments, hopes, and recriminations. Though the fate of one of the aunts figures as a recurring fugue theme, the novel is less plotted than painted. The coffee table with its doily, plastic flowers, and dish of sugared almonds; the family photographs; everything draped and dim and airless, and from the next room the muffled sound of someone sobbing: it is an achingly detailed tableau of lace-curtain Irish despair.

At Weddings and Wakes is the only novel I can think of told from a third-person-plural point of view, a narrative built on "The children saw . . ." and "To the younger girl it seemed that. . . ." Yet the children's individual identities are strangely blurred; we barely learn their names, and other than a few parenthetical asides which sweep us decades ahead, we get no glimpse of their subsequent, adult lives and selves. This too is an extension of an impulse already evident in *That Night.* Indeed, an odd disjunction between the extravagant detail of her descriptive writing and an unwillingness to individuate the point-of-view character has figured increasingly as a hallmark of McDermott's style. Reading *At Weddings and Wakes* is a bit like being carried to a window on the shoulders of anonymous porters. Inside is a world where wedding-party bands play "Galway Bay" as men tell stories of Gentleman Jimmy Walker or a voice calls out "Sweet Jesus, don't mention Parnell!"; where children are taught the lives of the saints by nuns with names like Sister Illuminata. *At Weddings and Wakes* took the lyrical sadness of *That Night* and joined it to something like ethnography. Written in a lovely prose that quivers at the brink of sentimentality—this is a writer who can make even a door, "easing itself closed with what sounded like three short sorrowful expirations of breath," seem wistful—it is a nostalgic and immaculately detailed valedictory to a vanishing corner of Irish Catholicism.

McDermott's new novel, *Charming Billy,* is her most challenging to date—incorrigibly digressive, brash with time, intricately layered and crammed full of life. Set in 1983, *Charming Billy* focuses on three days following the funeral of Billy Lynch, WWII veteran, long-time employee of Con Edison, and lifelong resident of Irish Catholic New York (Queens, to be exact). Through the reminiscences of family and friends we meet an incurable romantic who drank himself to death at sixty: a Billy who charms older ladies in restaurants; calms a woman's baby by murmuring Yeats's "Down by the Salley Gardens"; writes notes on napkins to send to the priest; calls his cousin and best friend, Dennis, in the middle of the night to rail drunkenly against death and the passing of all things. It is a rousing, tender rendition of that stock Irish figure, the poetic rogue in love with his sorrows. Is that a breviary in Billy's jacket pocket, or a flask?

Behind his sorrow lies a tale of deception and lost love. McDermott takes us to Long Island in the summer of 1945, where Billy meets and courts a young Irish nanny named Eva. Back in Ireland, she agrees to marry him, accepts the money he saves to send for her passage and then is heard from no more. Through a go-between Dennis uncovers the banal truth (Eva has married another man and used the $500 to open a gas station), but tells Billy instead she died of pneumonia. The impulsive lie inaugurates Billy's decades of grieving devotion to her memory—he eventually marries, but stays true in his heart to Eva—and places in the novel's foreground the proposition that a life of deluded passion is better than one of clear-eyed disillusion.

Critics have likened McDermott to Joyce; but there's also a lot of F. Scott Fitzgerald in this novel—Billy an Irish workingman's Gatsby, Eva his Daisy, and Ireland itself, perhaps, the green light over the water. Like Gatsby, Billy conflates romance with poetry; kissing Eva on the beach in 1945 he feels, McDermott writes, "a desire for life itself to be as sweet as certain words could make it seem. . . ." But McDermott frames Billy's life story in ironies, stinting neither the cost nor the complexity of his romanticism. First there are the ravages of alcohol and its punishing toll on the body: the downside of poetry is, literally, morbidity. Then there's the fact that Billy's tragedy is founded on a lie. And for whose benefit? His goodness of heart gets soaked up by friends and relatives whose hurting he does for them: he loves and loses; he keeps the faith.

The Christian echo of a redemptive, sacrificial quality to Billy's passion could be heavy-handed. But McDermott guards against bathos by making those mourners who explicitly construe Billy as a Christ figure *themselves* seem heavy-handed. Still, those who dismiss Billy's suffering as the "genetic disease" of alcoholism—there's an Uncle Ted, an evangelical AA member—come off as pinched and zealous proponents of our era's mistaken urge to collapse tragedy into (mere) pathology: a reductively pragmatic approach, McDermott clearly believes, to the mysteries of human existence.

Charming Billy is a stealthily ambitious work of fiction. Under the cover of a realist's reverence for descriptive detail and a romance writer's duty to affairs of the heart, McDermott conducts surprising experiments in form and voice. At times she's content simply to sit her characters around a table and quote speaker after speaker, or to compress their talk into a group monologue of page-spanning paragraphs that reads like an unedited transcript. Elsewhere, her narrator steps forward with pronouncements that have a Jane Austen–like ring: "In the arc of an unremarkable life, a life whose triumphs are small and personal, whose trials are ordinary enough, as tempered in their pain as in their resolution of pain, the claim of exclusivity in love requires both a certain kind of courage and a good dose of delusion." An elegiac impulse plays freely with her sentences, lending a curious, huffing quality:

> He had, at some point, ripped apart, plowed through, as alcoholics tend to do, the great deep, tightly woven fabric of affection that was some part of the emotional life, the life of love, of everyone in the room.
>
> How lonely they all seemed to me that night, my father's family and friends, lonely souls every one of them, despite husbands and children and cousins and friends, all their hopes, in the end, their pairings and procreation and their keeping in touch, keeping track, futile in the end, failing in the end to keep them from seeing that nothing they felt, in the end, has made any difference.

There's a fine line between the exquisite and the laborious, and such writing risks becoming a parody of lyricism. There's something almost willful in the baroque extravagance of McDermott's style. It's as if she feels her previous books haven't gone far enough, that this time she's determined not merely to write *about* loss, but to take it down into the basic structures of the novel itself, fashioning a syntax of melancholy, a prose that gasps with sadness and doubles back on itself like the tangled contingencies of fate.

So too with the profusion of characters and their stories. *Charming Billy* seems wildly discursive, chronicling not merely the principal players in Billy's life, but much of the large supporting cast as well. You may find yourself flipping back to check which Daniel Lynch this is (there are two) or whose Uncle Jim worked at Edison back in '37; or wondering how you got onto the story of Billy's cousin's mother's Great-Aunty Eileen. Who *are* all these people? Again, McDermott isn't content merely to describe a texture of consciousness; she wants to create it, taking the density of Irish Catholic working-class family life and pressing it into the very molecules of the novel. It's as if the welter of names and stories—or rather our resistance to it—reveals our own attenuated capacity for family life. Reading *Charming Billy* one feels at times something like the strangeness, the scratchy bewilderment, of things perceived across a cultural divide.

Which brings us, finally, to the narrator. *Charming Billy* is told by the daughter of Billy's cousin Dennis, but through much of the novel you'd hardly notice it. She's a rather ghostly presence, never named, often present in the room but listening far more than talking. Only in the margins of the story do we get the skimpiest hints at her own life: a college graduate, married, living in Seattle with her children and husband. Readers of McDermott's last two books, recognizing yet another version of the trademark stealth narrator, may wonder, why not dispense with her altogether? Why bother to bring the narrator in as an actual character if you're not going to fill her out? It would be easy enough to toss the crutch aside and let an omniscient narrator take the slow drift back through the decades of Billy's life.

But there's a reason for the elusive anonymous quality of McDermott's narrators. Third-generation Irish-Americans situated at the end of a progression that goes urban New York, suburban Long Island, Somewhere Else, they stand looking back through the one-way window of assimilation at the lives their parents and grandparents lived. It is a crowded picture, replete with emblems of a no-frills urban Irish Catholicism: a funeral party over roast beef and boiled potatoes; characters with names like Mickey Quinn or Bridie "from the old neighborhood" (famous for her pound cake, made with a full pound of butter); men who stop after work at Quinlan's for a quick drink before Friday Mass and who call their wives "Mama"; apartment living rooms where the brocade sofa with its plastic slipcovers stands beneath a framed copy of the Irish Blessing as a new widow sobs in grief, and the Monsignor, stopping to offer solace, is welcomed with awe and deference, like a movie star.

For better and for worse, this is the life of ethnic and religious community—loud, close-knit, restrictive. And it is a life McDermott's point-of-view characters have left behind. In *Charming Billy* the narrator's few comments about herself make clear who she is: "I married Matt and we headed off to Seattle. Lives of our own, we said. Self-sacrifice having been recognized as a delusion by then, not a virtue. Self-consciousness more the vogue."

Lives of our own, we said. The mildly deprecating irony McDermott reserves for what might be called post-Irish life suggests ambivalence about the trade-offs that come with breaking free of one's roots. Yes, things are gained: mobility, a change of scenery, freedom—including sexual freedom—education and professional status, and so on. But much gets lost. To shrug off the burdens of group identity is also to shrug off ferocious attachments; and McDermott's novels express doubt about whether, as ties attenuate and the old neighborhood sinks further into the past, anything as vivid and nourishing will take their place. The grand struggle to wrest one's self from the group delivers her protagonists to this deeply American paradox: that getting a life of your own brings a diminished sense of who you are. Hence the ghostly narrators.

Charming Billy bids farewell both to Billy and to his entire way of life, its nameless narrator sent back to inspect a world where everyone owned a piece of you from one where identity rests on the still more perilous ground of self-discovery. Who *is* this person looking back with such regret and longing?

SPIELBERG'S "SCHINDLER"

RICHARD ALLEVA

Since Oskar Schindler was the most magnificent con man who ever lived, a scam artist who bilked the Third Reich of the pleasure of torturing and killing more than eleven hundred human beings, it should not surprise us that he left a trap as his bequest to anyone trying to tell the story of his achievement. All honor then to director Steven Spielberg and scriptwriter Steven Zaillian (and, of course, Thomas Keneally, whose novel they adapted) for avoiding that trap, for succeeding in drawing from the contortions of Schindler's life and the horrors he surmounted, a movie that is always art, and sometimes great art.

What is the trap? Oskar Schindler was enormously attractive. He was attractive to men as a drinking buddy and raconteur, to women as a lover. Any storyteller worth his salt must reproduce that enveloping charm on the page or screen, or *there simply is no story to tell,* for charm (abetted by bribes) was Oskar's weapon of weapons. Charm made him a successful salesman for an electrical company in the economically depressed Central Europe of the late twenties; charm kept him out of the German army; charm gained him charge of the Cracow factory that made mess kits and field kitchenware and that earned Schindler a fortune. And Oskar's charm and money seduced Nazis into allowing him to siphon off the Jews of the neighboring workcamp of Plaszow into his factory. Forty-five workers at first, then two hundred and fifty, and finally, once Schindler had acquired a "subcamp" of his own, more than eleven hundred lives were held in the nicely manicured hands of this admirable fraud who kept them safe and never let even one slip through his fingers.

But Oskar's charm is the trap! It entrances us from beyond the grave. Not only Keneally (who has the excuse of being a novelist imagining his

RICHARD ALLEVA (1948–) has served as *Commonweal's* film critic since 1990.

way under the skins of his characters) but any journalist, historian, or critic writing about this entrepreneur soon starts calling him Oskar. Indeed, one wants to have known him and to have witnessed him luxuriating in his success, gloating in the glory of his fancy cars and expensive clothes, holding his cigarette at that peculiarly Central European, forty-five-degree angle while scanning all the beautiful women in the dining room of some expensive restaurant. Suave Oskar, courteous Oskar, unfailingly adept Oskar is so much more gratifying to be with than. . . .

Than the Jews he rescued. For prolonged, atrocious suffering does not render people pathetically attractive or lovable, though we may love and pity them anyway. Starvation and fear loosen bowels, create nasty smells, monotonous speech, lusterless eyes, ferret-like behavior. So, hide those Jews from us, Mr. Moviemaker, and spare our tender sensibilities. Well, don't conceal them entirely, for then we would have no one on hand for Oskar to rescue. Just keep them at a distance, in the background, in the shadows. Coax them into camera view when it is time for Our Hero to do his stuff, and then whisk them out of sight when they have served their purpose.

It's clear that Steven Spielberg was excited by Schindler's heroism for he cinematically glories in his protagonist's swashbuckling machinations. The scene in which the industrialist swoops down on a table of Nazis and their women and soon has them literally eating out of his hands is a triumph of leaping, synoptic editing: the rhythm emulates Oskar's dazzling bonhomie. But Spielberg has resisted making Schindler a star turn surrounded by supernumeraries. Instead, he has created a concerto. In any good concerto, the orchestra doesn't merely support the single instrument but creates the sonic world that gives the soloist a sonic destiny. In *Schindler's List,* the virtuosic con man finds his moral destiny and salvation in the world of suffering experienced by the Cracow prisoners. *En masse,* these victims become a character just as important as Schindler. This is their story as much as his. Spielberg and Zaillian and Keneally never let us forget that.

But nobody experiences suffering *en masse* but in his own body, in her own mind. Spielberg's camera isolates the face of an old man awaiting execution, the empty sleeve of a person whose armlessness cost him his life (one-armed people produce less slave labor), rivulets of blood in the corridor of a ghetto tenement, the upturned face of a child, up to his chest in the excrement of the jakes where he is hiding. Another director might have extracted a sentimental pornography out of all this woe, but in Spielberg's hands everything contributes to an overall feeling of monumental suffering.

Yet the avoidance of one trap leads perilously close to another. Against all this anguish, unflinchingly staged, must not Schindler's sleek, sexually busy existence seem an affront, no matter how great the man's heroism?

My answer is simple: no. This is a story not of unalleviated suffering but of succor and rescue. In any such story, the rescuer inevitably attracts the attention of the viewer precisely because he is in action, moving and transforming instead of awaiting and enduring.

Thoughtful people are coming out of this movie praising it but troubled by the question, "When did Schindler change? What was the motive for his self-sacrifice?" Which is perhaps just another way of asking the question, "How *can* this beefy sensualist be allowed as the hero of this movie if we can't clearly be shown the exact moment of conversion from sybarite to savior?"

Well, if you must have a turning point, there is the moment when Schindler sees from a hilltop the decimation of the Cracow ghetto and spots a little girl in a red coat. The moment is piercing because that red appears on the canvas of a black-and-white movie. (Horribly, that red will reappear later on a cart of corpses.) But that's only (only!) a moment of anguished realization on Oskar's part that he must act soon and radically. It's not really a turnaround of character, just an intensification of a concern he has already felt. So, again, where does Schindler's goodness come from?

We ask that question because we think we know what goodness looks like. It looks like Gandhi, skinny in his loincloth, or Mother Teresa, unostentatious in her nun's habit. Goodness doesn't gourmandize or sleep with pretty Polish stenographers. Since Oskar Schindler never puts on a loincloth or goes on a fast or pays the least attention to his marital vows, how can we pinpoint his conversion?

We can't. We can't because there is no fundamental conversion, only an ignition of a virtue that was waiting to be ignited. In truth, Schindler's goodness was aborning in the pleasure he took in food, in his several expensive cars, and, yes, in the beauty of the women he drafted into his personal seraglio. Godless, unstirred by and uncomfortable with ideas and ideals, unshakably a hustler to the very last day of his life, Schindler could imagine heaven only as a place here on earth, and he couldn't bear that anyone in his purview be forced to live in a hell on earth. The Final

Solution affronted his pleasure-instinct. Oskar Schindler is the saint of sybarites.

He is played by Liam Neeson, all silk and steel. There is a line of Keneally's that Neeson must have contemplated during his preparation for this role: "Oskar murmured away in that peculiar rumble of his which could at the same time contain threat and bonhomie." Not only his voice but Neeson's entire characterization is that compound. In the sequences in which Schindler moves against his foes, Neeson propels his big frame forward like a tank and, in some shots, recalls the legendary hulks of German cinema's golden age, Emil Jannings or Werner Krauss. There are even times when he looks like Field Marshal Goering, a resemblance that carries its own mordant irony. But, courting women or Nazis, Neeson can be as debonair (and as much of a clothes horse) as Boyer or Redford. Up to now a specialist in attractive weaklings, Neeson allows no fissure to show in Schindler until his very last scene. But, when it comes, that breakdown is harrowing, a sudden fit of self-accusation in front of the people he has saved. In its mixture of self-revulsion and compassion, and in its over-the-top emotionality, the scene is Dostoyevskian.

This movie is so good that it demands the ultimate judgment: Is it not only a movie of movies but among the best works of art in any medium? I think the answer is no.

As long as *Schindler's List* is, it's not long enough. (It really could have been a TV miniseries.) Spielberg tries to pack in nearly all the complexities Keneally found and consequently often skims rather than delves. This skimming mars the most fascinating relationship in the film, Schindler's friendship with Goeth, the commandant of the Plaszow prison camp (harrowingly played by Ralph Fiennes as a nihilistic baby). An entire movie could have been made about just these two men, and a full-scale contrast might have told us something startling about the human condition, for Goeth's evil is a materialism turned murderous as surely as Schindler's goodness is sensuality enacting itself as altruism. But Spielberg has dozens of other dramatic areas to cover and so he moves on, leaving us tantalized rather than enlightened. Also skimmed: the character of Schindler's wife who was as tough and enterprising as her husband and virtually ran the subcamp on the numerous occasions when her husband was being interrogated by the Gestapo.

One final thing must be said against this movie but it is no slur on Spielberg's individual artistry; it's rather a reservation about the capability of fiction in dealing with the Holocaust. The very greatest films on this subject—the twenty-minute *Night and Fog* of Alain Resnais or the seven-hour *Shoah* of Claude Lanzmann—are all documentary evocations of horror rather than reproductions. They vividly allude to the evils perpetrated and thereby spur us to imagine the horrors for ourselves. When Lanzmann's camera stares at the now empty trains that once transported Jews, or at the faces of survivors and witnesses, the spirit of evil seems to materialize before our eyes. In *Schindler's List,* we are always silently murmuring our astonishment at the filmic skill deployed on the recreation of horrors. But, in *Shoah,* skill disappears and we seem to be in the very presence of enormity.

These necessary ingratitudes I have just expressed are part and parcel of my much larger gratitude to Steven Spielberg for making this movie. Though the best, alas, is always the enemy of the good, *Schindler's List* is very good indeed. It is splendid.